The Dhimmi

Jews and Christians under Islam

Bat Ye'or

With a Preface by
Jacques Ellul

Translated from the French by
DAVID MAISEL   PAUL FENTON
(Author's text)   *(Document section)*
and
DAVID LITTMAN

Rutherford ● Madison ● Teaneck
Fairleigh Dickinson University Press
London and Toronto: Associated University Presses

First published as *LE DHIMMI: Profil de l'opprimé en Orient et en Afrique du Nord depuis la conquête arabe* (335 pages), by Editions Anthropos, Paris, 1980.

Revised and enlarged English edition.
© Bat Ye'or 1985, including translation copyright.

Associated University Presses
440 Forsgate Drive
Cranbury, NJ 08512

Associated University Presses
25 Sicilian Avenue
London WC1A 2QH, England

Associated University Presses
2133 Royal Windsor Drive
Unit 1
Mississauga, Ontario
Canada L5J 1K5

Library of Congress Cataloging in Publication Data

Bat Ye'or.
  The Dhimmi.

  Translation of: Le dhimmi.
  Bibliography: p.
  Includes indexes.
  1. Dhimmis. 2. Islamic Empire—Ethnic relations.
3. Arab countries—Ethnic relations. I. Title.
DS36.9.D47B3813 1985   909'.097671   84-47749
ISBN 0-8386-3233-5 (cloth)
ISBN 0-8386-3262-9 (paperback)

Printed in the United States of America

To my father Marc Aslan Orebi
who taught me respect for the humble
To my daughter Diana Avivah
who taught me compassion for the meek

Contents

PART TWO

DOCUMENTS

I

JURISTS' TEXTS

II
ASPECTS OF THE DHIMMIS' EXISTENCE
As Observed

ORIENT

THE ERA OF EMANCIPATION

12   Contents

14   Contents

                            III
             ASPECTS OF THE DHIMMIS' EXISTENCE
                       As Experienced

IV
MODERN PERIOD

Acknowledgments

I wish to record my indebtedness to Dr. Paul Fenton (Cambridge University) and Dr. Eliezer Bashan (Bar Ilan University, Israel) for having brought to my attention a substantial amount of documents, a number of which have been reproduced in this work. I also benefited from their suggestions and advice, as well as from that given to me by Dr. Moshe Ma'oz and Dr. Robert Wistrich (both of the Hebrew University, Israel) who, on short notice, read the entire manuscript in November 1982. Dr. Vivian Lipman gave precious editing aid. I extend to all of them my sincerest thanks. I am greatly obliged to Mrs. Marina Zeller for her tireless patience in typing a long manuscript that was continuously revised and enlarged. Finally, and above all, my deepest gratitude is reserved for my husband, whose aid and counsel have guided me throughout this long work, and whose collaboration in its translation has proved indispensable.

Permissions

The author wishes to acknowledge her debt to the Public Record Office (London) for its authorization to reproduce nineteenth-century documents from its archives. She is obliged to David Littman for material from the archives of the Alliance Israélite Universelle (Paris) published in documents 107, 108, as well as for the photograph illustration no. 27.

She would like to express her appreciation and thanks to the following publishers for permission to use material from their books, also listed in the bibliography. Exact page references are provided at the end of each "document":

The American Academy of Jewish Research (New York), for the English translation by Boaz Cohen, from Maimonides' *Iggeret Taiman*, edited by S. A. Halkin (1952)—"doc. 94"; the American Oriental Society (New Haven, Conn.), for the translation by Richard Gottheil, from Ghazi b.al-Wasiti, in *JAOS* 41 (1921)—"docs. 6, 23, 24, 25"; E. J. Brill (Leiden), for translations from Romanelli and *Dibray ha-Yamin*, in *A*

History of the Jews in North Africa, vol. 2 (1981), by H. Z. Hirschberg—
"docs. 56, 97, 101"; Victor Gollancz Ltd. (London), for *The Mufti of
Jerusalem* (1947), by Moshe Pearlman—"doc. 110"; the Jewish Publication Society of America (Philadelphia), for *Travels in North Africa*
(1927), by Nahum Slouschz—"docs. 80, 82", and for the translation of
al-Mutawwakil's decree, from al-Tabari, in *The Jews of Arab Lands: A
History and Source Book* (1979), by Norman Stillman—"doc. 8"; John
Murray (Publishers) Ltd. (London), for *Aden to the Hadhramaut* (1947),
by D. van der Meulen—"doc. 93"; the Oriental Institute (Oxford), for
the translation by A. Scheiber in his "The Origins of Obadya the
Norman Proselyte", *JJS* 5, no. 1 (1954)—"doc. 21"; Princeton University Press, for *The Muqaddimah: An Introduction to History,* vol. 1 (1958),
by Ibn Khaldun, translated by Franz Rosenthal, Bollingen Series 43—
"doc. 1"; the School of Oriental and African Studies (London), for the
translation from al-Asnawi, by Moshe Perlmann, in his "Notes on anti-
Christian propaganda in the Mamluk Empire", *BSOAS* 10 (1939–
42)"doc. 26"; the University of California Press (Berkeley), for the
translation from Shaykh Damanhuri's tract, by Moshe Perlmann, in
his *Shaykh Damanhuri on the Churches of Cairo* (1975)—"doc. 20"; the
University of Colombia (New York), for *The Origins of the Islamic State*
(1916), by al-Baladhuri, translated by P. H. Hitti—"doc. 2."

Illustrations. The author is grateful to Mr. Alfred Rubens for kindly
supplying six photographs from his private collection at very short
notice (illustrations nos. 8, 11, 15, 18, 20, 24) and for permission to
reproduce a photograph (illustration 23) from his *A History of Jewish
Costume* (London, 1973). Her thanks are also due to the Israel
Museum for three photographs provided in 1975 (illustrations nos.
25, 27, 31); the Schulmann Collection for two photographs received
from the late Prof. H. Z. Hirschberg in 1975 (illustrations nos. 19, 21);
A. S. Barnes & Co. for one photograph (illustration no. 30) and Keystone (illustration no. 34). Illustrations nos. 4 and 5 are from her own
family archives. The remaining illustrations, principally from the
nineteenth century, have been chosen from various publications. Exact references are provided in conformity with the specific system
adopted for all the "documents" of this volume.

Author's Note

Because there is no perfect solution to the problems of transcribing foreign words occurring in texts of varied origins, the policy here has been to simplify throughout. Thus, where conventional English spellings of such words exist (e.g., Koran instead of Qur'ān), these have been used in the author's historical analysis and in the translations of the texts. Where the latter were already in the English language, the original transcriptions, despite inconsistencies, have been retained, as is customary. Consequently, no attempt at standardization has been made, even if this has resulted in some orthographic discrepancies (e.g., Muslim, Moslem, etc.). Elsewhere a simplification has been employed, omitting all diacritical points with the exception of an apostrophe ('), which has been used without distinction to represent the *hamza* or the *'ayin*—occurring in the *middle* of a word only.

All quotations and texts in English— including translations into English from published works—are reproduced here *exactly* as in the original source, to which a reference is indicated. Where an authoritative French translation from the Arabic was used in the 1980 French edition of *The Dhimmi,* the translation into English was made basically from the French and not from the Arabic original.

The word "antisemitism" is spelled throughout following the usage initiated by Dr. James Parkes fifty years ago in his classic history of antisemitism.

Page numbers in ordinary brackets at the end of a paragraph indicate an ellipsis in the text—as does (. . .) —as well as providing the exact reference to the work quoted. In general, except for archival sources, only the author's last name is noted at the very end of documents, precise details of the article or book being confined to the bibliography.

Ordinary parentheses (within the text) are reproduced as they were originally published. Square brackets [containing clarifications] are by the author, as are the subtitles in italics.

The indexes and the selected list of Muslim historians and theologians have been prepared by Dr. Paul Fenton. The bibliography includes only publications actually mentioned in this work, but indications have been given regarding other specialized bibliographies.

For convenience, the King James Authorized Version of the Bible and Arberry's translation of the Koran have been used.

ABBREVIATIONS

AOH	*Acta Orientalia Hungarica* (Budapest)
AS	*Arabian Studies* (Cambridge)
BAIU	*Bulletin, Alliance Israélite Universelle* (Paris)
BIJS	*Bulletin of the Institute of Jewish Studies* (London)
BSOAS	*Bulletin of the School of Oriental and African Studies* (London)
EI[1]	*Encyclopaedia of Islam*, first edition
EI[2]	*Encyclopaedia of Islam*, new edition
EJ	*Encyclopaedia Judaica*, new English edition
HESPERIS	*Institut des Hautes-Etudes Marocaines* (Paris)
IOS	*Israel Oriental Studies* (Jerusalem)
JA	*Journal Asiatique* (Paris)
JAOS	*Journal of the American Oriental Society* (New York)
JESHO	*Journal of the Economic and Social History of the Orient* (Leiden)
JHSE	*Jewish Historical Society of England* (London)
JIMMA	*Journal Institute of Muslim Minority Affairs* (Jeddah)
JJS	*Journal of Jewish Studies* (London)
JNES	*Journal of Near Eastern Studies* (Chicago)
JPS	*Journal of Palestine Studies* (Beirut)
JRAS	*Journal of Royal Asiatic Society* (London)
JQ	*Jerusalem Quarterly* (Jerusalem)
JQR	*Jewish Quarterly Review* (Philadelphia)
JYCSR	*Journal of Yemen Centre for Studies and Research* (San'a)
MES	*Middle Eastern Studies* (London)
NC	*Nouveaux Cahiers* (Paris)
PI	*Politique Internationale* (Paris)
PAAJR	*Proceedings of the American Academy for Jewish Research* (New York)
RCAJ	*Royal Central Asian Journal* (London)
REI	*Revue des Etudes Islamiques* (Paris)
REJ	*Revue des Etudes Juives* (Paris)
RMI	*Rassegna Mensile di Israel* (Rome)
RSPT	*Revue des Sciences Philosophiques et Théologiques* (Paris)
SEFUNOT	*Sefunot, Annual for Research on the Jewish Communities in the East* (Hebrew) (Jerusalem)
SPS	*Studies in Plural Societies* (The Hague)
WLB	*Wiener Library Bulletin* (London)
YOD	*Revue des Etudes Hébraïques et juives modernes et contemporaines* (Paris)

ARCHIVES, etc.

AIU	*Alliance Israélite Universelle* (Paris)
PRO	*Public Record Office* (London)
FO	*Foreign Office* (PRO)
PP	*Parliamentary Papers* (London). See Bibliography under *PP*

F O   78/500
78/836
78/1452
78/1520
78/1538
195/369
195/524

Illustrations

Preface

by Jacques Ellul

This is a very important book, for it deals with one of the most sensitive problems of our time, sensitive owing to the difficulty of the subject—the reality of Islamic doctrine and practice with regard to non-Muslims, and sensitive owing to the topicality of the subject and the susceptibilities it now arouses throughout the world. Half a century ago the question of the condition of non Muslims in the Islamic countries would not have excited anyone. It might have been the subject of a historical dissertation of interest to specialists, the subject of a juridical analysis (I am thinking of the work of M. Gaudefroy-Demombynes and of my old colleague G.-H. Bousquet, who wrote extensively on different aspects of Muslim law and history without their research giving rise to the smallest controversy), or the subject of a philosophical and theological discussion, but without passion. That which was related to Islam and the Muslim world was believed to belong to a past that, if not dead, was certainly no more alive than medieval Christianity. The Muslim peoples had no power; they were extraordinarily divided and many of them were subjected to European colonization. Those Europeans who were hostile to colonization showed some sympathy for the "Arabs," but that was as far as it went! And then, suddenly, since 1950, everything changed completely.

I think that one can discern four stages in this development. The first was the attempt of the Islamic peoples to rid themselves of their conquerors. In this, the Muslims were by no means "original": the Algerian war and all that followed was only a consequence of the first war against the French in Vietnam. It was part of a general process of decolonization. This process, in turn, led the Islamic people to search for their own identity, to seek to be not only free of the Europeans but different, qualitatively different from them. This led to the second step: that which was specific to these peoples was not an ethnic or organizational peculiarity, but a religion. Accordingly, even in left-wing socialist or communist movements in the Muslim world there was a return to religion, so that the idea of a secular state such as

Atatürk, for instance, had envisaged was completely rejected. The explosion of Islamic religiosity is frequently considered specific to the Ayatollah Khomeini, but that is not correct. One ought not to forget that the terrible war of 1947 in India between the Muslims and Hindus was fought on a purely religious basis. More than one million people died, and since massacres had not taken place when the Muslims had lived within the Hindu-Buddhist orbit, one may presume that the war was caused by the attempt to set up an independent Islamic republic. Pakistan officially proclaimed itself an Islamic Republic in 1953, precisely at the time when other Muslim peoples were making their great effort to regain their identity. Hardly a year has since passed without its marking some new stage in the religious revival of Islam (e.g., the resumption of the conversion of Black Africa to Islam, the return of alienated populations to religious practice, the obligation for Arab socialist regimes to proclaim that their states were "Muslim" republics, etc.), so that at the present day Islam can be said to be the most active religion in the world. The extremism of the Ayatollah Khomeini can be understood only in the light of this general tendency. It is not something exceptional and extraordinary, but its logical continuation. But, together with this religious renewal, there arose an awareness of a certain unity of the Islamic world over and above its political and cultural diversity. This was the third stage in the Islamic revival. Of course, one ought not to overlook all the conflicts between Muslim states, their divergences of interests and even wars, *but* these differences should not blind us to a more fundamental reality: their religious unity in opposition to the non-Muslim world. And here we have an interesting phenomenon: I am tempted to say that it is the "others," the "communist" and "Christian" countries, that reinforce the unity of the Muslim world, playing, as it were, the role of a "compressor" to bring about its unification. Finally, and this is obviously the last stage, there was the discovery of Islam's oil resources and economic power, which hardly needs elaboration. Taken as a whole, this process follows a logical sequence: political independence, religious revival, and economic power. It has transformed the face of the world in less than half a century. And we are now witnessing a vast program to propagate Islam, involving the building of mosques everywhere, even in the USSR, the diffusion of Arab literature and culture, and the recovery of a history. Islam now boasts of having been the cradle of all civilizations at a time when Europe was sunk in barbarism and the Far East was torn asunder by divisions. Islam as the origin of all the sciences and arts is a theme that is constantly developed. This idea has perhaps been promoted more in France than in the English-speaking world (although one should not forget the Black Muslims in the United States). If I take the

French situation as my yardstick, it is because I feel that it can serve as an example.

The moment one broaches a problem related to Islam, one touches upon a subject where strong feelings are easily aroused. In France it is no longer acceptable to criticize Islam or the Arab countries. There are several reasons for this: the French have a guilty conscience on account of their invasion and colonization of North Africa, doubly so after the Algerian War (which, by a backlash, has brought about a climate of sympathy for the adversary), and then there has also been the discovery of the fact, true enough, that for centuries Western culture has underestimated the value of the Muslim contribution to civilization (and, as a result, now goes to the other extreme). The flow of immigrant workers of Arab origin into France has established an important group that is generally wretched and despised (with racial overtones). This has led many intellectuals, Christians and others, to be favorably and uncritically disposed toward them. A general rehabilitation of Islam has therefore taken place that has been expressed in two ways. On the intellectual level there is first of all an increasing number of works of an apparently scholarly nature whose declared purpose is to eradicate prejudices and false preconceptions about Islam, with regard to both its doctrines and its customs. Thus these works "demonstrate" that it is untrue that the Arabs were cruel conquerors and that they disseminated terror and massacred those peoples who would not submit to their rule. It is false that Islam is intolerant; on the contrary, it is held to be tolerance itself. It is false that women had an inferior status and that they were excluded from public life. It is false that the *jihad* (Holy War) was a war fought for material gain, and so on. In other words, everything that has been regarded as historically unquestionable about Islam is considered as propaganda, and a false picture of Islam has been implanted in the West, which, it is claimed, must be corrected by the truth. Reference is made to a very spiritual interpretation of the Koran, and the excellence of the manners and customs in Islamic countries is emphasized.

But this is not all. In some Western European countries, Islam exerts a special spiritual fascination. Inasmuch as Christianity no longer possesses the religious influence it once had and is strongly criticized, and communism has lost its prestige and is no longer regarded as being the bearer of a message of hope, the religious needs of Europeans require another form in which to find expression, and Islam has been rediscovered. It is no longer a matter of an exchange of ideas between intellectuals, but rather of an authentic religious adherence. Several well-known French intellectuals have made a spectacular conversion to Islam. Islam is presented as a very great advance over Christianity, and reference is made to Muslim mystics. It is re-

called that the three religions of the Book (Jewish, Christian, and
Muslim) are all related. All of them claim Abraham as their ancestor,
and the last one, the most recent, must obviously be the most advanced of the three. I am not exaggerating. Among Jews in France
there are even serious intellectuals who hope, if not for a fusion, at
least for a coming together of the three religions. If I have described
what may be observed in Europe, it is because—whether one likes it
or not—Islam regards itself as having a universal vocation and pro-
claims itself to be the only true religion to which everyone must
adhere. We should have no illusions about the matter: no part of the
world will be excluded. Now that Islam has national, military, and
economic power, it will attempt to extend its religion everywhere,
including the British Commonwealth and the United States. In the
face of this expansion (for the third time), one should not react by
racism, nor by an orthodox dogmatism, nor by persecution or war.
The reaction should be of a spiritual and psychological nature (one
must avoid being carried away by a guilty conscience), and on a scholarly level. What really happened? What was the reality: the cruelties
of the Muslim conquest, or the magnanimity and the beneficence of
the Koran? What is correct as regards doctrine and its application to
daily life in the Muslim world? And the search that is done must be
intellectually serious, *relating to specific points.* It is impossible to judge
the Islamic world in a general way: a hundred different cultures have
been absorbed by Islam. It is impossible to study all the doctrines, all
the traditions, and all their applications together. Such a study can
only be undertaken if one limits oneself to the study of specific questions, disentangling what is true from what is false.

It is within this context that Bat Ye'or's book *The Dhimmi* should be
placed: and it is an exemplary contribution to this crucial discussion
that concerns us all. Here I shall neither give an account of the book
nor praise its merits, but shall simply indicate its importance. The
dhimmi is someone who lives in a Muslim society without being a
Muslim (Jews, Christians, and occasionally "animists"). He has a particular social, political, and economic status, and it is essential for us to
know how this "refractory" person has been treated. But first of all,
one ought to realize the dimensions of this subject: it is much more
than the study of one "social condition" among others. The reader
will see that in many ways the *dhimmi* was comparable to the European
serf of the Middle Ages. The condition of serfdom, however, was the
result of certain historical changes such as the transformation of slavery, the end of the State, the emergence of the feudal system, and the
like, and thus, when these historical conditions altered, the situation
of the serf also evolved until his status finally disappeared. The same,
however, does not apply to the *dhimmi:* his status was not the product

of historical accident but was that which *ought* to be from the religious point of view and according to the Muslim conception of the world. In other words, it was the expression of the absolute, unchanging, theologically grounded Muslim conception of the relationship between Islam and non-Islam. It is not a historical accident of retrospective interest, but a necessary condition of existence. Consequently, it is both a subject for historical research (involving an examination of the historical sources and a study of their application in the past) and a contemporary subject, most topical in relation to the present-day expansion of Islam. Bat Ye'or's book ought to be read as a work of current interest. One must know as exactly as possible what the Muslims did with these unconverted conquered peoples, because that is what they will do in the future (and are doing right now). It is possible that my opinion on this question will not entirely convince the reader.

After all, ideas and concepts are known to change. The Christian concept of God or of Jesus Christ is no longer the same for the Christians today as it was in the Middle Ages, and one can multiply examples. But precisely what seems to me interesting and striking about Islam, one of its peculiarities, is the fixity of its concepts. It is clear enough that things change to a far greater extent when they are not set in a fixed ideological mold. The Roman imperial regime was far more susceptible to change than the Stalinist regime because there was no ideological framework to give it a continuity, a rigidity. Wherever the social organization is based upon a system, it tends to reproduce itself far more exactly. Islam, even more than Christianity, is a religion that claims to give a definite form to the social order, to human relations, and claims to embrace each moment in the life of every person. Thus, it tends toward an inflexibility that most other forms of society have not had. Moreover, it is known that the whole of Islamic doctrine (including its religious thought) took on a juridical form. All the authoritative texts were subjected to a juridical type of interpretation and every application (even on spiritual matters) had a juridical imprint. One should not forget that this legalism has a very definite orientation: to fix—to fix relationships, halt time, fix meanings (to give a word one single and indisputable significance), to fix interpretations. Everything of a juridical nature evolves only very slowly and is not subject to any changes. Of course, there can be an evolution (in practical matters, in jurisprudence, etc.), but when there is a *text,* which is regarded in some way as an "authoritative" source, one has only to go back to that text and the recent innovations will collapse. And this is exactly what has happened in Islam. Legalism has everywhere produced a rigidity (not an absolute rigidity, which is impossible, but a maximal one) that makes historical investigation essential. One should be aware that when one is dealing with some

Islamic term or institution of the past, as long as the basic text—in this case, the Koran—remains unchanged, one can always return to the original principles and ideas whatever apparent transformations or developments have taken place, especially because Islam has achieved something that has always been very unusual: an integration of the religious, the political, the moral, the social, the juridical, and the intellectual, thus constituting a rigorous whole of which each element forms an integral part.

However, the *dhimmi* himself is a controversial subject. This word actually means "protégé" or "protected person." This is one of the arguments of the modern defenders of Islam: the *dhimmi* has never been persecuted or maltreated (except accidentally); on the contrary, he was a protected person. What better example could illustrate Islam's liberalism. Here are people who do not accept Islam and, instead of being expelled, they are protected. I have read a great deal of literature attempting to prove that no society or religion has been so tolerant as Islam or has protected its minorities so well. Naturally, this argument has been used to condemn medieval Christianity (which I have no intention of defending), on the ground that Islam never knew an Inquisition or "witch hunts." Even if this dubious argument is accepted, let us confine ourselves to an examination of the meaning of the term *protected person*. One must ask: "protected against whom?" When this "stranger" lives in Islamic countries, the answer can only be: against the Muslims themselves. The point that must be clearly understood is that the very term *protégé* implies a latent hostility. A similar institution existed in early Rome, where the *cliens,* the stranger, was always the enemy. He had to be treated as an enemy even if there was no situation of war. But if this stranger obtained the favor of the head of some great family, he became his protégé *(cliens)* and was then able to reside in Rome: he was "protected" by his "patron" from the acts of aggression that any Roman citizen could commit against him. This also meant that in reality the protected person had no genuine rights. The reader of this book will see that the *dhimmi*'s condition was defined by a treaty *(dhimma)* between him (or his group) and a Muslim group. This treaty had a juridical aspect, but was what we would call an unequal contract: the *dhimma* was a "concessionary charter" (cf. C. Chehata on Muslim law), something that implies two consequences. The first is that the person who concedes the charter can equally well rescind it. It is not, in fact, a contract representing a "consensus" arrived at between the two sides. On the contrary, it is quite arbitrary. The person who grants the treaty is the only one who decides what he is prepared to concede (hence the great variety of conditions). The second is that the resulting situation is the opposite of the one envisaged in the theory of the "rights of man" whereby, by the mere fact of being a human being, _one is endowed_ automatically with certain rights and _those_ who fail to respect them are at fault. In the case of the "concessionary charter," on the contrary, one enjoys rights only to the extent that they are recognized in the charter and only for as long as it remains valid. As a person, by the mere fact of one's "existence," one has no claim to any rights. And this, indeed, is the _dhimmi_'s condition. As I have explained above, this condition is unvarying throughout the course of history; it is not the result of social chance, but a rooted concept.

For the conquering Islam of today, those who do not claim to be Muslims do not have any human rights recognized as such. In an Islamic society, the non-Muslims would return to their former _dhimmi_ status, which is why the idea of solving the Middle East conflicts by the creation of a federation including Israel within a group of Muslim peoples or states, or in a "Judeo-Islamic" state, is a fantasy and an illusion. From the Muslim point of view, such a thing would be unthinkable. Thus the term _protected_ can have two completely opposite meanings according to whether one takes it in its moral sense or in its juridical sense, and that is entirely characteristic of the controversies now taking place concerning the character of Islam. Unfortunately, this term has to be taken in its juridical sense. I am well aware that it will be objected that the _dhimmi_ had his rights. Yes, indeed; but they were _conceded_ rights. That is precisely the point. In the Versailles Treaty of 1918, for example, Germany was granted a number of "rights" by the victors, and that was called a _Diktat_. This shows how hard it is to evaluate a problem of this kind, for one's conclusions will vary according to whether one is favorably or unfavorably predisposed toward Islam, and a truly scholarly, "objective" study becomes extremely difficult (though personally, I do not believe in objectivity in the humanities; at best, the scholar can be honest and take his own prejudices into account). And yet, precisely because, as has been said, passion is involved, studies of this kind are nevertheless indispensable in all questions concerning Islam.

So now it must be asked: is this book a serious, scholarly study? I reviewed _Le Dhimmi,_ when it first appeared, in a major French newspaper* (the French edition was far less complete and rich than this one, especially with regard to the documents, notes, and appendixes, which are essential). In response to that review I received a very strong letter from a colleague, a well-known orientalist, informing me that the book was purely polemical and could not be regarded seriously. His criticisms, however, betrayed the fact that he had not read the book, and the interesting thing about his arguments (based on

*_Le Monde,_ 18 November 1980.

what I had written) was that they demonstrated, on the contrary, the serious nature of this work. First of all, he began with an appeal to authority, referring me to certain works whose scholarship he regarded as unquestionable (those of Professors S. D. Goitein, B. Lewis, and N. Stillman), that in his opinion adopt a positive attitude toward Islam and its tolerance toward non-Muslims.

I conveyed his opinion to Bat Ye'or, who assured me that she was personally acquainted with all three authors and had read their publications dealing with the subject. Given the scope of the author's researches, I would have been surprised if this was not the case. She maintained that an attentive reading of their writings would not justify such a restrictive interpretation. One may now ask: what were the principal arguments that our critic advanced against Bat Ye'or's analysis? He claimed, first, that one cannot generalize about the *dhimmi*'s condition, which varied considerably. But this is precisely the point that Bat Ye'or makes in her very skillfully constructed book: using common data, from an identical basis, the author has provided documents that permit us to gain an exact idea of these differences, in accordance with whether the *dhimmi* lived in the Maghreb, or in Persia, Arabia, and so on. And, although we perceive a very great diversity in the reality of the *dhimmi*'s existence, this in no way changed the identical and profound reality of his condition. The second argument put forward by our critic was that the "persecutions" to which the *dhimmi* was subjected had been greatly exaggerated. He spoke of "a few outbursts of popular anger," but, on the one hand, that is not something that the book is particularly concerned with, and, on the other hand, it was here, precisely, that our critic's bias clearly revealed itself. The "few" outbursts, in fact, were historically very numerous, and massacres of *dhimmis* were frequent. Nowadays we ought not to overlook the considerable evidence (which was formerly *over*stressed) of the slaughter of Jews and Christians in all the countries occupied by the Arabs and Turks, which recurred often, without the intervention of the forces of order. The *dhimmi* did, perhaps, have recognized rights, but when popular hatred was aroused, sometimes for incomprehensible reasons, he found himself defenseless and without protection. This was the equivalent of pogroms. On this point it was my correspondent who was not "scholarly." Third, he claimed that the *dhimmis* had personal and communal rights, but, not being a jurist, he failed to see the difference between personal rights and conceded rights. This aspect has been stressed above and the argument is unfounded, as Bat Ye'or demonstrates by a careful and convincing examination of the rights in question.

Another point raised was that the Jews attained their highest level of culture in Muslim countries, and that they regarded the states in which they resided as *their own*. With regard to the first point, I would say that there was an enormous diversity. It is quite true that in certain Muslim countries at some periods, Jews—and Christians—did attain a high level of culture and affluence, but Bat Ye'or does not deny that. And, in any case, that was not anything extraordinary: in Rome, for instance, in the first century A.D., the slaves (who remained *slaves*) enjoyed a very remarkable position, being active in nearly all the intellectual professions (as teachers, doctors, engineers, etc.), directed enterprises, and could even be slave-owners themselves. Nonetheless, they were slaves! The situation of the *dhimmis* was something comparable to this. They had an important economic role (as is clearly shown in this book) and could be "happy," but they were nevertheless inferiors whose very variable status rendered them narrowly dependent and bereft of "rights." As for the assertion that they considered as their own the states which ruled them, that was never true of the Christians. And, with regard to the Jews, they had been dispersed throughout the world for so long that they had no alternative. Yet we know that a real current of "assimilationism" came into existence only in the modern Western democracies. Finally, Bat Ye'or's critic states that "a degradation of the condition of the Jews has taken place in recent times in Islamic countries," but that the *dhimmis'* condition ought not to be evaluated by what happened to them in the nineteenth and twentieth centuries. I can only ask whether the author of these criticisms, like so many other historians, has not given way to the temptation to glamorize the past. It is enough to notice the remarkable concordance between the historical sources referring to events, and the basic, authoritative texts to realize that such an evolution was not so considerable.

If I have dealt with the criticisms at some length, it is because I feel that it is important in order to establish the "scholarly" nature of this book. For my part, I consider this study to be very honest, hardly polemical at all, and as objective as possible (always bearing in mind the fact that I belong to the school of historians for whom pure objectivity, in the absolute sense, cannot exist). *The Dhimmi* contains a rich selection of source material, makes a correct use of documents, and displays a concern to place each situation in its proper historical context. Consequently, it satisfies a certain number of scholarly requirements for a work of this kind. And for that reason I regard it as exemplary and very significant. But also, within the "living context" of contemporary history, which I described earlier, this is a book that carries a clear warning. The Muslim world has not evolved in its manner of considering the non-Muslim, which is a reminder of the fate in store for those who may one day be submerged within it. It is a source of enlightenment for our time.

Bordeaux, May 1983

Antoine Fattal

Introduction

Over the last forty years the countries of the Middle East and North
Africa have undergone radical transformations which, among other
things, have brought about the near-extinction of Jewish communities
after two to three thousand years of existence. Today the descendants
of the Jews of the Islamic world, scattered in the Diaspora or settled in
Israel, do not know what to make of their past. Yet any quest for
identity implies a return to one's roots. I have therefore searched
among the remnants of more than a thousand years of history without having any idea of the directions in which my inquiries would
lead. The material gradually fell into place, clarifying the mysteries
and contradictions of history. A portrait emerged out of the mists of
time, imprisoned in the silence of its centuries-old shrine.

That silence, however, appeared increasingly artificial as my researches progressed, for only forgetfulness had disconnected the cir-
cuit. A multitude of voices spoke out from the documents
accumulated over the ages, and the picture that emerged, overflowing
into present reality, revealed the various aspects of human hope and
suffering.

This preamble indicates the framework and prescribes the limits of
my research.

This study does not seek to investigate the legal status of the *dhimmi*
peoples—that is, the non-Arab and non-Muslim nations and communities that were subjected to Muslim domination after the conquest
of their territories by the Arabs. That has already been done by Antoine Fattal, who has analyzed its theoretical and legal aspects, as well
as its practical applications.[1] Nor is this book concerned with a straight
chronological description of the course of events that made up the
history of each of the *dhimmi* peoples, for that falls within the province
of the specialized historian.

Its aim is much more modest. It has grown out of an independent
reflection on the relationship between conqueror and conquered, established as a result of a special code of warfare, the *jihad*,[2] for in the
"drama" acted out by humanity on the stage of history, it is clear that
the *dhimmi* peoples bore the role of victim, vanquished by force; and
indeed, it is after a war, a *jihad*, and after a defeat, that a nation

35

becomes a *dhimmi* people. "Tolerated" in its homeland, from which it has been dispossessed, this people lives thereafter as if it were merely suspended in time, throughout history. For the pragmatic political factor that decides the fate of a *dhimmi* people is essentially a territorial dispossession.

Obviously, one cannot ignore the religious elements of this specific condition, but I have refrained from examining it from a religious viewpoint, being unsure to what extent the persecution of the *dhimmi* in the Middle Ages was in contradiction with the principles of Islam itself. Could not the oppression of the *dhimmi* be the Islamic reflection of the fanaticism of Byzantine pre-Islamic institutions? Did not Muslim domination, on the contrary, mitigate an intolerance whose sanguinary excesses endangered the very survival of all "dissidents"?

Moreover, it is well known that political power inevitably betrays the spiritual tenets of a religion: history abounds in examples. The Bible reveals a respect for humanity by confronting it plainly and uncompromisingly with its own tragedy—that of a conscience torn by the contradiction between its weaknesses and its ethical ideals. Did not the Almohad and Catholic Inquisitions of Spain betray the spiritual values of both the Koran and the Gospels? And, with regard to modern "religions," what connections are there between socialist ideals and the Soviet gulags?

For such reasons, I have refrained from suggesting that Islamic religious doctrine was responsible for the status of the *dhimmi* as it developed through the centuries. The complexity of the problems concerning the relationship of power and religion caused me to locate the *dhimmi* condition—as revealed by the facts—within the victor-vanquished relationship, especially since this condition was first and foremost the result of a conquest. An examination of this relationship as it was experienced by its victims led me to present the account from the viewpoint of those who endured it and lived it daily, generation after generation, century after century.

The other version of the facts, that of the conqueror, is of course quite different, and there is no lack of books by Muslim and non-Muslim writers to expound it. This is why, in these pages, the *dhimmi* will speak for himself and will tell his own story, even if it is through the mediation of others, for the silence that follows in his wake confirms his bondage.

The first part of this study outlines the historical currents that gave rise to the general elements of the *dhimmi* condition in its diversity. It is for the specialists to distinguish the variations in this condition according to periods and regions. Here, only the different facets have been indicated: political, social, religious. As the work advanced, the typological character of the *dhimmi* condition, both in its legal structure and its human context, seemed to exceed the bounds of history, overflowing into the philosophical area that treats of man's oppression.

I have endeavored to distinguish between the people, instruments of an oppressive power, and that power itself as the practical realization of a system of values. This is a very ambiguous point in Islam, for politics and religion are intimately interconnected within the dogma itself. Notwithstanding this, a deliberate attempt has been made here to disassociate the religious sphere—a system of moral values and the relationship of man to God—from the political, that is, the relationship of man to his neighbor, even if political institutions seek to justify themselves by religious dogmas.

It is possible that a confusion between the two spheres has nonetheless remained. The reader is asked to impute this failure to the complexity of the subject, which does not always allow a clear distinction between the religious and the political, rather than to a deliberate partiality.

The Western reader may be bewildered by a subject concerned exclusively with religious groups, but in their historical and geographical birthplace in the Orient, religions assumed very complex and varied territorial and national forms deriving from historico-cultural institutions and traditions. The expansion of Islam having transferred the exercise of power exclusively to the Islamic community, the collective historical consciousness of the conquered peoples was reduced to a religious dimension, which was the only one tolerated in their Islamized territory. Resistance to the Arabian conquerors took various forms: religious for the Jews and Christians, cultural for the pagans—Persians, Berbers, Kurds, and so forth—who adopted Islam but endeavored to resist Arabization.

No society, however liberal, can escape the burden of history. The group's social heredity is transmitted from age to age, from generation to generation, by laws, traditions, customs, and social behavior-patterns fixed in ancient institutions. Unchanging stereotypes, the product of archaic ways of thinking, persist throughout the centuries and survive in modern prejudices and ideologies. The persistence of these social behavior-patterns and collective myths that are here described, both in contemporary Arab political ideologies and among the descendants of the *dhimmi* groups themselves, forms the subject of the conclusion of this section.

The second part of the book consists of documents selected in accordance with their relevance to the plan of this work. Legal texts reveal the sociopolitical world of the *dhimmis*, whereas the documentary material of various origins illustrates, by events, attitudes, or observations, the diverse aspects of their condition in different countries. As far as possible, they have been classified in chronological order, according to regions and subjects. The abundance of the documents and the fear of tiring the reader influenced me to reduce the number of documents from the fourteenth to the eighteenth century, many of which have been published in other works.[3]

I have, however, included some texts representative of behavior-patterns and ways of thinking, despite their partiality and the obvious prejudices that they reflect. The reader may perhaps be surprised by the broad areas of time and space covered, but throughout this diversity will appear the persistence of one and the same condition. This apparently ambitious method of approach seemed the most appropriate way to understand the objective condition of the *dhimmi*. A study of a single minority arbitrarily detached from the whole picture might produce a distorted image, particularly in the case of the Arabo-Islamic empire created out of a mosaic of different ethnic groups. Some documents may seem repetitive, but each one provides, by a fact or a nuance, a new insight into the subject.

It might be objected that European and *dhimmi* sources—from which the majority of the documents are drawn—provide only a partial image of the reality. The argument is valid enough, but would not the conqueror's version be even more partial? It was in his interest to denigrate the defeated, to exaggerate their economic power or their insolence in order to justify his reprisals. Would a historian, one thousand years hence, judge Western values exclusively from the description left by the Ayatollah Khomeini or Colonel Qaddhafi, or the history of the Arab-Israel wars simply from Arab accounts? Convinced that in history there is not *one single truth,* but *a multiplicity of constantly changing and contradictory situations,* interdependent one with another, I have drawn on versions other than those of the conquerors in order to investigate this subject more deeply. The reader thus forewarned may be better equipped to discern between prejudice and facts. Moreover, this study does not even pretend to be an outline, however vague, of a historical presentation of the subject. At most, it claims to put the questions: what was the human reality of the *dhimmi* as he saw himself—not as his master saw him—and how did he manage to bear his condition?

Beyond the religious relationship of Muslim, Christian, and Jew, which is beyond my competence, I have attempted to define the human aspects of a historical situation. And, because this particular situation is my own cultural heritage, I have dared, despite my limitations, to delve into this past. May the specialist not judge too harshly such a rash intrusion into his field, and may better equipped historians correct and improve this picture revealed by the long-neglected testimonies of centuries.

Postscriptum

This study, begun in 1974, was completed in 1976. Many of the themes developed there on Jews and Christians under Islam were already sketched in the first edition of my *Les Juifs en Egypte* (Geneva, 1971; enlarged Hebrew edition, January, 1974) and in numerous articles published in French and English from 1973 to 1979.

Working alone, independently of academic circles (any advice received from scholars was either cursory or restricted to facts), the results of my research led me toward an innovative historical analysis that freed the remnants of *dhimmi* peoples from the rhetoric of "toleration," and at the same time restored them to the heart of the *jihad*-strategy, that had determined their destiny since the seventh century.

In the early 1970s such a historical interpretation went against commonly accepted ideas and the writings of most contemporary scholars. The affirmation that *dhimmi* peoples had been reduced to religious minorities and were despised and persecuted over the centuries was not well received. To state that European colonization had emancipated these subjected peoples was taboo—at a time of Western culpableness over the issue of colonization. The pro-Arab policies of many states encouraged by Arab financial power, the appeasement of PLO terrorism, as well as left-wing and Third-World trends did not facilitate a new approach, free from general *clichés*.

Le Dhimmi was finally published in 1980. Throughout the 1970s, its themes were exposed not only in articles, but also in lectures and in correspondence.

Today, fifteen years after my initial timid research on this vast and complex subject, the recent trends in some Islamic countries and the tragic Lebanese conflict give a pale reflection of Islamic societies in which the *dhimmis* lived, where the *shari'a* was the only recognized jurisdiction. These contemporary events confirm, actualize and integrate the themes analyzed in *The Dhimmi*, within the dynamics of a history that was often avoided or was obfuscated.

July 1984

Notes to Introduction

1. A. Fattal, *Le Statut légal des non-musulmans en pays d'Islam* (Beirut, 1958) covers the period from 622 to the advent of the Ottomans in 1516–17. The author is principally concerned with the situation of the Christians in Egypt, Syria, Iraq, and Arabia; the Maghreb is mentioned incidentally. This scientific work and the clarity of its analysis render all the more regrettable some generalizations and comparisons concerning Judaism.

2. Muslim dogma divides the world into two parts: the *dar al-Islam*, which includes all the areas governed by the law of Islam, and the *dar al-Harb* (territories of warfare),

subject to the law of the infidels. A permanent state of war *(jihad)* exists between these two regions, but temporary peace treaties may be agreed upon. *Jihad* refers to the two struggles that the Muslim should make: to improve his own faith, and to strengthen and propagate Islam—either through warfare, or by persuasion, teaching, and the consolidation of Islam. Armed combat and missionary proselytism are the two tactics of *jihad* that are incumbent upon the Muslim community. R. Peters, *Jihad in Mediaeval and Modern Islam*, in *Nisaba* (Leiden, 1977), 5:86–90, provides a bibliography of translations of classical sources on the *jihad*. See also n. 10, chap. 1 (part I), below. Also see *Encyclopaedia of Islam*, 2d ed. *(EI²)*, "Dar al-Harb" (A. Abel), 2:126.

3. Fattal; A. S. Tritton, *The Caliphs and their Non-Muslim Subjects: A Critical Study of the Covenant of Umar* (London, 1930; reprint 1970); idem, "Islam and the Protected Religions", in *JRAS* (1931): pp. 311–38; E. Strauss (Ashtor), "The Social Isolation of Ahl adh-Dhimma," in *P. Hirschler Memorial Book* (Budapest, 1949), pp. 73–94. Concerning the situation of Jews in Muslim lands, see, *inter alia*, S. W. Baron, *A Social and Religious History of the Jews* (Philadelphia, 1957), 3:120–72 (and notes), 5:95–108 (and notes); S. D. Goitein, *Jews and Arabs: Their Contacts through the Ages*, 3d rev. ed. (New York, 1974); E. Fagnan, "Le Signe distinctif des Juifs au Maghreb," in *REJ* 28, no. 56 (1894):294–98; idem, *Arabo-Judaica*, in *Mélanges Hartwig Derenbourg (1844–1908)* (Paris, 1909), pp. 103–20; G. Vajda, "Juifs et Musulmans selon le Hadit," in *JA* 219 (1937): 57–127; idem, "L'Image du Juif dans la tradition islamique," in *NC* 13–14 (1968): 3–7; N. A. Stillman, *The Jews of Arab Lands: A History and Source Book* (Philadelphia, 1979). Further information on the history of Jews and Christians and their situation in the Middle Ages is to be found in Ibn Naqqash, "Fetoua relatif à la condition des Zimmis et particulièrement des Chrétiens en pays musulmans," trans. Belin, in *JA* 18 (1851): 417–516, and 19 (1852): 97–140. See also R. J. H. Gottheil, *Dhimmis and Moslems in Egypt*, in *Old Testament and Semitic Studies in memory of W. R. Harper* (Chicago, 1908), 2:353–414; idem, "An Answer to the Dhimmis," in *JAOS* 41 (1921): 383–457; C. Cahen, "Histoire économico-sociale et islamologie: le problème préjudiciel de l'adaptation entre les autochtones et l'Islam," in *Les Peuples musulmans dans l'histoire médiévale* (Damascus, Institut Français, 1977), pp. 169–88; S. A. Aldeeb Abu-Sahlieh, *Non-Musulmans en pays d'Islam: cas de l'Egypte* (Fribourg, Switzerland, 1979).

For an insight into the situation of the *dhimmis* under the Ottomans, see H. A. R. Gibb and H. Bowen, *Islamic Society and the West: A Study of the Impact of Western Civilization on Muslim Culture in the Near East*. Vol. 1: *Islamic Society in the Eighteenth Century*, Part 2 (Oxford, 1957), ch. 14, pp. 207–61.

Information on the position of the *dhimmi* may be found in the Ottoman-Turkish archives (Istanbul): *Bashvekalet Arshivi (Archives of the Prime Minister's Office)* and in the Arabic sources, *Sijjil* (Registers) of Muslim *Sharia* Courts. See Asad Rustum, *Al-Mahfuzat al-Malikiyya al-Misriyya (The Royal Archives of Egypt)*, 4 vols. (Beirut, 1940–1943). See also B. Lewis, "The Ottoman Archives as a Source for the History of the Arab Lands" (1951), in *Studies in Classical and Ottoman Islam (7th–16th centuries)*, Variorum reprints (London, 1976). S. Shamir, "Muslim-Arab attitudes towards Jews: The Ottoman and modern periods," in *Violence and Defence in the Jewish Experience* ed. S. W. Baron and G. S. Wise (Philadelphia, 1977); and K. Binswanger, *Untersuchungen zum Status der Nichtmuslime im Osmanischen Reich des 16. Jahrhunderts:mit einer Neudefinition des Begriffes "Dimma"* (Munich, 1977); for a valuable bibliography pertaining to the Jews of the Maghreb, see R. Attal, *Les Juifs d'Afrique du Nord: bibliographie* (Jerusalem, 1973); and its supplement, R. Attal & Y. Tobi, *Oriental and North African Jewry: An Annotated Bibliography (1974–1976)* (Jerusalem, 1980). And a recent study, P. B. Fenton, "Jewish Attitudes to Islam: Israel Heeds Ishmael," in *JQ* 29 (1983): 84–102.

PART ONE

1
Historical Outline

In the year 622, on the invitation of the Ansar—a group of pagans converted to Islam—Muhammad and his small band of followers left Mecca for Yathrib (Medina). The population then consisted of numerous polytheistic clans, of Jewish tribes that had long been established in Arabia, and of Arabs converted to Judaism. The Jews practised agriculture and various specialized handicrafts, while paying dues in money or in kind to pagan Arab tribes allied with them.

The arrival of Muhammad and his followers in Medina provoked no opposition from the Jews. The Prophet organized the Muslim immigrants into a community—the *umma*. He preached to them an egalitarian moral system founded on the principles of solidarity, charity, and mutual confidence and respect that ought to prevail among Muslims. These principles, revolutionary for a heathen Arab society, were applicable only within the *umma*.[1] Relations with non-Muslims were elaborated progressively, on the basis of a strategy of hostilities and truces pursued in accordance with the requirements needed to assure the Muslim victory. Razzias in the cause of Allah, during which war and religion were inextricably mingled, inspired many verses of the Koran regarding the *jihad* (Holy War) and its twofold reward: booty in this life and paradise in the hereafter.[2]

The doctrine preached by Muhammad was a simple one. The Koran is a book of divine origin revealed progressively to Muhammad through the angel Gabriel. Islam is the only true and eternal religion (Koran 3:17). The prophets of Israel and Jesus had already preached it and foretold the coming of Muhammad, but the Jews and Christians, jealous of the perfection of the new religion, had rejected him and falsified their own sacred Scriptures. The Muslim faith stresses the divine character of the Koran and of Muhammad's preaching: "Whosoever obeys the Messenger obeys God."[3] Muhammad, being the last of the messengers sent by God to instruct humanity, is the *seal* of the prophets.

In 624 Muhammad, joined by more followers, called upon the Qaynuqa, one of the Jewish tribes of Medina, to recognize his prophetic mission. When they refused, he besieged and overcame them. On the

intercession of one of their protectors—a recent convert to Islam—
their lives were spared, but they were expelled from the city, their
lands and a part of their possessions being confiscated by the Muslims.
The following year the Jewish Nadir tribe suffered a similar fate:
Muhammad burned down their palm groves and divided all their
fields and houses among the community of the Believers.[4]

In 627 the Meccans sent a united force to lay siege to the Muslims in
Medina, but they withdrew suddenly on a stormy night without
fighting. However, guided by the angel Gabriel, Muhammad then
turned his host against the Jewish tribe of the Qurayza, who had been
neutral during the siege. Because the Jews refused conversion,
Muhammad attacked and overwhelmed them. Trenches were then
dug in the marketplace of Medina, and the Jews—six to nine hundred
of them, according to traditional Muslim sources—were led forth in
batches and decapitated. All the menfolk perished in this way, with
the exception of one convert to Islam. The Prophet then divided the
women, children, houses, and chattels among the Muslims.[5]

Shrewd in political matters, Muhammad then endeavored to win
over the powerful tribes of Mecca. In 628, taking advantage of a
treaty of nonbelligerency (Hudaybiya) with the Meccans,[6] he attacked
the oasis of Khaybar, one hundred and forty kilometers northwest of
Medina, cultivated by another Jewish tribe. The assailants came to the
oasis at night and in the morning attacked the peasants as they were
coming out to work in the fields, carrying spades and baskets.[7] Their
palm groves were burned down. After a siege lasting a month and a
half, the inhabitants surrendered under the terms of a treaty known
as the *dhimma.* According to this agreement Muhammad allowed the
Jews to continue cultivating their oasis, on condition that they ceded
to him half of their produce; he also reserved the right to break the
agreement and expel them whenever he wished.[8] Subsequently, all the
Jewish and Christian communities of Arabia submitted to the Muslims under the terms of a *dhimma* similar to that granted at Khaybar.
The peasantry were expected to provide assistance and provisions to
the Muslim forces and pay a tribute in money or kind known as the
jizya, to be distributed among the Prophet and his followers according
to the circumstances of the conquest. In addition, they were to make
available an area within their synagogues and churches, if required by
the Muslims. On his side, Muhammad undertook to respect their
religious observances and to defend them. Thus, newly converted
Bedouin permitted sedentary cultivators to continue tilling their own
soil as share-croppers in exchange for a tribute.

The *dhimma* of Khaybar, which fixed the relationship between the
Muslim victors and the vanquished local inhabitants, was thereafter to

serve as a model for the treaties granted by the Arab conquerors to the conquered peoples in territories beyond Arabia. Henceforth, the term *dhimma* will be used in the sense of the unequal agreements that regulated the relationship between the Muslim conquerors and the vanquished populations.

These episodes in the life of Muhammad are recalled since they inspired Koranic revelations and thereby gave a definitive form to the main features of future relationships between Muslims and infidels concerning the strategy of warfare *(jihad)*, Muslim rights of conquest, the laws pertaining to the division of booty, and the fate of the vanquished populations whose lands were taken over by the Islamic community, for according to Muslim tradition Muhammad said at the siege of Khaybar: "The land belongs to Allah and his Messenger."[9]

The fate of the Jews of Arabia has been outlined because it foreshadowed that of all the peoples subsequently conquered by the Arabs. The primary guiding principle of the *jihad* was to summon the non-Muslims to convert or accept Muslim supremacy, and, if faced with refusal, to attack them until they submitted to Muslim domination.

As the Muslims grew increasingly powerful, the Holy War spread out beyond Arabia. Initially a razzia for spoils, the *jihad* developed into a war of conquest subject to a code of legislation, the principal aim of which was the conversion of the infidels. Truces were allowed but never a lasting peace.[10] Polytheists generally had to choose between death or conversion; life, freedom of worship, and the inviolability of their belongings was, on certain conditions, conceded to Jews, Christians, and Zoroastrians, and later, of necessity, to Hindus.

The *jihad* is a global conception that divides the peoples of the world into two irreconcilable camps: that of the *dar al-Harb*, the "Territory of War," which covers those regions controlled by the infidels; and the *dar al-Islam*, the "Territory of Islam," the Muslim homeland where Islamic law reigns. The *jihad* is the normal and permanent state of war between the Muslims and the *dar al-Harb*, a war that can only end with the final domination over unbelievers and the absolute supremacy of Islam throughout the world.[11] In the fourteenth century, a jurist, Ibn Taymiyya, justified this permanent state of war by asserting that because the possession of lands by infidels is illegitimate, such lands should *revert* by Divine Right to the adherents of the true religion. Thus the *jihad* became the means by which the Muslims *received back* that which had been usurped on earth by the infidels (see doc. 4). In this sense it is a holy and legitimate war because it *restored* to the Muslims the lands and possessions that should be a part of the *dar al-Islam*, but which the *dar al-Harb* retains illegally. For that reason,

any warlike act in the *dar al-Harb*—which has no legal right to exist—
may be regarded as just and legitimate and is exempt from any moral
disapproval.[12]

Since the *jihad* is a state of permanent war, it excludes the possibility
of true peace, but it does allow for provisional truces in accordance
with the requirements of the political situation. These truces, which
should not last for more than a maximum of ten years, can be ended
unilaterally by the Muslim ruler, but only after he has first warned the
enemy. Finally, the *jihad* lays down the conditions for treaties with the
dar al-Harb, always within the framework of this concept of a provisional truce. Regarded by Muslim theologians as one of the fundamental articles of the faith, participation in the *jihad* is held to be a
duty incumbent upon all the Believers, each of whom must contribute
to it as best he can, either in person through military service, or by
material contributions or through writings and militantism.

Muslim jurists fixed the rights of conquest on the basis of Muhammad's treatment of the Jews of Arabia. This treatment became a
model serving as a universal norm to be applied to all Jews, Christians, Zoroastrians, and others vanquished by *jihad.* In the same manner as Muhammad had spared the Jews of Khaybar, who had
recognized his suzerainty, so the Arab conquerors concluded "toleration" treaties with all the other peoples who, faced with *jihad,* submitted to their domination. The *dhimmi* condition, which is a direct
consequence of *jihad,* is connected with this same contract. It suspends
the conqueror's initial rights over the adherents of the revealed religions on payment of a tribute such as the Jews had agreed to give the
Prophet at Khaybar. Thus the hazards of history, or Providence, chose
some obscure Jewish tribes of Arabia to symbolize the fate awaiting
the powerful and populous Byzantine and Sassanian empires, and of
a multitude of peoples in Africa, Asia, and Europe who, in the course
of history, had fallen to the advance of Islam during a millennium of
expansion and annexation. The ideological web of the *jihad* has linked
the fate of Israel to the destiny of multitudes. Thus Israel's fate in
Arabia became the fate of many tribes, peoples, and nations. Its destiny was in no way exceptional, but rather it became the ominous
mirror reflecting the historical subjection of a large section of humanity.

The cities of the Byzantine and Sassanian empires, exhausted by
half a century of wars and internal struggles, succumbed to the Arab
hosts. The pacts made with the Christian and Zoroastrian populations
varied according to whether the victory had been obtained through a
capitulation, a war, or by means of a treaty. In the first two cases the
harbis who had taken up arms and fought could be put to death or
reduced to slavery, redeemed, exchanged, or set at liberty, and their

wives and children—according to the precedent of the treatment meted out to the Jews of Arabia—could be taken as slaves. If, however, the *harbis,* like the Jews of Khaybar, submitted to the rule of Islam, the conquerors agreed to respect their lives, their religion, and their property according to the provisions of the treaty *(dhimma),* which was binding on the two parties. Meanwhile the Muslim armies continued their march of conquest, securing their hinterland by the establishment in the annexed territories of military garrisons and settlers from Arabia. In the *dhimma* conceded to Hira (Iraq) in 633, a specific clause was introduced dealing with the principle of a vestmental distinction between Muslims and non-Muslims.

In 640 the caliph Umar b. al-Khattab expelled the Jews and Christians from the Hijaz, basing his action on the *dhimma* of Khaybar. He quoted the Prophet: "The land belongs to Allah and his Messenger, the Messenger of Allah can annul his pact if he so wishes." He is also said to have cited the Prophet's advice: "Two religions shall not remain together in the peninsula of the Arabs."[13]

The ninth-century Arab historian al-Waqidi recorded a story, purported to have been told by a notable of Medina who visited Khaybar following the hostilities between Muhammad and the Jews:

> When we were in Medina and famine would strike us, we would go to Khaybar and stay there a while before returning, or sometimes we would go to Fadak or Tayma.[14] The Jewish inhabitants always possessed fruit and an abundant supply of water. . . . All this was before the rise of Islam. When the Prophet came to Medina and conquered Khaybar, I said to my companions, "Shall we go to Khaybar for we are stricken with hunger?", and they replied, "The countryside has changed, for, as Muslims, we now encounter a people who harbour animosity and malice towards Islam, whereas beforehand we had no religion". However, as we were tormented by hunger, we made our way to Khaybar where we found that the owners of the land and palm trees had changed, for the Jewish owners and rich proprietors had been killed and those who remained were poor people who lived by the work of their hands.[15]

Origins of the Dhimma

For the Muslims the Koran is the word of Allah, and Muhammad is His Messenger to mankind:

> It is not for any believer, man or woman, when God and His Messenger have decreed a matter, to have the choice in the affair. Whosoever disobeys God and His Messenger has gone astray into manifest error. (Koran 33:36)

The Koran is thus the divine and sacred foundation of Islamic law. The victory that delivered up the most advanced civilizations of the

time to the Muslims created complex administrative problems that
Muhammad had not anticipated. An Islamic system of legislation was
required in order to govern the multitudes of subject peoples. Since
Muhammad was now dead, theologians sought to discover the will of
Allah in the Prophet's words and deeds *(hadith)*. A sacred record of his
doings and sayings, handed down by a chain of transmitters *(isnad)*
was compiled into a corpus of Traditions *(Sunna)*, which was completed toward the end of the ninth century. The different interpretations of the *Sunna* were codified by the four principal orthodox
Muslim schools of law: the Hanafi, the Maliki, the Shafi'i, and the
Hanbali.

Because religion is inseparable from politics in Islam, it was necessary to discover a definition of the Good, as a practical guide no less
than a spiritual one. The theologians agreed unanimously that, since
Islam was the only true religion, what the Muslim community *(umma)*
accepts as being true and just, must be so.[16] This is the principle of the
ijma, or the consensus of the Islamic community.

Controlling a huge empire, the invading Arab armies were a small
minority among the mass of non-Muslims, mainly Christians and
Zoroastrians. The Byzantine and Persian systems of administration
were retained for practical reasons, but a special legislation regulated
the relations between the Arabs and the indigenous peoples, between
Muslims and non-Muslims. Basing themselves on the Koran and the
Traditions, Muslim theologians elaborated the *dhimmi* status—that is,
that of the non-Muslim indigenous populations now under Islamic
rule. This body of rules, also known as the Covenant of Umar, is
variably attributed by Arab historians to Umar I (634–644), or to
Umar II (717–720).[17] It is generally agreed by Western orientalists,
however, that this legislation was inconsistent with the liberal policies
of the first four caliphs and the ninety-year dynasty of the Umayyads
(661–750). It appears to have evolved under the early Abbasid rule, at
the time when the intolerant religious authorities were occupied in
suppressing heresies and in brutally crushing local revolts.

The legal status of the *dhimmis*—defined by the *dhimma*—was based
on the contracts between Muhammad and the Jewish and Christian
tribes of Arabia, but it differed from them in its coercive components.
It was elaborated long after the conquest, at a time when Arab economic and military colonization was gaining strength. Its humiliating
character may be explained in a context of power, which facilitated
the institutionalization of oppression by a military organization, in full
control of the means of domination. Thus the *dhimma*, losing its original character of an agreement binding the parties concerned, became
the formal expression of a legalized persecution. It was the *dhimma*
that was largely instrumental in the success of the policies of Arabiza-

tion and Islamization of vast regions outside Arabia and the progressive disappearance of indigenous peoples and cultures.

The inferior status of Jews, Samaritans, Christians, Sabaeans, and Zoroastrians passed through various modifications at different times and places. In traditionalist regions the *dhimmi* status was maintained, as in North Africa up until European colonization, and in Persia and Yemen into the twentieth century. On the other hand, the *dhimmis* were granted the right of self-administration according to the laws of their religions as well as—subject to certain restrictions—freedom of worship, movement, and residence, which proved precious guarantees except in times of fanaticism and anarchy.

The Islamic power granted the subjected Jewish and Christian peoples the right to collect taxes for their own communal institutions, the right to administer justice in matters of personal law, freedom of religious education and worship, and recognized the official status of the head of each community. Such privileges were not an innovation. In its struggle for survival amidst a heathen multinational empire, the Jewish people, on its land and in the Diaspora, managed to secure similar privileges from the Greek and Roman emperors. But under the Byzantines, the Greek Orthodox clergy endeavored to curtail them. The subsequent Arab rulers restored the traditional Roman administrative regulations applicable to the Jews, and extended them to all the tolerated religions.

In the Ottoman Empire, a clause of the Hatti Humayun edict (1856), inserted on the insistence of the European powers, abolished the discriminatory status of the *dhimmi* (*raya* in the Ottoman Empire, a word previously applied to the Muslim peasantry), but effective emancipation was granted them only somewhat later.

Muslim legal writings, Arab and *dhimmi* chronicles, and the accounts of European consuls and travelers over the centuries provide a valuable documentation on the *dhimmis*.

Notes to Chapter 1

1. The ordinance allegedly granted by Muhammad on his arrival at Medina and known as the *Constitution of Medina*, included both Jews and pagan Arabs within the Islamic community, but it proved ephemeral. See Ibn Ishaq (d. 767), *Sirat Rasul Allah (The Life of Muhammad)*, trans. A. Guillaume (Oxford, 1955), pp. 231–33; Stillman, pp. 115–18; M. Gil, "The Constitution of Medina: A Reconsideration," in *IOS* 4 (1974): 44–65.

2. The perfection of the Koran, the duty of Muslims to engage in *jihad*, and the inferiority of infidels are recurrent themes in the Koran and the Traditions (*Sunna*). To avoid repetition, no further references to the Koran have been made on these themes. All Koranic quotations are taken from A. J. Arberry, *The Koran Interpreted* (Oxford: World Classics, 1964).

3. Koran 4:82, 106, 135; 5:22; 6: 114, 126; 11:17, 20; 12:2, 104. See n. 2 above.

4. al-Bukhari (d. 869), *Les Traditions Islamiques (Al-Sahih)*, trans. O. Houdas and W. Marçais (Paris, 1903–1914), vol. 2, title 41, chap. 6; title 56, chap. 80: 3, chap. 154: 2. This compilation of the acts and sayings attributed to Muhammad, completed in the ninth century, constitutes one of the two pillars of Islamic jurisprudence, the other being the contemporary compilation made by his younger disciple, Muslim (d. 875).

→ 5. Ibn Ishaq, pp. 461–69; M. Gaudefroy-Demombynes, *Mahomet* (Paris, 1969), pp. 142–46; W. Montgomery Watt, "Muhammad", in the *Cambridge History of Islam* (Cambridge, 1970), 1:39–49.

6. Gaudefroy-Demombynes, p. 154; Bukhari, vol. 2, title 54, chap. 15.

7. Ibn Ishaq, p. 511; Bukhari, vol. 2, title 56, chaps. 102: 5, 130.

8. Ibn Ishaq, pp. 524–25; Bukhari, vol. 2, title 41, chaps. 8, 9, 11, 17, and title 57, chap. 19: 10. For an example of the treaties between Muhammad and the Jews living in Makna (near Eilat), see al-Baladhuri (d. 892), vol. 1, *The Origins of the Islamic State (Kitab Futûh al-Buldân)*, trans. P. K. Hitti (New York, 1916), pp. 93–94.

9. Muslim, *Traditions (Al-Sahih)*, trans. A. H. Siddiqi (Lahore, 1976), vol. 3, chap. 723 (4363); Bukhari, vol. 2, title 57, chap. 1: 3, and title 58, chap. 6: 1.

10. Koran 8: 40; 9: 124; 24: 56. See n. 2 above. On the aim and rules of *jihad*, see below, documents 1, 2, 3. Also Bukhari, vol. 2, chaps. *De la Guerre Sainte* (t. 56), *De la Prescription du Quint* (t. 57), *La Capitation* (t. 58). Muslim, vol. 3, chaps. 704–53 *(The Book of Jihad and Expedition);* Fattal, pp. 14–18, 372–73. The code concerning *jihad* or Holy War has been studied and described by all Muslim jurisconsults.

11. See *EI¹*, "Djihad" (D. B. Mac Donald) 1: 1141–42; *EI²*, "Djihad" (E. Tyan) 2: 538–40; *EI²*, "Ahl al-Kitab" (G. Vajda) 1: 264–66; *EI²*, "Dhimma" (C. Cahen) 2: 227–31; M. du Caurroy, "Législation musulmane sunnite, rite Hanéfi", in *J.A.*, 4th ser. 17, 18 (1851), and 19 (1852); Tabari (d. 923), *Kitab al-Jihad (Book of Holy War)*, ed. Schacht (Leiden, 1933); Shaybani (d. 805), *Siyar (The Islamic law of nations)*, trans. M. Khadduri (Baltimore, Md., 1966); M. Khadduri, *War and Peace in the Law of Islam* (Baltimore, Md., 1955). For the modern period, Al Azhar University, ed., *The Fourth Conference of the Academy of Islamic Research* (1968) (Cairo: Government Printing Offices, 1970), pp. 23–250 and D. F. Green, ed., *Arab Theologians on Jews and Israel: Extracts from the Proceedings of the Fourth Conference of the Academy of Islamic Research (1968)*, 3d ed. (Geneva, 1976), pp. 61–68; Abd al-Qadir, as-Sufi, *Jihad, a Groundplan* (London, 1978); Peters, *Jihad . . .; idem, Islam and Colonialism: The Doctrine of Jihad in Modern History* (The Hague, 1979), contains a comprehensive bibliography (pp. 201–25).

12. Gaudefroy-Demonbynes, p. 521.

→ 13. Ibn Ishaq, p. 525; Bukhari, vol. 2, t. 41, chap. 17; t. 54, chap. 14; vol. 4, t. 89, chap. 2; Muslim, vol. 3, chap. 723 (4366); Fattal, p. 85.

14. Oasis cultivated by Jewish tribes.

15. al-Waqidi (d. 823), *Kitab al-Maghazi*, ed. M. Jones (London, 1966), 2:713; see also I. Ben Zvi, *The Exiled and the Redeemed* (London, 1958), p. 172.

16. Koran, 3:105; I. Goldziher, *Le Dogme et la loi de l'Islam* (Paris, 1973), pp. 44–45.

17. See Theophanes (758–817), in *Corpus Scriptorum Historiae Byzantinaea* (Bonn, 1892), §334; Ibn Abd ar-Rabbih (864–940), *al-Iqd al Farid* (Cairo, 1884), 2:339–40.

2
Aspects of the Dhimmi Condition

Conquest and Annexation of Territories

Basing himself on the precedent of Khaybar, where the Jewish lands became the property of the whole Islamic community, Umar I forbade the division of the conquered lands amongst the Muslim warriors. Except for individual fiefs (qata'i), the conquered territories became *fay* lands—that is, the property of the Muslim community.[1]

The *dhimmi* peoples became a valuable source of assistance for the conquerors. Making up the entire economic infrastructure of the ever-expanding empire and skilled in professions unknown to the Arabs, they maintained the Arab military apparatus through their taxes and payments in kind, enabling it thereby to pursue the *jihad* without hindrance.

The conquest of the Byzantine Christian provinces by the Arab-Muslim armies ended civil strife, as well as the Orthodox Church's violent persecutions of both the dissident Churches and the Synagogue. However, the oppressive fiscal system provoked revolts and peasant insurrections that were harshly repressed by the Arab colonialists. The insurgents were put to the sword, large sections of the local populations (e.g., Persians, Armenians, Copts, etc.) were reduced to slavery, and many were deported.

The first Arab colonies were military camps, controlling the highways and frontiers, which gradually grew into towns. In the wake of the victorious Arab armies, waves of emigrants swept across the conquered lands to the east and west. This continual influx, century after century, accelerated the process of Arabization. The invaders enjoyed special privileges when they settled in the new territories. Expropriation and fiscal oppression resulting from the conquest and colonization thinned the ranks of the *dhimmi* peasantries, who emigrated to the new towns or to regions beyond Muslim domination.

However, in numerous *hadith*, Islamic teaching recalls the Prophet's warnings against the mistreatment of subject peoples and against placing too heavy a burden upon them. Baladhuri relates that when

some people in the Lebanon revolted against the collector of the
kharaj (land tax) at Ba'labakk (Baalbek), Salih ibn-Ali ibn-Abdallah ibn
Abbas sent in troops to crush the insurrection. Some of the rebels
went back to their villages where they were allowed to retain their
Christian faith, but others were expelled. When al-Awza'i heard this,
he reproached Salih, saying:

> Thou hast heard of the expulsion of the *dhimmis* from Mt. Lebanon,
> although they did not side with those who rebelled, and of whom
> many were killed by thee and the rest returned to their villages.
> How didst thou then punish the many for the fault of the few and
> make them leave their homes and possessions in spite of Allah's
> decree: "Nor shall any sinning one bear the burden of another"
> (Koran 6:164), which is the most rightful thing to abide by and
> follow? The command worthy of the strictest observance and obedi-
> ence is that of the Prophet who says, "If one oppresses a man bound
> to us by covenant and charges him with more than he can do, I am
> the one to overcome him by arguments."[2]

The destructive consequences of the wars and of continual foreign
invasions were prolonged and reinforced by the laws of the conquerors. In reserving the right to revoke the *dhimma* unilaterally at
any time, the victors placed the *dhimmis* in a situation of permanent
insecurity. The tolerated status granted to them on their own land, in
return for submission, established for centuries a form of protection
that was provisional and conditional upon the will of the ruler. The
expulsions of the Jews and Christians from Arabia set a precedent for
similar actions in later periods. These expulsions, however, were rare
and were often rescinded.

Discriminatory Taxes

a) Kharaj

The rights of conquest first established at Khaybar led to the expropriation of the vanquished peoples by the transfer of their lands to
the Islamic community. The *dhimmi,* thus dispossessed by the victors,
retained the right to cultivate his land in exchange for the payment of
a tax to the Muslim ruler. This tax, called *kharaj,* represents the Islamic community's rights of ownership over the conquered lands of
non-Muslim peoples. The *kharaj* thus transformed the former peas-
ant-owner into a tributary, who tilled his land as a tenant—his heirs
retaining this same right—whereas the freehold ownership was
confiscated by the ruler.

As the *dhimmis* were forbidden to possess arms, they became totally
dependent on the occupying power. In certain rural areas, the servile

character of the *dhimmi*'s condition worsened with the passage of time. In 1884 Charles de Foucauld described areas in southern Morocco where the Jews and their families belonged body and soul to their Muslim master and were unable to leave him. Here the condition of serfdom was determined by religion and was passed on from generation to generation: these people were part of the master's inheritance in exactly the same way as his lands and livestock. As late as 1913, the Jews of Dadès in the Greater Atlas of Morocco were serfs, the property of their Muslim master.[3]

The *kharaj* was subject to varying interpretations in different times and places. In the Ottoman Empire it was sometimes confused with the *jizya*. It should be noted that a similar land tax had already been in existence prior to the Muslim conquest in the Byzantine and Persian empires. If its adoption by the Arabs did not alter the essential nature of the tax, it endowed it with a sacred and definitive significance. It represented the inalienable rights over the territory of the vanquished that Allah had conferred upon the victors.

The payment of the *kharaj* guaranteed protection to the *dhimmis*. However, this relationship often lapsed, owing to the disparity between the two parties—on the one hand, a sedentary culture founded on daily labor, and on the other, warlike Bedouin traditions. Whereas the caliphs had been able to protect the laboring non-Muslim peasantries at the beginning of the conquest, in periods of instability the latter suffered from Arab internecine bellicosity that, added to other factors, ruined the agricultural system.

b) Jizya

In addition to the *kharaj*, the *dhimmi* had to pay a poll tax, the *jizya* (Koran 9:29), which was assessed at three rates in accordance with the economic condition of each individual male above puberty.

According to some jurists, this poll tax was to be paid by each person individually at a humiliating public ceremony in which the *dhimmi*, while paying it, was struck either on the head or on the nape of the neck. However, Abu Yusuf Ya'qub (d. 798) recommended clemency and justice in the collection of the *jizya* (see note 63 and doc. 3). Women, paupers, minors, the chronically sick and the crippled were theoretically exempted from this tax.[4]

When oppressive taxation provoked a wave of conversions to Islam, the administration imposed a collective sum on each *dhimmi* community which their notables apportioned between them, irrespective of their numbers.

Possession of the receipt for the *jizya*—originally a piece of parchment worn around the neck or a seal worn on the wrist or on the chest—enabled the *dhimmi* to move from place to place. A *dhimmi* travelling without this receipt could be put in jail. The seal of the *jizya*, characteristic of the *dhimmi*, was soon regarded as a mark of dishonour. Later, in the Ottoman Empire, the receipt had to be produced at the demand of tax-collectors on pain of immediate imprisonment, for the *dhimmis* were easily recognisable by their distinctive costume and could be stopped in the street. The French consular archives show that one of the chief objections to the employment of Jews or Christians as *dragomans* (interpreters) in the consulate during the Ottoman period was their subjection to the *jizya*, with all the humiliating conditions which it entailed. The prestige attached to this function was felt to be quite incompatible with the necessarily abject status of the *dhimmi*, as his degraded condition might reflect upon the consul himself.[5]

Dhimmis were allowed to practise usury—in theory forbidden to Muslims—but this commerce sometimes led to the murder of the creditor. Moreover, in loaning capital to their *dhimmi* "bankers," the authorities insisted in receiving a high rate of interest, a condition which increased the unpopularity of the usurer.

(c) Other Taxes (avariz: irregular taxes)

Dhimmis also paid higher commercial and travel taxes than the Muslims. Apart from taxation, large sums were extorted from the *dhimmi* communities at the ruler's pleasure. In the Middle Ages, if these burdens were not met, women and children would be reduced to slavery. As late as the eighteenth century, Church leaders and notables in the Ottoman Empire were imprisoned and tortured until a ransom was paid for them. From the middle of the sixteenth century until the early nineteenth, the Jewish community of Fez was ruined by such demands. In Tripoli about 1790, Ali Burghul put the whole Jewish community to ransom, threatening it with a general massacre.[6] In Yemen, Persia, and other places the Jews were often victims of fiscal oppression.

In several regions throughout Syria, Palestine, and Iraq the periodic insecurity that prevailed until the late nineteenth century forced the *dhimmi* communities to protect themselves from pillage and massacre by paying protection money to emirs, sheikhs, and leaders of marauding bands. The practice of buying one's security became established whenever the central authority failed and local power fell into the hands of nomadic tribes seeking plunder. It brought about the ruin of unarmed and sedentary populations (including Muslims), constantly threatened and exploited by rival clans.

The necessity of having to pay for their security and survival became the norm for the *dhimmi* communities. This custom legalized financial abuses and extortion and, in the end, shattered the indigenous pre-Arab populations, almost totally eliminating what remained of its peasantry.[7]

At the end of the eighteenth century, Sheikh Dahir al-Umar, who had extended his rule over Galilee and Samaria, raised an unusual tax which was referred to in a letter from the French consul in Sidon.

> A peculiarity in the life of this man, now aged ninety, is that he marries or rather takes a young girl of thirteen or fourteen each year. The religious of the Holy Land—in other words, the Order of St. Francis—must cover the costs of the ceremony. They have allowed a custom to become established whereby they pay 1000 écus to the sheikh for the first night. If only to gain this sum, he will marry every year until his last breath.[8]

François Charles-Roux has defined the *avania:* "To use a modern expression, an *avania* was blackmail—a sum of money extorted from the nation [community] under the threat of persecution."[9] The methods of extortion sometimes included confiscation and torture. In 1849 the Jews of Tiberias envisaged exile because of the brutality, exactions, and injustice of the authorities.[10] In addition to ordinary taxes, their coreligionists in Hebron were accustomed to pay five thousand piastres annually to an Arab sheikh for the protection of their lives and property;[11] nonetheless, the same sheikh added a further ransom in 1852, threatening to attack and expel them from the town if it was not paid. In the second half of the nineteenth century, the pressure exerted by European powers put an end to these ransoms, which had reduced whole communities to utter destitution.

Public Administration

The exclusion of *dhimmis* from public office was based on several verses of the Koran (3:27, 113; 5:56) and on *hadiths*, according to which an infidel ought never to exert authority over a Muslim. In spite of this, *dhimmis* frequently did hold public office; detested and often discarded, they were nevertheless indispensible. Although Umar I (634–644) had forbidden the employment of *dhimmis* in public office, Umar II (717–720) found many *dhimmis* employed in the civil administration and ordered their dismissal. In the Middle Ages, the holding of high administrative positions by *dhimmis* could lead to an insurrection (e.g., Granada in 1066, Fez in 1275 and 1465, Iraq in 1291 and frequently in Egypt under the Mamluks: 1250–1517). The populace, stirred up by the *ulama,* demanded their re-

moval; the emirs sometimes tried to protect them by offering them
the choice between either resignation or conversion. A number accepted conversion in order to keep their positions.

Inequality before the Law: Invalidity of the Dhimmi's Oath

Every legal case involving a Muslim and a *dhimmi* was judged according to Koranic law. Although the very idea of justice implies an
equality between parties, a *dhimmi* was not allowed to give evidence
against a Muslim. Since his oath was unacceptable in an Islamic court,
his Muslim opponent could not easily be condemned. In order to
defend himself, the *dhimmi* was obliged to purchase Muslim witnesses
at great expense. In Bosnia, the British vice-consul noted in a report
of 1877:

> The present Cadi [Muslim judge] of Travnik resolutely refuses to
> admit all Christian evidence before the Tribunals, and though the
> Mussulman witnesses are always, it is true, to be found for money,
> nothing but a miscarriage of justice can be expected where such
> practices prevail.[12]

In 1895 the British consular agent in Jaffa noted: "False witnesses
are always ready to appear in any accusation or claim brought by
Mussulmans against Christians and Jews."[13]

The refusal of the Muslim religious courts to accept the testimony
of the *dhimmi* was based on *hadiths* which maintained that the infidels
were of a perverse and mendacious character because they deliberately persisted in denying the superiority of Islam.[14] For the same
reason, a Muslim was never to be put to death on account of an
infidel. According to a *hadith,* attributed to Muhammad (in the compilation of Muslim, d.874), "No Muslim would die but Allah would
admit in his stead a Jew or a Christian in Hell-Fire."[15]

Lane observed in Egypt, about 1830: "A Jew has often been
sacrificed to save a Muslim."[16] The refusal to accept the *dhimmi*'s testimony was particularly serious in view of the frequent accusations
against Jews and Christians of having blasphemed the Prophet, Islam,
or the angels—an offence punishable by death. In such a case, the
dhimmi was in no position to contradict the testimony of the true
believer in a court of law and could save his life only by conversion to
Islam.

Nonetheless, there were exceptions to this rule and some cases are
recorded where even in Muslim religious courts *(sharia),* the testimony of *dhimmis* was accepted. In the nineteenth century the Ottomans introduced new systems of legal administration—the *mejjelé*
(1840)—which dealt with civil and criminal affairs according to

modified codes of law, derived from European, predominantly French jurisprudence. This change provided the base of a different system of justice, which recognized the *dhimmis'* testimony. Most of the Muslim judges continued to discriminate against Christians and Jews, but such a procedure was no longer legal throughout the Ottoman Empire and this was already a significant improvement.

Muslim law (Koran 2:174–75) applies the *lex talionis* (law of retaliation), which may be applied only between equal parties: that is, between Muslims. The punishment that a guilty Muslim received for a crime would be greatly reduced if the victim were a *dhimmi*, and, conversely, in practice if not in law, a *dhimmi* would often be sentenced to death if he dared raise his hand against a Muslim, even in legitimate self-defence. Such penalties were reported by travelers in Persia and Yemen until the end of the nineteenth century, and in the Maghreb until the European colonization.

Sometimes collective punishments would be imposed. In Persia, at the end of the nineteenth century, a whole community was held responsible for the offence of one of its members. In 1866, when a Jew wounded a Muslim who had tried to kill him in Fez, thirty Jews were immediately wounded in retaliation, and only vigorous action by the authorities prevented a general massacre. According to Slouschz, who in 1908 visited the Jabal Gharian (Libya), the accidental killing of a Muslim would condemn the whole Jewish community to death or exile.[17]

Religion

a) Places of Worship

The laws concerning places of worship depended on the circumstances of the conquest and the terms of the treaties. The construction of new synagogues, as well as churches and convents, was forbidden by law, but the restoration of pre-Islamic places of worship was permitted, subject to certain restrictions and on condition that they were neither enlarged nor transformed.

Perhaps this penalization of non-Muslim religions reflected a desire to protect the conqueror's new faith, which—being foreign and uninstitutionalized—was at a disadvantage when faced with the more ancient religions practiced by the subjected local populations. The Bedouin, many of whom had been recently converted from paganism to Islam, could have been attracted by the civilizations of the conquered peoples among whom they were a minority. Thus the abasement of the other religions, no less than the privileges of the conquerors, served to reinforce the Muslim Arabs' feelings of superiority. Religious restrictions, which were probably derived from the needs of colonization, became customary. Although these restrictions frequently fell into desuetude, nonetheless the *ulama* demanded their reactivation, even after Arab colonization had succeeded in stamping out the indigenous cultures.

Dhimmi places of worship were not considered inviolable. They could be ransacked, burned, or demolished as acts of reprisal against the community, on the pretext that some of their members had exceeded their rights. The exterior of these buildings looked dilapidated and the extreme wretchedness of their interiors and contents was at times the result of looting, or a deliberate policy of the *dhimmis* to discourage predatory attacks. This state of decay was often mentioned by *dhimmi* chroniclers and described by European consuls and later by foreign travelers. In 1852 soldiers housed their horses and donkeys in a Tiberias synagogue.[18] In 1855, when a synagogue was renovated in Jerusalem, its enlargement and embellishment were forbidden.[19] Early photographs dating from the middle of the nineteenth century show the disrepair of the Church of the Holy Sepulchre in Jerusalem and confirm that a cross was only permitted to surmount its dome a few years after the 1856 edict of emancipation.[20] A traveler visiting Sulaymaniyah in northern Iraq reported in 1909 that troops had occupied one of the rooms of the synagogue and made it a shambles, covering it with filth. The provisioning of the army, one of the obligations that fell to the *dhimmis,* gave rise to numerous abuses. Descriptions from Morocco, Libya, and Palestine in the second half of the nineteenth century inform us that the lodging and maintenance of troops exposed the *dhimmis* to maltreatment, pillage, and sometimes even death.

Conversely, nineteenth-century European travelers give examples where, if Jews or Christians entered a mosque in North Africa, it was regarded as a capital offence. Their impure nature was said to defile the Muslim places of worship, which they were not supposed to approach. In 1869 a Jew passing in front of the great Zaytuna Mosque in Tunis was killed on a false charge of having intended to enter it. In 1888, when a Jew from Isfahan was falsely accused of having struck a Muslim and profaned a mosque by his presence, the Jewish community was collectively punished and almost massacred. The delegate of the *Alliance Israélite Universelle* in the Yemen, Sémach, noted in 1910 that a Jew who dared to enter a mosque would not leave it alive. On the other hand, in the second half of the nineteenth century the authorities of the Ottoman Empire tried to accustom the population to a more tolerant attitude.

Solely because of the special relationship between Turkey and Great Britain, in 1862 the Prince of Wales became the first Christian since

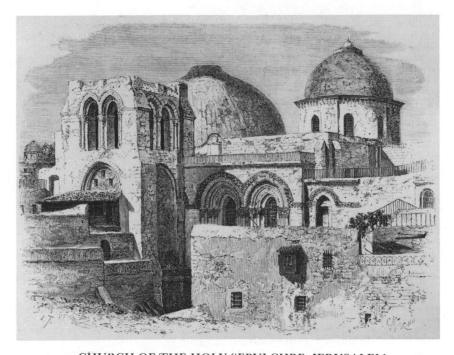

CHURCH OF THE HOLY SEPULCHRE, JERUSALEM
Neither Cross, nor Belfry
Engraving by C. Maurand, from a drawing by E. T. Thérond, after a photo-
graph by A. Salzmann (1856)
Anon, *Voyage*, in *Le Tour du Monde* (1st sem. 1860), p. 397

1266 to be allowed to enter the Machpelah cave in Hebron.[21] Under
the British Mandate (1922–1948), Christians were henceforth given
free access to the tombs of the Hebrew patriarchs, Abraham, Isaac,
and Jacob, but Jews were able to worship or visit the interior of the
building only in 1967, after the Six Day War. The abolition by the
State of Israel of this religious discrimination, which had prevailed for
seven centuries, incensed the Arab-Muslim population and provoked
riots whose motivations hardly differed from those of the Middle
Ages. Hebron is the classic example of the exclusive appropriation by
the Muslims of numerous Jewish and Christian holy sites.[22]

b) Liturgy

The ringing of bells, the sounding of the ram's horn (*shofar*), and
the public exhibition of crosses, icons, banners, and other religious
objects were all prohibited.

Although Judaism and Christianity were tolerated according to the terms of the *dhimma* concluded with Muhammad, in practice freedom of worship was not respected. Since the Arab army, at the beginning of the Muslim conquest, was a small foreign element among the indigenous peoples, it was obviously not in a position to restrict religious practices throughout the conquered territories. Intolerance increased with the reinforcement of the Arab-Muslim element. Some theologians allowed religious processions of *dhimmis,* but only in towns where they formed the majority.[23] In the fourteenth century, the traveler Ibn Battuta, hearing the sound of bells for the first time at Kafa, a port on the Black Sea, was so alarmed that he asked for the Koran to be read from the top of the only mosque.[24] Manifestations of non-Muslim worship offended the Muslims. If the *dhimmis* sometimes succeeded in purchasing some rights at an exorbitant cost, the population often revolted and thwarted all attempts at liberalization. Thus the *dhimmi* was placed in the center of a conflict between the venality of the authorities and the fanaticism of the people who, led by the *ulama,* demanded a strict application of the degrading law. Such a policy of discrimination encouraged bribery and proved to be a source of enrichment for the rulers. The more meddlesome the oppression, the more remunerative it became.

Muslim tombs had to be distinguished from those of the *dhimmis* so that a Muslim would not accidentally pray over the grave of an infidel. The latter had to bury their dead discreetly without mourning. Their cemeteries—considered as being within the realm of hell—were not respected. They were often completely destroyed and the tombs profaned, practices that have persisted until our days.

A criminal who converted to Islam was absolved of all his sins.[25] Apostasy[26] or blasphemy against Islam, the Prophet, or the angels incurred the death penalty.[27] An accusation of blasphemy, whether true or false, often led to the summary execution of the *dhimmi.* One well-known case in the nineteenth century was that of the Jew Samuel (Batto) Sfez, executed in Tunis in 1857.[28] Accusations of blasphemy provoked acts of collective retaliation, for example, against the Jews in Tunis (1876), Hamadan (1876), Aleppo (1889), Sulaymaniyah (1895), Teheran (1897), and Mosul (1911).

c) Persecutions and Forced Conversions

The Koran forbids forced conversions, but the wars and the necessities of colonization caused this prohibition to be violated. In 704–5, the caliph Walid I (705–715) assembled the nobles of Armenia in the church of St. Gregory in Naxcawan and the church of Xram on the

Araxis, and burned them to death. Others were crucified and decapitated and their wives and children taken into captivity. A violent persecution of Christians in Armenia is recorded from 852 to 855.[29] It is reported that in 1033, between five and six thousand Jews were massacred in Fez, and in 1066 about three thousand in Granada.[30] In Yemen the Jews were forced to choose between death and conversion in 1165 and 1678. The Almohad persecutions (1130–1212) in the Maghreb and in Muslim Spain put an end to what remained of the Christian population of North Africa. The Jews, who had been forced to accept Islam, formed a mass of "new converts" who practiced their former religion in secret. The Almohad inquisitors, doubting their sincerity, took away their children and raised them as Muslims. A similar law also existed in Yemen, where every Jewish orphan child had to be converted to Islam.[31] Abrogated by the Turks during their brief occupation of the country after 1872, it was reintroduced by the Imam Yahya in 1922 and confirmed again in 1925 (see doc. 107). In 1896 the Armenians of the area of Biredjik on the Euphrates, compelled to embrace Islam, had to go into exile in order to revert to their former religion.[32] During the great massacres of 1915–1916, a small number escaped death by accepting Islam.

Records concerning Morocco, Algeria, and Yemen reveal that during changes of reign and times of instability, the Jewish quarters were regularly pillaged, some of the menfolk massacred, and many women abducted and held for ransom by the soldiery or by tribes from the surrounding regions. Eyewitnesses have described the destruction of the Jewish quarter at Fez in 1912 at the beginning of the French protectorate,[33] and at San'a in Yemen as late as 1948, after the assassination of the Imam Yahya.[34] Such ordeals, over the centuries, resulted in many conversions to Islam. Thus a number of Judeo-Berber tribes of the Atlas, and Muslim families in Fez, are known to be descended from Jews who accepted Islam to save their lives in 1165, 1275, 1465, and 1790–92. There are Muslims in Tripolitania and elsewhere who are the descendants of Jews forcibly converted at different periods. The Jews of Tabriz were obliged to convert in 1291 and 1318, and those of Baghdad in 1333 and 1344. Throughout Persia, forced conversions from the sixteenth century to the beginning of the twentieth century decimated the Christian and, even more, the Jewish communities. In the reign of Shah Abbas II (1642–1666) a law of 1656 gave the convert to Islam, whether Christian or Jewish, exclusive rights of family inheritance. As a concession to Pope Alexander VII, it was mitigated for Christians, but remained in force for the Jews till the end of the nineteenth century.[35] Cazès mentions the existence in Tunisia of similar inheritance laws favoring converts to Islam.[36]

Segregation and Humiliation

The *dhimma* required the humiliation of the *dhimmis,* who were accused of perpetuating false versions of the Old and New Testaments, in which, supposedly, the divine prophecies foretelling the mission of Muhammad had been suppressed, distorted, and omitted. Their persistence in error was held to be the mark of a diabolic nature, necessitating their segregation from the Islamic community and their abasement.[37] Toward the end of the Middle Ages, with a few exceptions, special quarters had been set aside for infidels, outside of which they were not permitted to acquire either lands or buildings; both in size and appearance, their houses had to be inferior to those of the Muslims, shabbier and smaller. Houses of *dhimmis* were demolished for being higher than was authorized by tradition.

There were various exceptions, however. These laws have not been recorded for Muslim Spain. In Tunisia under the Hafsids there were Jews who owned fields and fine houses. The Turkish conquest inaugurated a much more tolerant era, and the situation of the *dhimmis* greatly improved in the regions under Ottoman rule, particularly during the sixteenth century.

A *dhimmi* was not permitted to have slaves who converted to Islam; he was also forbidden to possess arms. But there appear to have been exceptions to this rule, such as some of the Jewish tribes of the Moroccan Atlas and central Asia. In 1785 Volney, who visited Mt. Lebanon where the Maronites were not subjugated and therefore not generally treated as *dhimmis,* described these mountaineers:

> From a habit founded on distrust, and the political state of the country, every one, whether Shaik, or peasant, walk, continually armed with a fusil and poniards. This is perhaps an inconvenience, but this advantage results from it, that they have no novices in the use of arms among them when it is necessary [as in defence of their country] to employ them against the Turks.[38]

Arab honorific titles and the use of the Arabic alphabet were forbidden to the *dhimmis.*[39] Consulting them as physicians and pharmacists was discouraged, for they were generally suspected of poisoning Muslims; yet, due to their talents, these learned *dhimmis* often distinguished themselves at the courts of the caliphs.[40] Marriage or sexual relations between *dhimmis* and Muslim women were punishable by death, but a Muslim could marry a *dhimmi* woman.

The Jews, Nestorians, and Armenians of Kurdistan were subject to tallage and corvées at their master's command.[41] In Tunisia the Jews could be assigned to public undertakings such as the digging of cisterns, the construction of bridges, and so on, and had to supply the army with clothing, tents, and whatever was required.[42]

The most degrading tasks fell to the *dhimmis*. In Yemen an edict of 1806, which remained in application until they left for Israel in 1950, obliged the Jews to carry away dead animals and clean the public latrines, even on Saturdays. In Yemen and Morocco the *dhimmis* were obliged to extract the brains and salt the decapitated heads of the sultan's enemies, which they then exposed upon the walls of the town. Louis Frank, the physician of the Bey of Tunis at the beginning of the nineteenth century, noted:

> When a Turk [Muslim] is condemned to death by strangulation, some Christians or Greek innkeepers from the town are commandeered and forced to act as executioners. Two of them tie a rope, well rubbed with soap, around the neck of the victim; two others grab the rope, which they also fasten to their foot; and all four pull together with feet and hands until death ensues. . . .
> Usually, the bey orders the hands of thiefs to be cut off. Once the sentence has been pronounced, the condemned men are led to the Moorish hospital for the operation, which is performed by a Jew, who carries out the judgment as best he can with a bad knife, amputating the hand at the joint.[43]

It was regarded as a grave offence for a *dhimmi* to ride upon a noble animal such as a horse or camel. Outside the towns he was allowed to ride on a donkey; but at certain periods this concession was restricted to special cases. In 1697 a Frenchman visiting Cairo noticed that Christians could ride only on donkeys and had to dismount when passing distinguished Muslims, "for a Christian must only appear before a Muslim in a humiliating position."[44] The Spaniard Domingo Badia y Leblich, who traveled and wrote under the name of Ali Bey at the beginning of the nineteenth century, related that no Jew or Christian was allowed even to ride a mule in Damascus. When, under the lenient Egyptian occupation, the newly appointed French consul was authorized to ride through the streets of Damascus in 1833, riots broke out. The prohibition against riding on a horse or camel was still in force for the Yemenite Jews in 1948, and it was specified that they had to sit sidesaddle when riding a donkey.

In Yemen and in the rural areas of Morocco, Libya, Iraq, and Persia, up until the beginning of the twentieth century a Jew had to dismount from his mule when passing a Muslim. If he did not do so, the Muslim was justified in throwing him to the ground.[45]

Dhimmis were not permitted to group together to talk in the street. They had to walk with their eyes lowered and pass to the left of the Muslims, who were encouraged to push them aside. In Yemen it was an offence to screw up one's eyes on seeing a Muslim naked. When standing in front of a Muslim, a *dhimmi* had to speak in a lowered voice and only when authorized to do so. Until the middle of the nineteenth century the Jews were ill-treated and humiliated in the streets of Jerusalem, Hebron, Tiberias, and Safed. Travelers to the Maghreb and Yemen reported similar customs even later in the century. Slouschz, in the early twentieth century, mentions that in Bu Zain in the Jabal Gharian (Libya), it was customary for Arab children to throw stones at Jewish passersby.[46] The teaching of contempt at such a tender age was neither confined to desert regions nor directed only against Jews. British missionaries to the Jews who visited Jerusalem in 1839 wrote:

> While we were leaning over the parapet [of the pool of Bethesda] and musing over the past, some Moslem boys began to gather stones and throw them at us, crying "Nazarani" [Christians]. We had approached nearer the gate of the mosque than Christian feet are permitted to do.[47]

Travelers in Persia and Yemen at the beginning of the twentieth century noticed the low doors that forced the *dhimmis*—as an additional humiliation—either to bend down or knock their heads when entering their own houses.[48] The Jewish quarter of San'a, inhabited by several thousands, lacked lighting at night, in contrast to the rest of the town, and had no garbage collection.[49] In Bukhara a piece of cloth had to be hung on Jewish houses to distinguish them from those of the Muslims; their height also had to be lower. Forced at certain periods to wear only black, the Jews of Bukhara had to crouch down in their shops so that their Muslim clients would see only their heads and not their bodies,[50] a practice that recalled the obligation, in early sixteenth-century Damascus, of keeping the threshold of the shops of Jews and Christians below street level.[51]

The locked doors of the *dhimmis'* quarter were not always adequate to protect their inhabitants from rape and pillage. In Yemen the Jewish houses were like labyrinths, allowing fugitives to hide or put pursuers off their track. Local Jewish chronicles from the Maghreb give us a glimpse of the misery of the Jewish quarters, as well as of the terror and anguish that frequently gripped their inhabitants, who often became the defenseless victims of pillage and massacre.[52]

The restrictions imposed on the *dhimmis'* movements and places of residence varied according to regions and periods. Deportation and expulsion from some towns and territories were also practised, although infrequently.

In Persia, Yemen, and North Africa, until the nineteenth century the Jews were not allowed to enter certain streets of a town. They lived in separate quarters, where they were locked in at sunset, a practice that continued in Yemen until their emigration to Israel in 1949–50. Certain towns were completely out of bounds to them, because their presence would desecrate the sanctity of the place, for the same reason as no non-Muslim is allowed to enter Mecca or Medina today.

The restrictions imposed on foreign Christians could be even more stringent than those applied to the local *dhimmis*. In North Africa they were allowed to reside only in a few coastal towns, where they were grouped together in a *funduq* (inn) under the authority of a consul. If they wished to visit the interior of the country, they had to obtain special permits or disguise themselves as Jews. If they came to a town, they were regarded as too impure to stay in the Muslim section and so had to lodge in the Jewish quarter. Throughout the nineteenth century, Europeans who for reasons of security or because of discrimination had found shelter among the Jews left full and detailed descriptions of the wretched existence of the latter. Despite the prejudices of the period, the sight of so much suffering and injustice aroused the shocked compassion of travelers, and particularly of missionaries, who thought that such tribulations might induce the Jews to become Christians, thereby fully benefiting from the considerable privileges that went with the protection of the foreign power.

In certain regions (i.e., the interior of Tripolitania, the Atlas mountains, and Yemen) the Jews were often the property of their Muslim master and were unable to leave him. They were able to survive only by submitting to this condition of servitude, the master exploiting, yet also protecting, his Jews in the same way as he protected his property, tents, and flocks.

Although many regulations concerning the *dhimmis* were derived from the provisions of the Code of Justinian (534) concerning Jews and heretics in the Byzantine empire, a differentiation of costume appears to have been an innovation of the Arabs. From the beginning of the conquest, the Arabs were imbued with the idea that they belonged to the superior race of the Prophet; they set themselves above the other peoples and refused to share their privileges with the local converts. However, as the Islamization of the conquered territories took root under the Abbasids, the racial discrimination between Arabs and non-Arabs decreased, while religious discrimination intensified.

Thus there were many laws regulating the clothes worn by the *dhimmis* (color, shape, and dimensions), the shapes of turbans, footwear, and saddles, as well as the attire of wives, children and servants of *dhimmis*.

The *dhimmis* often broke these humiliating regulations and were punished accordingly. The wars between Islam and Christendom in the Middle Ages provided a suitable climate for anti-*dhimmi* riots, as well as for the reinforcement of the discriminatory laws. As the Christians formed a large part of the population of the *dar al-Islam,* they became—for this and other reasons—the chief victims of religious persecution. Often accused of collusion with neighboring Byzantium and with the enemies of Islam, they also suffered from the consequences of the Crusades and the Spanish Reconquista, as well as from the persecutions of Muslims living under Christian rule.

Many sources attest that the *dhimmis* were still subjected to vestmental regulations throughout the nineteenth century. Until 1875 the Jews of Tunisia could wear only a blue or black burnous; also their shoes and caps had to be black. Toward the end of the century, a traveler noted the distinctive headdresses of the Tunisian Jews.[53] In Tripoli (Libya) the Jews had to wear a distinctive blue badge.[54] At the same period, throughout Morocco, with the exception of a few coastal towns, the Jews were obliged to go barefoot outside their quarter *(mellah).* Slouschz reported that at Zenaga in the Algerian Sahara in 1912, the Arabs allowed the Jews neither to wear shoes, nor to ride an animal. In the Mzab (Southern Algeria), before the French colonization, the Jews paid the *jizya* and lived in their own quarter, leaving it only when dressed in black. They were forbidden to emigrate. The same conditions applied to the Jews in Tafilalet and the Atlas mountains.[55] Ali Bey mentioned the dark colors that the Jews and Christians were forced to wear in Jerusalem in the early nineteenth century.[56] Dr. Lortet noticed the black turbans worn by the Jews in Safed in 1880. This headgear may simply have been a custom inherited from the past, for the Ottoman government had abolished religious discrimination and proclaimed the equality of all its subjects in 1856.[57] An Anglican missionary, Wolff, who visited Bukhara in 1831–34, mentioned that the Jews, in addition to having to submit to the usual restrictions regarding synagogues, were obliged to wear a discriminatory badge.[58] In 1892 the clergy of Hamadan in Persia forced the Jews to wear a visible red circular patch on the upper part of their garment, and in 1902 they again made them wear a special costume. At the same period in Shiraz, fanatical fundamentalists seized Jews in the streets, shaved their beards, cut off their hair, and made them wear the distinctive badge. In Teheran in 1897 the *mullahs* published a *fatwa* requiring the Jews to wear the badge and to cut their hair in order to distinguish themselves from the Believers. Under strong British pressure the Shah issued an edict forbidding its implementation (doc. 86). In Yemen, Sémach described the special costume worn by the Jews, which was intended to make them look ridiculous (doc. 91); a French woman, resident in San'a, noted in 1947:

The women were unveiled but the men were subject to a strict rule that they had to wear a white cotton shirt with stripes of black. They were not allowed to own horses and generally were bullied by the Arabs. I saw a tribesman whose badly loaded donkey had shed its lucerne [alfalfa], seize the nearest Jew and compel him to pick it up and replace it.[59]

[These examples are intended to indicate the general character of a system of oppression, sanctioned by contempt and justified by the principle of the inequality between Muslims and *dhimmis*. Superimposed upon this pattern of daily life throughout the centuries were calamities such as wars, invasions, despotisms, famines, epidemics, and waves of fanaticism. These misfortunes afflicted the whole population, but especially the *dhimmis*. Singled out as objects of hatred and contempt by visible signs of discrimination, they were progressively decimated during periods of massacres, forced conversions, and banishments. Sometimes it was the prosperity they had achieved through their labor or ability that aroused jealousy; oppressed and stripped of all their goods, the *dhimmis* often emigrated.]

The disappearance of those *dhimmi* communities concerning which records of their destruction have been fortuitously preserved, prompt a reflection upon the fate of the many communities that were destroyed without leaving a trace. Their annihilation was not the result of wars, which often occurred, but of the fact that, not being Muslims, hence unarmed, they could live only in a state of perpetual insecurity and contemptuous tolerance.

Process of Colonization

The Arabization of the territories conquered by the Muslims took place in two stages:

(1) the *jihad*—the military conquest and annexation of territories, governed by specific rules and based on a concept of election that justifies world domination;

(2) the *dhimma*—a system of dispossession and colonization, aimed at protecting and safeguarding the domination of the triumphant Islamic community.

The condition of minorities in Christian countries has often been compared with the fate of the *dhimmis* under Islam, although such generalizations concerning vast territories and periods of time are inappropriate. Rather than looking for similarities between the two, one should acknowledge an essential difference. During the first two centuries of their conquest—and certainly at the outset—the Arabs were themselves a minority. In order to impose their laws, their language, and their foreign culture on ancient civilizations, they had to

proceed with caution. A general uprising of the subject populations
would have compromised the success of their conquest. Baladhuri
related that when Iraq fell to the Arab conquerors, the soldiers
wanted to "share out" the region of Sawad between themselves. The
caliph Umar b. al-Khattab permitted them to divide the booty, but
decreed that the land and the camels should be left to the local
farmers so as to provide for the Muslims: "If you divide them among
those present, there will be nothing left for those who come after
them." And Ali, the Prophet's son-in-law, said of the non-Muslim
peasants of Sawad, "Leave them to be a source of revenue and aid for
the Muslims." Sulayman b. Ya'sar explained:

> Umar left al-Sawad for posterity, considering the people as *dhimmi;*
> *jizya* is taken from them and *kharaj* from their lands. They are
> therefore *dhimmis* and cannot be sold as slaves.[60] (see doc. 2)

Here a difference in character between the *jihad* and the *dhimma* is
clearly apparent. Booty—the immediate reward of the *jihad*—includes
slaves from among the conquered, leaving the majority of the vanquished, bound by the *dhimma,* to continue the long-term economic
function of supporting the conquering Islamic community. (see doc.
3: *Battle procedures*). It should be remembered that the Arabs did not
invent these taxes that the *dhimmis* paid to the conquerors, but only
preserved and adapted the system of taxation existing in the Byzantine Empire. Baladhuri states that in Syria and Palestine, the Jews had
been the *dhimmis* of the Christians and had to pay to them the *kharaj*
on their lands.[61]

The *dhimma* prepared the way for Arab colonization in the political, economic, religious, and cultural sectors. The divine rights of
conquest transformed the foreign lands into "Arab territories," while
Arabization reinforced the military conquests. Conquered peoples
who revolted, such as the Copts, Armenians, Berbers, and Persians,
were massacred or deported from one region to another, while successive waves of Bedouin settled in the depopulated territories, the
state having appropriated all the lands and resources of the conquered regions. This constant policy of repopulation with Arab tribes
diminished the huge numerical gap between the occupying army and
the colonized peoples, who were reduced, as their condition deteriorated, to a cheap source of manpower that could be drawn on to
perform the most menial tasks.

In the opinion of medieval Muslim jurists, the *dhimmis* had been
tolerated because their advantages to the conquerors had outweighed
their disadvantages. Skilled at building, navigation, agriculture,
medicine, science, and art, subject to tallage and liable to forced labor
at any time, the *dhimmis* as a whole provided the conquerors with the

ARMENIAN ARCHITECT OF CONSTANTINOPLE
"Most of the architects and carpenters of Constantinople are Armenians" (p. 47)
Engraving (no. 88) by J. de Franssières from a painting by J.-B. Vanmour
(1707–08)
Antoine de Feriol (Louis XIV's ambassador to the Sublime Porte)

means and resources for the strengthening of the Islamic society and
the continuation of the *jihad*.[62] It is known that the Muslim masses also
suffered from the despotism of the military castes. Famine, misery,
and injustice were the cause of many revolts. But one should nevertheless distinguish between these vicissitudes, derived from the faults
of a given political system, and, on the other hand, the in-
stitutionalized persecution of the *dhimmis* who survived on the fringe
of that system.

Yet it should not be forgotten that there were many *hadiths* that
reminded the Muslim political authorities of the principles of charity
and mercy laid down by the founder of Islam:

> "Allah would torment those who torment people in the world";
> "Beware of the supplication of the oppressed, for there is no bar-
> rier between him and Allah"; "Whoever will kill a tributary [a
> *dhimmi*] will not smell the fragrance of paradise; although its fra-
> grance makes itself felt at a distance of forty years walk."

Before dying, Umar b. al-Khattab told the future caliph Uthman:

> And I send you again recommendations with regard to the people
> [of the Book], who are under the protection of Allah and his Mes-
> senger; it is necessary to faithfully keep the agreements made with
> them, fight to defend them and not impose upon them overwhelm-
> ing burdens.[63]

When traveling in Palestine, Umar released some *dhimmis* who were
being maltreated because they were unable to pay the poll tax.[64]

Under the Abbasids (750–1258), many non-Muslims held public
office, despite degrading legislation concerning infidels in edicts proclaimed under Harun al-Rashid (786–809), al-Ma'mun (813–833), al-
Mutawakkil (847–861), al-Muqtadir (908–932), and the Buwayhid
emirs in Iraq (945–1055). The Seljuk Turks (1038–1194) were more
tolerant, although the caliph al-Muqtadi (1075–1094) revived al-
Mutawakkil's legislation and extorted high ransoms from the *dhimmis*.
In the twelfth century the condition of the non-Muslims in Iraq improved. The pagan Mongol Il-Khan dynasty (1265–1353) abolished
religious discrimination, but when Ghazan was converted to Islam in
1295, the *dhimmis* were again subjected to the customary humiliating
legislation and suffered from reprisals that decimated whole communities.

Under the rule of the Fatimids (909–1171) the *dhimmi* communities
in Egypt, Syria, Palestine, and part of the Maghreb enjoyed considerable liberty, except under the reign of Caliph al-Hakim bi-Amr
Allah (996–1021). Persecutions of the *dhimmis* by the Almoravids and
Almohads (1042–1269) wiped out the Christian communities of Mus-

lim Spain and North Africa. The Jews, threatened with forced conversions by Yusuf ibn Tashfin (1061–1106) were able to avoid the same fate only by paying a heavy ransom. Under the Almohads, in 1159, however, the Jews were again left with three choices: conversion, exile, or death (see doc. 94). Those who were converted became outwardly Muslims, but continued to practice Judaism in secret. The Hafsids (1228–1534), comparatively tolerant, allowed them to return to Judaism on condition that they paid the *jizya* and other heavy taxes, adopted a special costume, and complied with other humiliating measures.

In Egypt, Syria, and Palestine, Saladin (1169–1193) revived the Covenant of Umar. Persecution of Jews and especially Christians increased during the rule of the Mamluks (1250–1517). Under the influence of the *ulama*, discrimination, humiliation, massacres, fiscal extortions, forced conversions, and the destruction of churches and synagogues occurred. The condition of the *dhimmis*, however, improved considerably with the more tolerant Ottoman regime. Sultan Bayazid II (1481–1512) allowed the Jews expelled from Spain in 1492 to settle in his empire and practise their religion. The periodical accusations of ritual murder that the Greek Orthodox Church leveled against the Jews were forbidden by the Turkish authorities.

In Persia, Shah Abbas I (1588–1629), although tolerant, under the pressure of the Shi'ite religious leaders imposed a special badge on all the Jews of the kingdom at the end of his reign and obliged those of Isfahan to convert to Islam. His successor, Shah Safi (1629–1642), permitted them to revert to Judaism; the Christians were also less oppressed. In the latter part of the reign of Abbas II (1642–1666), however, the Jews throughout the empire were obliged to choose between forced conversion and banishment. The synagogues were closed and the converts were made to break with their past, change their names, and marry their daughters to Muslims. Armenians and other Christians were expelled from Isfahan, but owing to the intervention of the Pope and the European states, their fate was less wretched than that of the Jews. In 1661 the Jews were allowed to practice their religion anew on condition that they paid the *jizya* and also made a retroactive payment, calculated from the time of their conversion to Islam. Oppression and persecution of the Jewish and Christian *dhimmis* continued in the following reigns, with the exception of that of a remarkably tolerant ruler, Nadir Shah (1736–1747). Under the Qajar dynasty (1794–1925), the oppression and humiliation of the Jews increased. Between 1834 and 1848 a wave of persecutions broke out. The Jews, subjected to discriminatory laws, had to wear a distinctive badge and headdress; the community was made collectively responsible for the offence of any individual.[65]

This brief historical survey shows how the same type of persecution can take a large number of forms, varying from one region to another and from one period to another according to economic and political circumstances. Persecutions were at times abolished or diminished by a benevolent governor or sultan, and revived in periods of war or fanaticism at the demand of the theologians. Often a community that was persecuted in one region fled and managed to survive by placing itself under the authority of a more merciful Muslim ruler. Thus *dhimmis* from Persia often found refuge in Afghanistan, and at some periods the Jews of the Maghreb and Yemen would emigrate to the Ottoman Empire.

Some discriminatory practices were generally applied in the *dar al-Islam;* others remained local. In Yemen, for instance, a decree was passed in 1667 forbidding the Jews to cover their heads; a few years later they were authorized to do so with a piece of cloth, thereby protecting themselves against the heat or the cold. The decree of 1846, forcing them to clean the latrines and carry away dead animals, was also a purely local one. It remained in application until 1948. The obligation to go barefoot outside their special quarters existed only in Yemen and the Maghreb. The legislation based on their impurity was particularly harsh in Yemen and Persia, but not elsewhere.

The *dhimmi*'s condition also depended on the code of legislation applied in each country. The Hanafi and Maliki schools, dominant in Turkey and Egypt, were more tolerant. On the other hand, the most fanatical school, the Hanbali, developed in Syria and Iraq and was dominant in Palestine until the fifteenth century.

This system of oppression and humiliation was practised over a vast area for more than a thousand years. The practice of contempt affected manners, shaping traditions, ways of thinking, and patterns of behavior. Habits and customs would spring up, sometimes without any specific legal justification. That the Jews should go barefoot in the Maghreb or expose their legs in the Yemen, wearing short black tunics, was justified in the eyes of the Arabs through immemorial custom based on religion, even though the Koran had nothing to say on the matter.

Arabic sources relating to early Muslim history rarely refer to *dhimmis,* a silence probably based on the scorn felt toward inferiors (see doc. 1). Sometimes the guile of the *dhimmis* is mentioned in connection with a particular incident so as to demonstrate the tolerance of the Muslims, a fact that tells us, if not the truth, at least something about the attitude of mind. That is why the tragedy of the *dhimmis* can be expressed in all its aspects neither by Muslim authors, who are apologists for the triumphant faith, nor by the oppressed, alienated and ready to corroborate the victor's version. Often the observations of Western travelers, who belong neither to the rulers nor the oppressed, may complement the other sources, although allowances must be made for the prejudices of the period. Indeed, the reader cannot be warned too strongly against the prejudices of Westerners, where Jews, Oriental Christians, and Muslims are concerned, but it is precisely these testimonies which, in spite of frequent antisemitic overtones, provide us with some of the most valuable information on the condition of the *dhimmis.* Perhaps one of the most moving accounts of the grim situation of the Jewish *dhimmis* was given by Charles de Foucauld, a French officer and aristocrat. It is also one of the most accurate, because he was obliged to disguise himself as a rabbi-emissary from Jerusalem in order to visit Morocco in 1883–84, even though his inveterate dislike of the Jews affected his attitude to those whose hospitality was necessary to his security.[66]

The *dhimmis* were often accused of practicing usury. This accusation was commonly made against Christian *dhimmis* in Egypt and Syria—and elsewhere. It appears to be older than similar accusations against the Jews in the Maghreb which, for obvious reasons, are often reiterated in the period of European colonial expansion. If usury was, in fact, practiced by the *dhimmis,* it was principally because the despotic system and the unstable economic conditions forced it upon them. Money was a vital necessity to them as well as an economic function that enabled them to survive.

European sources often describe the moral degradation of the *dhimmi.* Forced to endure foreign rule, living in a situation of permanent injustice and insecurity, the *dhimmis* could survive only by following the few paths imposed on them by oppression, and by circumventing the laws which consecrated that injustice. This tragedy of the *dhimmi*—that of a man who allows himself to be oppressed and destroyed in soul and spirit for the sake of his convictions—redeems this image of humility and abasement.

Only the sociohistorical frame in which the *dhimmi* peoples evolved has been sketched in this chapter. It remains for specialists to examine the religious, political and economic factors determining the variations of the frame, the enforcement of the legislation or its neglect according to periods of fanaticism or toleration. One might object to a compilation of disabilities which were not equally and simultaneously applied throughout immense regions and over centuries, since this multiplicity of prohibitions, separated from their historical background, could convey a darker picture than was the daily reality. In order to compensate for this aspect due to the subject matter of this book, attempts have been made wherever possible to underline brighter periods and to stress the fact that the condition of the *dhimmi* changed and evolved according to historical circumstances.

Notes to Chapter 2

1. *EI²*, "Fay" (F. Lokkegaard) 2:869–70; *EI²*, "Kharadj" (C. Cahen) 4:1030–34; *EI²*, "Djizya" (C. Cahen) 2:559–62; D. C. Dennet, *Conversion and the Poll Tax in Early Islam* (Cambridge, Mass., 1950); Khadduri, chap. 11 ("Spoils of War").

2. al-Baladhuri, 1:251. For the taxation of the *dhimmis*, 1:221, 244–45; Fattal, chap. 7; Tritton, chap. 13; E. Ashtor, *A Social and Economic History of the Near East in the Middle Ages* (London, 1976), chaps. 1 and 2; A. Cohen, *Palestine in the 18th Century: Patterns of Government and Administration* (Jerusalem, 1973), pp. 249–59. See Documents section: "Jurists' texts."

3. C. de Foucauld, *Reconnaissance au Maroc (1883–1884)* (Paris, 1888), pp. 398–400; N. Slouschz, *Travels in North Africa* (Philadelphia, 1927), p. 483. For the Jabal Nefusa, see M. Hakohen, *Highid Mordekhai* (sec. 91), in H. E. Goldberg, ed. and trans., *The Book of Mordechai: A Study of the Jews of Libya* (Philadelphia, 1980), p. 74.

4. Theory was not always followed in practice. Many sources stress that the elderly, the impotent, women, children not having attained puberty, and sometimes even the dead, were constrained to pay the *jizya*. See S. D. Goitein, "Evidence on the Muslim Poll Tax from Non-Muslim Sources," in *JESHO* 6 (1963): 278–95; idem, *A Mediterranean Society* (Berkeley and Los Angeles, 1971), 2:132, 380–94. See doc. 21 below. It is probable that political and economic factors over the centuries must have influenced the application of the taxation system of the *dhimmis* as well as that concerning Muslims. How a theoretical law was actually implemented within complex and changing realities will always remain a hypothetical question for the historian. For practical implementation of the *jizya* in nineteenth-century Morocco, see doc. 59 (1815) [the original source is J. Riley, *Loss of the American Brig Commerce (1815)* (London, 1817), pp. 441–42] and doc. 79 (1894).

5. F. Rey, *La Protection diplomatique et consulaire dans les Echelles du Levant et de Barbarie* (Paris, 1899), pp. 251–53.

6. Slouschz, p. 21.

7. Eighteenth- and nineteenth-century accounts from British and French diplomatic correspondence describe the continuous process of elimination of the *dhimmi* communities in Palestine by nomadic tribes of Arabs and Turkomans, and in Armenia by Arabs and Kurds. For an earlier period, in Palestine, see M. Sharon, "The Political Role of the Bedouins in Palestine in the Sixteenth and Seventeenth Centuries," in M. Ma'oz, ed., *Studies on Palestine during the Ottoman Period* (Jerusalem, 1975), pp. 11–30.

8. F. Charles-Roux, *Les Echelles de Syrie et de Palestine au 18ème siècle* (Paris, 1928), pp. 86–87.

9. Idem, p. 53.

10. A. M. Hyamson, *The British Consulate in Jerusalem (1838–1914)* (London, 1939), 1:136–39, 149–51.

11. Idem, 1:198–99, 202, 260.

12. Report by Freeman in Despatch of Holmes (Bosna-Seraï) to Derby (London), 15 May 1877, in *P.P.* 1877 [C. 1768], 92:554. An American noted that the testimony of a Jew of Morocco (in 1815) ". . . cannot be taken against a Moor, any more than that of a negro slave in the West Indies and the Southern States of America, can be given against a white man . . ." (see Riley, p. 459).

13. Hyamson, 2:501.

14. Bukhari, vol. 2, t. 52, chap. 29; Koran 3:16–19, 71–72, 5:70–71. In 1851 and 1858 the British Consul in Jerusalem noticed that the testimony of a Jew against a Muslim was refused in Islamic courts (Hyamson, 1:171 and 261).

15. Muslim, vol. 4, chap. 1149 (6666); and, "When it will be the Day of Resurrection,

Allah would deliver to every Muslim a Jew or a Christian and say: That is your rescue from Hell-Fire" (6665); "There would come people amongst the Muslims on the Day of Resurrection with as heavy sins as a mountain and Allah would forgive them and He would place in their stead the Jews and the Christians" (6668); Bukhari, vol. 2, t. 56, chap. 180:2. In contrast, see the verses mentioned by al-Awza'i: "Nor shall any sinning one bear the burden of another" (Koran 6:164). See n. 2 above.

16. E. Lane, *The Manners and Customs of the Modern Egyptians* (London, 1836; London: Everyman Library, (1963), pp. 559–60.

17. Slouschz, p. 146.

18. Hyamson, 1:211. On the profanation or confiscation of places of worship, see Tritton, p. 49; Fattal; also M. Perlmann, "Notes on Anti-Christian Propaganda in the Mamluk Empire," in *BSOAS* 10 (1939–1942): 844–61; R. J. H. Gottheil, *Dhimmis and Moslems . . .* 2:353–414. In 1697–1698, a French traveler noticed that many churches were used as stables throughout Ottoman Palestine. See A. Morison, *Relation historique d'un voyage nouvellement fait au Mont Sinaï et à Jérusalem* (Paris, 1705).

19. Hyamson, 1:235.

20. The absence of a cross on the dome of the Church of the Holy Sepulchre and other churches, as well as their dilapidated state, is confirmed by old prints and photographs. See E. Schiller, ed., *The Holy Land in Old Engravings and Illustrations* (Jerusalem, 1977): A. Forbin (1817–1818), pp. 48, 51, 55; A. Dausatz (Taylor) (1830), p. 81; J. M. Bernatz (1837), p. 102; D. Roberts (1839), p. 118; E. Schiller, *The First Photographs of the Holy Land* (Jerusalem, 1979), pp. 198, 200 (1862), pp. 201–2 (1868, replacement of the cupola and the raising of a cross on the dome); and Schiller, *The First Photographs of Jerusalem and the Holy Land* (Jerusalem, 1980), pp. 87 (1856), 64 (1865).

21. C. Wilson, ed., *Picturesque Palestine* (London, 1882), 3:198–99.

22. Concerning the sequestration of holy sites in North Africa, see frequent references in Slouschz, *Travels;* E. Doutté, *Missions au Maroc: En Tribu* (Paris, 1914), pp. 210–12.

23. Fattal, p. 203.

24. Ibn Battuta, *Voyages* (1325–1354), trans. C. Defremery and B. R. Sanguinetti (1854; reprint Paris, 1979), 2:357–58; idem, 1:124.

25. Bukhari, vol. 2, t. 54, chap. 15.

26. S. M. Zwemer, *Law of Apostacy in Islam* (1925; Amarko reprint, New Delhi, 1975.) There had been cases where the *dhimmis*, converted by force to Islam, were allowed to return to their original religion, for the Koran forbids compulsion in religion. R. Lebel refers to forced conversions of Jews in Morocco, as well as the case of a young girl of fourteen (Zulaika Hajwal), who, having been obliged to become a Muslim but wishing to remain Jewish, was decapitated in public at Fez in 1834 by order of the sultan. See his *Les Voyageurs Français du Maroc* (Paris, 1936), pp. 125–26; but particularly (on Zulaika) H. Z. Hirschberg, *A History of the Jews in North Africa*, Leiden, 1981), 2:304.

27. Bukhari, vol. 2, t. 56, chap. 144; vol. 3, t. 64, chap. 55; 1, 3; Koran 3:79–83; 101, 171; 4:91, 115, 118; 22:56; 32:22; 61:7; 83:10.

28. This incident provoked an explosion of popular fanaticism in the *hara* of Tunis, where the Jews were attacked and pillaged. The Europeans prepared to defend their own quarter. See J. Ganiage, *Les Origines du protectorat français en Tunisie (1861–1881)* (Paris, 1959), pp. 71–72.

29. J. Muyldermans, *La Domination arabe en Arménie*, extract from *Histoire Universelle* by Vardan (d. 1271) (Louvain and Paris, 1927). See also *EI*[1], "Armenia" (Streck), 1:435–49; *EI*[2], "Arminiya" (M. Canard), 1:634–50. On the subject of conversions to Islam in general, see the bibliography in N. Levtzion, ed., *Conversions to Islam* (New York, 1979).

30. Hirschberg, 1:108; M. Perlmann, "Eleventh-Century Andalusian Authors on the Jews of Grenada," in *PAAJR* 18 (1949): 285.

31. Muhammad is recorded as having said that all children are born Muslims, but that their parents raise them as Jews or Christians. See Muslim, vol. 4, chap. 1107 (6423) (6426); Bukhari, vol. 1, t. 23; 92:3. The Ottoman military corps of Janissaries was made up of Christian children brought up as Muslims. The abduction of *dhimmi* children, mainly Christians, is well-known from the sixteenth century onward, particularly in the nineteenth century, because of the abundant documentation in consequence

of the increased number of European consular agents accredited throughout the Ottoman Empire and in Morocco. In Persia, Armenian children were forcibly converted in
the seventeenth century (see V. Moreen, "The Status of Religious Minorities in Safavid
Iran (1617–1661)," in *JNES*, 40 (1981): 129). As late as the early twentieth century,
during the periods of the Armenian massacres, large numbers of children were carried
off and brought up as Muslims. See doc. 45, p. 268, and doc. 94, p. 347.

32. L. de Contenson, *Chrétiens et Musulmans* (Paris, 1901), p. 84.

33. *Archives* (Maroc) and *Bulletins* (1911, 1912) of the *AIU*, translated in D. G. Littman, "Jews under Muslim Rule, II: Morocco 1903–1912," in *WLB* n.s. 29, nos. 37/38
(1976): 16–19. On the abduction of women and children in 1907 after the destruction
and pillage of the *mellah* of Casablanca, idem, (1976): 8–11.

34. L. Février, "A French Family in the Yemen," in *AS* 3 (1979): 134.

35. The pope's letter is dated September 21, 1658. See *A Chronicle of the Carmelites in
Persia and the Papal Mission of the 17 and 18 centuries* (London, 1939), 1 : 364–66, quoted
by W. J. Fischel, *The Jews in Medieval Iran from the 16th to the 18th Centuries: Political,
Economic and Communal Aspects*, paper read, posthumously, at the International Conference on Jewish Communities in Muslim lands, Institute of Asian and African Studies
and the Ben Zvi Institute, Hebrew University (Jerusalem, March 1974), p. 14; see also
E. Spicehandler, *The Persecution of the Jews of Isfahan under Shah Abbas II (1642–1666)*, in
ibid., p. 10.

36. D. Cazès, *Essai sur l'histoire des Israélites de Tunisie* (Paris, 1888), p. 103.

37. Koran 2 : 141; 4 : 48; 5 : 18; 6 : 114; 7 : 156. See *EI*¹, "Ghiyar," 2 : 159; *EI*², "Ghiyar"
(M. Perlmann) 2 : 1075–76.

38. C. F. Volney, *Travels in Egypt and Syria (1783–1785)* (London, 1787), 2 : 18–19.
The phrase in square brackets is to be found in the French first edition of 1786, but
does not appear in this English translation of 1787.

39. At Bukhara in 1832, a well-known Anglican missionary (Hebrew-speaking, formerly a Jew born in Bavaria) noted that Jews who read or wrote Arabic or Persian could
be forced to become Muslims. This assertion seems excessive. See J. Wolff, *Researches
and Missionary Labours (1831–1834)* (London, 1835), p. 177; also docs. 7, 8, and 16
below.

40. M. Perlmann, "Notes on the Position of Jewish Physicians in Mediterranean
Muslim Countries," in *IOS* 2 (1972): 315–19; Fattal; and doc. sec.: "Jurists."

41. I. J. Benjamin, *Eight Years in Asia and Africa (1846–1855)* (Hanover, 1859),
pp. 68–75. See also "Reports by Her Majesty's Diplomatic and Consular Agents in
Turkey Respecting the Condition of the Christian Subjects of the Porte (1868–1875)",
Parliamentary Papers: Turkey, no. 16 (1877). The Muslim peasantry were not exempt
from exploitation by their Muslim masters.

42. Cazès, p. 100.

43. L. Frank, "Tunis, Description de cette Régence", in, ed., J. J. Marcel, *l'Univers:
histoire et description de tous les peuples: Algérie, Etats Tripolitains, Tunis* (Paris, 1862), pp. 64–
65.

44. Morison, p. 155.

45. *Archives* (LIBYE I.C. 12) of the *AIU*, quoted by D. G. Littman, "Jews under
Muslim Rule in the Late 19th Century", in *WLB* 28, n.s. 35/36 (1975): 71. With reference to Palestine, early nineteenth century, see doc. 30. For Morocco, see Riley,
pp. 515–17, 537.

46. Slouschz, p. 153. See also the 1909 report of H. E. Wilkie Young, British vice-
consul in Mosul (Iraq), "Notes on the City of Mosul," enclosed with despatch no. 4,
Mosul, 28 Jan. 1909, in *FO* 195/2308, reprinted in *MES* 7, no. 2 (1971): 232, (ed.)
E. Kedourie.

47. A. A. Bonar and R. M. (Mc) Cheyne, *Narrative of a Mission of Inquiry to the Jews
from the Church of Scotland in 1839* (Edinburgh, 1845), p. 163. It was customary for the
Arab children of Palestine to throw stones at Jews and Christians, as is known from a
great number of European travelers. See, *inter alia* (for Jerusalem, Nablus, Ramla,
Khan Yunes), W. C. Bryant, *Letters from the East* (New York, 1869), pp. 193–95; (for
Hebron) J. W. Dulles, *The Ride through Palestine* (Philadelphia, 1881), p. 142.

48. Y. D. Sémach, *A travers les communautés israélites d'Orient* (Paris, 1931), p. 25; idem,

Une Mission de l'Alliance au Yémen (Paris, 1910), pp. 23, 31, 47. Touring the Black Sea region in the early nineteenth century, a traveler wrote, "At the village of Kourou-Chesné, the dark slate colour of the houses, approaching almost to black, indicates that they are occupied by *rayahs* [*dhimmis*], none of whom, except by express permission, are allowed to paint their dwellings with the gay colours in which the Orientals delight." J. Fuller, *Narrative of a Tour through Some Parts of the Turkish Empire* (London, 1829), p. 101.

49. Sémach, *Une Mission,* p. 76.

50. Ben-Zvi. See the list of restrictions imposed on the Jews of Bukhara, pp. 86–87.

51. E. Ashtor, "Levantine Jewries in the Fifteenth Century," in *BIJS* 3 (1975): 92. A similar practice is mentioned in Persia (1622) but may not have been applied. See L. D. Loeb, below, n. 65 (p. 292).

52. G. Vajda, "Un Recueil de textes historiques judéo-marocains," in *Hespéris* 12 (1951); D. G. Littman, "Quelques Aspects de la condition de dhimmi: Juifs d'Afrique du Nord avant la colonisation (d'après des documents de l'A.I.U.)", in *YOD,* 2, no. 1 (1976): 23–52; idem (above, n. 45) in *WLB* 28, n.s. 35/36 (1975) and (above, n. 33) in *WLB* 29, n.s. 37/38 (1976).

53. D. Bruun, *The Cave Dwellers* (London, 1898), p. 322.

54. Boody, *To Kairwan the Holy* (London, 1885), p. 34.

55. Slouschz, pp. 351–52.

56. (Domingo Badia y Leblich), *Travels of Ali Bey in Morocco, Tripoli, Cyprus, Egypt, Arabia, Syria and Turkey, between the years 1803 and 1807, written by himself* (London, 1816), 2: 242. Many travelers of the nineteenth century declared that the inhabitants of Jerusalem, Hebron, and Nablus were the most fanatical.

57. L. Lortet, *La Syrie d'aujourd'hui* (Paris, 1884), p. 535.

58. Wolff, *Researches,* p. 177.

59. Février, p. 132.

60. Qudama b. Ja'far (d. ca. 948), in D. R. Hill, *The Termination of Hostilities in the Early Arab Conquests* (A.D. *634–656*) (London, 1971), p. 103.

61. Baladhuri, 1:190–91

62. Shaykh Damanhuri, *On the Churches of Egypt (1739),* trans. and ed. M. Perlmann (Berkeley: University of California, 1975), p. 30.

63. Bukhari, vol. 3, t. 64, chap. 60:5; vol. 2, t. 58, chap. 5 and vol. 2, t. 56, chap. 174. See also the principles of equity and clemency recommended with regard to the poll tax and the prohibition to oppress and overtax the tributaries, in Abou Yousof Ya'koub (d. 798), *Le Livre de l'impôt foncier (Kitâb al-Kharâdj),* trans. E. Fagnan (Paris, 1921), pp. 159–95.

64. Muslim, chap. 1083 (6329).

65. D. G. Littman, "Jews under Muslim Rule: The Case of Persia," in *WLB* 32, n.s. 49/50 (1979). For the earlier period, D. d'Beth Hillel, *The Travels of Rabbi David D'Beth Hillel from Jerusalem through Arabia, Koordistan, part of Persia and India to Madras* (Madras, 1832), recently reedited by W. J. Fischel (ed.), *Unknown Jews in Unknown Lands: The Travels of Rabbi David d'Beth Hillel* (New York, 1973); Wolff, *Researches;* Benjamin. Two recent publications provide useful details on the Jews of Shiraz and the development of the Baha'i religion in nineteenth- and twentieth century Persia. L. D. Loeb, *Outcaste: Jewish Life in Southern Iran* (New York, 1977); M. Momen, ed., *The Bábi and Baha'i Religions (1844–1944): Some Contemporary Western Accounts* (Oxford, 1981).

66. Foucauld; R. Bazin, *Charles de Foucauld: explorateur du Maroc, ermite au Sahara* (Paris, 1921), pp. 46–47; Y. D. Sémach, "Charles de Foucauld et les Juifs marocains," in *Bulletin de l'Enseignement public du Maroc* (Juin 1936); M. Carrouges, *Foucauld: devant l'Afrique du Nord* (Paris, 1961), pp. 149–52.

3
Foreign Protection

The manner in which the *dhimma* was applied varied according to political circumstances or the disposition of the ruler. There were some periods during which the authorities favored one community to the detriment of another, and other periods when they governed with a tolerance recalling that of the first Caliphs. The Umayyads in Spain (710–1031), the Fatimids (except the Caliph al-Hakim) and the Ottomans in the early period of their expansion allowed the *dhimmis* a degree of freedom and even encouraged the social advancement of their elite. In Egypt also, at the beginning of the nineteenth century, Muhammad Ali (1805–1848) and his son Ibrahim succeeded in silencing the opposition of the *ulama* and in promoting the emancipation of the Christians. Gérard de Nerval, who visited Egypt in 1843, depicted the Egyptian people as hospitable, tolerant, and good natured. The contrast between this behavior and the fanaticism prevalent at that time in the Maghreb, Syria, Persia, and Yemen indicates the very great difference of conditions from one area to another.

Just as Islam today, at the call of the *mullahs*, has triumphed in Iran, so, throughout history, people blindly followed the directives of their religious and political leaders. If they were tolerant and in proper control of the country, the *dhimmis* could aspire to a certain security. However, these brighter periods, linked to particular political circumstances, were not only precarious but also exasperating to the common people, who saw a few *dhimmis* assume high office, wear silken garments and ride horses. As a result, either the ruler yielded to popular pressures, or reprisals against the entire community followed the fall of the impious regime, and the *dhimmi* survivors were put back to their degraded position.

In many cases the tiny minority of unbelievers singled out for favor by a ruler were detested by the majority of their own coreligionists, who lived in misery and had to endure the consequences of the social advancement of a few. As we have seen, the Muslim populations also suffered from the rapacity of the sultans and from cruel and tyrannical governors. They were no less oppressed and exploited than the *dhimmis,* but they could be protected by the powerful class of *ulama,* or, in extreme cases, would resort to an armed revolt. Such possibilities of mitigating injustice were not available to the unarmed *dhimmi* communities. Often the rulers exploited their people through *dhimmi* officials who, being more vulnerable than the Muslims, were also inclined to be more loyal to the authorities. The people therefore took vengeance against the sultan by slaughtering the *dhimmi* communities, religious fanaticism thus being reinforced by political and economic motives.

In the preceding chapter the legal framework of relations between Muslims and non-Muslims and the kind of toleration that the authorities were prepared to grant the latter within that framework have been briefly summarized. Christians who found themselves under Muslim rule sometimes benefited from the foreign protection of Christian rulers. It should be remembered that, whereas Islam controlled its holy places—Mecca and Medina—Christendom had seen the geographical and cultural origins of its faith fall into the hands of foreign conquerors. As the need to preserve contact with the Holy Land was a vital necessity for Christendom, the protection of pilgrims and of the Christian inheritance henceforth remained a constant preoccupation of the West. Thus, in exchange for important services granted to the sultans, as well as regular gifts, Christian princes succeeded in gaining a relative security for pilgrims and, later, in alleviating certain restrictions of the *dhimma* such as those forbidding the improvement of old churches and the construction of new ones.

By the *firman* of October 1596, France obtained from the Sublime Porte the assurance that foreign Christian pilgrims would be neither molested nor forced to embrace Islam. In the following year, at the request of Henri IV of France, the sultan revoked a decision to imprison the monks and priests of the Holy Land and to convert the Church of the Holy Sepulchre into a mosque.

However, the Muslim officials continually inspected the churches to ensure that no repairs had been carried out without authorization, and always found a pretext for extorting money from the clergy. Monsieur de Bonnac, the French ambassador in Constantinople, succeeded, by the *Capitulations* of 1740, in obtaining the limitation of these troublesome visits to one a year, and in gaining the right to repair some churches at the ambassador's request. After forty years of negotiations, this same ambassador obtained permission to repair the roof of the Church of the Holy Sepulchre. Over the centuries, the Byzantine Empire, European countries, and Russia attempted to protect the local Christian communities. Consular budgets were heavily burdened by the gifts or sums of money that the Muslim authorities insisted upon receiving before they would respect agreements, which were constantly in dispute or arbitrarily withdrawn.[1]

(?) ## Commercial and Political Protections

In addition to the protection of religious interests, economic protections also developed. From the most ancient times, trade links had been established around the Mediterranean coast that had facilitated the spread of the Hellenistic and Judeo-Christian cultures. Though the Arab domination impeded this process, it did not end it. This is not the place to examine the origins of the European commercial trading companies (*Échelles*) allowed under the *Capitulations.* In view of the status of infidels in Islamic countries, and of the frequent wars, the regular conduct of commercial relations between the Orient and Europe required that foreign merchants should be shielded from local jurisdiction, thereby exempting them from the *dhimma.* These foreign merchants enjoyed an extraterritorial status, being thus subject to their own jurisdiction administered through consuls. They lived grouped together in *khans* or *funduqs,* whose doors were locked every night for their protection. As a measure of prudence, they were forbidden to marry local *dhimmis* or to have other than commercial relations with Muslims.[2]

The first *Capitulations* (1535) were basically economic. Consular protection applied to matters of personal status, of worship, and of trade and navigation; it also guaranteed fiscal and legal privileges. Apart from their own nationals, the consuls also protected a few foreigners without consular representation in the Orient, as well as Jews of Spanish origin who, in return for large payments, obtained certain rights, though without enjoying all the privileges available to other merchants.

Because Jews were regarded as a nation without a country and consequently without representation, the European consuls sold their protection to a certain number of them. Although the latter benefited from this arrangement, it was not in any way motivated by humanitarian considerations. Indeed, commercial and later political motives were conducive to an ever-increasing number of individuals placing themselves under consular protection. Jews were sometimes welcomed and protected in the Levant by the consuls of nations whose laws discriminated against them in Europe. These Jews, pleased to escape from their insecure condition, submitted willingly enough to the special payments that distinguished them from the other merchants trading under the *Capitulations* system: payments limited only by the rivalry of the consuls who solicited them. The European Christian merchants and other *protégés,* who were generally at odds among themselves, sought the expulsion of the Jews. Prejudice and greed motivated this hostility, because the Jews, through their knowledge of languages and their widespread contacts, were <u>serious competitors.</u> *AH*

In 1731 the French consul at Aleppo protested against the imposition of an additional tax on the Jews.

> If the Jews here, who have been for twenty-five years under the protection of the king were to relinquish it, this loss would oblige us to increase considerably the tax of the trading centres *(Échelles),* to the great disadvantage of those who trade here, as well as to all the resident merchants.[3]

The Jews often complained of the unjust treatment that singled them out from the other merchants. However, they possessed a powerful weapon: the threat of seeking protection from another consul, thereby enriching their new protector-nation with their contributions and their skills. The other merchants, who tolerated them only with reluctance, expressed their hostility by attempting to humiliate them. In public ceremonies in which a well-ordered protocol assigned janissaries, dragomans, ambassadors and consuls, foreigners and local *protégés* their respective places, the Jews always came last. Even the mere acceptance of their presence was constantly disputed by the Christian merchants, who demanded their total exclusion from all public ceremonies. The consuls, however, remained firm. In Salonica, the Jews were admitted to the ceremonies in 1738 for the following reasons:

> Monsieur de Villeneuve replied that it should be of no interest to the [Christian] merchants of Salonica, if the *protégés* were to accompany him on the visits which he made to the officials of the Grand Seigneur [sultan], as long as they were made to walk at the very end, and that this condescension could have a good effect by keeping them even closer to French protection, from which it was not advisable to allow them any pretext to abandon.[4]

In 1743 the merchants of Aleppo, supported by the Marseilles Chamber of Commerce, demanded the exclusion of the Jews from the official visits. The ambassador wrote to the minister:

> I will not conceal the fact that I am surprised that the Chamber of Commerce has been more affected by the capriciousness of the [Christian] merchants of Aleppo than by its own interest, which is to spare the foreigners, who, if they were to seek another protection, would diminish the taxes collected.[5]

The merchants, however, were successful, and the Jews were no longer admitted to the visits.

In 1770 the Jewish communities of Cairo and Alexandria were
ruined by the intrigues of Syrian Christians who were eager to take
their places. It is noteworthy that some Jews were Venetian *protégés*,
who, in order to keep their consular protection, were obliged to make
large payments to the Muslim authorities. Thus treaties and *Capitulations* did not always protect foreign merchants and local *protégés* from
the rapacity of the governors. One gains the impression from the
consular reports and contemporary descriptions that they were more
often violated than honored, as may be seen from the following story.

In 1748, when a French ambassador trying to settle a dispute referred to the *Capitulations,* the Ottoman Grand Vizier reacted by allowing the document to be carried off by the wind. After one of his
officers had brought it back, the Grand Vizier placed it in the same
spot, but weighted it down with a purse full of money. Then, turning
to the ambassador, he remarked:

> Do you see how one must give weight to the *Capitulations,* so that
> the wind does not carry them away as has just happened?[26]

Consular protection was also extended to the *dhimmis* who were
employed there as interpreters and in other official functions. But
these *dhimmis,* as subjects of the sultan, were obliged to wear special
clothes and paid the *jizya,* a symbol of shame. Molested in the streets,
they were humiliated and frequently assaulted. Sometimes the sultan
or pasha, displeased with a consul, would take revenge by ordering
the whipping, impaling, or hanging of his Christian interpreter. As a
result, the consuls attempted to remove their *dhimmi* employees from
the control of the local jurisdiction. This protection of local subjects
was a constant source of friction between the consuls and the Turkish
authorities, who insisted on the payment of taxes due from their
dhimmi subjects. The *protégés,* for their part, in order to validate their
privileges, had to obtain, for a fee, special documents from the sultan
and from the consul. The sale of such protections became a lucrative
trade for the consul, while the sultan sought every opportunity of
issuing and renewing them.

It has been shown that, within the *umma,* the non-Muslim stood at
the center of a conflict between the rapacity of the rulers and the
fanaticism of the populace, a situation that led the *dhimmi* to practice
guile. In the wider relationship between the *dar al-Islam* and *the dar al-
Harb,* the *dhimmi* was once more in the midst of clashing interests. The
increase in the number of European *protégés* actually conferred a
double advantage on foreign governments in Islamic countries.
Through protections, commercial privileges were obtained and national economic interests developed; moreover, they could influence

JEW OF CONSTANTINOPLE
"The Jews are dressed in black and wear a round violet turban with a gaudy Sesse
[kaveze]*" (p. 36)*
Engraving (no. 63) by B. Baron, from a painting by J.-B. Vanmour (1707–08)
Antoine de Feriol (Louis XIV's ambassador to the Sublime Porte)

the policy of Muslim governments. Whereas European politicians realized that the discriminations affecting the *dhimmi* allowed them to interfere and extend their rival political and economic interests, the *dhimmi,* for his part, felt that the only way of escaping from his debased status was to obtain the protection of a European power. Jews and Christians, tempted by the consuls' offers, sought this protection, which theoretically preserved them from fiscal extortion as well as arbitrary and summary justice, but made of them the involuntary instruments of European penetration. The *dhimmis* saw in the *protégé* status a first step toward emancipation. Because this emancipation introduced Christian influence into the *dar al-Islam* and because it contradicted the *dhimma* rules, it also aroused Muslim hostility against the *dhimmis.*

Consular protection developed in the Levant, particularly from the sixteenth century onward, owing to the political pragmatism and economic needs of the Ottomans. Though it stimulated trade, it was also the cause of many political abuses. Nevertheless, the continuous and tenacious efforts of generations of consuls eroded the constraints on the *dhimmi,* so that in 1856 the European powers were able to demand the dhimma's abolition throughout the Ottoman Empire.

The protection extended to the minorities also reflected the interplay of European rivalries (see doc. 53). Thus, at the Madrid Conference of 1880, the British delegate Sir John Drummond Hay, wishing to reduce commercial activity between Morocco and some European states, proposed—with the backing of the sultan for other reasons—that the existing system of European protections in Morocco should be abolished. As a result, the Jewish merchants whose abilities had largely increased trade in the area would have been placed in such a vulnerable situation that the flow of commerce between Morocco and the rival European nations would have been seriously weakened. The British diplomat hid the political motives for his proposal behind humanitarian reasons. He declared that the granting of equality to the protected Jews would so anger the Muslims that in revenge they might pillage and massacre thousands of men, women, and children.[7]

The question of protections had become crucial in Morocco, not because the Jews were more oppressed there than elsewhere—indeed, their condition was as bad in Persia and Yemen and parts of Tripolitania and Iraq—but chiefly because of the increased development of commercial activity between Morocco and Europe. In fact, this system could not be eliminated without establishing the principle of equal rights for all the sultan's subjects and the validity of the testimony of Jews and Christians in Muslim courts of law. But any attempts at such reforms inevitably led to popular indignation and riots; fanatics thus took their own revenge upon those whom the sultan, under European pressure, was obliged to protect. This fanaticism demonstrated the need for the retention of the protection system, imperfect as it may have been. Since any modification of the *dhimma* by the sultan would lead to retaliation against the *dhimmi* communities, the problem seemed insoluble (see docs., sec. "Emancipation").

Toward the end of the nineteenth century and the beginning of the twentieth, colonial-inspired writings, critical of the *dhimmis* and favorable to the Arabs, made their appearance. It was the period of colonization in North Africa, during which European and Levantine settlers, adventurers, and merchants flooded into the Maghreb and the eastern Mediterranean countries. The confrontation between these ambitious foreigners, who were imbued with European anti-semitism, and the local Jews, whose traditional economic structures had been strengthened and consolidated by the alleviation of the *dhimma* and, later, by its abrogation, encouraged this unsympathetic attitude. These writings, despite some blatant contradictions, usually praised the tolerance and generosity of the local authorities for improving the lot of the *dhimmis,* as if the few liberties that were grudgingly bestowed upon them were praiseworthy. In fact, the emancipation of the *dhimmis* imposed by the West was a very long process which, far from being achieved, is still questioned today by the *ulama.*

European protection greatly influenced the political, social, and economic situation of the *dhimmis.* It altered not only their relationship with the *umma* but also the relationships between the different *dhimmi* communities themselves. One group was favored rather than another, in accordance with the power of the protecting country and its influence on the sultan. The general condition of the Christians improved owing to the protection of the European countries and Russia, whereas the social situation of the Jews, in comparison with that of the Christians, and with that of the Armenians in Persia, deteriorated in Syria, Palestine, and Egypt.

Through the system of protections, Europe developed its trade and, later, its colonial interests. In order to increase the number of *protégés,* missionary institutions such as hospitals, hospices, and schools were set up, and proselytism was encouraged, although coordination between Church and State did not always exist in the nineteenth century. This missionary zeal exasperated the *dhimmi* religious leaders, who turned to the Muslim authorities for help. At the beginning of the twentieth century, a large number of Christians of the Nestorian Church in Azerbaidjan accepted the Greek Orthodox rite in order to place themselves under Russian protection. One of the targets of this proselytism, though not the only one, was Oriental

Jewry. Here one should mention the activities of the London Society
for promoting Christianity among the Jews, which dispatched converted European Jews to some of the most vulnerable Jewish communities. Disposing of large funds, this society distributed
translations of the New Testament in Hebrew, Arabic, and Yiddish,
and provided hospitals, schools, and workshops for its *protégés*.[8]

Would the *dhimmi* peoples have completely disappeared in the
course of the Arabization and Islamization of their former homelands
without the protection and intervention of the European powers? In
Yemen, where European influence was never exercised, Jewish communities still existed in the early twentieth century, but one of their
members described their condition as that of animals rather than
human beings (see doc. 91). On the other hand, the Jews—and the
Samaritans—were virtually eradicated from the villages and towns of
Palestine. The same can be said of the Armenians in their former
homeland, and of the numerous Christian rural populations of
Mesopotamia (Iraq). It is difficult to assess the degree of influence
that Europe had on the evolution of the *dhimmi* peoples, but in help-
ing Greece, the other Balkan countries, and Lebanon to regain their
national independence, it also opened up new hopes of dignity and
freedom for the remnants of other oppressed peoples.

Western influence set in motion two contradictory forces. It cur-
tailed or delayed the process of the extinction of the *dhimmi* peoples,
but it intensified Muslim anti-*dhimmi* feelings and inflamed fanaticism,
leading to bloody attacks, since the contract of toleration no longer
existed. Thus, paradoxically, Western influence sometimes stimulated
this process of the extinction of *dhimmi* communities—faced with massacre and expulsion—in a context of national uprisings intermingled
with European colonial interests.

Interfaith Relations

Arab rule, succeeding Byzantine theocracy, asserted itself over peoples steeped in religious intolerance. A system of legalized persecution, segregation, and humiliation had already been elaborated by the
Greek Orthodox Church, the true creator of the future *dhimma*. The
Theodosian code (438), the Justinian code (534), and the conciliar
laws constituted a coherent and ordered system of legislation that
justified the persecution of pagans, heretics, and Jews throughout the
Byzantine Empire. These laws were taught and interpreted in the
academies, convents, and schools founded by Justinian and disseminated throughout the empire. Many of the imperial officials who
were responsible for the implementation of these laws later incor-
porated them into the legislation of the conquerors, the desire of the

Christian ruling classes to retain their dominant positions having been a major cause of their conversion to Islam. These Byzantine laws, conceived in the context of a particular system of values, thus passed into Islamic legislation, where they were justified by another system of values. Both systems, however, rested on one and the same principle: namely, that the power and domination of a religion are proofs of its veracity, while the abasement and humiliation of other faiths demonstrate their error. It is indeed an irony of history that in the territories that came under its rule, Islam was able to use, for the destruction of Eastern Christendom, the remarkable system of oppression which the Byzantine Church had elaborated and perfected for use against the Synagogue. In imposing its anti-Jewish legislation, the Church Fathers—unconscious agents of history—having arrived at the height of their power, were simultaneously laying the ground for the destruction of Eastern Christianity. And, in exactly the same way as the Church proved the superiority of its dogma through the abasement of the Synagogue, so Islam, in turn, asserted its own superiority through the humiliation of the Church. The more the enemies' creeds were debased, the more the truth of the victorious faith, heightened by temporal power, confirmed Allah's Will.

Similarities exist in both systems of legislation: in the laws relating to the possession of slaves, to proselytism, blasphemy, apostasy, places of worship, conversions (including children), social segregation, the prohibition of mixed marriages, the inadmissibility of legal testimony and exclusion from the administration. These laws of Byzantine origin gradually became the substance of the *dhimmi* condition. The Arab conquerors added the *jizya*, a poll tax, whereby the *dhimmi*'s life was spared on his submission to specific regulations.

Subsequently, humiliating laws brought this persecution to a high level of refinement. Rules governed the color and shape of the *dhimmis'* clothes, the cut of their hair, and sometimes the shape and colour of their footwear. Specifications applied to the type of animal that *dhimmis* could ride, the way in which they could mount it, and the kind of saddles they could use, and also their behavior in the street, the manner in which they should be greeted, and the like. On the other hand, the *dhimmis* enjoyed a limited judicial and legal autonomy, which was inherited from Roman and Byzantine law.

In the early period, the Arab conquerors benefited—in different parts of the Byzantine Empire—from the collaboration of Jewish, Samaritan, and Christian groups who had been oppressed by the Greek Orthodox Church. The invaders knew how to take advantage of the dissensions between local groups in order to impose their own authority, favoring first one and then another, with the intention of weakening and ruining them all through a policy of "divide and rule."

However, the role played by the Muslim powers as arbiter and protector in settling the quarrels between non-Muslim communities, as well as in righting injustices committed by the Muslims against *dhimmis*, should not be forgotten.

The Arab conquest changed the position of the Orthodox Christians from that of the oppressors (of pagans, Jews, and members of other Christian Churches) into that of the oppressed. Even worse, they were relegated to the degrading condition that the ruling Byzantine Church had formerly imposed upon those whom it had persecuted. The former oppressors now joined their victims, but the hatreds remained alive—even if less explosive—between the Greek Orthodox Church and the Synagogue, and also, in different variations, between the several Eastern Churches.

Common misfortune did little to reconcile the various *dhimmi* communities. On the contrary, their degradation only reinforced their mutual hostility. The abasement of the Jews reflected onto the Greek Orthodox community its own image, an image doubly painful since it had originated within the Church. As for the Jews, Islam—although more tolerant—perpetuated an oppression that, in many respects, they had endured under the Byzantine Church. For them nothing had really changed, except for the abasement of their proud oppressor and the sharing—with the other Churches—of a common distress, which was to endure as long as did the *dhimma* and its motivations.

Factors of Political Manipulation

An analysis of the subtle complexity of intercommunal relations throughout the centuries does not fall within the scope of this study. The interplay of hostile but frequently of conniving and friendly relations between oppressed communities is the very thread of history. When the Copts of Cairo, for instance, were massacred if they ventured into the streets in 1343, the Jews lent them their own discriminatory garments, and it was owing to this disguise, borrowed from another persecuted community, that they were able to leave their houses. In 1853 the Rumanian traveler Benjamin described the good relations between Jews and Armenians in Kurdistan. In the nineteenth century, Jews and Christians often joined forces to protest against injustice in Tunis. The sheikh of Merv welcomed some Jews from Meshed who had been forced to become Muslims in 1839, and allowed them to revert to their former religion. In fact, the Muslim notables of Meshed saved most of the Jews from death by declaring publicly that the whole community would convert to Islam. During the Damascus massacres of 1860, some Muslims tried to save Christians, notably the emir Abd al-Qadir, and Jews took refuge in Muslim houses (see docs. 45, 46, 51). The numerous examples of interfaith solidarity between oppressed groups, as well as with Muslim groups, would require a specific monograph. Here, however, some constant factors have been noted, which made the *dhimmis'* condition not only one of oppression, but also one prone to intrigue and manipulation.

The choice of a spiritual leader for each *dhimmi* community had to be ratified by the caliph or governor. Venality often favored the more corrupt elements among the *dhimmis,* so that the moral and cultural level of the communities declined, bringing them into discredit not only in the eyes of the *umma* but also in those of their own members. Despotism and corruption decided the fate of communities that wished to curry the favor of authorities in order to survive or develop. In periods of crisis the deportation and dispossession of one group for the benefit of another fostered rivalries and hatreds that lasted for centuries.

For instance, in 1856–60, the Ottoman government, worried by the rise of Christian nationalisms within its empire, incited the Druses against the Maronites with whom they had lived peacefully for centuries. In order to crush the Armenian autonomist movement, the Turkish authorities, in conformity with their policy of stirring up strife between the communities, used the Kurds to massacre the Armenians in 1894–96. At Urfa on the Euphrates, the Jews were made to bury them and disinfect the area.[9] Nonetheless, as has already been stated, it would be a mistake to imagine that the various communities lived in a state of perpetual hostility.

The relationship between the various Churches, which had been supported and protected by Christendom, also depended on political conditions. Not only did the rivalries of European states affect the various communities, but, in addition, these latter were deeply concerned by the wars and the treaties signed with Islamic countries. In the nineteenth century the fear of European reprisals on the *umma* helped to improve the position of the Christians and earned them a certain respect.

Other factors were important. Intolerance, and consequently oppression, was greater if a *dhimmi* community was the only non-Muslim people in a particular region. This was the case with the Jews in the Maghreb and in Yemen. On the other hand, their condition was much better in Muslim Spain and in the Ottoman Empire, where they were a minority among the Christians. Exiled from their ancient homeland and without any foreign support, the Jewish people were of no political consequence.

This situation, however, favored them in relation to the Christian *dhimmis,* who, being much more numerous and linked with Christendom, were considered to be dangerous and potential traitors. Thus

the Jews sometimes held, between the Muslim oppressors and the
subjected Christian populations, a privileged intermediate position
that polarized hostilities. Unaccustomed to the refined civilizations
that they subjected, the Arab conquerors (and later the Turks) had
been wise enough to use the qualified elites which had been oppressed
by the dominant Church—Jews or heretical Christians—as a means of
controlling the conquered populations. The Judeo-Arabic "Golden
Age" in Spain and in the Ottoman Empire grew out of a political
situation that was generally favorable to those who had been dominated, but disastrous for their former oppressors who, under the
yoke of new foreign rulers, sank to the level of their former victims
and sometimes lower, depending on political circumstances.

The existence of Jewish and Christian court *dhimmis,* who shed a
temporary luster upon their respective communities, in no way implied the abrogation of the *dhimma,* inscribed in the sacred texts of the
Sunna. These men, whose talents were exploited by their masters and
oppressors and who succeeded through bribery in alleviating some
constraints, were anomalies in a system of injustice and inequality.
The manifest contradiction between their privileged existence and
their legal status provoked a fanatical reaction. Far from being an
authorized exception to the rule, in the eyes of the Muslim religious
class the situation of the court *dhimmis* constituted a sacrilege, a heresy
dangerous for the *umma* and punishable by collective reprisals. Despite their court financiers, the Jewish people in the *dar al-Islam* was
little more than a despised source of manpower, liable to forced labor
at any time. Owing to its very vulnerability, surrounded by the *umma,*
it fulfilled the useful function of scapegoat. The meteoric rise of
individual Jews, followed by a fall even more spectacular since it involved collective punishment, alleviated neither the discriminatory
laws nor the oppression weighing on the people. Moreover, the power
gained by some Jewish *dhimmis,* forbidden by the religious laws of the
umma (and previously by the Byzantine codes) only increased hostility.
In 1856, when the sultan granted equal rights to the minorities of his
empire, some Christian leaders protested because the Jews received
rights equal to their own.

It may well be that the role that some Jews assumed as intermediaries for the Muslims accounts for the extreme forms of anti-
Jewish persecution in the period of the *Reconquista* of Spain, and in
nineteenth-century Greece and in other Balkan countries. During the
independence wars in the Balkanic provinces of the Ottoman Empire,
the Jewish communities—being apolitical and vulnerable—suffered
persecutions and expulsions in this context of religious fanaticism,
which prompted the sultan to protest on behalf of his former subjects.

X. Economic and Religious Rivalries

Christians didn't fair well

The emancipation and liberation movements that took place in the Ottoman Empire during the nineteenth century excited Muslim anti-Christian hatred, thus provoking numerous massacres of Greeks, Slavs, Maronites, and Armenians.[10] More timid, humble and, of necessity, apolitical, the Jewish communities were spared or even favored by the Turks, who wished to appear liberal and tolerant in the eyes of their European allies. This political disparity, together with the economic advancement of the Jewish elite heightened intercommunity tensions even more.

In those professions where *dhimmis* were in competition, religious hostility was intensified by economic rivalry. This rivalry was all the greater as opportunities were limited and were subject to the whims of despots who encouraged corruption.

It was this fierce competition between *dhimmi* minorities, subject to the most arbitrary oppression, that underlay the false accusation of ritual murder made in Damascus in 1840 against the Jewish community by the Syrian Christians and the French consul Ratti-Menton.[11] A relationship was then established between an emancipated European Jewry and the *dhimmi* Jewish communities of the Orient and North Africa, which completely changed their structure.

From 1860 onward, the tireless representatives of the *Alliance Israélite Universelle* and, from 1872, of the Anglo-Jewish Association, devoted themselves to the emancipation of the Jews of North Africa and the Orient. A considerable number of letters and reports reveal to us the wretchedness and decay—but also the nobility—of those oppressed communities. In the last decades of the nineteenth century, European Jewry, assisted by the consuls, managed to modify the balance of forces between the Jewish and Christian *dhimmis*. But differences still remained. The Christian *dhimmis*, emancipated earlier, enjoyed European protection, both on a national level (e.g., schools and political institutions in Lebanon) and on an individual level, owing to the many missionary institutions. More numerous and more powerful than the Jews in economic life, they provided a strong encouragement to the traditional Muslim judeophobia. Indeed, the slow economic emancipation of the Jews stimulated old animosities, bringing into existence a modern virulent form of Oriental Christian anti-Judaism, against which the Jews defended themselves within their limited possibilities.

Indeed, Oriental Jewry counted on the assistance of European Jewry, which itself had only recently gained emancipation and was already the object of modern forms of political and economic antisemitism. Yet this weakness, as compared with the power of Christian communities, was counterbalanced by the strong desire of the Jews for dignity and education—a desire which was apparent in the reports on even the most deprived communities. From 1840 onward, this desire became a realizable goal. The time of liberty—of moral and cultural redemption—emerging from nebulous Messianism, was foreseeable in the context of human realities. If justice had not triumphed during the Damascus Affair, at least injustice had been circumscribed.[12] A people who had been forced to live in moral degradation, humiliation, and ignorance now glimpsed the light at the end of the tunnel.

If the struggles for the emancipation of the Jewish and Christian communities appear similar, in fact they were quite different, their similarity consisting solely in the reactions which they aroused in their common oppressor. The forms of pressure available to the protectors of the two groups were also different. The Christian nations could exert political pressure backed up by military force, while the Jews of Europe (and later the United States) could act only in the name of a universal ethic, denouncing fanatical excesses before public opinion in Parliaments and in the European press. Such excesses discredited Muslim regimes which incited or tolerated them, or the Christian clergy when they were responsible. Either by necessity or out of sincere conviction—it is hard to disentangle the two in the labyrinths of power—the authorities took measures to check racial and religious persecution. Church leaders disavowed accusations of ritual murder and other public antisemitic practices particularly common among the Greek Orthodox communities,[13] and Muslim political leaders issued edicts for the protection of minorities. After 1860 there was unceasing effort on the part of Jewish organizations in France and England, in cooperation with the foreign consuls, to extend to the Jews—and consequently to all the oppressed minorities—the emancipation first granted to the Christian *dhimmis.* Although the Ottoman government had promulgated the Gülhaneh (1839) and Humayun (1856) edicts of toleration, they were not effective as far as the Jews were concerned.

These attempts to promote religious equality in the Ottoman Empire, although important, were only operative at the highest political level. The main task—getting the regional governors and the people, among whom the minorities lived, to respect the sultan's orders—still remained to be performed. Indeed, the Turkish authorities, themselves a minority, would often fail to apply the reforms for the liberalization of the *dhimmi* status, out of fear of antagonizing the common people, who were convinced of their superiority and were attached to their traditions of domination (see docs. 39 and 53). Incapable of controlling rebel clans or of diminishing the general condition of corruption and insecurity in the provinces, the central Ottoman administration often abandoned the minorities to the tyranny of local governors or tribal leaders. Henceforth, the contact with Europe started a vast struggle that placed all the *dhimmi* communities, although divided among themselves, in opposition to the traditional values of the *dhimma,* which had sanctified the usurpation of their territory and their degraded status. This struggle was carried on simultaneously by the different communities, but in a spirit of disunity, hatred, and rivalry, including servile alliances—a situation that could only benefit their common oppressor.

Nationalism

At the beginnning of the twentieth century, the rivalry between the movement for political emancipation of the Jews, on the one hand, and of the Arabic-speaking Christians, on the other, further poisoned relations that were already very complex. These movements, which expressed themselves in Zionism[14] and Arabism respectively, were both threatened by pan-Islamism.

The Christian stream of Arab nationalism, active from the second half of the nineteenth century, sprang from two sources: French imperialism and the aspirations of the Christian *dhimmis* to emancipation.

In claiming to be the champion of Arabism, France aimed at carving out for itself colonial territories at the expense of the Ottoman Empire. It also endeavored to weaken the economic and political influence of Great Britain. French ideological and strategic support for the autonomy of the Ottoman Arab provinces hardly differed in its motives and methods from that of other contemporary imperial powers. The desire for emancipation of the Arabic-speaking Christians was used to discredit and weaken Turkey and benefit French colonial policy. In exactly the same way, Russia justified its seizure of Turkish and Persian provinces because of the persecution of Orthodox Christians, and Great Britain protected Jews and later supported Zionism in order to control Palestine.

The other current of Christian nationalism was linked to an emancipation movement. Essentially religious, it originated and developed in clerical circles and missionary institutions that were either French or under French influence. After the 1856–1860 massacres of Christians in Syria and Lebanon, and in Nablus (Palestine), this movement aimed at substituting the concept of a secular Arab nation for the religious concept of the *umma*. This conception was by no means original. It was the Arab equivalent of the Ottoman movement (en-

couraged by Great Britain), which in the nineteenth century had tried
to prevent the decay of the Ottoman Empire by integrating the
numerous *raya* (i.e., *dhimmi*) ethnic groups into an Ottoman nationalism. In other words, the religious imperialism of *jihad* attempted to
retain its territorial acquisitions within a modern nationalist ideology,
by transforming itself into a secular Ottoman nationalist movement.

Inspired by Western liberal ideologies, Ottomanism advocated the
equality of all Ottoman subjects. Thus it uncompromisingly contradicted the theocratic policy of the *umma,* which justified discriminations against conquered infidel peoples. But Ottomanism overlooked
one fundamental aspect of the ethnic revolts of the *raya* peoples: their
movements for religious emancipation were essentially wars for national liberation. The struggle of the Serbs, the Rumanians, the Bul-
gars, the Greeks, the Armenians, and the Jews was principally a
struggle for their land, their language, their history, and their culture,
rather than for their religion, which was officially tolerated.

This same territorial and cultural Ottoman imperialism was in turn
appropriated by pan-Arabism and for similar motives, the Arab Empire having expanded by the conquest of non-Arab territories and the
suppression of indigenous peoples and cultures. The Christian *dhimmis* who tried to gain emancipation through Arab nationalism with the
aid of France later found themselves faced with a dilemma: Arab
values, linked to Islam, justified the very discriminatory laws of the
dhimma from which they were attempting to free themselves by means
of Arabism. This movement of Arab renaissance in which the Christians were active contained within itself the seeds of the Islamic renaissance, the rejection of the West (embodying the *dar al-Harb*), its
values, and its secularism, and pointed to the future reestablishment
of the *dhimmi* status for Jews and Christians.

The recent disintegration of Lebanon derives from this dichotomy
in Arab nationalism: on the one hand, the emancipation of the Christians, and on the other, the *dhimmi* condition, which is inherent in
Arabism. Because they never wished or were never able to specify
clearly the conditions they required for their independence, the
Maronites, together with the other Christian communities, today find
themselves trapped in a culture conflict with the *umma,* reconstituted
through Arabism. The struggle of the Oriental Christians for emancipation appears to form a tragic cycle of history, spreading over more
than a century of suffering and massacre and ending at its starting
point: the reestablishment of the *dhimma* in modern terms. Thus the
violent anti-Zionism of the Christian branch of Arab nationalism—
particularly among some adherents of the Orthodox Church—may
be explained by its religious origins and by a historical survival in
conditions of vulnerability conducive to manipulation.[15]

Three points are worth making before concluding this rapid survey of intercommunity relations during the nineteenth and twentieth centuries. The first is the condition of the Jews, a people without a country which, exiled and scattered as a result of the occupation of its territory, was condemned by that very fact to be the victim of the conflicts between Islam and Christendom. The second is the process by which an independent state was achieved by the people of Israel, compared to the fanatical excesses accompanying the *Reconquista* of Spain and the wars of independence of the Greeks, the Balkan peoples and, in recent times, the Arabs. The third point concerns a historical parallel: the possibility that the *jihad* directed against the Armenians at the beginning of the twentieth century served as a model for the genocide of the Jews carried out some thirty years later. The Germans, allies of the Turks in the First World War, were present at the attempt to liquidate a whole people that was striving for its freedom. They saw how civil populations were shut up in churches and burned, or gathered *en masse* in camps, tortured to death, and reduced to ashes, or led in interminable convoys toward their place of execution, forced to dig their graves, or abandoned in the desert, or, again, sold as slaves to Arab tribes and compelled to accept Islam. After the sultan's proclamation of *jihad* on 1 November 1914, the governments of Germany and Austria-Hungary knew that the local Muslim populations in Anatolia, Armenia, Iraq, and Syria actively participated in the 'final solution' of the Armenian people. They saw the paralysis of the European governments confronted with a slaughter that was reported in the world's newspapers and known to all.

This history lesson was remembered one generation later, when Hitler planned a genocide with all the technological refinements and efficiency of modern times. One can point to similarities in the behavior of the victims, the murderers, and those who were passive spectators. It is worth recalling the convoys of docile Armenians deluded by the pretext that they were being transported to a temporary change of residence, when in fact they were being taken to their place of executions. Victims were selected for various purposes—for immediate death or slavery, for ransom, or for prostitution—before finally being killed. Children were used as a form of target practice. All of this shows the similarity in the collective behavior of peoples when historical circumstances repeat themselves.[16]

Notes to Chapter 3

1. See Rey; Charles-Roux.
2. Rey, pp. 395–400. These measures were particularly harsh in Syria and Palestine because of local fanaticism; see Charles-Roux, chap. 3.

3. Charles-Roux, p. 48.
4. Rey, p. 419.
5. Idem, p. 420.
6. Idem, p. 181.
7. N. Leven, *Cinquante ans d'Histoire: L'Alliance Israélite Universelle (1860–1910)*, 2 vols. (Paris, 1911/1920), 1:245; for the Madrid Conference, idem, pp. 236–60, and J. L. Miège, *Le Maroc et l'Europe (1830–1894)*, (Paris, 1961), 3:274–92.
8. W. T. Gidney, *History of the London Society for Promoting Christianity amongst the Jews from 1809 to 1908* (London, 1909).
9. Contenson, pp. 57–62. The Jews were obliged to bury the bodies of thousands of Armenians, men, women, and children massacred at Urfa during two days.
10. Reports of that period show a contempt and hatred for the Greeks, Maronites, and Armenians, not unlike the contemporary anti-Israel policy of the Arab League states and most Muslim leaders. The Ottoman government and the *umma* would not accept that subjected and humiliated non-Muslim peoples could achieve national independence in their historic homelands. See below, doc. sec. II: *The Era of Emancipation*, and, inter alia, *P.P.*, 1860 [2734] 69; 1861 [2800] 68; 1877 [C. 1739] 92; 1877 [C. 1768] 92; 1877 [C. 1806] 92.
11. An Italian Capuchin friar, Father Thomas, disappeared in Damascus on 5 February 1840, with his Muslim servant. A blood-libel accusation was brought against the Jewish community by the local Christians, the charges and legal process being conducted by the French consul in Damascus, Count Ratti-Menton, supported by the Egyptian governor Sherif Pasha. Seven venerable leaders of the community were arrested and tortured; two died; one accepted Islam to save his life; while sixty-three Jewish children were imprisoned and many homes were destroyed in the vain search for the bodies (and blood). See A. J. Brawer, "Damascus Affair", *EJ* 5:1249–52 (and bibliography); A. M. Hyamson, "The Damascus Affair–1840", Transactions, *JHSE* 16 (1945–51): 47–71; Stillman, pp. 105–6, 393–402. Strong anti-Christian hatred was aroused at this time as a consequence of European and Russian imperialism and the national movements of Christian nations under Ottoman rule. As several European Christians had been murdered in Syria at that time, it is possible that the French consul decided to divert French public opinion away from such incidents by making a scapegoat out of the Damascus Jewish community in order to safeguard France's good relations with Muhammad Ali, whose control of Syria-Palestine was then being challenged by Great Britain. If in fact Father Thomas had been killed by a Muslim soldier (or civilian), a condemnation for the death of a Christian would have aroused more popular resentment against the French, then in process of "pacifying" Algeria. In 1860, after the massacre of thousands of Christians in Damascus, attempts were made to incriminate the Jews. See doc. 51 below.
12. In 1841, the Ottoman sultan Abdülmecid I declared the blood-libel fallacious and forbade its propagation in the empire. Sir Moses Montefiore was instrumental in obtaining this *firman*.
13. On the blood libel in the Orient, see M. Franco, *Essai sur l'histoire des Israélites de l'Empire Ottoman* (Paris, 1897), pp. 47–48, 87–88; J. M. Landau, "Ritual Murder Accusations and Persecutions of Jews in the 19th Century Egypt," in *Sefunot* 5 (1961) (Hebrew): 417–60, and in *Middle Eastern Themes* (London, 1973), pp. 99–142; idem, *Jews in Nineteenth-Century Egypt* (London, 1969), pp. 182, 199, 203, 215, 289, 294, 307, 320, 324ff. At Jaffa, a tradition existed during the fast of Lent when small children from Greek families would go from house to house begging for contributions to buy the wood necessary for "burning the Jew." On the evening of Easter Thursday, the pyres were lit, on each of which a strawman wearing Jewish apparel was burned amidst the clamor and the boos of the crowd. See V. X. Fontanier, *Voyage dans l'Inde, dans le Golfe Persique par l'Egypte et la Mer Rouge* (Paris, 1844–1846), 2:607; and, in Egypt (1883), Landau, *Jews*, pp. 225–26. Besides the accusation of blood-libel, the persecutions against the Jews by the Eastern Churches took various forms, which caused the death and torture of unnumbered innocent victims over the centuries.
14. Bat Ye'or, *Jews in Egypt* (Hebrew) (Tel Aviv, 1974), chap. 13; idem, "Zionism in Islamic Lands: The Case of Egypt," in *WLB*, n.s. 30, nos. 43–44 (1977): 16–29;

D. Bensimon-Donath, *Immigrants d'Afrique du Nord en Israël* (Paris, 1970); M. Abitbol, "Zionist Activity in the Maghreb", in *JQ* 21 (1981): 61–84. It is unfortunate that the meager historical research on Zionism in the Orient and North Africa (and that recent work has mainly been published in Hebrew) has strengthened the common belief that Zionism was an exclusively European-inspired political doctrine. When referring to Zionism in the Orient, it is essential to bear in mind the *dhimmi* condition. The severe massacres that became the lot of the Greeks, the Maronites, the Armenians, and other *dhimmis* made it mandatory on Oriental Jewry to express its loyalty to a movement of national liberation with the greatest prudence, or face mortal danger for whole communities.

15. Imperial Russia recruited its agents from among its *protégés*, members of the Arab-speaking Greek Orthodox and Armenian communities. See M. Ma'oz, *Ottoman Reform in Syria and Palestine, 1840–1861: The Impact of the Tanzimat on Politics and Society* (Oxford, 1968), p. 216; A. L. Tibawi, "Russian cultural penetration of Syria-Palestine in the Nineteenth Century," in *Royal Central Asian Journal* 52 (1966), pts. 2 and 3.

16. J. Brycc, ed., *The Treatment of Armenians in the Ottoman Empire, 1915–1916* (London, 1916), particularly pp. xxxiii–xxxiv, 72–75, 86.

4

Emancipation

European protection is linked to the emancipation movement of the *dhimmis,* for it not only provided an ideological inspiration, but also gave it practical support—if necessary, with military force. Ideologically, emancipation derived from the Declaration of the Rights of Man, as well as from the principle of national self-determination. In its most radical expression, this movement of emancipation became a war of national liberation of a *dhimmi* people.

The emancipation of the *dhimmis* implied a fundamental transformation of values. A new universalist concept came to the fore: *rights* replaced the former concept of *toleration,* which was the product of a hierarchical relationship between a superior and an inferior—a concept that had created, sustained, and perpetuated a situation of inequality. Rights are inalienable, but toleration, based on goodwill or political opportunism, can be withdrawn at will. Rights guarantee dignity and security, but toleration, being the negation of rights, generates guile, intrigue, and corruption as the sole possible means of survival in a condition of permanent insecurity.

In nineteenth-century Islamic societies, where inequality between *dhimmis* and Muslims still represented the norm, the concepts of rights and equality appeared to Muslim traditionalists as subversive heresies, imposed by Christendom in order to weaken Islam.

The introduction of Western ideas of equal rights for individuals and peoples raised traumatizing religious and political problems in the Ottoman Empire. The introduction of reforms—particularly religious equality—which Europe insisted upon in return for military and technological assistance, brought the Ottoman government into conflict with the Muslim religious circles. Indeed, the emancipation of the *rayas* formed part of a larger context of cooperation, exchanges, and cultural interaction between the *dar al-Harb* and the *dar al-Islam.* This modified relationship constituted the ferment of a political, social, and ideological revolution. The traditional concept of permanent war (*jihad*) was to be replaced by a peaceful relationship, favorable to the adoption of reforms and ideas inspired by the *dar al-Harb,* which was no longer to be viewed solely with theological contempt and

98

hatred. The rehabilitation of the *dar al-Harb* opened the way for the emancipation of the *rayas*, themselves former *harbis*. However, this process inevitably led to territorial conflicts, owing to the fact that the "tolerated religions" were mainly nations dispossessed of their homelands. Thus the inner logic of the *jihad* could not tolerate religious emancipation. Permanent war, the wickedness of the *dar al-Harb*, and the inferiority of the conquered *harbis* constituted the three interdependent and inseparable principles underlying the expansion and political domination of the *umma*.

In the Ottoman Empire the consular correspondence and reports of the period provide a vivid daily account of the situation. The same political pattern is conspicuous everywhere. The *ulama*, custodians of the traditional politicoreligious values, stirred up the fanaticism of the people. The motivation of these uprisings was religious—the desire to maintain the *dhimma* and the wish to punish the insolence and arrogance of the *rayas*. But their aim was political—to intimidate the Turkish governors responsible for carrying out the reforms. In Syria and Lebanon, Palestine, Herzegovina, and the Morea the officials disregarded the reforms, fearing to be assassinated as traitors to Islam (see doc. sec. II: Emancipation). As an alternative to collective or individual reprisals, which might anger the Christian protecting powers, pressures and threats were brought to bear on *dhimmis* who sought emancipation.

In 1841, two years after the proclamation of the Hatt-i Sherif of Gülhane, which, on the insistence of the European powers, promised equal rights to all Ottoman subjects, the British Consul-General at Beirut noted:

> It is a curious fact that only a little more than half a year after the reading and proclamation of the Hatti Sheriff of Gülhané in this country there has been a general reaction in favour of the Koran and of the exclusive privileges of the Mahometans over Christians in diametrical opposition to the doctrine of equality of all before the law which is the essence of the Hatti Sheriff.[1]

When Western technical and military assistance became essential for the survival of the Ottoman Empire, France, Britain, and Austria succeeded in forcing the sultan to issue a proclamation in 1856 recognizing the equality of all his subjects before the law. In return for their cooperation, the European powers insisted that the rights of the *dhimmis* to dignity, equality, and security for themselves, their families, and their property should be recognized and guaranteed. A European in the sultan's service could not see the non-Muslim religions degraded by oppression and injustice without his own prestige's being seriously affected.

In Egypt the emancipation of the Christians, followed by that of the Jews, took place relatively smoothly. Muhammed Ali, eager to preserve the economic and military support of France, succeeded in silencing the religious opposition. In the Maghreb the emancipation of the *dhimmis* sponsored by the European powers provoked a confrontation between the Muslim authorities, threatened with European intervention, and the fanaticism of the populace. Thus the fundamental law ("Pledge of Security") imposed by France on the Bey of Tunis in 1857 had to be rescinded in 1864 following an insurrection. This pattern recurred in the third quarter of the nineteenth century in Morocco and Persia, where the sultan and the shah respectively, were incapable of imposing reformist policies upon the people, who were led by the *ulama*.

If one makes due allowance for regional differences, it is clear that the process of emancipation developed everywhere according to a similar pattern, no less in the Ottoman Empire than later in the Maghreb and Persia. Wherever the decay or disintegration of an empire produced a climate favorable to the European policy of encouraging emancipation of the *dhimmis*, the attempt to end discrimination gave rise to a conflict between reformist elements—however weak—among the Muslims, and hostile religious circles manipulating the people. Indeed, this emancipation was part of a wider program of reform that shattered the political and hierarchical traditions of the *umma*.[2] The emergence of modern societies involved reforms implying respect for the individual and equal justice for all. The archaic social rules, which consecrated the abasement of the infidel and encouraged oppression and legal and administrative corruption, were incompatible with the new society envisaged by realistic Muslim politicians, eager to improve the cultural and economic level of their peoples. European consuls frequently referred to the evils of the Ottoman justice. Holmes, the British Consul in Bosna-Seraï summarized this situation in his letter of 1871 to Foreign Secretary Granville:

The unnecessary delay and neglect, to the prejudice often of innocent persons, the open bribery and corruption, the invariable and unjust favour shown to Musulmans in all cases between Turks and Christians, which distinguish the Turkish administration of what is called "justice" throughout the Empire, cannot fail to suggest the question—what would be the lot of foreigners in Turkey were the European Powers to give up the capitulations? I am convinced that their position in the provinces, at all events, would be intolerable, and that they would quit the country to a man, while the outcry and feeling in Europe against Turkey would ultimately cause her ruin. The universal ignorance, corruption, and fanticism of all classes precludes all hope of an efficient administration of justice for at least another generation.[3]

The traditionalists, for their part, believed that emancipation—in freeing the *dhimmis* from their state of humiliation—annulled, *ipso facto,* the *dar al-Islam*'s pact of protection (see doc. 45). For the laws of *jihad* tolerated the *dhimmis* only in a context of discrimination, within which the payment of the *jizya* symbolized their subjection. Thus, according to this logic, the suppression of the *jizya* and the granting of equal rights for all Ottoman subjects broke the *dhimma*. This breach— according to the laws of *jihad*— restored to the *umma* its initial right to kill the *dhimmis,*seize their property, reduce their women and children to slavery, or expel them, actions that had been suspended only by their original pact of submission. (See doc. sec.: "Jurists") These reprisals against their persons and property were consequently regarded not only as justified but also as mandatory and even praiseworthy.

It should be stressed that the adherents of the tolerated religions were protected only within the context of a particular political ideology of territorial conquest *(jihad),* and not in accordance with a universal moral code recognizing equality of rights for all human beings. Clearly, the very idea of equal rights was regarded as sacrilege, and for that reason it could be imposed on the *umma* only by an external force backed by military might. However timidly the reforms were carried out, they shocked the *ulama* and the common people. *Dhimmis* were frequently assaulted and sometimes killed, often with the tacit approval of the authorities, who, on the pretext of preventing a bloodbath, hastened to revoke unpopular measures. Thus, the *dhimmi* found himself once again in the center of a conflict between a Muslim movement for liberalization—eager to modernize the country's military potential—and a reactionary movement attached to Muslim fundamentalism. This conflict between reformist and conservative forces—and sometimes their collusion, notably in the genocide of the Armenians—gives the nineteenth and early twentieth centuries its contradictory character as a period of hope but also of bloodshed, a period of emancipation but also of massacres, persecutions, and genocide.

It is important to emphasize that the absence of disturbances in Egypt was a remarkable exception to the rule. This is because the reforms were decided on willingly and introduced by Muhammad Ali himself, and not, as elsewhere, strongly influenced by outside forces. Thus, at the beginning of the nineteenth century, Egypt attempted to modernize itself and to abolish religious inequality. By embarking upon reforms that were revolutionary for the period, Egypt appeared to some Europeans as an example of a reforming Muslim society. Indeed, documents attest that the condition of the *dhimmis* was less difficult in Egypt and Turkey than in Palestine, Syria, Iraq, the Mag-

IN THE LIBERAL AGE: A TITLED JEW OF CAIRO
Aslan Levy Orebi Bey (1860–1915)

HIS CERTIFICATE OF CONGRATULATIONS (1913)
On Receiving a Second Title of Bey

hreb, Persia and Yemen. In Palestine and Syria, the reforms imposed on the Arab population by the Ottoman sultan provoked violent disturbances. In the Maghreb a total upheaval—that of colonization— was necessary in order to change traditional behavior-patterns. In Persia, the minorities were emancipated by a revolution after the First World War, and in Yemen the persecution ended only with the mass emigration of the Jews to the State of Israel in 1949–50. The different behavior-patterns correspond to various historical currents, and to the different characteristics of the numerous peoples of the *dar al-Islam.*

In general, one may discern three distinct but simultaneous forces that destabilized the multinational Islamic lands: the *dhimmi* liberation movements, *dhimmi* emancipation, and European colonization. These three movements, linked to the intellectual and economic development of Europe, shook the traditional Islamic societies and hastened the disintegration of the Ottoman Empire. They accclerated a phase of regression which succeeded the phase of expansion that had brought its armies to the gates of Vienna in 1683. For obvious geopolitical reasons, the first revolt of subject peoples took place in the Turkish territories in Europe. This revolt of Christian populations, supported by rival Western and Russian ambitions, ravaged the territory of the *umma* throughout the whole of the nineteenth century. The expulsion of the Turks from Transylvania (1691), Hungary (1686–1697), Wallachia, and Moldavia (1829) was followed, in the course of a century of struggles, by the liberation of Serbia and parts of Greece (1830), Bulgaria, Bosnia, Montenegro, and Herzegovina (1878), most of Thessaly, and part of Epirus (1881), Crete (1908), Macedonia, and all European Turkey (1911–1913). In Central Asia, Islam withdrew before the Russian occupation of the Crimea (1783), Bessarabia (1812), Georgia (1813), the Caucasus (1841–1859), Turkestan (1864–1885), and the Khanates of Bukhara (1868), Khiva (1873–1881), and Khokand (1875), followed by the loss of Merv (1884). This disintegration was contemporary with the European wars of colonization in India, Algeria (1830–1843), Tunisia (1881), Egypt (1882), Tripolitania (1911), Morocco (1912), and the granting after 1918 of mandates over the Arab Middle Eastern provinces of the Ottoman Empire to Great Britain and France.

The nationalist movements of the *dhimmi* peoples and their struggle for emancipation complemented one another. Although they were sustained by Russian and European colonial interests, they were often its victims, easily manipulated according to imperialist interests.

The alliance of the *dhimmi* peoples with the Western powers was founded only on a convergence of interests. The *dhimmis* sought

European help in order to rid themselves of the *dhimma*, while the Europeans supported their struggle in order to weaken the Muslim theocracies. The *dhimmi* peoples were hardly more than pawns, manipulated or sacrificed on the international chessboard.

Although nationalism and emancipation were two distinct processes—nationalism aiming at the liberation of a homeland, and emancipation seeking the abolition of legal discrimination—these two movements were nevertheless interconnected. Each *dhimmi* group took part in both movements stemming from its dispersion within the *dar al-Islam*. Although the Greeks, the Armenians, and later the Jews—due to historical circumstances—demanded equal rights within the Ottoman Empire, yet in Greece, Armenia, and Palestine they sought to liberate their countries. This is why persecutions and massacres struck the *dhimmis* indiscriminately, the *umma* embracing in its hatred both Europe—which patronized movements of liberation and emancipation—and its *protégés*. The *umma*'s contraction left its mark on many *dhimmi* communities. Persia's defeats at the hands of the Russians provoked the massacre of the Jewish communities in Tabriz (1830), Ardabil, Zanjan, and other towns in Azerbaidjan, and the slaughter and forced conversion to Islam of the Jews of Meshed in 1839, as well as other persecutions during the nineteenth century. In the Maghreb the Jews suffered as a result of Muslim frustration and humiliation caused by French colonialism. Massacres at Chios and "Bosnian horrors" accompanied the Greek and Balkan wars of liberation. The process of emancipation caused the extermination of twenty thousand Christians in Syria, Palestine, and Lebanon in 1860. Armenian nationalism was crushed by a genocide. The *dhimmi* movements, both of national liberation and of emancipation, aroused the same opposition and the same reprisals on the part of the *umma*, restrained only by the power of the European colonial armies and navies. Indeed, the emancipation of the *dhimmis* raised insuperable problems, rooted as it was in territorial and cultural claims.

It is against this background that one must set the European attempt to encourage local nationalism (Ottomanism or Arabism) in the Orient. It might have allowed the separation of religion from politics and opened the way to the emancipation of the *rayas*. By placing international relations in a secular context based on the principle of equal rights for all citizens and the legitimacy of nations, nationalism suppressed the concept of *jihad* and its direct consequence: the *dhimma*. After the 1860 massacres in the Levant, the Syrian Christians became the most ardent advocates of Arab nationalism. However, the basic tenets of Islam and Arabism were to lead the Christians into an ideological *cul-de-sac*.

Muslim Reaction

The reformist current, inspired by abstract concepts imported from abroad—from the *dar al-Harb*—remained superficial. The reaction, on the other hand, was deeply implanted in history, in tradition, in law. New forces constantly invigorated it: an uninterrupted stream of Muslim refugees fleeing from the lost Islamic provinces, burning with a desire for vengeance that revived fanaticism. These Muslim refugees from Europe—the descendants of Muslim settlers *(muhajirin)*, or Christians who had accepted Islam in order to retain their lands after the Muslim conquest—strengthened the intransigence of the Islamic religious party. The Ottoman government settled these emigrants in troubled regions, thereby tightening its control through a policy of Muslim colonization. The emigrants of the Balkan provinces were directed to Armenia. In 1874–1875 the Circassian Muslim emigration from the Caucasus settled in the Danube provinces, then in the full fever of nationalism, in Galilee and on the Golan Heights. In 1878, after the annexation of Bosnia-Herzegovina by Austria, Bosnian Muslim colonists arrived in Macedonia and on the coastal plain of Palestine. In 1912 Russia tried to prevent their immigration into Armenia. From the nineteenth century into the twentieth, a continuous stream of more than two million Muslim colonists from the Crimea and the Balkans were settled in Anatolia, Armenia, Lebanon, Syria, and Palestine by the Ottoman government, hoping thereby to counter the *dhimmis'* indigenous national aspirations by a massive Islamic colonisation.[4]

In 1878 an Ottoman law granted lands in Palestine to the Muslim colonists, with a twelve-year exemption from taxes and military service. In the Carmel region, Galilee and the plain of Sharon and Caesarea, lands were distributed to the Muslim Slavs from Bosnia and Herzegovina; Georgians were settled around Kuneitra on the Golan Heights and Moroccans in lower Galilee. In Transjordan and Galilee, Turkmenians and Circassians, driven out by the Russian conquest of the Crimea, the Caucasus, and Turkestan, were added to tribes who had preceded them in the eighteenth century and had settled at Abu Ghosh near Jerusalem. About eighteen thousand Egyptian fellahs immigrated to Jaffa, Gaza, and Jericho in the 1830s; Algerians who had gone into exile with Abd al-Qadir settled in Galilee, the Golan Heights, and Jerusalem.[5]

Islamic conservative movements, particularly strong in the Arabized provinces under Turkish rule, sprang not only from religious prejudice but also from the nature of Arab-Islamic imperialism, which had structured the Muslim multinational empire. When that

MUSLIM COLONISTS FROM THE CAUCASUS
Settled in Palestine by the Sultan, 1900
Collection, "American Colony" (Jerusalem)

empire was created, the seizure of territories and the degradation of
conquered indigenous peoples had led to the destruction of their
cultures. However, the interest of European scholars in the Ancient
World reawakened the pride and the desire for freedom of peoples
formerly subjugated by Islam, and this precisely at a time when the
Ottoman reforms were depriving the Arabs of their traditional privileges. Jews, Greeks, Armenians, and Maronites became increasingly
aware that they had not always been religious minorities, but that
they, too, had once been proud nations, tolerated—after the conquest
of their territory—only in a religious context, and at the cost of
humiliations and the payment of tribute. It was thus with profound
hostility that the Muslim populations viewed national patrimonies
from the pre-Arab past emerging from destruction and oblivion. The
emancipation of the *dhimmis* and their cultural rebirth appeared to
them to contain the seeds of nationalisms that could threaten their
domination. The destruction of a community therefore required not
only its physical annihilation, but also the eradication of its culture,
language, and art, symbols of its national creativity. In late nineteenth
century Palestine, recently-arrived Muslim colonists deliberately destroyed what remained of ancient Israel's civilization that had sur-

vived the ravages of the occupiers. These colonists were deliberately settled to check any *raya* national aspirations. In Armenia, physical liquidation was accompanied by forced conversions, massive deportations, the destruction of churches or their conversion into mosques.

The tribulations here briefly surveyed explain the motivations that gave to the struggles for emancipation and liberation of the *dhimmi* peoples in the Ottoman Empire the violent and fanatical character of religious wars.

From Emancipation to National Independence

It was difficult for the Muslim rulers to distinguish where the religious emancipation of a minority ended and where its claim to a usurped homeland—as well as rights to its own language, culture and institutions—began. Here was a dichotomy, inherent in the *dhimmi* condition, that affected the policies of the Ottomans and the Young Turks: on the one hand, the repression of Greek and Armenian nationalism, but, on the other hand, the protection of submissive Christian *rayas* throughout the empire. In the same manner, restrictive laws, applying to Jews only in their Palestinian homeland, were

DHIMMI RUINS IN GALILEE
Third Century Synagogue (Baram)
Engraving from a drawing
C. Wilson (1882), vol. 2, p. 95

intended to counteract Zionism, the most recent movement of national liberation and, as it then seemed, the least likely to succeed. In 1887 a law was passed forbidding Jews to immigrate into Palestine, to reside there, to buy land, to restore houses, or to live in Jerusalem. It applied only to Jews—whether *rayas* or those protected by foreign powers—but not to Christians or to Muslim immigrants.[6]

This aspect of Turkish policy can be illustrated by a specific example. When the massacre of the Armenians in 1895 provoked religious fanaticism, the Muslims of Aleppo threatened the local Jews and Christians with a similar fate. Order was restored only through the energetic action of the Turkish military commander Adham Pasha, who protected the Jewish and Christian quarters and threatened to turn his cannons on the Muslim quarter if they attempted to slaughter the non-Muslims.[7] The atmosphere of insecurity that emerges from the documents of that period was not confined to the Armenian crisis alone, but was a constant feature of the *dhimmi* condition. The new factors in the situation, however, were the struggle for independence, the political protection of the European powers, together with a better diffusion of information.

Just as the West had penetrated the Islamic states by means of its protections, so European colonial interests manipulated, for their own purposes, the national aspirations of the *dhimmi* peoples. The latter were an easy prey because their security depended essentially on an external force, ready to back them, even at their expense, in order to extend its influence. Thus, the traditional antagonism of the *dhimmi* peoples toward each other developed into political struggles sustained or even waged by European powers. Arab nationalism, which was originally an ideological support for the emancipation of the Christians, helped France, which promoted it, to weaken Turkey, Britain's ally. European and Russian imperialism clashed with regard to Arabism and Zionism, while Austria and Russia stirred up revolts in the Balkans and Armenia.

Under European colonization, radical transformations took place within the *dhimmi* communities. The emergence of a petty bourgeoisie, which received a European education, accentuated class tensions. The democratization of the communities' institutions eroded the power of the notables. This development, initiated by the European model, was not without its disadvantages. Roots were lost, group identity, already weakened in an oppressive environment—a phenomenon especially marked within the Christian communities—was obliterated. Cultural alienation resulted from the impact of Western civilization, which was all the more attractive for the *dhimmi* in that it liberated him. The new intelligentsia, having first been marginalized by the *umma,* was now receptive to every European cliché.

Since the European decolonization of Arab countries coincided with the revival of the Jewish state, the situation of the Oriental *dhimmi* communities changed completely, according to the separate paths they followed from the nineteenth century onward. Oriental Jews immigrating to Israel regained their national sovereign rights in an independent State, whereas Christian communities were marginalized within panarabic ideologies.

Christian Arab anti-Zionism is derived from two parallel sources: Byzantine judeophobia, and the traditional *dhimmi* mentality, which reflects the vulnerability and misery of a minority condemned to shifts, to compromises, and to an existence steeped in servility. Today the rise of fundamentalism is shaking the doctrine of Arab nationalism, itself in danger of being absorbed by the movement of pan-Islamism.

Notes to Chapter 4

1. H. H. Rose (Beirut) to Earl of Aberdeen (London), PRO (London) F.O. 78/449, no. 110, 12 Oct. 1841, in Ma'oz, p. 200. The emancipation of the Christians provoked a rebellion in Aleppo in 1850. The Greek Catholic Patriarch Maximos made a triumphal entry with great pomp and ceremony, displaying costly religious objects. Already irritated by military conscription, some Muslims attacked the Christian quarters and once they had control of the town, they began pillaging and raping. They agreed to a truce only on the following conditions: bells must not be rung and no crosses should be carried during religious processions. "The Christians will not ride on horses; they will no longer wear the *tarboosh;* they will return to using their old discriminatory clothing; they will no longer be allowed slaves, and, lastly, they will be reduced to their traditional ignominious status." (Berlin, in *JA* 19 (1852): 125–26, n. 3). Maximos declared that the reforms established equality between Christians and Muslims (Rose to Canning [Constantinople], F.O. 78/836, no. 48 [31 Oct. 1850], and Ma'oz, pp. 190–91). The Jews kept a low, humble profile and were not attacked.

2. B. Lewis, *The Emergence of Modern Turkey* (London, 1968).

3. Holmes (Bosna Seraï) to Granville (London), no. 21 (24 February 1871), in *P.P.* 1877 [C. 1739] 92, p. 665. See also Report of Holmes to Elliot on the subject of the injustices and corruption in the Ottoman Empire, enclosure in no. 21, idem, pp. 666–72.

4. Revealing details on the subject of the nineteenth-century colonization by European and Caucasian Muslims in Syria and Palestine are to be found in K. H. Karpat, "The Status of the Muslims under European Rule: The Eviction and Settlement of the Cerkes," in *JIMMA* (King Abdulaziz University, Jeddah), 1, no. 2 & 2, no. 1 (Winter 1979–Summer 1980): 7–27. In 1863 a French scholar noted that the ancestors of the 750 Muslims of Ain Karem near Jerusalem were considered—according to the local tradition—to have come from the Maghreb, principally from Spain, expelled by Ferdinand the Catholic. See M. V. Guérin, *Description de la Palestine* (Paris, 1868), *Judée,* 1 : 84. Quaresmius *(Elucidatio Terrae Sanctae)* referred to the numerous Moors who resided in Palestine when he was custodian and apostolic commissary for the Holy Land (1619–1626). Eighty years later, another traveler mentioned that in Samaria: "The few inhabitants who are to be seen there are Turks, Moors and Arabs" (Morison, p. 225). He found the same situation in Galilee and Judea, and particularly in the village of Bethany, near Jerusalem (p. 442). The constant immigration to Palestine of Muslims forced to leave Christian countries (see also chap. 4, below) may partially explain a tradition of intolerance and fanaticism that shocked contemporary travelers to Pales-

tine. On the Bedouinization of vast regions over the centuries and its effects on agriculture and sedentary societies, see X.de Planhol, *Les Fondements géographiques de l'histoire de l'Islam* (Paris, 1968).

5. L. Oliphant, *Haifa, Life in Palestine (1882–1885)* (London, 1887; reprint, Jerusalem, 1976), pp. 61, 116, 141, 255, 301, 310 and doc. 108; idem, *The Land of Gilead* (London, 1880), pp. 45–47; J. Marcel and A. Ryme, *Egypte* (Paris, 1848), pp. 12–13; Lortet, pp. 156, 231, 379–80, 458, 464, 536. Details on the sparse population of Palestine during the nineteenth century, the political objectives of Muslim colonization, practiced by the Ottomans, and the immigration and strengthening of the Christians element of the population—under European protection, notably French and Russian—are to be found in the descriptions of European and American travelers. This dual process of colonization was taking place at a time when restrictive measures—including expulsion—were being applied to Jewish immigration, particularly coming from the Ottoman Empire.

6. Hyamson, 2:439, 441, 442, 461, and 474.

7. N. J. Raffoul (Aleppo) to S. H. Goldschmidt (Paris), Archives, *AIU* (Paris), Alep., I.C.3., 8 Nov. 1895.

PART TWO

5

Jihad and Dhimma: Modern Formulations

Just as throughout history broad currents of thought and political tendencies have coexisted, and individual or collective behavior has ranged from fanaticism to understanding, so today the concepts of *jihad* and *dhimma* represent only one of the many tendencies of contemporary Arab political thought. Notwithstanding, this analysis will be limited to the survival of those concepts within the modern Arab world.

After the abolition of the *dhimma*—by a Muslim ruler (in the Ottoman Empire and in Persia), by the expulsion or departure of the *dhimmis*, or as a result of European colonization—it may be questioned whether the term "*dhimmi*", which defined a particular historical condition, is still appropriate in regard to contemporary realities. Indeed, it appears that thought and behavior-patterns shaped by the past, by education and tradition, do indicate the persistence of a "*dhimmi* syndrome." Fettered and often alienated by a specific historical conditioning, members of religious minorities tend to perpetuate the *dhimmi*'s marginal status. Thus the factors governing the traditional coexistence between the minority and the *umma*, involving the submission and alienation of the former and the tolerance of the latter, still remain operative. But the master only remains tolerant as long as the *dhimmi* is submissive. The force and persistence of these traditional attitudes throughout history may be explained by their constant renewal within social and psychological structures, owing to the revival in certain modern political ideologies of the same values that originally validated and defined these structures. Therefore, the term "*dhimmi*" will be retained, since it remains an actual concept in the context of political systems and attitudes. As the status of the *dhimmi* was determined by the *jihad* and the *dhimma*, it is necessary to examine the survival, the evolution, or the abandonment of these concepts in the contemporary Muslim world, although it is obvious that other political factors coexist with them.

In the Arabic-speaking countries, a transfer of Muslim religious

113

values to political Arabism may be observed. The former President of
Algeria, Ahmad Ben Bella, president of the "League of Muslim
Rights," declared in a 1982 interview:

—It is my impression that a form of osmosis is developing between
Arabism and Islam. I am very optimistic and I profoundly believe
in the realisation of fine and great projects, in the Arab genius and
in victory.
—You wish to say by that, "to the disappearance of the State of
Israel"?
—Exactly.[1]

The Jihad against Israel

On several occasions Arab leaders, either individually or collectively, have proclaimed a *jihad* against Israel, thus confirming their
attachment to a theocratic system embracing the whole of humanity
(see docs. 1 and 5). At the third Islamic Summit Conference on Palestine and Jerusalem, held in January 1981, thirty-eight Muslim heads
of State (Egypt not included), and Yassir Arafat, representing the
Palestine Liberation Organization (PLO), proclaimed from Mecca a
jihad against Israel. Since the *jihad* was proclaimed in the name of
Arab nationalism, and the PLO has always maintained that it was in
the vanguard of Arab nationalism, it is necessary to examine the
character of the PLO's *jihad*.

In 1970, Yassir Arafat stated:

The liberation of Palestine and [the] putting an end to Zionist
penetration, political, economic, military and propaganda, into
Moslem States, is one of the duties of the Moslem world. We must
fight a Holy War (Jihad) against the Zionist enemy, who covets not
only Palestine but the whole Arab region, including its holy places.[2]

The call to *jihad* in order to create a secular, democratic state in
which Muslims, Christians, and Jews would have equal rights represents a contradiction in terminology, since the aim of *jihad* is the
conversion of the infidels or their subjection to the *dhimma* (see docs. 1
and 3). Indeed, Arab leaders often stress the necessity to respect the
laws of *jihad*. Even Syria, engaged in a process of secularization, recalled in 1971 some of these tactical rules.

The laws of Holy War (Jihad) of Islam say that to fight the enemy it
is permitted to lay siege on his camps and civilian dwellings. It is
also permitted to destroy the enemy's houses and set fire to them, to
fell his trees and destroy his fields [in order] to force him into
surrender. It is also permitted to cut off the enemy's water supply,
even if there are women and children.[3]

The third Islamic Summit Conference in 1981 specifically endorsed the *jihad* at Taif, Saudi Arabia in the fifth of its six Resolutions:

> The Islamic countries made it clear in their resolution that the word *jihad* is used in its Islamic sense, which is not susceptible to interpretation or misunderstanding, and that the practical measures for its implementation will be taken in conformity with this and in constant consultation between the Islamic countries.[4]

Not every conflict is necessarily a *jihad*, but if it is proclaimed as such, the participants are bound to observe its tactics and strategy, which are governed by eternal, immutable laws, particularly the rule forbidding "collaboration between a believer and an infidel"—if the latter challenges or disregards its prescriptions (see doc. 3).

The first article of the PLO's Covenant asserts the Arab character of the "Arab Palestinian people," and thus its rights to a land situated nearly one thousand miles from the Arabian metropolis. In other words, Arab Palestinian rights to a non-Arab land (i.e., Israel) are based on its former annexation by *jihad*, and its Arabization through the *dhimma:*

> Palestine is the homeland of the Arab Palestinian people; it is an indivisible part of the Arab homeland, and the Palestinian people are an integral part of the Arab nation.[5]

Article 9 states:

> Armed struggle is the only way to liberate Palestine. Thus it is the overall strategy, not merely a tactical phase.

The importance of armed struggle was again stressed in article 2 of the "Fifteen Resolutions" of the thirteenth Palestinian National Council (PNC), held in Cairo in March 1977.[6] The seizure of lands by force in accordance with the laws of *jihad* gives the conquerors total ownership of the country. The conquerors may kill the inhabitants, expel them, or make them into tributaries (formerly constituting a part of the *fay*); places of worship may be destroyed, or their restoration and the construction of new buildings prohibited. In short, if the war is a *jihad*, conquest by force gives the conquerors absolute rights over the vanquished, while a treaty of submission obliges the victors to abide by the stipulated terms.

In the same manner as the Muslims shared collective responsibility for the *jihad*, so all Arabs are required to participate collectively in the PLO's *jihad* on behalf of the Palestinian Arabs:

> The liberation of Palestine, from an Arab viewpoint, is a national (*qawmi*) duty and it attempts to repel the Zionist and Imperialist

aggression against the Arab homeland, and aims at the elimination
of Zionism in Palestine. Absolute responsibility for this falls upon
the Arab nation—peoples and governments—with the Arab people
of Palestine in the vanguard. Accordingly, the Arab nation must
mobilize all its military, human, moral and spiritual capabilities to
participate actively with the Palestinian people in the liberation of
Palestine. It must, particularly in the phase of the armed Palestinian
revolution, offer and furnish the Palestinian people with all possible
help, and material and human support, and make available to them
the means and opportunities that will enable them to continue to
carry out their leading role in the armed revolution, until they
liberate their homeland. (Art. 15, PLO Covenant)

This point is reaffirmed in articles 4, 9, and 10 of the PLO's Fifteen
Resolutions (Cairo, 1977).

The laws of *jihad* forbid the massacre of innocent people, but permit the killing of combatants, rebels, and dangerous elements. The
vanquished who submit to the conquerors may live under their protection as *dhimmis*. This distinction is also made in the PLO's Covenant: the Zionists are to be killed or expelled, but the Jews who submit
to Arab laws are to be tolerated.

The aim of *jihad* had been the suppression of political and military
independence of infidel nations. Later the *dhimma* also extinguished
their cultural and social aspirations. Article 12 of the Agreement of 6
May 1970, signed by all the organizations belonging to the PLO,
proposed a similar policy (confirmed in Damascus, June 1980):

Therefore the aim of the Palestinian revolution is to liquidate this
entity [Israel] in all its aspects, political, military, social, trade unions
and cultural, and to liberate Palestine completely.[7]

The reiterated call for a *jihad* confirms the validity of this concept
which is the main cause of the Arab-Israeli conflict. Since Israelis are
to be regarded, perforce, only as a religious community, their national
characteristics—a geographical territory related to a past history, a
system of legislation, a specific language and culture—are consequently denied.

The "Arab" character of the Palestinian territory is inherent in the
logic of *jihad*. Having become *fay* territory by conquest (i.e., "taken
from an infidel people"), it must remain within the *dar al-Islam*. The
State of Israel, established on this *fay* territory, is consequently illegal.

The following affirmation by Ben Bella regarding his Arab rights to
Israel—rights claimed for all the Arabs of twenty countries—is derived from Umar b. al-Khattab's disposal of territories confiscated
from the conquered infidels (see docs. 2 and 3). It is noteworthy that
"95% of all cultivated lands" in early twentieth-century Ottoman
Palestine were *miri* (i.e., *kharaj*) lands.

I am an Arab, and Palestine does not only concern the Palestinians, but all the Arabs. Even if the Palestinians, under constraint, finally accept some sort of a solution, the Arabs will nonetheless never accept the State of Israel.[8]

As Spain, Greece, the Balkan states, and Armenia were also once *fay* territories, they should, according to the same logic, be regarded as illegal entities. Leaving aside Israel, this proclamation reveals the adherence to an ideology that implies permanent war against the whole of the *dar al-Harb*, destined to become *fay* territory.

The PLO's position on the exclusive *Arab* character of Lebanon is consistent with this conception. On 30 November 1975, Yassir Arafat declared in Damascus:

The civil war in Lebanon is not over and bloodshed will continue. The battle we are fighting in Lebanon is for the preservation of the country's Arab character. I declare in the name of the Palestinian revolution and the Lebanese nationalist and progressive movement that every inch of Arab land will remain Arab and Lebanon will remain Arab.[9]

Abu Iyad (Arafat's second-in-command) was even more explicit in 1976:

We accept in this country only the Lebanese Arab Army. . . . The way to Palestine passes through Lebanon. . . . it passes through Ain Tura and Ayun Al-Siman (Christian strongholds) and it must reach Junya (the Christian capital).[10]

It is this universal strategy of *jihad* that has given the local Israeli-Arab conflict its world dimension, Israel being merely a point of focus in the *dar al Harb*. The ramifications of the conflict have contributed to the devastation of Lebanon. Terrorism, originally directed against Israel and supported by the USSR, left-wing, and local neo-Nazi groups, has developed into a vast international network causing the death and mutilation of uninvolved individuals. Thus fanatical terrorism, constant blackmail, and internecine gang killings—inherent in *jihad* ideology and aimed at the *dar al-Harb*—incompatible with democratic institutions, have developed within Western countries, acutely endangering freedom of expression.

Today as in the past, Israel's prominence in the worldwide strategy of *jihad* may serve as a warning signal. As was stated in the first chapter, the fate of the Jews in Arabia was conceived as the prototype by later legislators and jurists in their relations with other nations. The present Arab policies adopted toward Israel may become normative for other nations if the ideology of *jihad* is not abandoned.

On the other hand, a Muslim government that rejects the ideol-

ogy of *jihad* might establish relations with Israel within a context of
the legitimacy of the sovereign rights of nations. Such an option implies the rejection of the *dar al-Harb* concept implicit in that of *jihad,*
that is, the "territory of war" where all warlike acts are legitimate,
except when limited by treaties of a temporary and conditional nature
that interrupt but do not end the state of permanent hostility. Therefore, consigning *jihad* to historical oblivion would open the way to a
policy of friendship and cooperation between peoples. It was President Sadat's commitment to a policy of global change, within the
dynamics of peace, that motivated his assassination by a fundamental-
ist group named, precisely, *"Jihad"*.

A contemporary apologetic school of thought tends to explain the
principle of the "major *jihad*" in terms of man's inner struggle, and
the "minor *jihad*" as a modern war of decolonization. This view over-
looks twelve centuries of history, forgetting that the Arab-Muslim
expansion did not occur in a vacuum, but in villages and towns, in
lands and territories conquered from other peoples.

The Palestinian Dhimma

The stage following the *jihad* (the destruction of Israel) would involve the Arabization of Israel by the denial of the national rights of
its people in conformity with article 12 of the Agreement of 6 May
1970. The Palestinian *dhimma* would transform the free Israeli citizen
authorized to remain in the country into a Jewish *dhimmi* tolerated
exclusively within the framework of Arab nationalism:

> The object of Palestinian struggle is the liberation of the whole of
> Palestine in which all citizens will coexist with equal rights and obli-
> gations within the framework of the aspirations of the Arab nation
> to unity and progress. (Art. 5, Agreement of 6 May 1970)

This form of toleration to be granted within the framework of Arab
national aspirations is reminiscent of the traditional *dhimma* conceded
by the *umma*:

> The land of Palestine will utterly spew out all that is on it, with the
> exception of the sons of Palestine, and none will remain except the
> Arabs, so that they may rebuild the glory of their homeland and
> cleanse it from the traces of the Jews, and it shall remain a land of
> the Arabs for the Arabs.[11]

The ideas of uncleanliness and impurity associated with the *dhimmi*
are transposed to the Israelis. The Israeli presence on the esplanade
of the Temple Mount—the site of the Aqsa Mosque and the Dome of
the Rock—or at the tombs of the Hebrew patriarchs in Hebron of-

fends the Arab-Muslim community, for the Jewish *dhimmi* religion is thereby encroaching on the prerogatives of the dominant Islamic religion. In a UNESCO (Paris) declaration, a PLO representative in 1976 stated that the Israeli presence was desecrating the sanctity of the mosques in those places.[12] Was this a nostalgia for former times when *dhimmis* entering the precincts of Muslim sacred shrines were punished by death? The PLO spokesman did not limit himself to this religious observation, but declared that the Israeli (hence Jewish) presence defiled the whole of Palestine. The link with tradition and with the archetype of the Jew is unmistakable: it was this religious idea of impurity that prompted the expulsion of the Jewish and Christian tribes from the pure soil of Arabia in the seventh century. To this day no church or synagogue is permitted to defile it. The same religious discrimination is therefore paradoxically applied to the "Arab territories of Palestine" by the ideologues of a future secular and democratic Palestinian state, through a PLO Christian spokesman.

The restrictions traditionally imposed on *dhimmi* property in order to facilitate Arab-Muslim settlements are similar to those put forward by the PLO with regard to "Arab Palestine" (i.e., British Mandatory Palestine), and, in fact, from 1948 to 1967 no Jews were allowed even to visit Jordan (i.e., Eastern Palestine, Judea and Samaria). Freedom of movement and settlement of Jews in Jerusalem, Judea, Samaria, Galilee, and in the whole of the historic area of the Land of Israel (Palestine)—Arabized by the *jihad* and the *dhimma*—are categorically prohibited by the PLO. Because Judaism, according to the PLO, is a religion without national characteristics, this prohibition is consequently a religious discrimination only and thus inconsistent with the secular, democratic principles asserted by the PLO.

If the several massacres of Jews in the twentieth-century Arab world were simply a manifestation of age-old habits of behavior, the killing of Jews in Mandatory Palestine was more precisely an extension of the nineteenth-century wars against the Greeks, the other Balkan peoples, and the Armenians—the same ideology inspiring in the descendants of Muslim settlers in Palestine a conduct identical with that of their forebears when confronted with similar situations. Thus Arab terrorism in Israel and terror against Jews and Zionists throughout the world appears to be the modern version of the right to kill indiscriminately rebellious *dhimmis,* while the denial of Israel's right to exist recalls the Ottoman wars against the Greek, Balkan, and Armenian nationalisms.

Arab Nationalism and Dhimmi Condition

Despite its many different motivations and its various and even cosmopolitan origins, Arab nationalism today is a political movement aiming at the reestablishment of an Arab supremacy similar to that of the Arab-Muslim Empire of the caliphs—an empire that came into being through the Arabization of the *dhimmi* lands and the subjection of indigenous peoples. Ideologically and historically, therefore, Arab nationalism is linked to *jihad* and *dhimma.* Because Arabism has served as the vehicle for Islamic values, it is understandable that Arab nationalism and pan-Islamism sometimes overlap or clash, due to their diverse components.

The continuing validity of the *dhimmi* status in recent times was recognized at the fourth conference of the Academy for Islamic Research, held in September 1968 at Al-Azhar University in Cairo, where a distinguished theologian stated:

> It may be said that they are non-Muslim subjects, living in our midst, and, thereby, we have to take care of them. Within this group are cited the Jews, residing in certain Muslim states the heads of which, together with men in authority, favour them with amity and shield them from the masses of Muslims. But we say to those who patronize the Jews that the latter are *"dhimmis"*, people of obligation, who have betrayed the covenant [i.e. the *dhimma*] in conformity with which they have been accorded protection. . . . These people have broken their covenant and violated their pledges: how then are we going to retain our obligation to protect them?[13]

It follows that if, according to Islamic dogma, the Jews in contemporary Arab society are still considered to be *dhimmis,* the Christians should also be *dhimmis,* and if that is the case they cannot have equal rights with Muslims.

The process of osmosis between Arabism and Islam to which Ben Bella referred does not augur well for a future of liberty and equal rights for "Arab" Christians. Since the nineteenth century, they had fought for assimilation in a *secular Arab democracy,* which would replace the *Islamic state,* where, traditionally, *Arabs* could only be Muslims (see doc. 3).

President Qaddhafi of Libya, replying to a question on the fate of the ten million Christians living in Arab lands, declared in 1980:

> —The Christians have followed a mistaken path and they must change their ways, to the extent that they really and truly are Arabs.
> —But there is no doubt about their Arab identity.
> —If so, they must convert to Islam.[14]

However, if they will not change their religion, Arab-Islamic history has already resolved this problem and will provide them with the well-tried, established *dhimmi* condition.

Thus the traditional values of the *umma,* recycled within Arab nationalism, perpetuate in modern times the contradiction between the cultural and linguistic aspirations of the pre-Arab peoples and pan-Islamism. The conflict affects various aspects of religious life (i.e., freedom of worship, the status of religious buildings, the holding of processions, the use of church bells, and matters of proselytism, conversions, apostasy, mixed marriages, and rights of inheritance), as well as questions of legal equality and employment opportunities.

This is not the place to give a detailed account of the wave of violence that during and after the Second World War swept over the whole of the Near and Middle East and the Maghreb.[15] The xenophobia that succeeded decolonization revived the old traditions of the *dhimma*, expressed in the language of Arab nationalism. For modern Arab nationalism, the obliteration of the humiliating consequences of European colonialism consisted above all in withdrawing from the *dhimmi* groups the rights to their religious and cultural emancipation that they had obtained through European intervention. The Muslim *dhimma* was now transformed into the Arab *dhimma*. The Islamic *umma* became the Arab nation, and the Oriental pre-Arab nationalisms reemerged as *dhimmi* nationalisms. The Israeli-Arab conflict released the pent-up hatred held in check only a short while previously by European colonialism. Breaking out sporadically like a recurrent fever, it reached a climax in the late nineteen-thirties, reawakening in the masses an age-old aggressiveness against the *dhimmis*. Rooted in popular psychology, these manifestations spread throughout the Arab world. Some governments, such as those of Morocco and Tunisia, attempted to stem the tide of popular fanaticism, but in Libya, Egypt, Syria, and Iraq it was the authorities themselves who stirred up the mob, already inflamed by demagogues. The Arab nationalists who released these collective emotions spoke the language of hatred and contempt of earlier centuries, but since these persecutions brought international discredit on their countries, they sought instead to apply the principles elucidated by Mawardi (see doc. 5). Stripped of all their possessions, most of the Jews were obliged, mainly by unofficial means of coercion, to leave Arab countries. Only 20,000 remain in 1984 of a population of nearly one million—approximatively 5,000 in Syria, where they are still held as hostages. In this way the ancient pre-Islamic Jewish communities, accused of rebelling against the Arab *dhimma*, have disappeared almost completely from the Middle East and North Africa.

After the Second World War, the situation of the religious minorities in Muslim states varied considerably from country to country. Their freedom and security increased to the extent that religious domination over politics (as well as Arab nationalism) diminished. This happened in Turkey, particularly after Mustapha Kemal became president (1923), and in Persia under Shah Reza Pahlavi and his son Muhammad Reza (1925–1978). In Egypt this process occurred toward the end of Anwar Sadat's rule, as the country withdrew from the Arab orbit and adopted a more liberal policy, in keeping with Egypt's history, her interests and with modern concepts of peaceful coexistence.

The instability now confronting these nations recalls those periods of conflicts, particularly in the nineteenth century, when the Islamic forces of change and progress were obstructed by conservative tendencies hostile to innovation. As in these earlier periods, the fate of the non-Muslim communities and the aggressiveness of the *jihad* will depend upon which one of the two parties gains the upper hand.

All attempts at secularizing Arab nationalism, initiated over the past one hundred years by the Christians of the *dar al-Islam*—who even more than the Israelis are in danger of being reduced to a state of "dhimmitude"[16]—appear Utopian in the light of the contemporary Lebanese conflict. Maronites and Israelis were then drawn together by the same threat, as well as by a common past, in which the vulnerability of both *dhimmi* groups, and their respective political manipulation, had hitherto engendered mutual enmity.

Arab Umma and Dhimmi State: Israel—the Ideological Conflict

In the historical Arab context, Israel represents the successful national liberation of a *dhimmi* civilization. On a territory formerly Arabized by the *jihad* and the *dhimma,* a pre-Islamic language, culture, topographical geography (biblical towns), and national institutions have been restored to life. This reversed the process of centuries in which the cultural, social, and political structures of the indigenous Jewish population of Palestine were destroyed.

In 1974 Abu Iyad, second-in-command to Arafat in the Fatah hierarchy, announced: "We intend to struggle so that our Palestinian homeland does not become a new Andalusia."[17] The comparison of Andalusia to Palestine was not fortuitous, since both countries were Arabized and then de-Arabized by a pre-Arabic culture.

Moreover, the Jews having generally been the most degraded of the *dhimmis,* the resurgence of Israel could appear as an even greater humiliation for the *umma.*

As Nasser said in 1953:

To the disaster of Palestine there is no parallel in human history.[18]

He added in 1955:

The mention of Palestine is sufficient to remind every Arab— indeed, every free man—of the greatest international crime that has been committed in the entire history of mankind.[19]

Moreover, it was feared that Israel might serve as an example for other *dhimmi* nationalisms surviving in the territories conquered by the *jihad,* which would have the effect of relegating Arabism to its original Arabian homeland:

The goal of the criminal State of Israel is that the Arabs should move to the Arabian Peninsula, their first homeland 2,000 years ago [*sic*],[20]

wrote Abdallah al-Tall in 1964, thus implicitly recognizing Arab expansionism, which in fact began in the seventh century.

Nasser was more explicit in 1959:

I cannot speak of Arab nationalism without speaking of Israel, for the existence and idea *(fikratuha)* of Israel are a threat to Arab nationalism in Palestine and the establishment *(ihlal)* of Zionist nationalism in its place, followed by expansion and the liquidation of Arab nationalism in the region.[21]

In 1961 Abd al-Rahman al-Bazzaz, professor of law at the University of Baghdad and a former Prime Minister of Iraq, explained how in his view the values of Arabism were threatened by the Jewish national movement:

The great danger of Israel is due to its being an ideological threat to our nationalism which challenges our entire national existence in the entire region. The existence of Israel nullifies the unity of our homeland, the unity of our nation and the unity of our civilization, which embraces the whole of this one region. Moreover, the existence of Israel is a flagrant challenge to our philosophy of life and the ideals for which we live, and a total barrier against the values and aims to which we aspire in the world.[22]

An Arab Palestinian writer, Fayez A. Sayegh, emphasized this view:

Apart from the political conflict, there is a basic philosophical and spiritual incompatibility between the two contending nationalisms. Even if all political disputes were to be resolved, the two movements, Zionism and Arab Nationalism, would remain, spiritually and ideologically, worlds apart—living in separate "universes of discourse" which are incapable of communication or meaningful dialogue.[23]

In the same way as the *dhimmis* were considered inferior, *dhimmi* nationalisms were despised. Ahmad Shukeiry, head of the PLO before the Six-Day War, summarized this attitude at the United Nations in 1961:

Zionism was nastier than Fascism, uglier than Nazism, more hateful than imperialism, more dangerous than colonialism. Zionism was a combination of all these evils. Its motive power was aggression and expansion.[24]

Similarly, in the PLO's Covenant:

Zionism is a political movement organically associated with international imperialism and antagonistic to all action for liberation and to progressive movements in the world. It is racist and fanatic in its nature, aggressive, expansionist and colonial in its aims, and fascist in its methods. (Art. 22)

Hichem Djaït, a Tunisian writer, stated that the existence of Israel raises doubts as to the definitive character of the Arabization and Islamization resulting from the Arab conquest.[25]

Opprobrium as a Necessity

Within the *umma*, the degradation of the *dhimmi* had a necessary function. The inner dialectic of power and conquest required the humiliation of the vanquished, the justification for the monopolization of Virtue and Rights by the victors. In the subsequent colonial phase (the *dhimma*), Evil—made publicly visible through the abasement of the *dhimmi*—magnified, by contrast, the power and solidarity of the *umma* (see docs. 19–20). In much the same way, Evil (the *Dhimmi* State), depraved and corrupted in its essence as were the populations destined to subjection by *jihad*, plays a similar role in the contemporary Middle East conflicts.

In recent times some ways of expressing the hatred of Israel recall the fastidious regulations concerning the shape and color of the right shoe as distinct from the left shoe of the *dhimmi*, the length and width of his sleeves, the shape of his belt and his saddle, the way his hair should be cut, and all the meticulous and degrading daily rituals intended to humiliate him constantly, together with his wife, his children, his servant, his animal, and even the deceased members of his family. The continual anti-Zionist invective in international forums has revived the old tradition of vilifying the *dhimmi*. Israel is the scapegoat, responsible for every evil that afflicts the Arab world as well as other regions. Israel is mocked and defamed, just as the *dhimmi* was forced to wear despicable clothes. In fact, Israel symbolizes the isolation, the hatred, the contempt that formerly crushed the *dhimmi* communities. The perception of Israel in the Arab world perpetuates the traditional behavior of the *umma* toward the *dhimmis*, who today happen to be the Israelis but tomorrow might be the Maronites or any other national community targeted by *jihad*. Moreover, the very terms applied to Israel—*insolence, arrogance, punishment*—are the traditional terms of abuse used to penalize the former *dhimmis* aspiring to liberty and human dignity.

Production of Hatred

Hatred, as has been shown, is an integral part of *jihad,* since without it the *harbi* would be regarded as an equal human being. The seizure of the American Embassy in Teheran in 1979 demonstrated the power of such hatred, orchestrated for political purposes through contemporary techniques of mass communication on a universal scale. Huge funds are invested in the worldwide dissemination and exploitation of hatred against Israel; "anti-Zionism" affects education, culture, and information. In international forums, the world can today observe the age-old hatred toward the rebellious *dhimmis* projected onto Israel.

Notes to Chapter 5

1. A. Ben Bella, "Tous contre Israël," in *PI* 16 (1982): 105–14.
2. *Al-Hayat* (Beirut), 25 Dec. 1970 (quoted from MENA, Cairo), in *The Arab View* (Research Division, Israel Foreign Ministry, September 1971), p. 72.
3. *Radio Damascus,* 15 March 1971, (Ibid., September 1971), p. 161.
4. *al-Riyadh* (Saudi Arabia), 29 Jan. 1981, in *JPS* 39 (Beirut, 1981):184.
5. All references to the PLO's 1968 Covenant are taken from Y. Harkabi, *The Palestinian Covenant and Its Meaning* (London, 1979). In an interview given in May 1982, Bashir Gemayel (elected president of Lebanon three months later and promptly assassinated) explained that "Arab nationals felt at home in any Arab country" because the notion of nation-state was absorbed into that of the *umma* and because of the desire to restore the Muslim caliphat. (B. Gemayel, "Libérer le Liban," in *PI* 16 (1982:118.)
6. Harkabi, *Palestinian Covenant,* pp. 149–59. Reaffirmed till Nov. 1984, Amman.
7. Harkabi, *Palestinians and Israel* (Jerusalem, 1974), p. 127.
8. Ben Bella, p. 106. See G. Baer, "The Development of Private Ownership of Land," in *Studies in the Social History of Modern Egypt* (Chicago, 1969), p. 73 (quoting Doukhan), regarding *kharaj* land; Bat Ye'or, "Terres arabes: terres de "dhimmitude'", In *La Cultura Sefardita,* vol. 1, *RMI* 44, no. 1–4, 3rd series (1983): 94–102.
9. Broadcast of Yassir Arafat's speech of 30 Nov. 1975 to the administrative council of the Palestine Student Association (Damascus), in *Voice of Falastin* (Lebanon), 1 Dec. 1975 and *Jerusalem Post* (Israel), 3 Dec. 1975.
10. Speech of Abu Iyad in Beirut, 23 May 1976, in *Al-Nahar* (Beirut), 24 May and in *Al-Nida* (Beirut), 25 May 1976, quoted by A. H. Yodfat and Y. Arnon-Ohanna, *PLO: Strategy and Politics* (London, 1981), p. 36. See also, J. Laffin, *The PLO Connections* (London, 1982).

J. Becker: *The PLO: The Rise and Fall of the Palestine Liberation Organisation* (London, 1984) gives the statement of an eyewitness at the massacre of 582 Christians in Damur by the PLO and its Muslim allies on 23 January 1976: *"The attack took place from the mountain behind. It was an apocalypse. They were coming, thousands and thousands, shouting 'Allahu Akbar! God is great! Let us attack them for the Arabs, let us offer a holocaust to Mohammad!' And they were slaughtering everyone in their path, men, women and children"* (p. 124).

Khomenist *fedayeen* were trained for the *jihad* in PLO Lebanese camps (p. 166). This fascinating book throws light on the use of terror and assassination to gain political power, an endemic plague in the Middle East. The *umma*'s enthusiastic and frenetic backing for the PLO springs from a shared history, tradition, and moral values. The endorsement today by the Muslim World of the PLO's treatment of Christians (Lebanese or hostages) and Jews confirms the traditional method used for eliminating the *dhimmi* peoples.

The collusion with the PLO by many Western governments (including the Vatican), political leaders and influential mass media resulted from corruption and terror (chaps. 29, 30). This behavior is reminiscent of those *dhimmi* notables who grew rich in the service of the triumphant caliphs. Then—traitors to their own people—they led them into "dhimmitude", amid a chorus of praise and flattery, since the punishment for criticism was death. Drugged by the opium of "petrolatry," the West balked at Israel's 1982 destruction of the PLO's terrorist infrastructure in Lebanon, which had been a training ground for international subversion.

11. Muhammad Husayn Sha'ban, *Ben Gurion . . . the Liar* (Arabic) (Government Publishing House Cairo, 1963), p. 59, in Harkabi, *Arab Attitudes to Israel* (Jerusalem, 1971), p. 39.

12. Ibrahim Suss, *Le Monde* (Paris), 2 April 1976.

13. Al-Azhar, p. 59 and D. F. Green, ed., p. 61.

14. *Al Safir* (Beirut), 15 Oct. 1980.

15. On anti-Jewish measures in modern times, see S. Landshut, *Jewish Communities in the Muslim Countries of the Middle East* (London, 1950); J. B. Schechtman, *On Wings of Eagles* (New York, 1961); Bat Ye'or, *Jews in Egypt* (Geneva, 1971; Hebrew ed., Tel Aviv, 1974); M. Roumani, *The Case of the Jews from Arab Countries: A Neglected Issue* (Tel Aviv, *Arab Countries: A Neglected Issue* (Tel Aviv, 1978).

16. B. Gemayel, "Liban: il y a un peuple de trop . . ." ("Lebanon: there is one people too many . . .") in *Le Nouvel Observateur,* Paris, 19 June 1982, p. 62 (". . . They are ready to tolerate us, to let us live and work in a condition of *dhimmitude*"). See also doc. 116.

17. *Le Monde* (Paris), 20–21 Jan. 1974.

18. 23 Dec. 1953, in Harkabi, *Attitudes,* p. 61.

19. 22 July 1955, in Harkabi, ibid.

20. Abdallah al-Tall, *The Danger of World Jewry to Islam and Christianity* (Arabic) (Cairo, 1964), p. 311, in Harkabi, *Attitudes,* p. 80.

21. 22 July 1959, in Harkabi, *Attitudes,* p. 93.

22. Abd ar-Rahman al-Bazzaz, *This is Our Nationality* (Arabic). (Cairo, 1964), pp. 253–54, in Harkabi, *Attitudes,* p. 97.

23. F. Sayegh, *The Encounter of Two Ideologies* (Washington: Middle East Institute, 1961), p. 90, in Harkabi, *Attitudes,* p. 99.

24. 4 Dec. 1961, Special U.N. Political Committee, in Harkabi, *Attitudes,* p. 180.

25. H. Djaït, *Le Personnalité et le devenir Arabo-Islamiques* (Paris, 1974), p. 120.

6

The Dhimmi Archetype in Modern Arab Nationalism

Archetype and Condition

While the condition of the *dhimmi* resulted from specific legislation constituted by numerous well-defined rules, the stereotype of the *dhimmi*, on the other hand, belongs to the sphere of collective psychology. This stereotype is the reflection of the *dhimmi* condition as perceived by the *umma*. A recapitulation of the basic elements of the *dhimmi* condition will provide a sketch of the *dhimmi* stereotype.

The *jihad*, a war of expansion for the Islamization of non-Muslim territories, constitutes the strategy by which a vanquished people is reduced to the status of a *dhimmi* people. The loss of their homeland condemns the vanquished to live forever as a landless nation. The choice is either to suffer in their homeland or, when threatened by extermination, to flee into exile. Forbidden to carry arms, the subjected people becomes powerless; its language, culture, and values are replaced by those of the invaders, thereby modifying both populations and towns. Its identity is extinguished; from a nation, or a specific community, it is reduced to the level of a tolerated religion, by which process "confessionalism" was developed.

Thus the *dhimmi* condition may be considered a collective and hereditary one. It characterizes the conquered group, regarded as morally inferior and hence afflicted with incapacity. The right to live is conceded, out of a policy of religious toleration and, on a practical level, in exchange for the benefits accruing to the conquerors. This dissymetric relationship between conqueror and conquered forms the basis of the covenant of toleration. The paternalism lasts as long as the exploitation of the *dhimmi* is profitable, an aim that requires the *dhimmi* to remain inferior and unequal. Toleration is withdrawn if the *dhimmi* rebels, or tries to recover his homeland and his independence—or if, rejecting the imposed degrading bondage, he acquires rights and privileges reserved exclusively for the dominant group. Such *insolence*—to use the term generally applied to such abuses— substitutes an equal relationship for the dissymetric one that guaran-

127

tees the *dhimmi*'s existence. From then on, his life and property are no longer protected and he can legally be put to death. The covenant can also be rescinded if the ruler decides unilaterally to withdraw his "protection." In both cases, the sentence hanging over the *dhimmis*, temporarily suspended by the grant of "protection," now becomes applicable.

The *dhimmi* communities not only are marginalized by their inferior status, but they also serve as scapegoats. Excluded from a society that only tolerated them the better to exploit and degrade them, they are the victims of every conflict. In times of instability, brute instincts and political and economic frustrations are unleashed, leading to pillage and massacre.

Uncleanness and impurity are attached to the *dhimmi* condition. This physical repugnance leads to the death penalty for sexual relations between *dhimmis* and Muslim women. The desire to restrict social contact with a group considered theologically unclean motivates the numerous meticulous laws governing the clothes, segregation, and movement of *dhimmis*, as well as the vexations and humiliating prescriptions restricting their religious and social activities.

This brief summary provides a general outline of the *dhimmi* archetype. At the political and collective level, it represents a nation whose land has been Islamized by *jihad*, a war process that theologically implies the purification of that land from sin. At the metaphysical level the *dhimmi* represents Evil, the perversity of the infidel who, refusing the superiority of the conqueror's beliefs, prefers his inferior faith. He suffers for his stubbornness, either by exile or, in his homeland, by a condition of humiliation, wretchedness, and servility—thus atoning for his shameful existence through submission to the terms of the "dissymetric contract."

Contingent political circumstances may abolish the *dhimmi* condition by abrogating the dissymmetric relationship, but the archetype will not necesarily be destroyed, since it exists independently of written laws within the collective psyche, from whence it can inspire the ideology. The archetype, having now become something fluid and abstract—a model of reference—draws its obsessive force from the past, and, making selective use of political factors in the present, it seeks a reincarnation in suitable circumstances in the future. Thus the archetype retains the potential of recreating the *dhimmi* condition in the future, even if this condition is temporarily abolished by historical contingencies, such as the successful revolt of the oppressed group or its expulsion. For the archetype, even though emptied of its substance, survives in its own ideological structure, whose function is to elaborate and select those factors which will eventually implement it in the future. The archetype fashions the condition, which is simply its incarnation in reality. Archetype and condition are dialectically interconnected, the one reinforcing the other.

This dynamic relationship between the archetype and its incarnation in reality may be observed in the Arab-Israel wars, which were caused, on the one hand, by the *umma*'s desire to restore a former condition through the Arabization of Israel, and, on the other, by the resistance of the Israelis. Here one sees an attempt to reaffirm the original acquisitions of the *jihad* and the *dhimma*. The archetype appears in the language used: the very fact of proclaiming that Israel is *Arab* implies that the Jews are necessarily a *dhimmi* people condemned to suffer Arab sovereignty in its homeland. In the logic of Arab history, "Arab Palestine" and "Jewish *dhimmi* status" are synonymous. They are two different aspects of one and the same reality. The terms *Arab Palestine* and even *"Palestine"*—the latter inherited from Roman imperialism—foreshadow the implementation of the *dhimmi* condition for the Israelis when the appropriate hour will come.

Should this condition once again bring about a national dissolution, the Jews would find themselves obliged, as before in their history, to seek refuge among other nations in order to survive. Thus the factors conducive to exile or degradation would again be reunited according to the *dhimmi* archetype, which, from an abstract project—albeit permeating ideology—would be accomplished in reality. The *dhimmi* archetype may also be discerned behind the repeated calls to *jihad,* in the affirmation that Israel is an *Arab* land, and, more directly and concretely, in the numerous declarations by Muslim political or religious leaders, which implicitly or explicitly confirm that the *dhimmi* condition is an obligatory status for Jews within the *dar al-Islam.*

Obviously, neither the average Muslim nor the popular consciousness understands the archetype and the *dhimmi* condition as clear concepts. Carried along by the currents of history, passing from the collective subconscious into a clear political formulation, these concepts find varied expression in proverbs and popular speech,[1] in literature and jurisprudence, in customs, tradition, collective psychoses, and political ideology. A critical reflection on Israel's rights to national sovereignty would consequently imply not only a complete reversal of contemporary Arab values, but also a reinterpretation of Arab imperialism along universalist lines, and not, as heretofore, in terms of an Arab epic. For various reasons, including social and cultural conditioning and a lack of freedom of expression, the Arab intelligentsia has never attempted such a retrospective examination. Instead, they have endeavored to update traditional modes of thinking so as to adapt them to changing historical circumstances. As for the submissive and sometimes servile behavior of *dhimmi* communities, which results from open threats, discrimination, and insecurity, it stems from their dual role as scapegoat and hostage.

The Dhimmi Archetype in the Arab-Palestinian Consciousness

Numerous books on racial persecution within societies reveal the harmful effects of discriminatory archetypes in the collective consciousness. It has been shown that a modification of the relations between oppressors and oppressed, whether through emancipation or assimilation, does not necessarily dispel the demonic image attached to the discriminated groups. Sometimes the emancipation gives rise to new forms of morbid collective psychoses. Indeed, the more the reality differs from the traditional image, the greater will be the emphasis laid on the stereotype in order to bridge the gap between phantasm and reality. Hence, the less the Israelis resemble the image of the Jewish *dhimmis,* the more distorted is the caricature.

It is well-known that the successful revolt of the colonized frequently traumatizes the colonizer. Vengefulness and hatred express the distress of the oppressor confronted by his victim's rebellion. An equality of rights with the inferior party *humiliates* the dominating group which, deprived of its superiority, seeks compensation in phantasms. Such reactions have been exhaustively analyzed in books dealing with the phenomenon of racism.

These general principles appear at two levels in the Israeli-Arab conflict. On the one hand, they influence collective Arab attitudes toward Zionism and toward the remnants of Jewish communities in the Arab world;[2] on the other hand, and on a much more traumatic level, they suggest an explanation of the relationship of the Palestinian Arabs to Zionism.

Whereas in the Diaspora the relationship of the Jews to their environment is that of a religious minority, in their ancient homeland their condition was and will remain that of a people living on its national territory. And this is true whatever the demographic dissymmetry resulting from oppression. The discrimination was greater in Palestine than anywhere else because of a political dimension: territorial dispossession. Rarely was a nation as systematically humiliated and destroyed in its national expression (demography, history, language, and culture) as was the Jewish remnant in its homeland. Making Palestine into an *Arab* land expressed the political intention of the victors to settle permanently and impose their values forever, since they had no doubt about their divine mission.

In modern times, however, the situation, formerly favorable to the occupier, altered radically. The weakness of the central Ottoman gov-

ernment in Palestine allowed the European governments to protect
the non-Muslims. Development of the press, as well as modern means
of communication and transport, enabled Zionism to emerge into a
coherent, worldwide movement of national liberation. Modern technology compensated for numerical inferiority. Times had changed:
the small groups of returning Jews—previously neutralized by persecution or expulsion—grew into a massive migration movement that
was to result finally in the establishment of an independent State of
Israel.

This historic context explains the traumatic effect that the progress
of Zionism had on the Arabs in Palestine. On the level of the collective
image, the behavior of European Jews did not conform to the archetype of the *dhimmi,* whose degradation confirmed and justified the
umma in its feelings of superiority and domination. The rise of the
dhimmi to equality with his oppressor was considered by the latter as a
humiliation, reducing him to the level of his former victim, whom he
had always regarded as a social outcast worthy only of toleration.
Politically, the rebellion of the *dhimmis* shook the Arab political consciousness, throwing into question the legitimacy of Arab domination—over territories conquered by *jihad,* and over distinct non-Arab
ethnic groups.

It is scarcely surprising, therefore, that these psychological elements trouble the Palestinian Arabs, who are directly concerned by
the territorial aspect of the conflict. The restitution of a territory—
Arabized by the *jihad*—to a *dhimmi* people, by the beneficiaries of the
dhimma, is considered as a catastrophe of cosmic dimensions. Arab
Palestinian anti-Zionist literature reflects down to the smallest detail
the Arab conception of the *dhimmi* and his destiny.[3] One may well ask
if Lebanon, through political manipulation, is not also a *dhimmi* State.

Toleration or Oppression?

Was the *dhimma* an oppressive system or a tolerant one? To reply to
this question in the abstract would be absurd. As a manifestation of a
particular civilization, it should be replaced within its historical context, including economic and political contingencies. It is in relation to
other contemporary systems of expansion and domination that its
positive and negative features, the variations in its interpretation and
in its implementation in different times and places have to be evaluated. This is not the object of this study, whose aim is to examine and
reflect upon this system from the *dhimmis'* point of view. No doubt an

interpretation from the viewpoint of the dominating group would give quite a different picture. Thus it has been asserted that Arab-Islamic rule provided a protection for its tributaries, to which it could be objected that originally this protection was rather in the nature of the domination over a disarmed population by an army of occupation. True, it deferred the carrying-out of a threat, but that threat after all proceeded from the dominating group and the rights it claimed for itself according to its code of war.

It is not uncommon to read that the *dhimma* remained an abstract concept and was rarely put into practice. Research and careful comparison of numerous documents from different origins suggests that this Utopian opinion is inspired by apologetics and rarely corresponds to historical reality. Last, it is sometimes claimed that the *dhimmis* suffered little from their lowly status. This is a subjective and racist argument, similar to the one that justifies slavery on the grounds that slaves suffer less than free men from the absence of dignity and freedom.

The ambiguous nature of this *toleration* is due to the complexity of its association with a unique system of universal war, considered as the only possible relationship between peoples—a relationship defined solely along religious lines. In theological systems devoid of such a concept, the confrontation between peoples or states was no less bloody and no less exacerbated by religious intolerance, but since war was not considered a religious obligation, nor an integral part of human relations, these systems could also adjust and evolve into a pluralistic coexistence, in a context of equality and reciprocal acceptance of *rights,* rather than into one of domination and *toleration.* It is this context of a perpetual and universal religious war that gives to Islamic *toleration* its peculiar characteristics. Indeed, the Prophet's protection granted to the "Peoples of the Book," his prohibition of compulsion in matters of religious belief, encouraged throughout the centuries a current of religious toleration that proved to be an important check to fanaticism in times of darkness and prejudices. It is sufficient to mention here this positive, permanent aspect that projects a brighter light upon the *dhimmi* condition.

It is undeniable that the Arab-Islamic colonization, especially at the beginning, was a considerable improvement over the theocratic Byzantine rule. Indeed, the period preceding the conquest was marked by the official legalization by the Greek Orthodox Church of religious persecution. Thus in contrast to Byzantine fanatical tyranny, Muslim rule, which recognized a place—albeit an inferior one—for other "revealed religions" represented a considerable advance for the period. The very idea of the coexistence of different peoples—even though in a state of inequality—and the granting of self-administration display a tolerance lacking in the Greek Orthodox theocracy. It can therefore be stated without contradiction that in the early period, before its progressive corruption by the adoption of Byzantine laws and customs, the *dhimma* had many positive features. According to a *hadith*, the Prophet is reported to have said: "Whoever kills a tributary will not inhale the scent of Paradise," and Umar b. al-Khattab, on his deathbed, said:

> I recommend to you the peoples protected by Allah's pact, for the covenant of your prophet covers them; and they shall provide subsistence for your families.

This system, at once paternalistic and oppressive, which decimated the *dhimmi* peoples at the same time as preserving (or fossilizing) them, appears today by its religious structure to be the main obstacle to the establishment of a relationship of equality between the *dhimmi* groups or nations and the Muslim environment. This same religious factor which, with its reference to the Divine Will was once a protection, has today become a stumbling block, since the status of the *dhimmi*—according to this religious interpretation—should be perpetuated until the end of time. One can only hope that Muslim thinkers, by a new interpretation of traditional texts, will be able to modify or abolish the concepts of *jihad* and *dhimma*.

Fundamentalism

This study does not attempt to analyze the present situation, by definition fluid and ever-changing, but one example illustrates traditional ways of thinking. Iran's 1979 rupture of relations with Israel, simultaneously with the Islamization of its political regime, confirms the rooting of anti-Zionism within the Islamic values of *jihad* and *dhimma*. Judaism as a religion is tolerated by the *umma*, but Zionism, the national, territorial liberation movement of the Jewish people, is opposed by it. This distinction explains the apparent contradiction between anti-Zionism and the apparent sympathy for Judaism by anti-Zionists.

In a speech of 16 August 1979, the Ayatollah Khomeini named Israel, the United States, and all those countries which would not participate in a special solidarity day with the Palestinians as enemies of Islam. He added:

> The governments of the world should know that Islam cannot be defeated. Islam will be victorious in all the countries of the world, and Islam and the teachings of the Koran will prevail all over the world.[4]

In the light of past experience, one may assume that these words suggest an intention of spreading the *jihad* and consequently the *dhimmi* condition throughout the world. Similarly, the Lebanese and the Arab-Israel conflicts reveal ideological policies that concern mankind, especially at a time of renascent Muslim fundamentalism. This recent development is by no means a revolutionary ideological innovation. Islamic fundamentalism has always been a permanent current in history. Sometimes eclipsed, sometimes prominent, it returns to the scene in times of social and political stress when the common people are drawn to religious leaders who radiate charisma and an aura of sanctity.

Contemporary Muslim fundamentalism expresses the violent tensions and confusion of traditional religious societies under the impact of modernity, the crisis of values, and the stresses of transition and readaptation.[5] In authoritarian regimes that forbid all form of political opposition, religion serves as a channel and a cover for various and contradictory forces aiming at sociopolitical changes.

During the 1920s in Egypt and recently in Iran, fundamentalism, expressing a popular discontent, was fueled by a conservative religious fervor. In the case of Iran fundamentalism also integrated the tactics of the communist party, as well as the aspirations of a Westernized middle-class intelligentsia seeking reforms.

These motivations aside, the aim of fundamentalism is the restoration of the Koran and the *Sunna* as the sole authority for jurisdiction and government in Muslim countries. However, the return to a strict orthodoxy first necessitates a purification of Islamic society from foreign legislation—i.e., from all legislation borrowed from the *dar al-Harb*. Indeed, all the problems of underdevelopment and all political setbacks are blamed on foreign influences that have brought Divine punishment upon the wayward *umma*. This rejection of the West is justified by the perception of the *dar al-Harb* through demeaning stereotypes—e.g., materialism, colonialism, imperialism, Zionism, enemy of mankind, and Great Satan.

In Iran the *mullahs* fomented revolution against the pro-Western Shah by stirring up fanaticism as a means of gaining power. The misery and ignorance of the masses were the leaven of an uprising which was controlled and guided by the religious classes. The tide of Muslim fundamentalism swept aside the Pahlavi dynasty that had attempted to modernize Iran since the twenties. In Egypt Sadat endeavored to win over the fundamentalists in order to control the movement from within, yet his approach toward the *dar al-Harb* (including Israel, after the Camp David Agreements) and his liberal global policy freed from the shackles of religion, earned him—like the

Pahlavis and the Turkish leaders faithful to the ideas of Ataturk—the title of "enemy of Islam."

Fundamentalism, however, does not only represent the rejection of the West and its scientific and technological civilization, but it also includes the hopes and sufferings of the Muslim masses. Thus fundamentalism is proclaimed as the way to the redemption of the *umma*, corrupted and weakened by Western civilization. The Muslim peoples, it is claimed, will regain their lost supremacy if only they apply to our own time the seventh-century principles that established the past strength and glory of Islam—a glory linked to *jihad*, the annexation of territories, the taking of booty in battle, the pillage of conquered civilizations and the amassing of huge reservoirs of manpower from Africa, the Middle East, Europe, and India. Thus the rejection of the West, coupled with a nostalgia for power based on conquest, help to make Muslim fundamentalism the vehicle and mainstay of *jihad*.

This is not to minimize other social, political and economic factors. Today world energy requirements recycled into petrodollars provoke the euphoria reminiscent of the heyday of the first caliphs. The products and technology of the West pour into Arabia. The labor of hundreds of millions of people is transformed into black gold at the disposal of the guardians of the faith. Economic power, through the control of energy resources, becomes a powerful instrument for political control of the Third World and Western Europe. By a curious reversal of history, the pressures, threats, orders and "punishments" brought to bear on the recalcitrant European states recall the diplomatic pressures exerted on the Ottoman Empire by Europe in the nineteenth century.

The social conditions conducive to Muslim fundamentalism are to be found in the dire poverty that disfigures Third World societies devastated by the impact of modernity. In the West technology is only one of the manifestations of a gradual cultural development that, because of its inner freedom, is constantly self-questioning and self-critical. But this same technology, imported into the Third World, cut off from its source and taken out of its cultural context, lacks an accumulation of the cultural strata that enables it to be assimilated and partly mastered. Technology becomes an independent force with a magic and corrupting power for its possessors,[6] while it subjects the poor and the illiterate to an infernal system of human exploitation and destruction.

The sub-proletariat spawned by this process thus perceives the West as a humiliating and oppressive power that degrades man, eroding his dignity as well as his traditional moral and religious values, replacing them with a foreign subculture. Driven to despair by seemingly un-

ending misery, the poor and humble blindly follow the religious doc-
trinaires who have arisen from their midst, know their troubles, speak
their language, and hold out the promise of a renewal of past glories
and religious redemption. This promise is all the more enticing on
account of the manna of petrodollars that these charismatic leaders
receive, a miraculous tribute exacted from the *dar al-Harb* and bestowed by Muslim heads of State who wish to win over these popular
forces, while gaining absolution for their own religious deviations.
Better that their subjects should seek the compassion of Allah rather
than turn to Marxism.

Thus the forces underlying Muslim fundamentalism appear at different levels. Culturally, fundamentalism stems from the traumatizing
confrontation with the West and the consequent rejection of its mate-
rialistic subculture, perceived as a system of oppression coupled with
cultural alienation. At the socio-political level, the reinforcement of
religious fervor provides a rampart against communist advances
among the masses, plagued by the woes of underdevelopment, although fundamentalism can also aid Soviet imperialism. The glories
of Muslim history serve as a proud banner to frustrated and confused
elites, deluded by phantasms related to a past bitterly-lamented
"Golden Age", allegedly destroyed by European colonization.

However diverse and opposed these forces are—whatever their social, political, or economic motivations and their polarization by the
East-West conflict—all these currents gain their coherence and orientation from the human context, the historical and religious texture
from which they stem, clash, or unite. The revolt against the Iranian
monarchy, for instance, had profound socio-economic roots, but was
also aimed at overthrowing a ruler considered as disrespectful of the
laws of Islam. Similarly, whatever combination of forces, foreign or
local, may have planned the murder of the pro-Western Sadat, the
terrorist cell involved was called *"Jihad"* and its aim was to execute the
traitor to Islam and to hasten the restoration of the caliphate. Since
then, *Jihad* organizations have carried out various bombings in Lebanon (1983) against American, French, and Israeli troops and against
civilian targets in Europe. Thus political actions are carried out, explained, and justified in terms of religion.

One may ask whether this political path was inevitable, or whether
there was a crucial moment in history that could have determined a
different course of events. If indeed this moment did exist, it must
have occurred during the period of choice between the path of war
and the path of peace. It is evident that the Arab-Israel conflict has
given the *jihad* its political framework. The Arab refusal to integrate
the Palestinian Arab refugees—as has always been done when ex-

changes of population have occurred[7]—using them instead as a
weapon against Israel, has transformed the refugee camps into breed-
ing-grounds of PLO *fedayeen* intent on war. Arab governments, prisoners of their own actions, were unable to make either peace or war.
Instead of limiting the conflict, they have internationalized it in order
to force other states—by means of threats and pressures—to collaborate in the destruction of Israel, over 60 percent of whose inhabitants
are the descendants of *dhimmis,* either indigenous to the country or
refugees from Arab lands. This universalization of the conflict contains the seeds of an all-embracing *jihad,* while unstable Arab governments accumulate stockpiles of sophisticated weapons. The Israeli-
Arab conflict, because of its worldwide dimensions, has today become
a test case.

Present and Future: a Challenge

The twentieth century confronts Muslim leaders with a great challenge—whether to continue their adherence to an ideology of *jihad,*
which might eventually engulf the whole world in a gigantic nuclear
jihad, or to strive for a profound renewal of hearts and minds, leading
to the acceptance of the infidel as a fellow human being with his hopes
and sufferings, who is everywhere the same.

A negative attitude was expressed in 1982 by Algeria's first president in a lapidary formula:

> Ce que nous voulons, nous autres Arabes, c'est *être.* Or, nous ne
> pourrons être que si *l'autre* n'est pas. (What we want, as Arabs, is to
> *be.* However we can only be, if the *other* is not)[8]

Although some contemporary leaders and intellectuals are facing
this challenge, the liberal minority in most Muslim countries today
feels overwhelmed by the rise of fundamentalism, by intellectual terrorism that has reached the West, and by an apologetic tendency that
seeks to justify traditional attitudes instead of paving the way for
reforms and changes through analysis and self-criticism.

Ben Bella openly approved the assassination of leaders whose
policies he disapproves of[9]—a common practice under the Mamluks—and then went on to justify, after the acquisition of nuclear
weapons by Arab states, a nuclear war to destroy Israel:

> If there is no other solution, then let there be a nuclear war, and
> that will be the end of it, once and for all.[10]

Such a public display of aggressiveness and moral irresponsibility is
rooted in a monolithic clear conscience, which has never been af-

fected by any scruples, regarding the tragedy of the *dhimmis*.[11] This attitude stems from an ignorance of history and a total rejection of Oriental non-Arab or non-Muslim peoples, whose history, sufferings, and rights are not even recognized.

It should be stressed that President Sadat initiated a revolutionary Arab policy, one that indicated an effort to understand the dangers of the nuclear epoch and the universality of national sovereignty. The very violence of the Rejection Front's reaction suggests how much perseverance is required to change thirteen-centuries-old political ideologies. However, the spontaneous fraternization between the Egyptian and Israeli peoples would seem to indicate that the bounty inherent in mankind may overcome the errors of political ideologies and governments.

Notes to Chapter 6

1. A. Galanté, *Le Juif dans le proverbe, le conte et la chanson orientaux* (Istanbul, 1935); R. Attal, "Le Juif dans le proverbe arabe du Maghreb" in *REJ* 122 (1963): 419–30; idem, "Croyances et préjugés; image du Juif dans l'expression populaire arabe du Maghreb," in *Les Relations entre Juifs et Musulmans en Afrique du Nord 19e–20e siècles),* Actes du Colloque International de l'Institut d'histoire des pays d'outre mer (Paris, 1980): 56–61.

2. Once the decolonization of their countries had been achieved, Arab heads of state (Muhammad V and Hassan II of Morocco, and President Bourguiba of Tunisia excepted) adopted indirect measures to expel the Jews from their respective countries or to retain them as hostages. The methods used were the arbitrary confiscation of their possessions, political, economic, and social discrimination, deliberate humiliation, imprisonment, and physical suffering, and summary executions and expulsions.

On the level of collective behavior, the numerous bloody pogroms perpetrated against the Jewish communities of the Orient and North Africa illustrate their role as scapegoats in an Arab world perturbed by Western colonization and control. In his study of the pogroms of Libya in 1945, H. E. Goldberg examines the mechanisms of the bloody ritual that constitutes the symbolism of the scapegoat in "The Tripolitanian Pogrom of 1945," in *SPS* 8 (1977): 35–56. These mechanisms functioned in a similar manner throughout the Arab world.

3. S. Abraham, "The Jew and the Israeli in Modern Arabic Literature," in *JQ* 2 (1977): 119–36.

4. *International Herald Tribune,* 17 August 1979. See recently, "Comment Khomeiny veut conquerir le monde," in *L'Express* (Paris), no. 1722, 13 July 1984, pp. 23–33.

5. Many studies have been devoted to this subject, among which are W. C. Smith, *Islam in Modern History* (Princeton, N.J., 1957); R. P. Mitchell, *The Society of the Muslim Brothers* (Oxford, 1969); M. Halpern, *The Politics of Social Change in the Middle East and North Africa* (Princeton, N.J., 1963). The bibliographies in the above works should be consulted. More recently, see G. Kepel, *Le Prophète et Pharaon: Les mouvements islamistes dans l'Egypte contemporaine* (Paris, 1984); O. Carré, "Juifs et chrétiens dans la société islamique idéale d'aprés Sayyid Qutb (d. 1966)", in *RSPT* 68 (1984): 51–72; J.–P. Pérouçel-Hugoz, *Le Radeau de Mahomet* (Paris, 1983).

6. The fetishism attached to imported modern gadgets is well apparent in the impressions and descriptions of the observant writer, V. S. Naipaul, *Among the Believers: An Islamic Journey* (London, 1981).

7. At no time in history have refugees been retained in camps for two generations by their own people. Without referring to the numerous deportations and exiles of

dhimmi peoples over the centuries, statistics attest that, since the Second World War, "exchanges of population" have affected about fifty million people in Europe, Africa and Asia.

8. Ben Bella, p. 108.

9. Idem, p. 107.

10. Idem, p. 108.

11. In the 1982 interview, to which frequent reference has been made here, Ben Bella repeats the commonly held opinion of Muslims that Islam, unlike Christendom, is free from any racist prejudice and has always treated its "minorities" well. He conveniently forgot the manner by which nations and communities were reduced to the status of religious minorities in their own countries. Without indulging in broad comparisons, it may be noted that Western countries allow minorities to research and record their own history without hindrance.

7

Psychological Aspects:
The Degradation and Nobility of the
Oppressed

The Super-Ego of the Dominating Group

All imperialisms seek to justify themselves by claiming that they are the bearers of a "civilizing mission," entrusted to a superior people whose victories testify to the progress of goodness, justice, and virtue upon the earth. The excesses linked to conquest—massacres, confiscations, deportations, and oppressions—are deliberately passed over in silence. The conquered peoples allegedly welcomed their benefactors with open arms. History itself becomes an epic justifying and glorifying the superior claims of the conquerors. Legends endow the vanquished with an imaginary Machiavellism, which enhances the mythical virtues of the victors, who are depicted as just and magnanimous heroes.

The free practice of oppression, sanctioned by law and by force, develops in the dominant group behavior patterns structured by tradition, customs, and history. Specialized sociologists have already analyzed the behavior of dominating and dominated groups.[1] It is sufficient for this present study to advance a few suggestions concerning the deteriorations detectable among *dhimmi* groups.

But first, let it be said that one cannot read the history of the *dhimmi* peoples in the partial versions of the conquering community. One should recall that the *umma* considered the behavior of the *dhimmis* according to its own values: for a *dhimmi* to ride a horse is ostentatious, and for him to wear green or white clothing becomes an act of insolence. Thus the accusations made against the *dhimmis* must be interpreted in the light of the values and taboos of the society that initiated them. Moreover, hatred and envy, apparent from the descriptions, often cast doubt on the authenticity of the facts. The charges leveled against the *dhimmis*—treachery, guile, affluence, economic monopolies, breaking the *dhimma*—by their frequent repetition seem pretexts for punishments, especially if one remembers that the dominant community reserved for itself the right to abrogate the *dhimma* whenever convenient. The consular reports in the nineteenth century give conflicting versions and interpretations of the same events. Bearing in mind that the *dhimmis* were denied the right to give sworn evidence in Muslim religious courts, prudence is necessary when interpreting these texts. Furthermore, the principle of collective punishment, making a whole community responsible for the transgressions of one or of a few members, even if not consistently applied, added another element of insecurity to their situation.

It is not intended here to suggest that the *dhimmis* were more virtuous than their conquerors. Human nature being the same everywhere, similar qualities and defects existed in both groups.

Yet the worst sin of the *dhimmis* in the eyes of their conquerors was that they were heirs to the civilizations, sciences, land, and wealth of the regions absorbed into the *dar al-Islam*. Because their tragedy was essentially political, one may say, with little fear of contradiction, that Islam as a religion was tolerant toward Jews and Christians, i.e., the "Peoples of the Book." Indeed, it was this very contradiction between, on the one hand, the Islamic religious toleration—which appears throughout history—and, on the other hand, political oppression, which enabled the *dhimmi* nations to survive albeit in a fossilized form.

Alienation of the Dhimmi

The moral and intellectual level of the *dhimmi* communities often depended on their leaders. If the latter were ignorant and corrupt, the already degraded community would sink into a condition of mediocrity and stagnation. The decisive role played by the leaders may be seen particularly in periods of forced conversions, when the hesitant congregation would follow the example of those who were responsible for directing the community and protecting its spiritual values. The situation of the notables, however, was not without a certain ambiguity. As intermediaries between the *dhimmi* masses whom they administered and the Muslim authorities who made use of them, the notables often became the agents and upholders of oppression, on account of the very privileges associated with their function.[2] This position, which enabled them to increase their personal fortunes, confirmed their hold over the community. These notables were all the more devoted to the rulers since their prestige and their precarious existence depended entirely on the tyrant's whim. Aware of their responsibilities, but also influenced by class interests, the notables, by maintaining the machinery of oppression, ensured the survival of the communities until conditions were ripe for the imposition of emancipation by Europe. The abolition of the *dhimma* permitted the forces opposed to the despotism of the notables and the spiritual domination of a bigoted clergy to be freed, causing an identity crisis among the minorities unassimilated by the *umma*.

The combined effect of the economic wealth of the notables, the spiritual aura of the scholars and the threats of the clergy helped to maintain the community's cohesion. However, the depreciation of a despised collectivity motivated some desertions. Ambitious individuals resented being excluded and humiliated by the dominant group, whose glory and culture fascinated them. In addition, the crushing power of the notables over the community thwarted personal aspirations. Hence, in extreme cases, some frustrated intellectuals experienced the individual and collective distortions of character associated with self-hatred. This phenomenon was mainly evident after 1860 as the emancipation of the Christian communities began and partly explains the "Arab option" of Christian intellectuals.[3]

The "conversion" of the Oriental Christians to Arabism had many consequences. It cut them off from their prestigious pre-Islamic history, reducing them to the level of the Bedouin-Arab conquerors, to whom they had transmitted their civilization. By this renouncement of their history, their language and their culture, they became rootless, mutilated, amnesic peoples. The traditional, cultural and religious links that had forged the solidarity and unity of the Christian *dhimmi* communities collapsed. On this erased palimpsest, myths grew. Masquerading as Arabs, Christians fought for their *Arab* rights, instead of for their human rights as Christians. During the period of European colonization, many were able to rise to influential cultural or political responsibility as *Arabs,* fighting for national (Arab) independence, but the rights of their own Christian communities were not modified after decolonization, with the exception of Lebanon. The Jews chose another path. They were rarely involved in pan-Arabism and therefore played no political role, yet they were nonetheless ousted from the *umma*. In conclusion, it can be said that the Judeo-Christian experience in the *dar al-Islam,* after thirteen centuries of sufferings and humiliations, has ended in failure.

The mass of the *dhimmis* naturally had the most reason to complain not only about the oppression exercised within the community by the notables, but also about that applied from without by the dominating group. But any rejection of the hierarchical structure of the community, necessary for its total liberation, would have required political thinking and organization. This, however, was not only impossible in the *dhimmis'* condition and environment, but would also have been suicidal. An internal uprising within the community might have disrupted payment of taxes. This would have invited Muslim collective reprisals, since the *dhimmis* were tolerated as tributaries. Thus the system of exploitation that functioned through the notables—this same system that guaranteed the levying of taxes and the payment of ransoms—was the very one that also assured the communities' existence. A revolt against the notables to end the system of taxation would at the same time have given legal sanction to the physical elimination of the *dhimmis* and the confiscation of their property.[4] Hence an appraisal of *dhimmi* communities that stresses the economic advancement of the notables—privileged collaborators with a political system—would fail to take into account the actual conditions of the majority of the community.

Furthermore, the conditions of the environment also rendered a revolt impossible. The absence of printing presses, the lack of roads, the dangers of travel, and the hostility of the surroundings emphasized the physical and moral isolation of the *dhimmi* enclaves, which were small in population, were scattered over an enormous area, and were helpless, confronted with violence and discriminated against in law courts. To all this must be added the dissensions between the different communities themselves, divided by factional hatreds carefully sustained, if not fomented, by the dominating power.

The Dhimmi Syndrome

Twelve centuries of humiliation impressed upon the individual and collective psychologies of the oppressed groups a common form of alienation—the *dhimmi* syndrome. On the individual level it was characterized by a profound dehumanization. The individual, resigned to a passive existence, developed a feeling of helplessness and vulnerability, the consequence of a condition of permanent insecurity, servility, and ignorance. Humiliated and discriminated against, he projected onto his group a scornful, accusatory, self-destructive hatred whose intensity varied in accordance with the extent of his desire to assimilate into the majority. This type of alienation may still today be observed in an acute form among the marginal minorities of the *umma*.

The basic characteristics of the *dhimmi* syndrome result from the psychological process of human debasement. Reduced to an inferior existence in circumstances that engender physical and moral degradation, the *dhimmi* perceives and accepts himself as a devalued human being. Realizing that a revolt would incur the death penalty, he has no other choice than to enter into the system or, in other words, to become the conscious instrument of his own destruction. The individual's liberty turned against itself is the most tragic aspect of alienation.

As a contemporary French philosopher has written: "The dissy-metric contract . . . is one of the main sources of alienation."[5] It is in the symbolism of the *jizya* rather than in the tax itself (the Muslims also paid heavy taxes, but of a different kind) that the origin of the *dhimmi*'s alienation is to be found. The vanquished had to pay the victor for the right to survive in his homeland, and the product of his labor was not merely paid to the state, but was intended to finance the *jihad* and consolidate its acquisitions. Thus the *dhimmi* worked for the benefit of the power that oppressed him, and for the community from which he was excluded (see doc. 3, "*Battle Procedures*").

In 1855 the *jizya* was abolished throughout the Ottoman Empire at the same time as the prohibition against *dhimmis*' bearing arms. This tax was replaced by another, the *bedel,* payable by non-Muslims in lieu of military service. But while this tax was optional for Muslims, it was obligatory for Christians and Jews, and assessed according to the individual's wealth. Thus, when the Christians of Damascus asked to be conscripted and refused to pay the *bedel,* which they considered a substitute for the *jizya,* they were regarded as rebellious *rayas* who had lost the right to protection, and this, together with other factors, provoked their massacre in 1860.[6]

Another essential element in the process of degradation was the victor's inalienable right of life and death over the vanquished. Understandable enough in the heat of battle, this right was per-petuated in peacetime from generation to generation. Saved from death, the *dhimmi* had constantly to redeem his life with money pay-ments and acts of submission to the victor who, because he had tem-porarily suspended a sentence of death, regarded himself as magnanimous (see doc. 19). A vicious circle developed whereby the master was considered just and tolerant, as the contempt for the degraded group increased. Finally, the dominator, now turned judge, reserved the right to eliminate at will his victim, who no longer reacted.

Exclusion of the Dhimmis from History

On the collective level, the *dhimmi* syndrome is evident in the oblit-eration of a people's history, culture, and political existence.[7] This obliteration is the consequence of the adoption or usurpation of the *dhimmi* past by the conquering group, which regards itself as the legiti-mate heir to all civilizations created on the colonized territories. In-deed, degradation and obliteration are dialectically connected, for the inferior group has no place in history. The silence on a *dhimmi* past is not accidental, but represents a deliberate eradication of the history of the *dhimmi* peoples. The change of status of a group from dignity to inferiority transfers to the superior group the cultural heritage—civilization, arts, and sciences—of the dominated group which, owing to its reduction in status, has forfeited its rights. This demotion of the legitimate heirs of a culture to a servile status, tolerated for reasons of economic expediency by the superior group, eliminates the only rival who could claim the rights the usurpers arrogate to themselves. Thus, the degradation of the *dhimmis* necessarily leads to an obliteration in terms of history and geography. Cultural imperialism justifies territorial imperialism; culture monopolized by the majority group, politicized and divested of its significance, becomes a supplementary instrument of domination and alienation.

The Arab-Israeli conflict emphasizes this tactic. PLO propaganda prepared for the Western media aims at substituting in history, by semantic perversion, Palestinian Arabs for Jews. The masquerade of Arabs (or "Palestinians") posing as "Jews" transfers to them Israel's historical rights and the merits or sympathy earned after 4,000 years of existence and hardships. By robbing the Jews of their past (i.e., the strategem of substitution), the PLO reduces them to a rootless, shadowy group, worthy only of Arab toleration.

During a press conference held on 2 September 1983 at the United Nations (Geneva), following his address to the "Conference on Palestine," Yasser Arafat stated:

> "*We* were under Roman imperialism. *We* sent a Palestinian fisherman, called St. Peter, to Rome; he not only occupied Rome, but also won the hearts of the people. *We* know how to resist imperialism and occupation. Jesus Christ was the first Palestinian *fedayeen* who carried his sword along the path on which the Palestinians today carry their cross" (UN simultaneous translation from the Arabic).

Thus, for the Palestinian Arab cause, Jesus Christ is metamorphosed into a Palestinian Super-*fedayeen* (i.e., fighter for Islam) and Yasser Arafat is directly associated with the founder of Christianity.

Moreover, everything related to culture is monopolized by the *umma*. Any intellectual distinction on the part of *dhimmis* was to be regarded as arrogance. To appreciate fully the ignominy of the *dhimmi* status, the term *humiliation* must be placed within the context of the value system of Arab societies, where honor has a predominant place.

Another important factor of psychological degradation is the rule of silence imposed upon a specific group. The refusal to accept a *dhimmi*'s evidence against a Muslim in a religious court determines an attitude and reveals a characteristic psychological pattern.

The *dhimmi* group, deprived of the means to defend itself, was placed in the situation of a potential hostage at the mercy of every unfounded accusation. Such a condition of perpetual vulnerability encouraged servility and flattery. After emancipation, European consuls noted the *dhimmis'* fear of asserting their rights and sometimes even of winning a court case, because "insolence" on the part of the *dhimmi* could be punished by death (see docs. 35 & 52).

For the dominant group, this refusal to accept the *dhimmi*'s testimony in court symbolized a greater refusal—the refusal of free speech, the distinctive sign of humanity. This refusal to listen, to make contact, to exchange and to share views was a denial of the sufferings and rights of the *other.* The suppression of speech reduces the witness to silence.

This refusal of testimony is transferred from the individual to the group, and is perpetuated in time. The effacement of its history abolishes its rights, thus allowing the official interpretation of events to become an epic in which only a single voice is to be heard.

Oriental Zionism

A *dhimmi* people not only has no history, but also does not even have the right to have one. This collective amnesia affects them indiscriminately. Oriental Jewry has been singled out in this study owing to contemporary events that have heightened this aspect. As a result of this amnesia, Israel's national struggle for independence has never been understood or explained in its full historical and geographical context. The collective memory having been circumscribed within the Ashkenazi branch of the Israeli nation, a comprehensive vision of the people's endeavors along the road to independence is lacking. The introduction of the Oriental dimension would complement the European account, thus permitting a more cohesive picture of the global historical process. Zionism would then appear in its true magnitude as an aspiration to national liberation, which found expression and acted freely only at a specific period in history from outside the *dar al-Islam.* Consequently, the role and activity of the Ashkenazi branch of Zionism would appear in a new historico-geographical perspective.

The fact that the Zionist struggle was active mainly in Europe and America, and the fact that ignorance has prevailed concerning the *dhimmi* condition and its after-effects (insecurity, fear, and silence), have led to Zionism's being viewed as an exclusively Western movement. The politico-cultural realities, which compelled the movement to be exclusively Western were obfuscated. The Ottoman sultan had already declared in the late nineteenth century that he would not allow Palestine to become "a second Armenia." It was clear that any vague manifestations of Hebrew nationalism within the sparse, isolated Jewish communities of his immense empire would probably have been crushed with as great a ferocity as was manifested in connection with Armenian nationalism, itself organized and armed by

JEWISH LADY OF PERA (CONSTANTINOPLE)
Engraving by F. Nash from a drawing by D. Wilkie (1840)
no. 2420, in A. Rubens (1981), and pl. 47 (1973)

neighboring Russia. The bloody struggles between the Ottoman government and its European Christian subjects, who were seeking national independence—including the early massacres of the Armenians in the 1890s—convinced the Jews of the *dar al-Islam,* virtually without the protection of a European power, that the price of liberty would be high. Oriental Jews therefore did not emerge either officially or publicly as militant Zionists, since their very existence was at stake, even if they felt somewhat safer during the transitory period of European colonization. Later events were to underline their vulnerability when Zionism became a capital crime in most of the independent Arab countries. However, other forms of activity existed, either masked or clandestine.

It is true that some incentives underlying Zionism in the West, such as antisemitic reactions against the emancipation and the assimilation of the Jews, did not exist in the Orient and North Africa. But a "Dreyfus Affair" is not an exclusive condition for triggering aspirations of national liberation, and in any case a "Dreyfus Affair" was an impossibility in the Orient, where no Jew or Christian could ever have held an important military staff rank. Moreover, a Muslim country could not have been morally split as was France by the unjust condemnation of a Muslim, let alone of a Jew or a Christian. Consequently, the study of Zionism within the *dar al-Islam* should not base itself on Western criteria, but should examine the historical and political elements in the *umma-dhimmi* relationship, with its modalities of evolution. The liberation of a *dhimmi* land, subject to the rules of *jihad,* could be initiated only from outside the *dar al-Islam*—as had happened in other cases, particularly for the Armenians—and this was indeed the role of Ashkenazi Jewry with regard to Palestine.

The growth of the Jewish population in their ancient homeland and their rights to the ownership of land—forbidden under Arab-Muslim rule—was only possible through the system of *Capitulations.* Due to these treaties signed between the Ottoman sultans and European governments, only European Jewry was able to embark upon this first and essential phase in the Zionist struggle. The efforts of the sultan to halt the return of the Jews to Palestine were partly ineffective, because the European Jews were now in a position to protest that the restrictions or ban affecting their visiting or residing in Palestine, and purchasing land there, was a religious discrimination against Jews which was not mentioned in the *Capitulations.* Oriental Jewry—Ottoman subjects or others—could not use this argument and were regularly refused entry, particularly toward the end of the nineteenth century. Here again their marginalized condition and the restrictions on the return of *dhimmis* to their homeland—among other factors—gave to the first phase of Zionist immigration into Palestine its mainly

European origin. The foregoing aspects are only summarized here in order to underline some essential factors of Oriental Jewry's history, which are virtually unknown to the general public.

The constant obfuscation of the Oriental dimension of Zionism has helped to foster the image of Israel as a colonial state of Western origin—even perceived as a reaction to Nazism. In this way Israel is defined within an exclusively Western framework, in contradiction to the realities of history, geography, and its demography. Without in any way denying the specific dynamics of European Zionism and its essential achievements, nothing can change the fact that the fate of Palestine and its Jewish population was determined by the laws of *jihad* and its ulterior consequences. It is the historical amnesia specific to Oriental Jewry that has caused Zionism to be interpreted as an exclusively European movement, even though it is the stream in which all the currents of a nation, dismembered by exile, converge and unite. This shortcoming is in part responsible for the difficulty of a dialogue with those who attribute the present situation of the Palestinian Arab refugees to European antisemitism and Nazism, whereas it is the consequence of a much more ancient tragedy. Only when the history of the *dhimmis* will have been taken into consideration will solutions be found to satisfy the rights of each party in conformity with historical realities.

The present situation of Israel provides an illustration of this historical nonexistence of the *dhimmi*. Effaced from Arab maps with the recent exception of Egypt, the State of Israel is not mentioned in the minutes or reports of international organizations where the *Jihad* Front enjoys an automatic majority.[8] Such policy perpetuates the principle of excluding from history the *dhimmi* peoples, heirs of the civilizations of the Ancient Orient. This process of obliteration—what Naipaul calls "killing history"[9]—linked to the conquest and subsequent Arabo-Islamic rights, continues to function today.

The cumulative effect of all those factors over the centuries has been to render the *dhimmi* peoples politically infantile—that is, irresponsible toward their collective historical destiny. Contemporary events in Lebanon have shown the feudal sectarian structures of the Maronites and the rivalries between leaders who pursued the independent policies of *dhimmi* notables, bankers of Arabism. One could point to a similar conduct in comparable past situations among Armenian and Jewish notables, and, in the nineteenth century, among the Greeks.

In Israel the apolitical attitude of the Oriental Jewish masses constitutes an aspect of the *dhimmi* syndrome. In this respect, the political activism of the "Palestinian Arabs," substantial sections of whom are the descendants of eighteenth- and nineteenth-century Muslim colonists from Eastern Europe and the Caucasus, may be compared to the silence of the Israelis of Oriental origin, who could not only vindicate their priority rights to their ancestral land, but could also prove that in the Arab countries—where they had been exploited and which they were obliged to leave—their communities had preceded the Arab conquest.[10] This contrast between activism and *dhimmi* silence reflects the difference between those accustomed to domination and others steeped in a tradition of exploitation, servility, and silence. The reason is that the *dhimmi* conscience is unable to think in terms of *rights;* rather, it confines itself to concepts of gratitude and toleration. This attitude was principally due to the oppression of the dominating group, but it also derived from the internal structure of the communities.

Generalizations would be out of place, but it would appear that, in some difficult historical circumstances, the officially appointed leaders of the *dhimmi* communities failed to rise to the level of their peoples' courage and endurance. The alienating dependence on protection, the abdication of responsibility due to the absence of political freedom, the recourse to a traditional economic role evolved under oppression, which still survive in *dhimmi* groups as so many forms of servitude inherited from the past—all these are typical characteristics of groups that have neither reached their political maturity nor acquired full national sovereignty.

The history of the *dhimmis* with its variety of oppressed groups shows that tyranny determined behavioral defects, which in turn justified oppression in the eyes of the tyrant. The form of reasoning that consists in attributing a harmful or perverse nature to a particular group in order to preserve a monopoly of virtue and to justify one's tyranny is contrary to logic. It is noteworthy that, even if the *dhimmis'* condition recalls that of a colonized people, in certain respects it is infinitely more tragic. Its typical characteristics of wretchedness, solitude, and a lingering torment resemble rather a martyrdom deliberately assumed for the sake of spiritual freedom.

The Existential Significance of the **Dhimmi's Condition**

The study of the documents that follow—a minute proportion of the mass of corroborative material—produces, among other feelings, a certain bewilderment. How could groups of human beings survive such oppression, even if—as has been pointed out—it was not applied in all times and places, in the same form and to the same degree? In his description of the condition of the Jews in the Moroccan Atlas in 1901, a French writer reflected:

> One is amazed that under such a tyranny a people could preserve intact the faith which earned it this martyrdom. One can still imagine the hatred which inspires the conquerors faced with the resistance of these wretches and the frequent massacres which decimated them.[11]

The problem is undoubtedly so complex that it is beyond the scope of this study to provide a satisfactory answer. The most one can do is to try to understand it more fully by stating it in question form.

First, it may be asked whether there was a genuine survival, or if the present remnants of the once-flourishing populations of the Ancient Orient are merely the relics of a policy that testify to their extinction rather than to their continuity. Some historians describe these remnants as fossilized cultures. This extinction does not necessarily refer alone to physical elimination, but also to the defection of large Christian and Zoroastrian majorities, for it is unlikely that without external pressures a people would freely abandon its own culture for that of its conqueror. The silence surrounding the first two centuries of the conquest reduces one to suppositions. Can it be argued that the enormous material and honorific advantages accruing to the conquerors were among the chief causes of conversions to Islam? It should be remembered that massive conversions always followed periods of great persecution. The term "extinction" thus implies the physical or cultural extinction of a group, whatever the means of coercion employed. The abduction of children and the forced conversion of orphans are examples of coercion that do not involve physical destruction, e.g. the Ottoman compulsory levy and conversion of young Christian boys (devshirme).

If indeed there was any survival, it may be evaluated by two criteria: quantitative and qualitative. The qualitative aspect concerns the preservation of a people's characteristics: history, language, literature, codes of law, and a nation's consciousness of its past, as well as its aspirations for the future. Numerous factors determine the degree of alienation suffered by each group. For instance, the Coptic community and the Armenian people, respectively, regard themselves as united by a specific culture and history, while the Orthodox Christians define themselves only as a religious minority. In modern times the only non-Muslim peoples of the Middle East to have regained their political independence are the people of Israel, and, to a limited extent, the Lebanese Christians; but whereas in Israel, Hebrew has been revived as the national language, the Christians speak the language of their conquerors—Arabic. There are three main reasons for

ROUNDING UP CHRISTIAN CHILDREN
IN THE BALKANS FOR SLAVERY
The Turkish Devshirme *system*
Engraving
A. Thevet (1575), vol. 2, fol. 272b

SALE OF CAPTIVE CHRISTIAN FAMILY AT CONSTANTINOPLE
Engraving
Anon, *Het Ellendigh* (1663)

Israel's successful national revival: a historical memory, the preservation of national-religious institutions, and dispersion (exile).

One may speculate concerning the factors that, in abnormal circumstances such as the loss of territory and submission to a foreign power, enabled the preservation of an ethnic consciousness in the indigenous *dhimmi* groups. The subject is too vast and complex, and the circumstances so different in each case (e.g., the Maronites who resided in Mt. Lebanon, for geographical reasons, retained their arms and were never treated as *dhimmis*) that it will be possible in this study only to hazard a few hypotheses, while recognizing the existence and major importance of internal elements of cohesion and solidarity.

Community Ties

On the communal level, group cohesion resulted from a solid structuring that bound each member by a sense of collective responsibility, acknowledged, moreover by the authorities. The various community institutions provided for religious requirements, education, charity, and health. The *jizya* for the old, the sick, and the poor, as well as special impositions and the money for the repurchase of their respective coreligionists (Jewish and Christian hostages) were paid out of community funds. The distribution of food, money, clothing, and free medical attention for the needy, the aged, widows, and orphans was also provided from this source, which was likewise used to assist travelers and other communities in distress.[12]

On the level of collective psychology, the elements are more complex. Two of them seem to predominate. The theme of redemption through suffering, expressed with such intensity in the prophetic literature of the Hebrew Bible and in the Gospels, constituted a spiritual refuge for Jews and Christians, although it affected each minority on different levels. For these two *dhimmi* groups, the despotic power imposed and maintained by force of arms hardly seemed superior to the spiritual value of their own culture, which they continued to develop despite all forms of oppression—especially the Jews, since their culture remained more alive. The *dhimmis* had an inner conviction that their obligatory external wretchedness, far from dishonoring them, degraded those who had imposed it, and they drew from their destiny a spiritual power and dimension that strengthened their moral resistance and directed their lives. They probably saw themselves, over the centuries, as an embodiment of Jeremiah's striking vision:

> He sitteth alone and keepeth silence,
> because He hath borne it upon him.

> He putteth his mouth in the dust;
> if so be there may be hope.
> He giveth his cheek to him that
> smiteth him: he is filled full with reproach.
>
> (Lam. 3:28–30)

Despite internal theological disagreements, the comforting theme
of the regeneration of the humiliated and the oppressed, so characteristic of biblical literature, sustained the *dhimmis'* passive resistance
over the centuries and gave them a deep spiritual identity. It was the
clergy who assumed the transmission of the national heritage: religion, language, history. But owing to the degradation and the humiliation of the representatives of the despised religions, the clergy
gradually came to symbolize, for those *dhimmis* wishing to assimilate
into the majority, the shameful survival of a hated condition.

Messianic Expectations

The other factor of survival—the most central and inherent in Israel's nationalism—was Messianic expectation. The people of Israel,
who for centuries considered themselves as Prisoners of Zion or Sons
of the Exile, kept alive the hope of returning to their liberated homeland.[13] This return to Zion was part of a vision of universal peace in
which a new world order would end the rule of tyrants and would
rehabilitate the exiled, the humiliated, and the persecuted. The absence of Messianic nationalism among the Christians was one of the
causes of defections from the masses and the elites, and of the disar-
ray and disenchantment of present-day Christian intellectuals. The
case of the Maronites is exceptional. Privileged by geographical conditions, they were able to resist the invader. Their feudal system, their
weapons, and their connections with Europe secured them a certain
autonomy and cohesion and gave them a sense of religious mission as
defenders of other persecuted Christian minorities.

Some have tried to explain this phenomenon of survival or lingering torment—it is not easy to decide which term is more applicable—by alleging that the Covenant of Umar was rarely applied, but
this explanation begs the question.

No doubt some of the *dhimmis* managed to bribe officials, thereby
evading the restrictions of the *dhimma,* but they were punished as soon
as they were caught. And how else should one interpret the constant
meticulous regulations that vilified the *dhimmis,* if not that it betrays
the frantic and unremitting tenacity of fanatics in avenging themselves on the subdued populations? Yet, despite the degradation to
which they were subjected, the latter refused to acknowledge the
superiority of their conquerors. It has been asserted that the occupa-

tion of important posts by *dhimmis* proves the tolerance and protection enjoyed by all the *dhimmi* communities within the *umma*. Besides the fact that the situation of a few notables was not representative of the condition of the majority, their privileges were in contradiction to laws and customs. In this respect the opinion of the renowned *dhimmi* philosopher Moses Maimonides, physician of Saladin's vizier in Egypt at the end of the twelfth century, is instructive (see doc. 94).

The statement that Muslim Judeo-Christian hatred resulted from European colonization and Zionism is contradicted by history and Muslim codes of law. In fact, the hostility against the *dar al-Harb* is central to the *jihad* and to Muslim expansion over the world. It is fallacious to infer from the abundance of European reports in the eighteenth and nineteenth centuries, confirming the intolerable state of the *dhimmis'* condition, that previously their situation was better. Actually, the increase in European descriptions resulted from the development of commercial and diplomatic ties that facilitated communications and travel, and consequently an outpouring of accounts on alien societies. A dearth of material in itself does not allow of generalizations concerning conditions of life. The growth of Western power exacerbated tensions already existent and latent, but it did not create them.

Indeed, the heart of the matter was glossed over. The human drama of the *dhimmi* was played down on the grounds that his familiarity with humiliation and suffering rendered him insensitive. In other words, the endurance of the oppressed is supposed to prove the tolerance of the oppressor.

This attitude, which implicitly accepts the right of one group to dominate another (the domination being defined as tolerant, and therefore worthy of gratitude, only because the dominated are despised) is fundamentally opposed to the ideology underlying the revolt of the victim. For it is precisely this revolt of the victim that contests this ethic. Far from praising despotic tolerance, the rebel, by his very revolt, contests the privileges that the dominator arrogates to himself. For the *dhimmi*, it is not a question of determining the degree of happiness that is possible within the framework of oppression, but of breaking out of that framework and asserting the equality of all human beings.

One should not look for literary, historical, or scientific greatness in the past of the *dhimmi* communities, even if one does find it occasionally, for these communities were excluded from history and relegated to the servile paths of exploitation and misery. The contribution of the *dhimmis* to the annals of universal history is different from the glorious materialization of power and force. Rather, it appears to be its reverse side, for it is to be found in humility and suffering, and in those long silences of history which constitute the hecatombs of nations. However humble and distressing this contribution may be, it is nevertheless considerable, since it reveals the legalized machinery of despotism and the sufferings assumed for the sake of spiritual liberty. A study of the *dhimmi* condition thus leads to a reflection on a type of resistance that was heroic in its humble passivity.

Indeed, one finds among the *dhimmis* all the social vices that injustice breeds: servility, greed, fraud, guile, and heaven knows what else, but these were the only means by which they were able to survive. A system that could produce such behavior is more discreditable than its victims.

Epilogue

The fundamental evil in alienation is forgetfulness.[14]

If in the first part of this work attention was given to different aspects of the *dhimmi* condition, it was because of a conviction that the past puts the present in perspective and clarifies it. First an analysis of the *dhimmi* condition was sketched, not as history but as a historical *situation*. From *dhimmi* communities one passes in modern times to the *Dhimmi* State, victim of the same ideologies and attitudes. The problems of minorities that are denied their rights are transferred to the national plane: the national sovereignty of a *Dhimmi* State is denied.

In concluding this study one feels that the questions raised by the history of *dhimmi* communities have not really been covered. Questions for the historian studying the relationship of victor and vanquished, questions for the sociologist examining the consequences of the marginalization of a group persecuted and exploited by an oppressive majority, and finally, reflections suggested to the philosopher by the survival of spiritual liberty, which is the core of the *dhimmi* condition.

Because there can be no history without rationalization, and all rationalization implies a justification (or a finality), one may ask what, in the final analysis, is the meaning or justification of a destiny of suffering. George Santayana's reflection, which is inscribed on the gate of the museum at the Nazi extermination camp of Dachau, will serve as a conclusion: "Those who cannot remember the past are condemned to repeat it".

If a knowledge of this past could inspire enemies to build a peaceful future by respecting each other's rights, then the fate of the *dhimmis* would have served a purpose. It is to be hoped that this research may induce both scholars and students to delve deeper into the subject.

Notes to Chapter 7

1. Among other works see A. Memmi, *The Colonizer and the Colonized* (New York, 1963); idem, *Dominated Man* (New York, 1966); L. Poliakov, *Le Racisme* (Paris, 1976).

2. A Jewish chronicler, writing in Fez (Morocco) in 1650, reports the intrigues of a notable and his supporters and the exorbitant bribe they offered to the sultan and his favorite so that the notable would receive the title of *nagid (rais al-Yahud:* chief of the Jews) against the wishes of the community. The chronicler adds that from that day the weight of oppression became unbearable on the community. See Vajda, *Un Recueil,* pp. 49–50.

3. S. G. Haïm, ed., *Arab Nationalism: An Anthology* (Berkeley: University of California, 1976), pp. 57ff.; E. Kedourie, *Arab Political Memoirs and Other Studies* (London, 1974), chaps. 5 and 6. Until the end of the nineteenth century the Christians who followed the *Orthodox* rite were referred to solely as *Greeks* (see, particularly, in Guérin). The assimilation of these Christians to Arabism has its roots in historical myths of modern "nationalisms." The greater part of the Greek Orthodox inhabitants of Akko (Israel) who claim to be *Arabs* are in fact the descendants of Greek colonists brought from Cyprus by the emir Dahir al-Umar in the eighteenth century.

4. See n. 2 above. The same chronicler mentions that the community discussed the possibility of abolishing the title of *nagid:* "The community decided to abolish the function, but the decision had to be rescinded as the post had to be maintained because of the oppressor" (Vajda, *Un Recueil,* p. 47).

5. R. Misrahi, *La Philosophie politique et l'État d'Israël* (Paris, 1975), p. 141.

6. Ma'oz, p. 233.

7. In his detailed description of Palestine, Guérin referred to the destruction of the ancient monuments of Israel by nineteenth-century nomads who were unaware of the history or even the former place names of the areas on which they camped.

8. For the situation of the State of Israel in international organizations since the late 1960s, see J. Givet, *The Anti-Zionist Complex* (with an Introduction by D. P. Moynihan) (New Jersey, 1982), chap. 5.

9. Naipaul, chap. 4.

10. In 1975 the World Organization of Jews from Arab countries (WOJAC) was created in Israel and in the Diaspora. This organization may be considered as the first expression of a political consciousness emanating from Oriental Jewry and the first time that a recognition of *rights* was demanded from the Arab countries, instead of *toleration.*

In a moving novel, a Jewish writer from Iraq has well described the *dhimmi* mentality as one of fear and humility. N. Kattan, *Adieu Babylone* (Montreal, 1975).

11. Doutté, p. 137; quoted in Littman, in *WLB* 28, n.s. 35/36 (1975): 4.

12. Goitein, *A Mediterranean Society,* vol. 2; E. Bashan, *Shibya u-Fedut ba-Hebrah ha-Yehudit be-Arsot ha-Yam ha-Tikhon (1391–1830) (Captivity and Ransom in the Mediterranean Jewish Society)* (Jerusalem, 1980).

13. A nineteenth-century traveler reported that at Pentecost the Jews of Mosul, Aronel, Arbil, Kirkuk, and from the mountains of Kurdistan, assembled at the traditional tomb of the prophet Nahum and danced in a warlike manner, imitating the battle they would one day have to fight. "This war performance is said to be a representation of the great combat which, according to the belief in those parts, the Jews, at the coming of the Messiah, will have to maintain against those nations, who oppose their entrance into the promised land, and the formation by them of a free and independent kingdom." (Benjamin, p. 73.)

14. Misrahi, p. 122.

DOCUMENTS

I
Jurists' Texts

1. Jihad

Jihad is a precept of Divine institution. Its performance by certain individuals may dispense others from it. We Malikis [one of the four schools of Muslim jurisprudence] maintain that it is preferable not to begin hostilities with the enemy before having invited the latter to embrace the religion of Allah except where the enemy attacks first. They have the alternative of either converting to Islam or paying the poll tax *(jizya)*, short of which war will be declared against them. The *jizya* can only be accepted from them if they occupy a territory where our laws can be enforced. If they are out of our reach, the *jizya* cannot be accepted from them unless they come within our territory. Otherwise we will make war against them. . . .

It is incumbent upon us to fight the enemy without inquiring as to whether we shall be under the command of a pious or depraved leader.

It is not prohibited to kill white non-Arabs who have been taken prisoner. But no one can be executed after having been granted the *amân* (protection). The promises made to them must not be broken. Women and children must not be executed and the killing of monks and rabbis must be avoided unless they have taken part in battle. Women also may be executed if they have participated in the fighting. The *amân* granted by the humblest Muslim must be recognized by other [Muslims]. Women and young children can also grant the *amân* when they are aware of its significance. However, according to another opinion, it is only valid if confirmed by the *imâm* (spiritual leader). The *imâm* will retain a fifth of the booty captured by the Muslims in the course of warfare and he will share the remaining four fifths among the soldiers of the army. Preferably, the apportioning will take place on enemy ground (p. 163).

Ibn Abi Zayd al-Qayrawani (d. 966)

In the Muslim community, the holy war is a religious duty, because of the universalism of the (Muslim) mission and (the obligation to) convert everybody to Islam either by persuasion or by force. Therefore, caliphate and royal authority are united (in Islam), so that the person in charge can devote the available strength to both of them (religion and politics) at the same time.

The other religious groups did not have a universal mission, and the holy war was not a religious duty to them, save only for purposes of defense. It has thus come about that the person in charge of religious affairs (in other religious groups) is not concerned with power politics at all. (Among them) royal authority comes to those who have it, by accident and in some way that has nothing to do with religion. It comes to them as the necessary result of group feeling, which by its very nature seeks to obtain royal authority, as we have mentioned before, and not because they are under obligation to gain power over other nations, as is the case with Islam. They are merely required to establish their religion among their own (people).

This is why the Israelites after Moses and Joshua remained unconcerned with royal authority for about four hundred years. Their only concern was to establish their religion (1:473).

Thereafter, there were dissensions among the Christians with regard to their religion and to Christology. They split into groups and sects, which secured the support of the various Christian rulers against each other. At different times there appeared different sects. Finally, these sects crystallized into three groups, which constitute the (Christian) sects. Others have no significance. These are the Melchites, the Jacobites, and the Nestorians. We do not think that we should blacken the pages of this book with discussion of their dogmas of unbelief. In general, they are well known. All of them are unbelief. This is clearly stated in the noble Qur'ân. (To) discuss or argue those things with them is not up to us. It is (for them to choose between) conversion to Islam, payment of the poll tax, or death (1:480).

Ibn Khaldun (d. 1406)

2. Conquest

*Peace Treaty between Habib b. Muslama[1] and the Christians of Tiflis
(Georgia, ca. 653)*

In the name of Allah, the compassionate, the merciful. This is a statement from Habîb ibn-Maslamah to the inhabitants of Taflîs,

---

[1] Habib b. Muslama (617–662), military commander under Mu'awiya, responsible for the conquest of Armenia.

which lies in Manjalis at Jurzân al-Hurmuz, securing them safety for their lives, churches, convents, religious services and faith, provided they acknowledge their humiliation and pay tax to the amount of one *dînâr* on every household. Ye are not to combine more than one household into one in order to reduce the tax, nor are we to divide the same household into more than one in order to increase it. Ye owe us counsel and support against the enemies of Allah and his Prophet to the utmost of your ability, and are bound to entertain the needy Moslem for one night and provide him with that food used by "the people of the Book"[2] and which it is legal for us to partake of. If a Moslem is cut off from his companions and falls into your hands, ye are bound to deliver him to the nearest body of the "Believers," unless something stands in the way. If ye return to the obedience of Allah [become a Muslim] and observe prayer, ye are our brethren in faith, otherwise poll-tax is incumbent on you. In case an enemy of yours attacks and subjugates you while the Moslems are too busy to come to your aid, the Moslems are not held responsible, nor is it a violation of the covenant with you. The above are your rights and obligations to which Allah and his angels are witness and it is sufficient to have Allah for witness (pp. 316–17).

The Conquest of Christian Armenia

After that, Marwân[3] made his entrance to the land of as-Sarîr, slaughtered its inhabitants, and reduced certain forts in it. Its king offered him submission and allegiance and made terms, agreeing to give every year 1,000 youths—500 lads and 500 maids—with black hair and eyebrows and with long eyelashes, together with 100,000 modii[4] to be poured in the granaries of al-Bâb. Marwân took from him a pledge.

The people of Tûmân made terms with Marwân, agreeing to give every year 100 youths—50 maids and 50 lads—each 5 spans in height, with black hair and eyebrows and with long eyelashes, together with 20,000 modii for the granaries (p. 326).

The Conquest of Christian Egypt

'Amr an-Nâkid from Sufyân ibn-Wahb al-Khaulâni:—When we conquered Misr [Egypt] without making a covenant with it, az-Zubair[5]

---

[2] Name, based on the Koran 9:29, given by Muslims to the adherents of revealed religions, i.e., Jews and Christians.
[3] Marwan b. Muhammad (d. 750), last of the Umayyad Caliphs of Damascus and formerly governor of Armenia.
[4] *Modius,* Latin, *modium.* A wheat measure equal to 8.75 lbs.
[5] az-Zubayr ibn al-Auwam, a military commander.

rose and said to 'Amr, "Divide it"; but 'Amr refused. Then az-Zubair said, "By Allah, thou shouldst divide it as the Prophet divided Khaibar."[6] 'Amr wrote that to 'Umar who wrote back, saying, "Leave it as it is, so that the descendants of the descendants may profit by it."

A tradition to the same effect was communicated to me by 'Abdallâh ibn-Wahb on the authority of Sufyân ibn-Wahb (p. 337).

Umar b. al-Khattab's Letter to Sa'd b. abi-Wakkas,[7] the Conqueror of as-Sawad (Iraq)

I have received thy letter in which thou statest that thy men have asked thee to divide among them whatever spoils Allah has assigned them. At the receipt of my letter, find out what possessions and horses the troops on "horses and camels" have acquired and divide that among them, after taking away one-fifth. As for the land and camels, leave them in the hands of those men who work them, so that they may be included in the stipends [pensions] of the Moslems. If thou dividest them among those present, nothing will be left for those who come after them" (p. 422).

How The Land And The Inhabitants Of As-Sawad Should Be Considered

Al-Husain from 'Abdallâh ibn-Hâzim:—The latter said, "I once asked Mujâhid regarding the land of as-Sawâd and he answered. "It can neither be bought nor sold. This is because it was taken by force and was not divided. It belongs to all the Moslems."

Al-Walîd ibn-Sâlih from Sulaimân ibn-Yasâr:—"'Umar ibn-al-Khattâb left as-Sawâd for those who were still in men's loins and mothers' wombs (i.e., posterity), considering the inhabitants *dhimmis* from whom tax [*jizya*] should be taken on their person, and *kharâj* on their land. They are therefore *dhimmis* and cannot be sold as slaves. . . .

'Umar ibn-al-Khattâb, desiring to divide as-Sawâd among the Moslems, ordered that they [the inhabitants] be counted. Each Moslem had three peasants for his share. 'Umar took the advice of the Prophet's Companions, and 'Ali said, "Leave them that they may become a source of revenue and aid for the Moslems." Accordingly, 'Umar sent 'Uthmân ibn-Hunaif al-Ansâri who assessed on each man 48, 24, or 12 [*dirhams*] (p. 423).

al-Baladhuri (d. 892)

---

[6] The terms of settlement accorded by Muhammad to the Jews of Khaybar became a precedent in Islamic military tactics. It amounted to a form of métayage (*muzara'a*) whereby land tenure was maintained against a rent from its produce. This kind of settlement was often preferred on account of the Arabs' reluctance to till the soil.

[7] Arab general (d. 671).

3. Fate of the Annexed Territories and the Conquered Peoples

Umar b. al-Khattab (634–644) replies to the Muslims who demand the sharing-out of the lands of Iraq and Syria (-Palestine) among the conquerors.

But I thought that we had nothing more to conquer after the land of Kesra [Persia], whose riches, land, and people Allah has given us. I have divided the personal possessions among those that conquered them after having subtracted a fifth, which under my supervision was used for the purpose for which it was intended. I thought it necessary to reserve the land and its inhabitants, and levy from the latter the *kharaj* by virtue of their land, and the capitation *(jizya)* as a personal tax on every head, this poll tax constituting a *fay*[1] in favor of the Muslims who have fought there, of their children and of their heirs. Do you think that these borders could remain without warriors to defend them? Do you think that these vast countries, Syria [-Palestine], Mesopotamia, Kufa, Basra, Misr [Egypt] do not have to be covered with troops who must be well paid? Where can one obtain their pay if the land is divided up, as well as its inhabitants? (pp. 40–41).

Umar's decision against the dividing up among the conquerors of the conquered territories, as soon as Allah had shown him the decisive passages of his Holy Book [the Koran] concerning this subject, constituted for him and his work a sign of divine protection and a blessing for all the Muslims. His resolution to levy the *kharaj*, so that the revenues could be shared among the Muslims was beneficial to all the Community [*umma*], for had it not been reserved to pay the wages and food of the warriors, the border provinces would never have been populated, the troops would have been deprived of the necessary means to carry on the holy war [*jihad*], and one would have been afraid that the infidels would return to their former possessions, since these would not have been protected by soldiers and mercenaries. Allah knows best where is the good! (p. 43).

The People Of The Countries Of War And The Bedouin Who Converted To Preserve Their Lands And Possessions

Prince,[2] you also demanded what are the rules applicable to those of the inhabitants of the countries of war[3] who convert in order to save

---

[1] *Fay*, "booty." The traditional Muslim commentators derive the word from the verb *afa'a* "to bring back" (cf. Koran 59:7), that which belongs by right to Allah and consequently to the Muslims. It was normally the spoils of an unconditional surrender, a fifth of which went to the imam and the rest of which was apportioned among the soldiers.

[2] The author, a jurist, is giving advice to the Caliph Harun al-Rashid (786–809).

[3] Countries of the *dal-Harb*, conquered by *jihad*.

their lives and their possessions. Their life is sacred, those belongings for whose preservation they converted remain their property, and likewise their lands, which thus become lands liable to tithes in the same way as in Medina, where the inhabitants converted at the arrival of the Prophet and whose land is liable to tithes. The same goes for Ta'if and Bahrayn, as well as for the Bedouin who converted in order to save their water-holes and their territory, which remained their land and which they continue to hold (pp. 94–95).

Every polytheistic people with whom Islam has made peace on condition that they recognize its authority, are subjected to the division of spoils and pay the *kharaj* as a tributary [people]. The land they occupy is called land of *kharaj:* it shall be taxed according to the stipulations of the treaty, but in good faith and without overcharging. All land over which the imam [sovereign] has become master by force may be apportioned—if he so decides, for he enjoys complete freedom in this respect—among those who have conquered it, whereupon it becomes tithe land; or, if he deems it preferable, it can be left in the hands of its inhabitants, as Umar b. al-Khattab did in the case of Sawad, whereupon it becomes land liable to *kharaj*, which cannot be retaken. The conquered have full possession of it, which they transfer by inheritance and by contract, and the *kharaj* that is liable on it must not exceed the capacity of its taxpayers (p. 95).

Arab territory differs from non-Arab territory in that one fights Arabs only to oblige them to embrace Islam without making them pay the poll tax: nothing but their conversion is acceptable, and their land, if it is left to them, is tithe land. If the imam does not leave it to them and decides on its division, it still remains tithe land. The decision in respect of non-Arabs is different because they are fought not only to convert them but also to oblige them to pay the poll tax, whereas only the first of these objectives applies to the Arabs since they must either convert or be put to death. We are not aware that either the Prophet or any of his companions, or any caliph since then accepted the payment of a poll tax by the idolatrous Arabs, who had only the choice between conversion or death. If they were conquered, their wives and children were reduced to slavery, which was done by the Prophet toward the Hawazin[4] at the time of the Hunayn affair; subsequently, however, he gave them back their freedom. He only acted in this manner toward those who were idolaters.

The Arabs who possess Revealed Scriptures [Jews and Christians] are treated as non-Arabs and are allowed to pay the poll tax. Umar acted in this way with regard to the Banu Taghlab [Christians][5] whose

[4] A confederation of North Arabian tribes, which were routed by Muhammad at the battle of Hunayn in 630.

[5] A tribe of Christian Arabs of the Wa'il branch, established in Arabia.

alms tithe he doubled as replacement of the *kharaj,* and the Prophet acted in a like manner when he levied a dinar from every pubescent person in the Yemen—or its equivalent in clothes—which in our eyes is similar to (the procedure to be followed in the case of peoples) having Revealed Scriptures. He acted likewise in granting peace to the people of Najran [Christians] for a ransom.

In the case of non-Arabs: Jews or Christians, polytheists, idolaters, fire-worshippers, the poll tax is to be levied on the males. The Prophet made the mages of Hajar pay it; yet the mages are polytheists and do not possess a Revealed Scripture. We consider them to be non-Arabs and we do not marry the women of their race, neither do we eat the animals that they slaughter. Umar b. al-Khattab levied on the non-Arab male polytheists of Iraq a poll tax divided into three categories: poor, wealthy, and middle-class.

In the case of Arab and non-Arab renegades, they are to be treated as Arab idolaters: they have the choice between conversion or death and they are not liable to the poll tax (pp. 100–101).

The inhabitants of villages and the countryside, as well as the towns, their inhabitants and all that they contain, can be left on their land, their dwelling places, or houses, as the imam decides, and may continue to enjoy their property in return for the payment of the poll tax and the *kharaj* (or all may be shared out among the conquerors). The only exception is the male Arab idolaters, who are not allowed to pay the poll tax and must choose between conversion or death (p. 103).

Thus the imam has the choice between two options, each of which is equally acceptable: either divide up [the land] as did the Prophet, or leave things as they were, as was the case elsewhere than at Khaybar. Umar b. al-Khattab made no changes in the Sawâd [Iraq]. Most of the countryside of Syria and Egypt was taken by force and treaties were required only when negotiating with the inhabitants of fortified places. Since the countryside had been occupied by the conquerors and taken by force, Umar relinquished it to the Muslim collectivity then existing, as well as to those who would come after them. He preferred to adopt this option, and similarly the imam is free to act as he pleases, providing the necessary precautions are taken (for the security) of the faithful and of religion (Islam) (pp. 103–4).

Difference between Tithed Land and Kharaj Land

Prince of the Believers, as to your question concerning the difference between tithed land and that of *kharaj,* any land, whether Arab or non-Arab, for which the inhabitants converted, remains in their possession and is considered tithed land, following the example of Medina, whose inhabitants converted for this purpose, as did those of the Yemen. Likewise, the land of idolatrous Arabs, from whom no poll tax can be accepted and who have to chose between conversion or death, is considered tithed even if it was conquered by the imam. Indeed, after having conquered the lands belonging to the Arab populations, the Prophet left them as they were, and they will remain tithed land until the day of the Last Judgement.

Any non-Arab inhabitable place, which has been conquered by the imam and left by him to the conquered, is to be considered land liable to *kharaj* but is tithable land if he shares it among the conquerors. It is not known that the non-Arab lands conquered by Umar b. al-Khattab and left by him to the conquered owners are lands liable to *kharaj?* Any non-Arab soil, concerning which the inhabitants negotiated and became tributaries, is liable to *kharaj* (p. 104).

Thus be sure, O prince of the Believers, to choose a reliable man, trustworthy, reserved, a loyal adviser, who is a guarantee both for you and for your subjects. Entrust him with the collection of all the charitable tithes from various countries, to which, according to your instructions, he will dispatch men of his choice, after whose manners, means, and collections he will inquire, and they will remit to him the tithes of the various regions. When they have been remitted, give him instructions regarding them in accordance with what Allah has stated, so that he should then carry them out. Do not entrust the collectors of the *kharaj* with the matter of tithes, for the product of the former must not be mixed with that of the latter. I have indeed heard that the *kharaj* collectors have sent out men to collect the charitable tithes who use unjust and abusive means and make impositions that are neither legal nor acceptable. For (collecting) the tithes, only reserved and virtuous people must be chosen. . . .

The product of the *kharaj* must not be united with that of the charitable tithes or with other tithes, for the former is a *fay* for all the Muslims, whereas the charitable tithes belong to those whom Allah has designated in His Holy Book (p. 121).

In order to collect payment of the poll tax, one must not beat the taxpayers nor expose them to the sun nor resort to other such methods, or inflict upon them repulsive physical torments. They must be shown gentleness, or imprisoned in order to extract payment from them for what they owe, and they are not to be released until they have paid in full. The *wali* [governor of a province] is not allowed to exempt any Christian, Jew, Magean, Sabaean, or Samaritan from paying the tax, and no one can obtain a partial reduction. It is illegal for one to be exempted and another not, for their lives and belongings are spared only because of payment of the poll tax, which, levied on one's possessions, replaces the *kharaj* [levied on the land] (p. 189).

Concerning the Costume and Appearance of the Tributaries

Furthermore, you must set a seal upon their necks when the poll tax
is collected and until all have been passed in review, though these seals
may later be broken at their request, as did Uthmān b. Hunayf. You
have succeeded in forbidding any of them the freedom to resemble a
Muslim by his dress, his mount, or his appearance; that all should
wear a belt *(zunnâr)* at the waist similar to a coarse string, which each
must knot in the middle; that their bonnets be quilted; that their
saddles carry, instead of a pommel, a piece of wood like a pome-
granate; that their footwear be furnished with double straps. That
they avoid coming face to face with Muslims; that their womenfolk do
not ride on padded saddles; that they do not build new synagogues or
churches within the town and restrict themselves to using, as places of
worship, those which existed at the time of the treaty that transformed them into tributaries, and which were left to them without
having been demolished; the same applies to the funeral pyres [of the
Zoroastrians]. Their residence in the main towns and Muslim markets
is tolerated and they may buy and sell there, but neither wine nor
pigs, and without displaying crosses in the main towns; but their
headgear will be long and coarse. Consequently, command your representatives to oblige the tributaries to respect these requirements in
their appearance, as Umar b. al-Khattab had done, as he said: "in
order to distinguish them from the Muslims at a glance."

I have it from Abd ar-Rahman b. Thabit b. Thawban, in the name
of his father, that Umar b. Abd al Aziz[6] wrote the following to one of
his governors: "After the preliminaries [greetings]; do not allow any
cross to be exhibited without smashing and destroying it; no Jew or
Christian may be allowed to ride upon a saddle, but must use a pack-
saddle, and let none of their womenfolk use a padded saddle, but only
a pack-saddle; formal decrees must be issued in this respect and the
public restricted from disobeying them. No Christian may wear a
kaba, nor a fine cloth nor a turban! It has been reported to me that
several Christians under your jurisdiction have relapsed into the custom of wearing turbans, no longer wear belts at the waist, and let their
hair grow freely without cutting it. Upon my life! if this happens in
your entourage, it is on account of your weakness, your incompe-
tence, and the flatteries that you heed, and these people know, in
resuming their former customs, what kind of person you are. Keep a
watch on all I have forbidden and do not contradict those who have
done it. Peace" (pp. 195–96).

[6] Umayyad caliph (717–720).

Letter from Umar to Abu Ubayda after the conquest of Syria and Palestine:

Leave that which Allah has made to return[7] to you, in the hands of those who hold it and impose upon them a poll tax, in accordance with their capacity, the produce of which is to be distributed among the Muslims. These are the people that till the soil, a task that they know well and for which they are more capable. There is no way, either for you or for the faithful who are with you, to make of it a *fay* that.you could distribute, on account of the agreement that was drawn up between them and you and because you are already collecting their poll tax according to their means. This was set out both to us and to you by Allah in His Book: "Fight those that believe not in God and the Last Day and do not forbid what God and His Messenger have forbidden—such men as practice not the religion of truth, being of those who have been given the Book—until they pay the tribute out of hand and have been humbled" (Koran 9:29). When you collect their poll tax, you can reclaim nothing more, nor have you any reason to do so. Reflect thereon! Were we to take those who are subjected to it and were we to share them out, what would be left for the Muslims that will come after us? By Allah, they would find no one to address, nor any work to exploit; the Muslims of our time would eat these people as long as they remained alive; once they were dead, and we also, our sons would devour their sons indefinitely, as long as any continue to exist, and these people would remain enslaved to the followers of Islam as long as it should last! So, impose upon them the poll tax, free their women and children from bondage, prevent the Muslims from oppressing and harming them, from devouring their possessions except within the legal limits, and fulfill the conditions upon which you have agreed with them concerning that which you have conceded to them. As for the display of crosses outside the town during their festivals, do not prevent them from doing it, but without banners or flags, just as they have requested, once a year; but within the walls of the town, amongst the Muslims and their mosques, no crosses must ever be displayed! (pp. 217–18).

Battle Procedures

It seems that the most satisfactory suggestion we have heard in this connection is that there is no objection to the use of any kind of arms against the polytheists, smothering and burning their homes, cutting down their trees and date groves, and using catapults, without, however, deliberately attacking women, children, or elderly people; that

[7] See n. 1 and doc. 4.

one can yet pursue those that run away, finish off the wounded, kill prisoners who might prove dangerous to the Muslims, but this is only applicable to those on the chin of whom a razor has passed, for the others are children who must not be executed.

As for the prisoners who are led before the imam, the latter has the choice of executing them or making them pay a ransom, as he pleases, opting for the most advantageous choice for the Muslims and the wisest for Islam. The ransom imposed upon them is not to consist either of gold, silver, or wares, but is only an exchange for Muslim captives.

All that the victors bring back to the camp, or the possessions and goods of their victims, becomes a *fay,* which is to be divided into five parts. One share is to be given to those numbered in the Holy Book, and the four remaining shares are distributed among the soldiers who captured the spoils in the ratio of two portions to each horseman and one to each footsoldier. If a certain territory is conquered, the decision is left to the imam as to the best course to take in the interest of the Muslims: if he decides to leave it, as did Umar b. al-Khattab, who left the Sawad [Iraq] to the indigenous people—the local inhabitants—in exchange for the *kharaj,* then he can do so; and if he thinks that it should be left to the victors, he divides the land between them after having deducted a fifth. I am inclined to believe that if he acts in this manner after having taken the necessary precautions in order to safeguard the Muslims' interest, then the act is admissible (pp. 301–2).

For my part I say that the decision concerning prisoners is in the hands of the imam: in accordance with whatever he feels to be more to the advantage of Islam and the Muslims, he can have them executed or he can exchange them for Muslim prisoners (pp. 302–3).

Whenever the Muslims besiege an enemy stronghold, establish a treaty with the besieged who agree to surrender on certain conditions that will be decided by a delegate, and this man decides that their soldiers are to be executed and their women and children taken prisoner, this decision is lawful. This was the decision of Sa'ad b. Mu'adh in connection with the Banu Qurayza [a Jewish tribe of Arabia] (p. 310).

The decision made by the chosen arbitrator, if it does not specify the killing of the enemy fighters and the enslavement of their women and children, but establishes a poll tax, would also be lawful; if it stipulated that the vanquished were to be invited to embrace Islam, it would also be valid and they would therefore become Muslims and freemen (p. 311).

. . . it is up to the imam to decide what treatment is to be meted out to them and he will chose that which is preferable for religion and for Islam. If he esteems that the execution of the fighting men and the

enslavement of their women and children is better for Islam and its
followers, then he will act thus, emulating the example of Sa'ad b.
Mu'adh. If, on the contrary, he feels that it would be more advantageous to impose the *kharaj* upon them and that this is preferable in
order to increase the *fay*, which enhances the resources of the Muslims
against them and the other polytheists, then he is to adopt this measure toward them. Is it not correct that Allah has said in His Book:
"Fight those . . . until they pay the tribute out of hand and have been
humbled" (Koran 9:29), and that the Prophet invited the polytheists
to embrace Islam, or, if they refused, to pay the poll tax, and that
Umar b. al-Khattab, after having subdued the inhabitants of Sawâd,
did not spill their blood but made of them tributaries? (p. 312).

If they offer to surrender and accept the mediation of a Muslim of
their choice together with one of their number, this is to be refused,
for it is unacceptable that a Believer collaborate with an infidel to
arrive at a decision on religious matters. If by error, the ruler's representative accepts and a verdict is proposed by both men, the imam is
not to declare it binding unless it stipulates that the enemies will be
tributaries or be converted to Islam. If this condition is adopted by
them, then they are reproachless and if they acknowledge that they
are tributaries, then they shall be accepted as such, without there
being need of a verdict (pp. 314–15).

Abu Yusuf (d.798)

4. Dhimmi Taxation and Its Usage

Booty

The State's revenues, which have their origins in the Koran and
Sunna, are three in number: booty *(ghanima)*, charity *(sadaqa)*, and the
fay. The booty consists of spoils taken from the infidels by force. Allah
has established their statutes in the *sura, al-Anfal*,[1] which he revealed
at the time of the battle of Badr and to which he gave the precise
name *al-Anfal*, because the booty represents an increase in the wealth
of the Muslims. Allah said: "They will question thee concerning the
spoils. Say: 'The spoils belong to God and the Messenger . . .'"
(Koran 8:1).

In the two *Sahihs* [the two canonical collections of religious tradi-
tions] the Prophet said according to Jabir b. Abd Allah: "I have been
endowed with five gifts, which no other Prophet has received before
me. I have triumphed through terror for a period of a month. For me

[1] Koran 8 ("The Spoils").

has the earth become a mosque and purity; any individual from my community who is overtaken by prayertime can pray wherever he may be. I received permission to take booty, a privilege that was never accorded to any of my predecessors. I received the gift of intercession. The prophets who preceded me were sent only to their own peoples; I was sent to all mankind." The Prophet said: "I was sent with the sword before the Day of Resurrection so that all men may serve only Allah, without associates. My resources lie in the shadow of my spear. Those who opposed my orders have been reduced to degredation and humiliation. He who wishes to ressemble these people must be considered as one of them" (pp. 27–28).

Fay

The *fay* is based on the following verses from the *sura, al-Hashr* (The Mustering), which Allah revealed at the time of the expedition against the Banu Nadir,[2] after the battle of Badr. Allah said: "And whatever spoils of war God has given unto His Messenger from them, against that you pricked neither horse nor camel; but God gives authority to His Messengers over whomsoever He will. God is powerful over everything. Whatsoever spoils of war God has given to His Messenger from the people of the cities belongs to God, and His Messenger, and the near kinsman, orphans, the needy and the traveller . . ." (Koran 59:6).

These possessions received the name of *fay* since Allah had taken them away from the infidels in order to *restore (afa'a, radda)* them to the Muslims. In principle, Allah has created the things of this world only in order that they may contribute to serving Him, since He created man only in order to be ministered to. Consequently, the infidels forfeit their persons and their belongings which they do not use in Allah's service to the faithful believers who serve Allah and unto whom Allah restitutes what is theirs; thus is restored to a man the inheritance of which he was deprived, even if he had never before gained possession.

In this category the capitation tax *(jizya)* to be paid by Jews and Christians is to be included; the contributions imposed on certain enemy countries or the presents that they offer the sultan of the Muslims, such as for example, the *palladium (haml)* made by certain Christian countries; the tithes *(ushr)* paid by the merchants of countries within the territory of war *(dar al-Harb);* the five percent tax levied on the protected peoples *(ahl al-dhimma)* who trade outside of their country of origin (this is indeed the rate employed by Umar b.

---

[2] One of the two main Jewish tribes of Medina expelled by Muhammad.

al-Khattab); the payments imposed on the people of the Book who violate their covenant of protection; the land tax *(kharaj)* that originally concerned only the people of the Book, but was applied later, in part, to certain Muslims.

Under the heading *fay* were also grouped all the possessions of the state that form the patrimony of the Muslims, like the possessions that have no particular owner: heirless goods, usurped goods, loans and deposits whose owners it is impossible to find, and, more generally, all personal and real estate that belongs to Muslims and that is in a similar situation. All property of this type constitutes the patrimony of the Muslims (pp. 35–36).

Concerning the men "whose hearts are to be won over" [by gifts], they can be either infidels or Muslims. If they are infidels, it is hoped that by these gifts an advantage may be obtained: for example, to induce them to convert, or avoid some misfortune, on condition that it is impossible to act otherwise. If they are influential Muslims, it is hoped that some benefit will arise such as strengthening their conversion, forcing it on one of their fellows, enlisting their support in order to obtain the payment of the *sadaqa* from another group that has refused its payment, inflicting harm on an enemy or preventing him from harming Islam, providing always that this result cannot be achieved except at this cost.

These gifts, granted to the powerful and withheld from the lowly, resemble externally those which kings are wont to bestow. However, acts are what intention *(niyya)* makes of them: if these gifts are to serve the common interest of the Muslim religion and of Muslims, then they will be like those which the Prophet and the caliphs bestowed; if, however, they are motivated by ambition and corruption, then they will be like those granted by Pharaoh (p. 51).

The two other revealed religions were enfeebled by their incapacity to fulfill themselves, or through the fear that their followers experienced in the face of necessary ordeals. Consequently, these religions appeared devoid of power and greatness to men, who then understood that they were incapable of ensuring their own happiness as well as that of others. These two erroneous paths are those of men who have embraced a faith without perfecting it with all that is necessary for its own existence; power, *jihad,* material resources—or that of men who have sought power, fortune, or war without having had as their goal the triumph of [their] religion. These two paths are those of men who have incurred Divine Anger, and those of men who have gone astray. One is that of the Christians who, in their error, have wandered astray; the other is that of the Jews, who have incurred the Divine Anger.

The straight path is only that of the Prophets, saints *(siddiqin),* martyrs, and the pious. It is the path of our Prophet Muhammad, his caliphs, companions, their followers, and our forebears who have shown us the way: the *Muhajirs,* the *Ansar,* and the faithful of the second generation. Allah has reserved for them gardens where running water flows and where they will abide through all eternity. That is the supreme triumph (p. 178).

Ibn Taymiyya (d.1328), *in* H. Laoust.

5. Jizya and Kharaj (11th century)

Poll Tax and Land Tax

The poll tax and the *kharaj* are two levies that Allah has imposed upon the polytheists for the benefit of the believers and that have three aspects in common and three that differ, apart from the more complicated applications of the rules. The three points in common are as follows: (a) both taxes are imposed upon the polytheists in order to emphasize their inferior condition and their humiliation; (b) they increase the *fay* and the proceeds are reserved for those entitled to the *fay;* (c) the payment becomes due at the end of the year and is not payable before this date. The three points by which they differ are the following: (a) the poll tax is stipulated in a [Koranic] text, whereas the *kharaj* was devised by personal estimation *(ijtihad);*[1] (b) the lowest rate of the first is established by the [Koranic] Law, the highest being calculated by personal estimations, whereas both rates of the second are based on personal estimation; (c) the former is payable as long as the individual remains an infidel and disappears subsequent to his conversion, whereas the second is payable whether he has remained an infidel or converted to Islam.

The *jizya,* or poll tax, which is to be levied on the head of each subject, is derived from the verb *jaza* (retribution or remuneration), either because it is a remuneration due by reason of their unbelief, for it is exacted from them with contempt, or because it amounts to a remuneration because we granted them quarter, for it is exacted from them with meekness. The origin of this impost is the Divine text: "Fight those who believe not in God and the Last Day and do not forbid what God and His Messenger have forbidden—such men as practice not the religion of truth, being of those who have been given the Book—until they pay the tribute out of hand and have been humbled" (Koran 9:29) (pp. 299–300).

---

[1] Legal technical term signifying "an effort to form an opinion in a case or as to a rule of law."

The words *out of hand* may mean either despite their state of riches and opulence, or that they are convinced that we have the strength and power necessary to exact it from them. As for the words *and have been humbled,* they either signify that they are to be despised and humiliated or that they must be governed by Islamic prescriptions.

Every authority must impose the poll tax on the followers of the revealed religions who come under our protection, so that they may thereby dwell in Islamic territory, and the payment that they make confers upon them the following two rights: to be left alone and to be protected, so that, by virtue of the former, they have security, and by virtue of the latter, they find the shelter of our arm. . . .

Like the others, the Arabs are subjected to the poll tax (whenever it is applicable). However, Abu Hanifa[2] stipulated: "I do not require it of the Arabs in order that they should not be a target of humiliation." Thus neither the renegade, nor the materialist, nor the idol-worshipper was subjected to it. Nonetheless, Abu Hanifa did subject the latter to it when a non-Arab, but not in the case of an Arab.

The followers of the revealed books are the Jews and the Christians, whose sacred writings are respectively the Torah and the Gospels (pp. 301–2).

Whoever converts from a Jewish to a Christian sect is not free to do so. According to the more correct of the two opinions he is obliged to become a Muslim (p. 302).

When peace has been made with them [the infidels] on condition that hospitality be shown by them to passing Muslims, this obligation is to be limited to three days and cannot be increased. It was in this manner that Umar dealt with the Christians of Syria by imposing upon them the obligation to lodge in their homes any traveling Muslims, while providing them with normal food, but without requiring them to slaughter a sheep or a hen; as well as the obligation to provide shelter for their animals, but without supplying fodder for them; moreover, only the inhabitants of the countryside and not those of the towns accepted this obligation (pp. 304–5).

Two clauses appear in the poll tax contract, one of which is obligatory and the other recommended. The first entails six articles: (a) they must neither attack, nor deform the Holy Book; (b) nor accuse the Prophet of falsehood nor quote him with contempt; (c) nor speak of the Muslim faith in order to denigrate or question it; (d) nor approach a Muslim woman with a view to having illegal relations, or marriage; (e) nor entice a Muslim from his faith, nor harm him or his belongings; (f) nor aid enemies or lodge any of their spies. These are

---

[2] an-Nu'man b. Thabit b. Zuta Abu Hanifa (ca. 767), leading *fiqh* scholar and theologian and founder of the Hanafi school of jurisprudence.

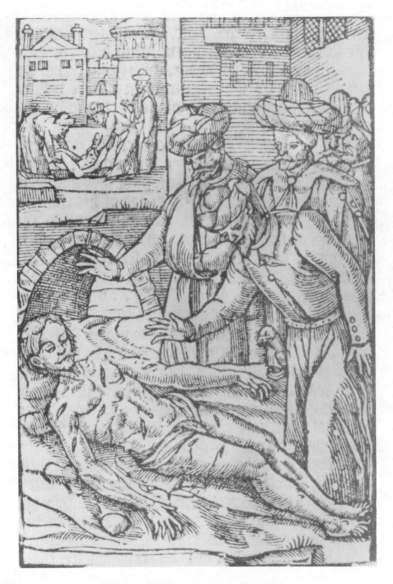

**MARTYRDOM OF A JEW WHO
CONVERTED TO CHRISTIANITY (CONSTANTINOPLE)**
Engraving of 1600, from an event of 1528
no. 2351, in A. Rubens (1981)

MARTYRDOM OF AN ARMENIAN
CATHOLIC IN CONSTANTINOPLE
Dergoumidas condemned by the Grand Vizier
Dergoumidas and two other Armenian Orthodox were beheaded on 5 Nov. 1707 for
becoming Roman Catholics (Franks). The deposed Orthodox Patriarch Saary and seven
other Armenian notables converted to Islam, thus escaping martyrdom (p. 44–47)
Engraving (no. 85) by J. de Fraussières from a painting by J.-B. Vanmour
(1707–08)
Antoine de Feriol (Louis XIV's ambassador to the Sublime Porte)

those duties to which they must strictly conform and which they must observe without its being necessary to stipulate them. If this is done, it is merely in order that they should be made aware of them, to confirm the solemnity of the obligation that is incumbent upon them and in order to emphasize that, henceforth, carrying out one of these acts will result in the nullification of the treaty that has been conceded to them.

The second clause, which is only recommended, also consists of six points: (a) changing their outward attire by the wearing of a distinctive sign (ghiyar), and a special belt (zunnar); (b) prohibiting the construction of buildings higher than those of the Muslims. They should be only of equal height, or lower; (c) prohibiting them from causing offence to Muslims by the ringing of their bells (nakus), the reading of their books, and their pretensions concerning Uzayr[3] and the Messiah; (d) prohibiting them from drinking wine in public, or displaying either crosses or pigs; (e) the obligation for them to conduct their funerals in secret, without overtly crying or lamenting; (f) prohibiting them from riding horses, be they thoroughbreds or crossbreeds, though leaving them the use of mules and donkeys. These six prescriptions are not necessarily to be included in the vasselage agreement, unless they were expressly stipulated, in which case they are strictly obligatory. Despite their having been stipulated, any offence does not result in the nullification of the pact, but the infidels are forcibly obliged to respect them and are punished for having violated them. They are not punishable if nothing was expressly stated in this respect (pp. 305–6). When allies and their tributaries unite in order to combat the Muslims, they immediately fall into the category of enemies and each of these combatants can be put to death. For those who did not take up arms, it must be decided whether or not they gave their approbation to the hostilities.

The refusal of tributaries to pay the poll tax constitutes a violation of the treaty that was conceded to them. According to Abu Hanifa, this refusal is not tantamount to a violation unless, in addition to this, they rejoin the "territory of war" [dar al-Harb]. This tax is levied by force, in the same manner as other debts. They are not allowed to erect new synagogues or churches in the territory of Islam [dar al-Islam] and any built are to be demolished without compensation. They can restore ancient synagogues and churches that have fallen into ruin.

Only when they combat us does the violation of their treaties by the tributaries permit them to be slain, their belongings to be pillaged and

---

[3] Uzayr is mentioned in the Koran 9:30. He is generally identified with Ezra, who, the Muslims allege, was believed by the Jews to be the Son of God.

their wives and children to be enslaved. Otherwise they are to be evicted from Muslim territory and afforded safe conduct until they reach their place of safety in the nearest polytheistic country. If they do not leave of their own will, then they are to be expelled by force (pp. 308–9).

Mawardi (d. 1058)

6. Expulsion of the Natives from State Administration

Traditions Concerning the Caliph Umar b. al-Khattab (634–644)

For this reason the Imam Ahmad ibn Hanbal said: "No help must be accepted from either Jews or Christians in any of the official acts of the Muslims, e.g., the poll-tax [*jizya*]." In like manner Abu Hanifah, al-Shafi'i and other legal authorities hold that it is not lawful to appoint one of them to a position of influence in any province or to any station of trust; for unbelief is inconsistent with authority and with trust. The injunction of Allah: "Do not ask help of an idolater" includes asking them for help in defence, employing them as governors, as clerks, and the like. The general term used must be applied in all cases and can not be confined to a special case. In saying this he strengthens his position by two considerations. The one is that he gives their idolatry as a reason for withholding the appeal for help; and this reason applies equally to all such appeals. The second is that since he has not asked help from them in military matters, in which there is neither official appointment, nor raising him to a position of trust, nor elevating in rank—when it comes to positions of authority and of dignity, it is even less meet and proper. For this reason the legal authorities are agreed that it is impossible to put them in governing positions or in stations of power or in places of weight in a council; nor can they be allowed to build their houses higher than those of Muslims, nor can they be greeted first. When they are met on the road, they should be compelled to take to the narrowest part of it. It will be seen that the prohibition of asking them for help is general in its tenor—it being understood to refer to all unbelievers (living) among the People of the Book. This decision he bases upon his belief in Allah and in his Prophet. For just as soon as any one of the People of the Book declares the law of Allah and of his Prophet to be untrue, and disobeys the demands as laid down by the Prophet of Allah, idolatry adheres to him.

In this respect Allah says: "They have taken their clergy and their monks as their masters, but not Allah and the Messiah son of Mary. They were commanded to serve only one God; there is none other than He. Praise be to Him; far be He from that which they associate with him" [Koran 9:31].

We have a tradition that has come to us from Abu Bakr al-Athram, one of the most important traditionists; it comes down to us through the Imam Ahmad ibn Hanbal and others and is cited in the (former's) collection of traditions, on the authority of Abu Musa al-Ash'ari, to wit: The Commander of the Faithful, 'Umar ibn al-Khattab, ordered him to bring an account of that which he had received and that which he had expended (written) upon a piece of parchment. Now, Abu Musa had a Christian for scribe; and this man brought the account to the Caliph. 'Umar wondered at Abu Musa['s] employing such a man and said: "Verily, this man is very careful; call him that he read the Koran for me." But, Abu Musa answered: "He will not be willing to come to the mosque." "Is he ritually unclean?" asked 'Umar. "No", answered Abu Musa, "he is a Christian." Whereupon 'Umar up-braided me, struck my thigh so hard with his hand as almost to break it, and said: "Have nothing to do with the Christians, seeing that Allah has put them at a distance, have no faith in them, seeing that Allah distrusts them; and do not esteem them, seeing that Allah has humbled them.". . .

Mu'awiyyah ibn Abi Sufyan wrote to the Commander of the Faithful, 'Umar ibn al-Khattab, as follows: "In my district there is a Christian scribe, without whom I can not complete the taking of the poll-tax. I am unwilling to continue employing him without some word from you." 'Umar answered his letter as follows: "May Allah keep us and you in good health! I have read your letter concerning the Christian. My answer is this. The Christian is to be considered as if he were dead and gone; in no tradition and in no narrative is there any mention of an idolater being given an administrative charge during the times of the Prophet, of Abu Bakr, 'Umar, 'Uthman or of 'Ali" [sic] (pp. 418–20).

Some of the Conquerors' Regulations in Syria-Palestine

So 'Umar laid a tax upon the wealthy of 48 dirhems; upon those of middling fortune, of 24 dirhems, and upon the poor, of 12 dirhems. He also gave orders that the Christians should not build new churches nor erect crosses, where Muslims lived, and that they should not ring their church-bells except in the interior of their churches; (saying) "we ought to have the power to divide up their dwellings with them, so that Muslims may share these with them." (He added): "I do not trust you; I shall take the southern part of the land around their churches as places for Mohammedan Mosques, as they are situate in the very middle of the various cities." It was, further, ordered that

they should not drive swine amongst the Muslims; that they should
entertain any guests that might come to them for three days and three
nights; that they should carry those who came on foot from one
village to another; that they should give such ones good advice and
not maltreat them, and that they should not show too much consideration for an enemy." He said further: "We consider it lawful to
shed their blood and to take captive their children and their wives. In
such manner a compact and an agreement are made with Allah, and
proper protection is assured the Muslims" (pp. 420–21).

Caliph Umar b. Abd al- Aziz (717–720) to the Imperial Governors

'Umar ibn Abd al-'Aziz, the chief of the Banu Umayah wrote to his
lieutenants in the various provinces as follows: 'Umar sends you
greetings. He cites to you from the Book of Allah, about which there
is no uncertainty: "O ye who believe! The non-Moslems are nothing
but dirt. Allah has created them to be partisans of Satan; most
treacherous in regard to all they do; whose whole endeavor in this
nether life is useless, though they themselves imagine that they are
doing fine work. Upon them rests the curse of Allah, of the Angels
and of man collectively." Know, then, that they who have gone before
you died simply because they refused to accept the truth and
stretched out the hand of wickedness. I have heard of some Moslems
in times gone by, that when they arrived in a certain country, the non-
Moslems came to them and asked them for assistance in their municipal affairs and in keeping their books, because the Moslems were
expert in book-keeping, in tax-gathering, and in running business
affairs.[1] There can be no prosperity, nor can there be any real management when one makes use of anything that angers Allah or his
Prophet. Indeed, there was a time—Allah has brought it to an end—
when one did not know of a governor, who, having a single man living
in his province connected with any religion other than Islam, did not
visit him with exemplary punishment. For the abolition of their own
governments, and their having reached the low station to which Allah
had degraded them was in itself abasement and derogation. Let every
one of you write to me what he has done in his province.

He commanded that both Jews and Christians should be forbidden
to ride upon saddles; that no one belonging to the "Protected Peoples" should be allowed to enter a public bath on Friday, except after
Prayer-time. He ordered, further, that a guard should be set to watch

---

[1] This spurious information probably suited the author's desire to see the *dhimmis*
replaced by Muslims in the public administration of his time.

both Jews and Christians whenever they slaughtered an animal, so that the guard should mention the name of Allah and of his Prophet (at such slaughter). His governor over Egypt, Hayyan, wrote to him: "O Commander of the Faithful! If things continue as they are now in Egypt, all the "Protected Peoples" will soon become Moslems and then we shall cease to get any money (taxes) from them." Whereupon 'Umar sent to him a messenger strong in character, saying: "Go down to Egypt and give Hayyan thirty stripes with a whip upon his head as a punishment for that which he has written, and tell him as follows: "Take care, O Hayyan; whosoever has become a Moslem, do not ask the poll-tax from him. I only wish that the whole bunch of them would become converted. Verily! Allah has sent Mohammed as a preacher, not as a tax-gatherer" (pp. 423–24).

Ghazi b. al-Wasiti (alive, 1292) in R. Gottheil, *An Answer.*

7. Constraints on Dhimmis

Malik b. Anas[1] said that it was not right for a Muslim to teach the Arabic script or anything else to a Christian. Furthermore, he should not place his children in foreign schools in order to learn an alphabet (language) other than Arabic. . . . When a *dhimmi* sneezes, one should no longer say, "may Allah bless you" but "may Allah lead you to the right path![2] or "may he improve your situation."

If a *dhimmi* had had a criminal relationship with a consenting Muslim woman, opinions are divided as to whether or not the pact is thereby annulled. If, on the contrary, he took her by force, as far as I am aware there is no disagreement and as far as that individual is concerned, his pact is ended. In this manner the pact of most of the *dhimmis* of Egypt has been annulled, for they insulted the Muslims and maintained, in one way or another, criminal relationships with Muslim women.[3] For the rest, Allah is all-knowing.

If the *dhimmi* refuses to pay the *jizya*, then his pact [*dhimma*] is broken and all of his possessions may be seized.

If he insults the prophet, he is to be put to death. It may be asked whether he can escape death by converting to Islam. Although there are two opinions on this subject, it would seem that whenever a *dhimmi*

---

[1] Muslim jurist and imam, founder of the Maliki school of jurisprudence (d. 795)

[2] Formula with which *dhimmis* were generally addressed. It really means "may you convert to Islam."

[3] The sexual immorality of the *dhimmis* is a recurring theme in Muslim literature. The Hebrew proverb says, "whosoever accuses does so with his own vice."

is condemned to death for violation of the pact, he can escape capital punishment by converting to Islam.

If he purchases a Muslim slave or a Koran he shall be punished.

Malik was asked the following question concerning the books that contain the Pentateuch and the Gospel: "Do you think that it is permissible to sell these books to the Jews and Christians?" "Be attentive," he replied, "first, can one be sure that these texts are really the Pentateuch and the Gospel? Notwithstanding, I do not think that we should sell them, nor receive payment for them."

Other *ulama* are of the opinion that, since Islam has abrogated all previous religions, it is not permissible to sell these books to men who believe in their precepts and who do not recognize the Koran, which has replaced them, even if they were the true Pentateuch and Gospel; but this also is not acceptable, for there is no means of knowing what was the authentic text, since Allah Himself has said "They have changed the Pentateuch and the Gospel" (18:510–12).

CHURCHES—It is related, according to the tradition, that the Prophet made this declaration: "No churches are to be built in Muslim lands, and those that will have fallen into ruin shall not be repaired." Another *hadit* is also quoted in his name: "No churches under Islam."

Umar b. al-Khattab (may Allah bless him!) commanded that every church that did not exist before the rise of Islam was to be demolished and he forbade the building of new ones. He also commanded that no cross was to be visible outside a church, otherwise it could be broken over the head of him who carried it.

Urwat b. Naj gave orders to destroy all the churches of San'a (Yemen). This is the law of the *ulama* of Islam.

Umar b. Abd al-Aziz went ever further than this and gave orders to leave neither churches nor chapels standing anywhere, be they ancient or recent. It is customary, says Hasan al-Basri,[4] to destroy the old and the new churches in any country.

Umar b. Abd al-Aziz also issued decrees prohibiting Christians to raise their voices while chanting in their churches, for these are the most distasteful hymns to the Most High. Moreover, he prohibited them from repairing those parts of their places of worship which fell into ruin. Concerning this latter point there are two opinions. If they resurface them on the outside, says al-Istakhari,[5] then they must be prevented from doing so, but if they merely restore the inside, the

---

[4]al-Hasan b. Abi l-Hasan al-Basri (642–728), prominent figure in the first century of Islam, renowned for his ascetic piety

[5]Abu Sa'id al-Hasan b. Ahmad al-Istakhari (898–940), Shafi'i jurist, resident in Baghdad and author of *Adab al-Qada* and other works on Muslim jurisprudence.

portion that is on their side, then this can be tolerated. However, Allah is all-knowing.

POLL-TAX

The *ulama* are of different opinions with regard to the *jizya*. According to some, it is determined and established in accordance with the sum fixed by Umar b. al-Khattab, and it is not permissible to increase or decrease it. Others, however, hold that it is fixed in accordance with the zeal of the imam, who is the most competent judge in the matter. Finally, a third opinion holds that while one cannot decrease the rate established by the imam, Umar b. al-Khattab, it can be increased. . . . The *jizya* established by Umar was forty-eight dirhams for the rich, twenty-four for the middle class, and twelve for the poor, but it is proper for the imam to show his zeal for the faith by increasing the sum of the *jizya;* and more so, in the times in which we live, it would be most fair to impose an annual levy of a thousand dinars on certain *dhimmis,* who, moreover, would not be incapable of paying such a sum, considering the riches that they have gotten out of the Muslims. Furthermore, once the imam has been informed of the treacheries that they have committed in order to accumulate these fortunes, he must dispossess them immediately. If he is not entirely convinced of their perfidy, he must share it with them, taking half of what they own, in the case, evidently, where they possessed a fortune before having entered the public administration *(wilaya);* however, if they were poor and needy at this time, then the imam is obliged to take all of their possessions. Moreover, this is how Umar b. al-Khattab acted toward the Egyptian notaries, by relying on the supposition that these individuals had become rich through their public office, and yet it was impossible to prove their guilt.

Praise be to Allah the Most High, the only God. May blessings and peace be bestowed upon Muhammad, his family and his companions (18:513–15)

Ibn Naqqash (d. 1362)

8. Decree of Caliph al-Mutawakkil (850)

In that year (235/850), al-Mutawakkil ordered that the Christians and all the rest of the *ahl al-dhimma* be made to wear honey-colored *taylasans* (hoods) and the *zunnar* belts. They were to ride on saddles with wooden stirrups, and two balls were to be attached to the rear of their saddles. He required them to attach two buttons on their *qalan-*

suwas (conical caps)—those of them that wore this cap. And it was to be of a different color from the *qalansuwa* worn by Muslims. He further required them to affix two patches on the exterior of their slaves' garments. The color of these patches had to be different from that of the garment. One of the patches was to be worn in front on the breast and the other on the back. Each of the patches should measure four fingers in diameter. They too were to be honey-colored. Whosoever of them wears a turban, its color was likewise to be honey-colored. If any of their women went out veiled, they had to be enveloped in a honey-colored *izar* (large wrap). He further commanded that their slaves be made to wear the *zunnar* and be forbidden to wear the *mintaqa* (Arab military belt).

He gave orders that any of their houses of worship built after the advent of Islam were to be destroyed and that one-tenth of their homes be confiscated. If the place was spacious enough, it was to be converted into a mosque. If it was not suitable for a mosque, it was to be made an open space. He commanded that wooden images of devils be nailed to the doors of their homes to distinguish them from the homes of Muslims.

He forbade their being employed in the government offices or in any official business whereby they might have authority over Muslims. He prohibited their children [from] studying in Muslim schools. Nor was any Muslim permitted to teach them. He forbade them to display crosses on their Palm Sundays, and he prohibited any Jewish chanting in the streets. He gave orders that their graves should be made level with the ground so as not to resemble the graves of Muslims. And he wrote to all his governors regarding this (pp. 167–68).

al-Tabari (d. 923), *Ta'rikh al-Rusul wa'l-Muluk*, in N. Stillman.

9. Zoomorphic Discriminatory Badges (9th century)

The Qadi, Ahmed b. Talib (9th century), compelled the *dhimmis* to wear upon their shoulder a patch of white cloth *(riqa')* that bore the image of an ape (for the Jews) and a pig (for the Christians), and to nail onto their doors a board bearing the sign of a monkey (p. 142).

[Muslims reviled Christians for eating pork, which they, like the Jews, considered unclean. According to the Koran (2:65), Jews were transformed into apes on account of their sins. See also: "Whomsoever God has cursed, and with whom He is wroth, and made some of them apes and swine, and worshippers of idols . . ." (Koran 5:65), which was considered by Muslim commentators on the Koran to refer to Jews and Christians. *Translator's note—P.B.F.*]

al-Maliki (11th century), *Riyad an Nufus* (Bibl. Nat., Paris: Ms. Arabe 2153, Vol. 52v), in H. R. Idris

10. Dhimmis' Servitudes in Seville (ca. 1100)

A Muslim must not act as masseur to a Jew or Christian; he must not clear their rubbish nor clean their latrines. In fact, the Jew and the Christian are more suited for such work, which are degrading tasks. A Muslim must not act as a guide or stableman for an animal owned by a Jew or Christian; he must not act as their donkey-driver or hold the stirrups for them. If it be noticed that a Muslim contravenes these prohibitions, he shall be rebuked (p. 108).

A Jew must not slaughter an animal for a Muslim. The Jews may be authorized to open their own special butcher shops (p. 110).

It is forbidden to sell a coat that once belonged to a leper, to a Jew or Christian, unless the buyer is informed of its origin; likewise if this garment once belonged to a debauched person (p. 112).

No tax-officer or policeman, Jew or Christian may be allowed to wear the dress of an aristocrat, nor of a jurist, nor of a wealthy individual; on the contrary they must be detested and avoided. It is forbidden to accost them with the greeting "Peace upon you!" *(as-salam alayka!)*. In effect, "Satan has gained the mastery over them, and caused them to forget God's Remembrance. Those are Satan's party; why, Satan's party, surely they are the losers!" (Koran 58:20) A distinctive sign must be imposed upon them in order that they may be recognized and this will be for them a form of disgrace (p. 114).

The sound of bells must be prohibited in Muslim territories and reserved only for the lands of the infidels (p. 123).

It is forbidden to sell to Jews and Christians scientific books unless they treat of their particular law. They have in fact translated scientific books and attributed them to their coreligionists and to their bishops, whereas they are really the work of Muslims! It would be preferable not to let Jewish or Christian physicians be able to heal Muslims. Since they are incapable of noble sentiments toward Muslims, let them treat their fellow infidels; knowing their feelings, how is it possible to entrust the lives of Muslims to them? (p. 128).

Ibn Abdun, in E. Lévi-Provençal

11. The Jizya's Meaning: Edict of Caliph al-Amir bi-Ahkam Illah (1101–1130)

Now, the prior degradation of the infidels in this world before the life to come—where it is their lot—is considered an act of piety; and the imposition of their poll tax [*jizya*], "until they pay the tribute out of hand and have been humbled" (Koran 9:29) is a divinely ordained obligation. As for the religious law, it enjoins the inclusion of all the infidels in the payment of the *jizya*, with the exception, however, of those upon whom it cannot be imposed; and it is obligatory to follow in this respect the line laid down by Islamic tradition.

In accordance with the above, the governors of the provinces in their administration must not exempt from the *jizya* a single *dhimmi*, even if he be a distinguished member of his community; they must not, moreover, allow any of them to send the amount by a third party, even if the former is one of the personalities or leaders of their community. The *dhimmi*'s payment of his dues by a bill drawn on a Muslim, or by delegating a real believer to pay it in his name will not be tolerated. It must be exacted from his directly in order to vilify and humiliate him, so that Islam and its people may be exalted and the race of infidels brought low. The *jizya* is to be imposed on all of them in full, without exception.

The [Jewish] inhabitants of Khaybar and others, in this respect, are on equal terms. The *Khaybaris* [inhabitants of Khaybar] had pretended that they were not to be subjected to the *jizya*, in consequence of an agreement concluded between themselves and the Prophet; but that is nothing but a deceit, an invention, and a lie, which men of religion and instruction will recognize without difficulty. These impostors have invented this tale, they have fabricated it; then they spread it abroad, thinking that the men of learning would not discern it and that it would be acknowledged by the Muslim *ulama*, but Allah allowed us to expose the absurdities and fraud of these impostors.

Now the traditions are in agreement, and it is authentic, that Khaybar was taken by force, and that the Prophet was resolved to expel the *Khaybaris*, just as he had done in other localities to the brethren-in-belief of their Scriptures. But they having conveyed to Muhammad that they were the only ones who knew how to irrigate the palm groves properly and till the soil of the region, the Prophet let them remain as tenants; he accorded them half of the harvest and this condition was expressly stipulated, for he told them: "We will allow you to remain in this land as long as it pleases us." He thus placed the *Khaybaris* in a state of abasement; they remained in the land, working on these conditions; and they were given neither any privileges, nor distinction, that might exempt them from the *jizya* and make an exception between them and the other *dhimmis*. . . .

In this same document, one also learns: "We have exempted them from taxes and corvées." Now, during the prophet's lifetime, there was nothing of the sort, nor for that matter in the time of the caliphs, who distinguished themselves by outstanding piety. When the Muslim territory grew and the bulk of the people converted to the faith and there were among the Muslims men capable of tilling the soil and irrigating the palm trees, Umar b. al-Khattab drove the *Khaybari* Jews out of the isle of the Arabs [Arabia] with the words: "If Allah prolongs my life, I shall certainly chase all the Jews and Christians from Arabia and will leave only Muslims" (18:475–78).

Ibn Naqqash (d. 1362)

12. Forced Conversions in the Maghreb

Toward the end of his reign [1198], Abu Yusuf [Abu Yusuf Ya'qub al-Mansur, 1184–1198, Almohad ruler of Spain and North Africa] ordered the Jewish inhabitants of the Maghreb to make themselves conspicuous among the rest of the population by assuming a special attire consisting of dark blue garments, the sleeves of which were so wide as to reach to their feet and—instead of a turban—to hang over the ears a cap whose form was so ill conceived as to be easily mistaken for a pack-saddle. This apparel became the costume of all the Jews of the Maghreb and remained obligatory until the end of the prince's reign and the beginning of that of his son Abu Abd Allah [Abu Muhammad Abd Allah al-Adil, the Just, 1224–1227]. The latter made a concession only after appeals of all kinds had been made by the Jews, who had entreated all those whom they thought might be helpful to intercede on their behalf. Abu Abd Allah obliged them to wear yellow garments and turbans, the very costume they still wear in the present year 621 [1224]. Abu Yusuf's misgivings as to the sincerity of their conversion to Islam prompted him to take this measure and impose upon them a specific dress. "If I were sure," said he, "that they had really become Muslims, I would let them assimilate through marriage and other means; on the other hand, had I evidence that they had remained infidels I would have them massacred, reduce their children to slavery and confiscate their belongings for the benefit of the believers" (pp. 264–65).

al-Marrakushi (d. 1224)

13. Prestige and Honor Forbidden to Jews and Christians
(ca. 1220)

It is related concerning him [Ibn Fadlan, d. 1233] that when he was
appointed inspector of the finances of the *dhimmis,* he sent the following letter to the Caliph Nasir ad-Din Allah [d. 1225]: "According to
the Shafi'i school, no religious principle prohibits increasing the
yearly tax levied from the *dhimmis,* i.e., the Jews and Christians, for
the purchase of their right to reside in Baghdad and to enjoy the
benefits that this city has to offer; however, the total amount must
[legally] not be less than one dinar. It is absolutely forbidden to accept
less than this sum, but there is nothing to prevent taking up to a
hundred dinars, dependent on the individual case, and if it is considered good then it is a praiseworthy act to double the sum exacted
from each of their members. Now it so happens that the law is at
present applied with regard neither to their status nor to their possessions, for the sum to be levied is even decreased. Some of them work
for the government *(diwan)* and receive a decent salary, not to speak
of the riches that they pilfer from the sultan and his subjects, the
money they get as tips and gifts. Thus it happens that one of them
may spend in one day the equivalent of his annual poll tax. Moreover,
one can add to the foregoing the excessive freedom that they enjoy,
the extreme honor and eminence over and above the Muslim notables. Your servant and other employees of the Treasury themselves
witnessed how Ibn al-Hajib dismissed Ibn Hajraj in order to appoint
[the Christian] Ibn Zatina in his stead.

It is related concerning Ali that he forbade us to allow the *dhimmis*
to sit amongst us on the councils, [for us] to accompany their funeral
processions, to visit their sick, and to greet them the first. I have
already been consulted by Ibn Mahdi and others in connection with
the appointment of Ibn Sawa as an inspector in al-Wasit [Iraq]. I
replied that this act was prohibited. Furthermore, I told him the anec-
dote about Umar b. al-Khattab, to whom Abu Musa al-Ash'ari had
submitted a record file that had just arrived from the provinces. He
was satisfied with it and asked who had written it. Umar was sitting in
the mosque and Abu Musa replied "That man at the door of the
mosque." Umar asked, "Why does he not enter; is he in a state of
impurity?" "No", came the reply, "he is a Christian". Umar flew into a
temper and cried, "Would you then draw near those whom Allah has
sent away? Have you confidence in those whom Allah has accused of
treachery? Would you raise up those whom Allah has cast down?" For
they [the *dhimmis*] cannot work in any of the countries of Islam.

Furthermore, in Baghdad they enjoy prestige and honor, the likes
of which they do not receive in any other country, so much so that

whatever increase in tax we would impose upon them, their fortune would never decrease. Among them there are doctors who have a considerable income for they frequent the homes of the nobles and are the acquaintances of the dignitaries, who, as is customary, pay them more handsomely than the official fee for their visits. What is more, these people do not refrain from donning elegant attire, amassing fortunes, and indulging in vulgar display on the occasion of their festivals, while debasing medicine [as a profession] which they exercise very badly; thus we see their youngsters, who, scarcely in possession of a few theories, change their garb, put on a large turban, and sit down on their benches, surrounded with instruments, on the public thoroughfare in order to establish a reputation and go the rounds of the houses. Others practice pharmacology. They use unjust weights and measures and reap great profits in this manner, at the cost of the Muslim merchants. Others are goldsmiths, substituting brass for the same weight of gold. When it is possible, they counterfeit silver and their moneychangers falsify the state currency. Moreover, they befriend Muslim men and women and lavish enormous sums of money on the gratification of their ends, which include lewdness, comfort, and the pleasures of the palate, whereas in former times they were obliged to show their inferiority by wearing distinctive signs [*ghiyar*] required by Islamic law.

Umar b. al-Khattab wrote to the governors of the provinces instructing them to oblige the *dhimmis* to shave their hair, to wear lead and iron seals around their necks, not to sit astride their saddles, to wear at the waist special belts that differentiated them from the Muslims.

And so it was in the time of the caliphs, but the last to have rigorously imposed these obligations was the Caliph al-Muqtadir bi-Amrallah,[1] who forced them to observe the laws that had been current in the time of al-Mutawakkil. He ordered them to hang bells about their necks and to put wooden effigies on their doors in order to distinguish them from Muslims houses. Their homes were not to be of the same height as those of Muslims. He obliged the Jews to wear a badge and a yellow turban, whereas Jewish women were to wear yellow veils and different-colored shoes, one white and the other black. They also had to wear iron necklaces around their necks when they entered the bath-houses. As for the Christians, they had to wear black or grey garments, a special belt around the waist, and a cross on their breast. They were not allowed to have a horse as a mount, but only a mule, or an ass without a pack or a saddle, which they were not allowed to ride astride, but on one side only. Although all this has

[1] Abbasid caliph, reigned in Baghdad 908–32.

been abandoned, no increase of tax has been enacted, whereas in most [Muslim] countries they are still forced to wear [distinctive] badges and are admitted to none but the most humiliating employments. Thus, for example, in Bukhara and Samarkand the *dhimmis* clean out the lavatories and sewers and carry away the rubbish and refuse. In the province of Aleppo, which is the closest to us, they are still bound to wear the badge. What is more, according to Islamic law, when the poll tax [*jizya*] is to be paid, the person who delivers the sum must be standing and he who receives it must be seated. The former places it in the other's hand so that the Muslim receives it in the palm of his hand, the Muslim's hand being above and that of the *dhimmi* below. The latter then stretches forth his beard and the Muslim strikes him on the cheek with the words: "Pay the dues of Allah, O enemy of Allah, O infidel." But today, it even happens that some of them no longer come in person before the officials, but send their messengers in their stead.

As for the Sabians, who are outright idol-worshipers, who live in the province of al-Wasit [Iraq], they are not *dhimmis*, although they were so in the past.[2] When the Caliph al-Qahir Billah inquired of Abu Sa'ad al-Istakhari the Shafi'i concerning their status, he declared their blood licit and refused their poll tax. When they had wind of this, they bribed him with 50,000 dinars and he left them alone. Consequently, today they do not even pay the poll tax and nought is demanded of them even though they be under Muslim domination. May the will of the sultan be done!

Ibn al-Fuwati (d. 1323)

[2] There is some discrepancy in Islamic law as to whether or not the Sabaeans were in possession of a Revealed Scripture and were therefore to be considered as *dhimmis*.

14. Dhimmis in the Maghreb and Egypt (1301)

In the month of Rajab al-fard in the year 700 [1301], the vizier of Gharb [in the Maghreb] came to Cairo on his way to the pilgrimage and he had a meeting with Sultan al-Malik an-Nasir Muhammad ibn Qal'un [reigned, 1294, 1299, and 1309–1341], his governor, the emir Sallar, and the emir Rukn ad-Din Baybar *al-Jashangir*, who offered him magnificent presents and received him with the greatest distinction. They discussed with him the status of the Christians and Jews in his country, where this class of people was maintained with constraints of humiliation and degradation. Thus they were not permitted to ride on horseback, nor to be employed in the public administration. Moreover, he voiced his disapproval of the fact that the *dhimmis* of

Egypt were attired in the most elegant clothes and that they rode on mules, mares, and expensive horses, and that they were considered worthy of being employed in the most important offices, thus gaining authority over the Muslims. He added that the pact of their protection *(dhimma)* had expired in the year 600 of the Hijrah [1203] and went on to cite a multitude of similar objections to the same effect.

These words impressed the state dignitaries and especially the emir Rukn ad-Din Baybars *al-Jashangir* and the other emirs. They unanimously declared that if similar conditions were to prevail in Egypt this would greatly enhance the [Muslim] religion. Consequently, they assembled the Christians and Jews on Thursday, 20 Rajab, and informed them that they would no longer be employed either in the public administration or in the service of the emirs. They were to change their turbans: blue ones for the Christians, who were moreover to wear a special belt *(zunnar)* about their waists; and yellow turbans for the Jews. Thus the Christians and Jews suffered in Cairo and Egypt a grievous return to the past. The leaders of both communities made vain attempts to have this decision repealed by approaching men of renowned piety, important people and the principle dignitaries, to whom considerable sums were even offered. But these offers were in no way accepted and on the contrary, stricter severity was shown in the execution of the decrees. The emir Rukn ad-Din Baybars *al-Jashangir* was held responsible for their enactment. The churches of Misr (old Cairo) and Cairo were closed and their portals were sealed after having been nailed up. By the twenty-second of Rajab all the Jews were wearing yellow turbans and the Christians blue ones; and if they rode on horseback, they were obliged to ride with one of their legs bent under them. Next, the *dhimmis* were dismissed from the public administration and the functions that they occupied in the service of the emirs. They were then prohibited to ride horses or mules. Consequently, many of them were converted to Islam, and, especially Amin al-Mulk *Mustawfi as-Suhba.*

The Sultan gave orders to send instructions to all the provinces recently added to his states and in which there were houses owned by Jews and Christians, in order that all those that were higher than the surrounding Muslim abodes should be demolished to their height. Furthermore all the *dhimmis* who owned a shop near that of a Muslim, should lower their *mastaba* [ground floor] so that those of the Muslims would be higher. Moreover, he recommended vigilance in the observance of the distinctive badges *(ghiyar)* in accordance with ancient custom.

The messenger *(al-barid)* who brought these orders arrived in Damascus on the first of Sha'aban and the following Monday, the seventh of the same month, the rules imposed *(shurut,* "conditions") upon the *dhimmis* of Damascus were read out in the presence of the sultan's *na'ib*, the emirs and qadis. The emirs agreed to dismiss the *dhimmis* from the posts they occupied, and the decrees whereby they were forbidden to ride either on a horse or saddled mount were published. Then on the 25th of the same month the edict of the viceroy was proclaimed in Damascus, whereby the *dhimmis* were enjoined to wear distinctive signs upon their heads: blue was the sign of the Christians, yellow that of the Jews, and red that of the inhabitants of Samaria [the Samaritans]. The order was enforced obligatorily and so it was that the following Sunday all the Jews had adopted the color assigned to them. Verily, it was a beautiful spectacle! The Christians and the Samaris [Samaritans] followed, give praise and glory to Allah!

Then began the work of destroying their churches, principally those of Cairo. For this occasion the *ulama,* jurisconsults and the *qadis* convened a council and it is even related that the *qadi* Ibn ar-Rafa'a, the *na'ib* (of the chief) of justice in Egypt, had already composed a *fatwa* permitting the churches to be demolished. However, after a lengthy deliberation and a heated discussion on the subject in the council of *ulama,* the *qadi al-qudat* [head of the judiciary officials in Egypt], Taqi ad-Din Ibn Daqiq al-'Id,[1] spoke up and produced a *fatwa* that stated that the churches were not to be touched unless it was proved that they had been built in recent times and that if this fact were to be established, then they were to be demolished. For my part [Ibn Naqqash], I esteem that this *fatwa* is to be counted among the errors committed by this *qadi al-qudat* (may Allah have mercy upon him). Besides, he is known for his lack of profundity in the sciences of traditions and in the knowledge of the procedures enacted during the Muslim conquests of infidel lands taken by force or surrender. For the rest, for understanding, explanation, and profound analysis of different expressions (of the Koran and the Sunna), the sheikh Taqi ad-Din was an ocean, whose depth, as the proverb says, could not be fathomed (18:482–90).

                                                          Ibn Naqqash (d. 1362)

[1] Taqi al-Din Ahmad Ibn Taymiyya (d. 1328), leading Hanbali jurist.

15. Synagogues and Churches

In the beginning of the fourteenth century, the dhimmi places of worship having been closed, the opinion of the jurist Ibn Taymiyya was sought on the subject.

What is your opinion (may Allah keep you in his grace) concerning the synagogues of Cairo and other places, which have been closed by order of the authorities, considering that the Jews and Christians protest that this is an injustice and request the reopening of these buildings, to which end they have demanded the intervention of the prince (may Allah guard, preserve, and protect him!)? Is it necessary to respond favorably to their request or not, for, according to them, these synagogues and churches are very old and date from the time of the prince of the believers, Umar b. al-Khattab and others? They ask that they may be left in the state in which they were at the time of Umar and the other caliphs and they claim that the closing of these synagogues is contrary to the provisions of the upright caliphs, the *"Khulafa ar-rashidin."*[1]

Ibn Taymiyya's reply:—With regard to their claim that the Muslims have committed an injustice by closing these *kana'is* [places of worship], this is a falsehood that is indeed in contradiction to the universal opinion of the Muslims. In fact, all the Muslims from the four schools of law, Hanifi, Maliki, Shafi'i, Hanbali, and the former imams, such as Sufyan ath-Thawri,[2] al-Awza'i,[3] al-Layith b. Sa'ad[4] and others, as well as the companions of the Prophet and their followers (may Allah bless them!) are unanimous in proclaiming that, had it been the imam's will to destroy all the synagogues and churches in the lands of the believers, for example in Egypt, in the Sudan, in the provinces of the Euphrates, in Syria, and other such countries, in accordance with the view of those who profess this opinion, it would not have been an injustice on his part and moreover one would be obliged to obey him. Whosoever opposed his efforts would have transgressed Allah's covenant and would have committed the most heinous sin. Furthermore, their claim that these synagogues and churches exist since the time of Umar b. al-Khattab and that "the upright caliphs" left them in their possession, is a further falsehood. Tradition has established that Cairo was founded some three hundred years after Umar b. al-Khattab, subsequent to Baghdad, Basra, Kufa, and Wasit. Moreover, the Muslims agree that it is forbidden for Jews and Christians to build synagogues and churches in the cities founded by the Muslims.

Even when the Muslim conquest was achieved through surrender and a peace treaty resulting in the Jews and Christians being allowed to retain their places of worship, nevertheless even then Umar laid down the condition that new ones were not to be erected in the conquered territories, and certainly not in the cities founded by Muslims. In the case of lands that had been conquered by force (the case of Mesopotamia and Egypt, where no surrender was offered to the Mus-

---

[1] The first caliphs of Islam: Abu Bakr, Umar, Uthman and Ali (632–61).

[2] Abu Abdallah Sufyan ath-Thawri (8th century), celebrated theologian and ascetic.

[3] Abu Amr al-Awza'i (8th century), main representative of the ascetic school of religious law.

[4] al-Layith b. Sa'ad (8th century). Famous theologian.

lims) and in which the Muslims have built cities, they are even em-
powered to remove the synagogues and churches already standing, so
that no more synagogues and churches would remain, unless authorization had been granted by a contract (pp. 9–10).

Ibn Taymiyya (d.1328), in M. Schreiner.

16. Places of Worship, Clothes, and Behavior of Dhimmis

Those who are of the opinion that to pray in a church or synagogue
is loathsome also say that they are places of infidelity and polytheism.
Indeed, their loathsomeness is greater than that of bathhouses,
cemeteries, or dunghills since they are places of Divine Wrath. Similarly, did not the Prophet prohibit prayer in the land of Babylon,
saying, "It is cursed," justifying the abstention from prayer therein on
account of this malediction? Verily, these churches are haunted by
malediction and Divine Wrath, displeasure descending on those that
congregate within them. As one of the Prophet's companions said,
"Avoid the Jews and Christians during their festivals, for wrath de-
scends upon them at that time." Moreover, are they not the houses of
the enemies of Allah, and Allah is not to be adored in the houses of
His enemies? (pp. 56–57).

They [the Christians] are prohibited to sound bells except noise-
lessly in the depths of their churches . . . for the sound of bells is the
banner of infidelity, as well as its outward sign. . . . Malik b. Anas said,
"When bells are sounded, the anger of the Compassionate is aroused,
whereupon angels descend to the four corners of the Earth and sing,
"Say He is One," until the anger of the Lord is appeased" (pp. 59–61).

The reason for their being sounded within the church is so that
they may eventually fall into disuse. For the bells are normally attached to the church steeple so that when rung they may be heard
from afar. If they are obliged to ring them within the church, then
none will hear them or pay heed to them and they will be abolished
altogether since they will serve no purpose. . . . Verily, Allah has
annulled the sounding of the Christian bell and the Jewish [ram's]
horn and has replaced them with the call of monotheism and devotion. He has raised the sound of the word *Islam* as a sign of the true
vocation so as to throw into obscurity the call of the infidel, and he has
replaced the bell with the [Muslim] call to prayer . . . just as He has
replaced the Satanic scriptures with the Koran (p. 62).

Distinctive Clothing

"Humiliation and derision are to be the lot of those that disobey my
word." The *dhimmis* are the most disobedient of His command and
contrary to His word; consequently it befits them to be humiliated by

distinguishing them from the comportment of the Muslims whom Allah has exalted through their obedience to Him and His Prophet above those that have disobeyed Him. These He has humiliated, belittled, and rendered abominable so that the sign of contempt is manifest upon them, so that they can be distinguished by their appearance. That a distinctive sign [*ghiyar*] must be imposed upon them is clear from the Prophet's statement, "He of the people who resembles them [the *dhimmis*] shall be deemed of their number.". . . It is obligatory to force the infidel to remain similar to his people so that the Muslims can detect him. For has not the Prophet said: "The rider shall greet the pedestrian, the pedestrian he who is seated, and the individual the assembly. . . . whereas it is forbidden to greet a Jew or Christian first. If one of them greets us [Muslims], then we reply, "and upon you."[1] If this is the custom of Islam then it is necessary to impose upon the *dhimmis* a special garb so that they can be recognized and Islamic custom be properly observed and a Muslim may know who has greeted him. Is he a Muslim who deserves to be greeted in peace or is he a *dhimmi* who is not deserving? . . . Moreover the distinctive dress serves other purposes. He [the Muslim] will thereby know that he is not to go to meet him, he is not to seat him among Muslim company, he is not to kiss his hand, he is not to stand up for him, he is not to address him with the terms *brother* or *master,* he is not to wish him success or honor as is customary toward a Muslim, he is not to give him Muslim charity, he is not to call him as a witness, either for accusation or defence, he is not to sell him a Muslim slave, and he is not to give him religious or legal books concerning Islam. Consequently, were it not for these prohibitions, then they would have treated him in a manner that is reserved for Muslims (p. 81).

The turban is the crown of the Arabs [*'arab*]. . . . Turbans are not the attire of the children of Israel, but that of the Arabs. Abu Qasim said, "It is forbidden for a *dhimmi* to don a turban, for he must have no honor in the land of Islam and therefore it is not his attire" (p. 84).

It is strictly forbidden to address a *dhimmi* as "sir" or "master," as it is stated in the *hadith:* "Do not call the unfaithful "sir," for if he is your "sir" then you have angered your "Lord." As for calling them, "Glory of the state," "Pillar of the state,"[2] etc., this is not allowed. If any one of them bears these titles, then a Muslim must not call him by them. If he be a Christian let him call him, "You, there, Christian," "You, there, O cross," and if he be a Jew, let him address him with the words, "You, there, Jew" (p. 115).

---

[1] I.e., without the word *Peace,* as a truncated reply to the customary greeting, "Peace upon you." Moreover, the *dhimmis* were accused of harboring malignant feelings toward the Muslims. Thus the formula "and upon you" would countervail any form of curse of which the *dhimmi* was suspected. See also below, docs. 20 (p. 204) and 35 (p. 237).
[2] Honorific titles given to distinguished officials.

"The *dhimmi* is bound to honor the Muslims in their assemblies, showing them respect and deference. He should not beguile them, nor must he enter their presence without their permission. He must not perform disrespectful or discourteous deeds in their presence. He must greet them as he would his fellows. He must not uncover his legs nor raise his voice in their presence (p. 118).

The neglect or substitution of these laws of Umar by others, even though accepted by the religious authorities, constitute a negligence on the part of him to whom Allah has commended the truth and a victory for the enemies of Allah. For, in allowing them to manifest their irreligion and to emerge from the status of inferiority, the religion of Allah, His Prophet, His Book, and the Muslims are thereby defamed . . . and the demonstrations that we have adduced confirm that *jihad* is obligatory until the word of Allah reigns supreme, and until all are of the religion of Allah [Islam], until the religion of Allah triumphs over all religions and until they pay the poll tax while in a state of inferiority (pp. 236–37).

Ibn Qayyim al-Jawziyya (thirteenth century)

17. Dismissal of Christian Officials in Egypt (1419)

The 7th of Jumada 1122 (1 June 1419), the sultan of Egypt (Mâlik Mu'ayyad Abu Nasr)[1] summoned the Christian Patriarch to appear before him in the presence of the Qadis and doctors of the Law. While remaining standing, he received reproaches and blows and was berated by the sultan on account of the humiliations to which the Muslims had been subjected by the prince of the Abyssinians; he was even threatened with death. Next the chief of the Cairo police, Shaykh Sadr ad-Din Ahmad b. al-Ajami, was summoned and reprimanded on account of the contempt of the Christians toward the laws relating to their [specific] costume and their outward attire. After a long discussion between the doctors of the Law and the sultan on this subject, it was decided that none of these infidels would be employed in government offices, nor by the emirs; neither would they escape the measures taken to maintain them in a state of humiliation. Thereupon the sultan summoned Al-Akram Fada'il, the Christian, the vizier's secretary, who had been imprisoned for several days; he was beaten, stripped of his clothes, and ignominiously paraded through the streets of Cairo in the company of the chief of police, who proclaimed "This is the reward for Christians employed in government offices!" After all this, he was thrown back into prison.

[1] al-Malik Sayfad-Din, Mamluk sultan of Egypt, of the Burji dynasty (1412–1421).

So thoroughly did the sultan carry out these measures, that nowhere in Egypt was a Christian to be found employed in the administration. These infidels, as well as the Jews, were obliged to remain at home, decrease the volume of their turbans, and shorten their sleeves. All were prevented from riding on donkeys, with the result that when the [common] people saw a mounted Christian, they attacked him and confiscated his donkey and all that he had. Consequently, none are to be found mounted on horseback, except outside of Cairo. The Christians made every effort to recover employment and offered great sums of money for this purpose; however, despite the support they had from the Coptic scribes, the sultan did not comply with their requests and refused to retract the prohibitions that he had decreed.

Whereupon I reflected: in view of this deed, Allah will perhaps pardon all the sins of Al-Malik al-Mu'ayyad! For, in acting thus, he effectively contributed greatly to Islam, since the employment of Christians in official functions is one of the greatest evils, which results in the exalting of their religion, since most Muslims need to frequent these officials in the course of their business. For every time they have some business that is dependant on an office run by such officials, they are obliged to behave humiliatingly and be polite to them, be they Christians, Jews, or Samaritans (pp. 115–16).

Thus the edict issued by this prince is tantamount to a second conquest of Egypt; in this manner was Islam exalted and infidelity humiliated, and nothing is more praiseworthy in the eyes of Allah (p. 117).

Ibn Taghribirdi (d.1469), *Nujum* (Bibl. Nat., Paris: Ms. Arabe 1783, fol. 159ff, in E. Fagnan, *Arabo-Judaica*.)

18. Contempt and Praise for Dhimmis

(Al-Maghili) (d.1504) showed an unbending stubbornness in upholding good and prohibiting evil. He thought that the Jews (may Allah curse them) no longer enjoyed the status of a protected minority *(dhimma);* this status was now abolished on account of their association with the Muslim ruling class. Such participation in governing is contrary to the degradation and scorn that accompany the payment of the *jizya*. It is enough that an individual (or a group) of them violate the status for it to be invalidated for all of them. (Our doctor) declared lawful the shedding of Jewish blood and the plundering of their belongings and he maintained that their repression was a more urgent duty than that of all other infidels. He wrote a book on the subject, consisting of several chapters that incurred the disagreement

of most of the jurists of his time, including shaykh Ibn Zakri[1] and
other (eminent personalities). A great discussion ensued. The work
arrived in Fez, the capital, where the jurists examined it at great
length. Some expressed their disdain, while others reacted equitably
(pp. 806–7).

Ibn Askar (d. 1578), *Dawhat an-nasir,* in G. Vajda, *Un traité*

Jewish Dietary Laws

If we were to discuss the mysteries of the dietary laws that Moses
established for them [the Jews] or to analyze their festivals and the
devotions that their prophet assigned to them and the great divine
mysteries therein, we fear that the ignorant will be misled and would
forsake our faith because of their ignorance of its mysteries. Therefore we will refrain from exposing the secrets of the devotion of the
people of the Book and discourse on that which is superior, that is, the
mysteries of the Islamic religion . . . for the religion of Muhammed is
the most perfect and his nation the most noble (p. 127).

al-Jili (fifteenth century)

Silence and Protection of dhimmis (16th century)

Observe with what modesty they (the *dhimmis*) conduct themselves
in the presence of the lowliest of people and you will see that their
manners are superior to and nobler than those of the majority of the
ulama. They are not offended if no one makes room for them when
they enter an assembly. If they are given water to drink that has been
fouled by the hands of children, slaves, or beggars, they remain composed and consider themselves, on the contrary, the meanest of men.
When they are permitted to join a gathering, they consider this a
favor. They seat themselves with their heads lowered, full of timidity,
asking Allah to conceal their iniquity from those present. Are these
not the real qualities of a scholar, for if knowledge does not increase
the humility of those who possess it, then it is baneful (p. 29).

ash-Sha'rani (d. 1565), *al-Bahr.*

We have taken the promise that none of our companions will harm
a *dhimmi*—certainly not a Muslim—especially if he recites his daily
prayers and is thus in the protection [*dhimma*] of Allah. For to harm

[1] Ahmad b. Zakri, Muslim jurist (d. 1500).

one who has said his daily prayers is, as it were, to despise the protection of Allah, heaven forbid. Beware not to inflict any harm upon him. If, however, he is first harmful to you, we may say that he who attacks you is to be met in the same manner, but it is better to be patient for the sake of Him who protects him. If a prince were to inform you that a particular individual was in his protection for a certain time would you not only refrain from harming him but also honor him? Thus is a servant of Allah to be treated (fol.70a).

ash-Sha'rani, *al-Bahr,* (Cambridge Univ. Lib. Arabic Ms. 1000)

19. The Manner of Collecting the Jizya

On the day of payment they shall be assembled in a public place like the *suq.* They should be standing there waiting in the lowest and dirtiest place. The acting officials representing the Law shall be placed above them and shall adopt a threatening attitude so that it seems to them, as well as to the others, that our object is to degrade them by pretending to take their possessions. They will realize that we are doing them a favor (again) in accepting from them the *jizya* and letting them (thus) go free. Then they shall be dragged one by one (to the official responsible) for the exacting of payment. When paying, the *dhimmi* will receive a blow and will be thrust aside so that he will think that he has escaped the sword through this (insult). This is the way that the friends of the Lord, of the first and last generations will act toward their infidel enemies, for might belongs to Allah, to His Prophet, and to the Believers (p. 811).

al-Maghili (d. 1504), *Ahkam ahl al-Dhimma,* in G. Vajda, *Un Traité*

On an appointed day the *Dhimmi*—Christian or Jew—must present himself in person, and not through the intermediary of an agent *(wakil),* before the emir responsible for the collection of the *jizya.* The latter must be seated on a chair raised in the form of a throne; the *dhimmi* will come forward bearing the *jizya* held in the middle of the palm of his hand, whence the emir will take it in such a way that his hand is above and the *dhimmi's* hand underneath. Following this, the emir will strike the *dhimmi* on the neck with his fist; a man will stand near the emir to chase away the *dhimmi* in haste; then a second [*dhimmi*] and a third will come forward to suffer the same treatment as well as all those to follow. All [Muslims] will be admitted to enjoy this spectacle. None [of the *dhimmis*] will be allowed to delegate a third party to pay the *jizya* in his stead, for they must suffer this degradation personally; for perchance they will eventually come to believe in Allah and his Prophet and be consequently delivered from this distasteful yoke (19:107–8).

al-Adawi

20. Traditions and Attitudes toward Dhimmis (18th century)

As Badr[1] says in *al-Durar al-Nafā'is,* quoting from Abū 'Ubayd:[2] The foundation of Muslim cities varies according to local conditions. Thus, for example, in Madina, Tā'if, Yaman, peace treaties were negotiated; uninhabited area[s] demarcated and settled by Muslims, such as Cairo, Kūfa, Basra, Baghdad, Wāsit; any village that was taken by force and that the caliph did not see fit to return to those from whom it had been taken. These are Muslim cities in which the protected people may not display any of their religious symbols, for example, erect churches, bring out wine or pork, or sound the clapper. No new synagogue, church, monk's cell, prayer assembly of theirs is allowed in these cities, by the consensus of the doctors. It has been mentioned above that our city, Cairo, is an Islamic town, started after the conquest of Egypt, under the reign of the Fatimids. Therefore, no church, synagogue, and the rest, may be erected in it. Among those who affirmed this was the mufti of Islam, the erudite Hanafi, Shaykh Qāsim b. Qutlūbughā[3] disciple of Ibn al-Humām.[4] The books of the school are unanimous in their prohibition of the erection of *dhimmi-*owned churches and the like in any Islamic territory. How then can it be permitted in this Islamic settlement, in a city over which unbelief has never had a hand, not since the city's inception? The Prophet, peace and blessing upon him, said: No emasculation and no church in Islam. The word "emasculation", *khisā,* follows the pattern *fi'āl,* as the verbal noun of *khsy,* "to emasculate." The relation between "emasculation" and "church" is that the erection of a church in Muslim territory denotes the elimination of manliness in the people of the territory, just as emasculation, in reality, is the elimination of virility in an animal, though the sense of the word in our context is withdrawal from women by attachment to churches. The connection is evident. By "no church" the Prophet meant no construction thereof, a prohibition, that is, that no church be built in Islamic territory because the

[1] Badr ad-Din Muhammad al-Qarafi (1533–1601), author of the work of jurisprudence, *ad-Durar an-Nafa'is.*
[2] al-Qasim Abu Ubayd (d. 838), scholar established in Iraq.
[3] Qasim b. Qutlubugha (1399–1474), leading Egyptian Hanafi scholar.
[4] Kamal ad-Din Muhammad Ibn al-Humam (d. 1457), Egyptian jurist.

erection of a new church in Islamic territory signifies the elimination of virility in the people of that territory, which is not permissible, even as the elimination of man's virility by castration is not (pp. 20–21).

Even though some data may be understood from the above, know that just as the *dhimmis* are prohibited from building churches, other things also are prohibited to them. They must not assist an unbeliever against a Muslim, Arab, or non-Arab; or indicate to the enemy the weak points of the Muslims, such as the Muslims' unpreparedness for battle. The *dhimmis* must not imitate the Muslims in garb, wear military attire, abuse or strike a Muslim, raise the cross in an Islamic assemblage; let pigs get out of their homes into Muslim courtyards; display banners on their own holidays; bear arms on their holidays, or carry them at all, or keep them in their homes. Should they do anything of the sort, they must be punished, and the arms seized. Neither Jew nor Christian should ride a horse, with or without saddle. They may ride asses with a packsaddle. They must not wear the *qabā* (full-sleeved garment), silk garments, turbans, but may wear quilted *qalan-suwa* [conical bonnet] headgear. If they pass by a Muslim assembly, they must dismount, and they may ride only in an emergency such as sickness or leaving for the country, and their path is to be made narrow. They must not imitate the garb of the men of learning and honor, or wear luxurious garb, silk, or, say, fine cloth. They must be distinguished from ourselves in attire, as the local custom of each area may have it, but without adornment, so that it indicates their humiliation, submission, and abasement. Their shoelaces must not be like ours. Where closed shoes are worn, not laced footwear, their shoes should be coarse, of unpleasant (unadorned) color. The Companions [of the Prophet] agreed upon these points in order to demonstrate the abasement of the infidel and to protect the weak believer's faith. For if he sees them humbled, he will not be inclined toward their belief, which is not true if he sees them in power, pride, or luxury garb, as all this urges him to esteem them and incline toward them, in view of his own distress and poverty. Yet esteem for the unbeliever is unbelief.

In *al-Ashbāh wa-l-nazā'ir*[5], it says:

> Deference for the unbeliever is unbelief. He who greets a *dhimmi* with deference is guilty of unbelief. He who says to a Magian "O, Master" in deference, is guilty of unbelief. That is so because they are the enemies of our beloved, the Lord of the Messengers; and he who honors the enemy of his beloved has humiliated his beloved. That is why it is not permissible to install infidels as officials. To let

[5] A title of several volumes on "the systematic structure of positive law." The work referred to is perhaps that of Ibn Nujaym (d. 1562) who was the Hanafi author of books of this type.

them gain sway over a Muslim by empowering them to beat, imprison, or oppress him in order to exact money turns the infidel into [a] tax collector from a Muslim, all on behalf of a chieftain or dignitary who, for the sake of worldly affairs and in disregard of punishment in the hereafter, fears not the consequences of endowing unbelievers with power over believers. If the infidel has behaved this way, he has violated the covenant [*dhimma*] with the Muslims as mentioned above, and is subject to death.

Kamāl b. al-Humām [d. 1457] says: "The *dhimmi* infidel who raises himself above the Muslims so as to become overbearing may be slain by the caliph."

It is prohibited to assign them a seat of honor in a session attended by Muslims, to show friendship for them, to extend greetings to them.

If you greeted one whom you considered a Muslim, only to learn he was a *dhimmi*, withdraw your word, pretending "he answered my salutations." If one of them salutes he is answered with "Same to you" only.[6] If you correspond with one, you say: "Salutation to him who follows right guidance." But avoid congratulating, consoling, or visiting them, unless you expect the person visited to convert to Islam. If you do expect so, visit him and proffer Islam to him.

Infidels are prohibited from raising a structure higher than that of a Muslim neighbor, even if the Muslim's structure is very low and the Muslim is reconciled to the infidel's high building. They are forbidden to buy a Koran, or a book of Islamic law or of prophetic tradition, or to take one as a pledge. Neither would be correct. One should not rise in their honor to start saluting them, as mentioned above. If a Muslim accompanies the greeted infidel, direct the salutation at him, and do not indulge in "How are you, how have you been, how do you feel?" One may say "May God honor and guide you," meaning toward Islam. One may say "May God give you long life, much wealth and progeny," because it implies the payment of many poll taxes.

Just as Muslims must be clearly different from infidels in life, so their graves must be clearly distinguished from those of the infidels, and must be remote from them (pp. 55–57).

                                        Shaykh al-Damanhuri (d. 1778)

---

[6]See above, doc. 16, p. 197, n. 1.

II
Aspects of the Dhimmis' Existence
As observed

ORIENT

21. Baghdad

A Description by Obadyah the Norman Proselyte (Johannes), Born in Oppido, Southern Italy, a Priest Converted to Judaism (1102).

The servant installed Obadyah, the Proselyte, in a house used by the Jews for prayers, and food was brought to him. Afterwards, Isaac, the head of the Academy, arranged that Johannes [Obadyah] should join the orphaned boys in order to be taught the law of Moses and the words of the prophets in the divine characters and the tongue of the Hebrews.

Before these events [in 1091], the Caliph of Baghdad, of the name of al-Muqtadi [1075–1094], had given power to his vizier, Abu Shuja, to introduce a change of policy in regard to the Jews of Baghdad and he had tried several times to destroy them. But the God of Israel had thwarted his intention (and) on this occasion also He hid them from his wrath. He (Abu Shuja)[1] imposed that each male Jew should wear a yellow badge on his headgear. This was one distinctive sign on the head and the other was on the neck—a piece of lead of the weight (size?) of a silver dinar (?) hanging round the neck of every Jew and inscribed with the word *dhimmi* to signify that the Jew had to pay poll-tax. Jews also had to wear girdles round their waists. Abu Shuja further imposed two signs upon Jewish women. They had to wear a black and a red shoe, and each woman had to have a small brass bell on her neck or shoe, which would tinkle and thus announce the separation of Jewish from Gentile [Muslim] women. He assigned cruel Muslim men to spy upon Jewish men and cruel Muslim women to spy upon Jewish women, in order to oppress them with all kinds of

[1] The Caliph al-Muqtadi's deputy. On him, see S. D. Goitein, in *JQR*, n.s. 43 (1952–53):63–64.

curses, humiliation and spite. The Gentile population used to mock at
the Jews, and the mob and their children used to beat up the Jews in
all the streets of Baghdad.

The law of the poll-tax, collected yearly by the Caliph's official from
the Jews, was as follows: Every Jew belonging to the wealthy class had
to pay four and a half dinars in gold; a Jew of the middle class two and
a half; and a Jew of the poorest a dinar and a half. When a Jew died,
who had not paid up the poll-tax to the full and was in debt for a small
or large amount, the Gentiles did not permit burial until the debt of
the poll-tax was paid. If the deceased left nothing of value, the Gentiles demanded that other Jews should with their own money meet the
debt owed by the deceased in poll-tax; otherwise (they threatened),
they would burn the body (p. 37).

Obadya (early 12th century), in A. Scheiber, *JJS*

22. A Courageous Copt in Twelfth-Century Egypt

*During the reign of Al-Amir bi-Ahkam Illah (1101–1130) in Egypt, a Copt
was admitted to public office and was very influential in affairs of state. The
Muslims took offence and one of their foremost writers criticized the conduct of
the Copt (Abu'l-Fadl?), known as "the monk".*

It was in the presence of several Egyptian [Muslim] writers, together with some Copts assembled in his diwan [reception room] that
he thus spoke to him; but the monk replied with the following words,
making himself heard by all present: "We are the masters of this
country, both from the point of view of population as well as for the
land tax. The Muslims took it from us, they appropriated it by force
and violence, and it is from our hands that they seized power. All that
we have been able to do against the Muslims is compensation for that
which we have suffered at their hands; moreover, a comparison can
never be made between today's events and the massacre that they
wrought on our kings and our ruling families during their conquest.
Furthermore, all the money that we conceal from their kings and
caliphs belongs to us legitimately, for it is only a fraction of what
righfully belongs to us. When we make a payment to them, it is a favor
from us for which they ought to be grateful."

Whereupon he recited the following poem:

They have seized a noble maiden from the arms of her mother;
they outraged her and trampled her beneath their feet;
Then they changed their minds and restored power to her,

and one knows what an enemy—to whose law one is subjected—is capable.

All those present, or rather the Christians and evildoers, applauded and asked the monk to repeat these verses, to which they listened with the utmost attention. . . .

At last the caliph awoke from his torpor and came out of his intoxication. The fervor of faith and the zeal of religion took hold of him and he broke into a holy rage, firmly decided to bring relief to Islam and uphold the true believers. He commanded the *dhimmis* to wear distinctive signs ("a differentiating garb"; a piece of cloth sewn onto the garment as a distinctive mark); he made them sink back to the rank of humiliation and lowliness to which Allah had assigned them. He prohibited their being offered any [government] employment and he ordered that an ordinance be proclaimed [to this effect], which everyone, young and old, had to read (18:460–63).

Ibn Naqqash (d. 1362)

23. The Copt's Testimony Refused

In the days of the Sultan al-Malik as-Salih Najm al-Din Ayyub [1240–1249], a Moslem went into the Suk al-Tujjar in Cairo. He had with him a title-deed to some money owing to him by a soldier. The document was all finished, and needed only the necessary signatures of the witnesses. The man came across two Christians. They were clothed in bodices and in garments that had wide sleeves, just as Moslems of the noble class are dressed. The Moslem really thought that they were nobles. He spread the document out before them and they signed it—their very act being a jeer at the Moslems. This fact was brought to the attention of the Sultan al-Malik al-Salih; and he gave orders that those Christians should receive a beating, that they should be forced to wear girdles and to put on the distinctive mark that they were not Moslems; that they should be prevented from making themselves look like Moslems, and that they should take the proper low and humble station to which Allah had degraded them (pp. 439–40).

Ghazi b. al-Wasiti (alive, 1292), in R. Gottheil: *An Answer.*

24. Conversion of Christians (Egypt)

Had I the power, or could I rely upon sufficient strength, I would relate particulars of many circumstances connected with the scribes of the Christians, and how many of them would have proclaimed Islam openly, had they not been afraid of being killed or punished—even giving their very names. I could recount the story of every one of them taken in by his own artifice, or by his own evil conduct counted among the trespassers—doing wrong, straying from the right path, a big fool, a bastard and one despised. I could disclose the state of every one who professed Islam (merely) with some trick in mind. I could explain the condition in which he was, due to those who were haughty in their ravings—by their lies condemning every learned Moslem as faulty, so that calamities came upon him like the falling of arrows— always going further in his treachery and robbery and increasing in his greed. In reality, his profession of Islam was only a blind. He was using it as a ladder to reach the height at which he was aiming—more devilish than the devil, the very elixir of lying and fraud. He would take an oath on the faith of Islam—which constituted an untruth. Out of clean cloth he would fashion that which never had occurred, by means of falsehood and misstatement. He had been amongst the lowest of the low among the Christians, the biggest liar, the one who possessed least shame and truthfulness, the greatest in impudence, with an inborn disposition to do things disgraceful and vicious. By such means he was able ostensibly to free himself from the lower position accorded the Christians, the ignominy of paying the head-tax, and to prevent himself from falling into despite [*sic*]. Openly, he would converse just like a Moslem—in order to preserve his fortune and his person, and that he might have an opportunity to cheat and to despoil. In fact, publicly he was a Moslem; but as soon as he entered his house he found his wife, his sons, his daughters, his relations and the relations of all his people Christian—and he was a Christian with them in very truth, fasting during their fasts, and breaking the fast at the same time they did. Had anyone taken the trouble to observe him, they would have found that he had led the life of a Christian for more than twenty-five years. Now, his appointment had lasted only for five; and during these years his fees could not have amounted to more than two-hundred dinars for all this time. Yet, you would have found his possessions and his manner of living to be such as to require thousands of dinars; not to mention the brocade, the dyed-goods, the precious stones that he had—the servants, the slaves, the marked horses, the flocks, the buffaloes, and the merchandise that had come over land and sea. On the other hand, imagine the condition of the greatest and most loyal Moslems, who have done service to kings and to sultans during the last fifty years—functionaries with high pay and of distinction—how they turned their pay and the moneys they expended into expressions of loyalty; each one of them spending the money received in his office in the interests of the Sultanate and in

increasing its splendor by means of horsemen and young men and by
his own fine experience. If ever these inherited anything, they spent
it. Indeed, at the end of their life they were in debt and poor, because
of the strength of mind they had shown and their fidelity (to the
ruling house) (pp. 444–45).

Ghazi b. al-Wasiti (alive, 1292) in R. Gottheil, *An Answer.*

25. A Jewish Vizier in Baghdad (1290)

In the days of the Sultan al-Malik at-Thahir, a lot of sincere Moslems from the country of the Tartars told him that al-Makin ibn al-
'Amid, the Secretary of War, was corresponding with Hulagu in
reference to the Egyptian army, its men and its commanders. Al-
Malik al-Thahir had him seized, with the intention of having him put
to death. His condition was much worse than that of those who were
governed by Christian Emirs—he was confined in prison for more
than eleven years. Then, through payments of money, his release was
effected. In order to put through this release, it was considered
proper by Moslems to seize the property of Christians, their wives and
their very lives. In the end, not a single Christian and not a single Jew
remained in the land. Now, Sa'id al-Daulah,[1] Chief Minister in Baghdad and Mesopotamia, was busy doing whatever injury he could to
the Moslems and elevating the status of the Jews. Then (Sa'id) struck
at Arghun and plotted against him with someone who gave him
poison,[2] after he had impounded the wealth of Islam, raised the condition of the Jews, and brought Islam into despite. Indeed, these two
cursed religions were always on the lookout for an occasion to arise in
which—Allah forbid!—they could do some injury to Islam by picking
a quarrel.

Now, when a knowledge of that which I have related had become
common property, I suggested to the high government to seize the
wealth of those dogs which they had stolen from the treasury of the
Moslems, and through which they had been able to establish busi-

[1] Sa'id (or Sa'd) al-Daulah was a Jewish physician who, in 1289, became vizier of the
pagan Mongol emperor Arghun (1284–1291). The nomination of a Jewish vizier
humiliated the Muslims and aroused hatred and fanaticism. The murder of Sa'd al-
Daulah unleashed a collective massacre and pillage of the Jews in the whole of Persia
and Iraq. See W. J. Fischel, *Jews in the Economic and Political Life of Mediaeval Islam,*
p. 117.

[2] This accusation was a classical one made against Jewish and Christian physicians.
See Moshe Perlmann, "Notes on the position of Jewish Physicians in Mediaeval Muslim
Countries," in *IOS* 2 (1972): 315–19. In this case it is particularly absurd, since Sa'ad al-
Daulah's life depended on Arghun's recovery. The vizier was killed on March 5, 1291,
before the death of Arghun.

nesses and to have dealings with merchants on land and on sea, in
Syria and in Egypt. Our master the Sultan became thoroughly informed of the audacity of these cursed peoples, who bought the captives of Tripoli—royal princes, rich women and Christian notables—
as well as of the hurt and the affliction that was being wrought by
them upon the Moslems, in their various provinces and to the very
limit of their power (pp. 450–51).

Muslim Censorship of the Dhimmis

Up to the end of the Nasirite dynasty, it was the custom of the Kings
of Syria and of their Sultans not to permit the Diwan known as the
Diwan al-Istifa[3] to be without Moslems, some of the most prominent
headmen belonging to the leading families who were renowned for
their good faith and for their activity. In such manner, no Jew or
Christian was alone in laying down the law in any matter relating to
Syria [-Palestine]. He was unable to speak or write (officially) about an
event that had happened, except after the truth had been established
by a Moslem. So, the Jew or the Christian would prepare the account;
and the prominent (Moslem) would countersign the reliability of the
document. Then, in the shortest possible time the Moslems turned
their attention to accustoming their children to uncovering the lies of
these vile and ignorant people, and, by their sagacity, to perfecting
themselves to a great degree and to excelling in unearthing the guile
(of others), as they already excelled in the religious sciences. Along
this line they composed thousands of works, wherein they developed
points of view which neither Jew or Christian could reach. They were
able to deal with the contents of the Moslem treasury as dictated by
the Moslem Scriptures and the traditions of Allah's prophet.

In this manner the contents of the treasury increased—through the
blessings (of Allah) and the equity (of the treasury's governors). All
noxious prejudices were rooted out, and all avenues of injustice
closed. Their guide-posts were battered down; their disgraceful and
shameful traces were extinguished. Our Master, the Sultan al-Malik
al-Ashraf Salah al-Din, (in doing all this) acted according to the traditions of the Prophet, and did exactly as did the righteous Caliphs and
the just Sultans. Verily, Malik[4] writes in his *Kitab al-Mudawwanah al-
Kubra,* that the Commander of the Faithful, 'Umar ibn al-Khattab
said: "There must not be chosen, either from among the Jews or the
Christians, diviners or money-brokers; they must be removed from
our market-places; Allah has made them unnecessary for the Moslems."

[3] General Treasury.
[4] The jurist, Malik b. Anas. This work is actually by his pupil, Sahnun.

Now, if this is so in questions of (ordinary) buying and selling, which are matters to which no importance and no (ethical) value can be attached, how much the more should it be the rule when the question of leadership in an affair is at stake. The Jews hold that interest may be taken from those who are not of their religion; for, according to their principles, the collection of fortunes is permitted. Now, then, can anyone who holds it is permissible to gain money out of Moslems be put in a superior position—either in argument or in law? Intelligent men have said: "What a wonder it is to see a believer take as a servant an unbeliever who differs from him in opinion, who is opposed to him in faith and belief!" They also have said: "What a wonder it is to see someone put aside a believing, intelligent friend and be contented with a foolish, unbelieving enemy!" Still another has said: "In a Moslem are to be found four qualities which you will not find in anyone else—excellent self-restraint in regard to women, plenitude of equity, consideration for people of (other) faiths, and liberality in advice to Moslems. In a Polytheist are also to be found four qualities— want of faith, abundance of perfidy, willingness to deceive Moslems, keeping at a distance people with faith" (pp. 456–57).

Ghazi b. al-Wasiti (alive, 1292) in R. Gottheil: *An Answer.*

26. Copts Claim Egypt as their Land (14th century)

Strangely enough, no country, either in the East or West, will recognize the appointment of *dimmis* in the management of the affairs of Muslims, Egypt being the only exception. By God, how strange! What is wrong with this country, of all Muslim lands? Is it not the greatest Muslim country, the richest in population and knowledge? Now the employment of unbelievers brings great evils and appalling conditions, such as one would not wish for his enemy, much less should Muslims wish them to come upon the community of Muhammad. The Copts declare that this country still belongs to them, and that the Muslims evicted them from it unlawfully. Then they often steal as much as they can from the state treasury, in the belief that they are not doing wrong. As to the possibility of confiscation and punishment, torture, they hold that the chances of these happening to them are about equal to that of falling sick; that is to say, sickness does sometimes come upon a man, but is not likely to be frequent.

They will deposit those funds in churches and monasteries, and other such institutions of the unbelievers; for they hold that so long as they, the Copts, are successful they are more entitled to these funds than are the Muslims. When they are put to torture they urge one another to bear the agony with fortitude, and display steadfastness. When they are compelled to pay they bring to light the smallest possible sum, hand over a portion of it, and pay some of it away in bribes until they are set free. Now, is it right to put in charge of public affairs people with such beliefs and capable of such acts? Moreover, they will appropriate much of the property of the Muslims, the land which is a source of income to the Sultan, or the fiefs of the emirs and the troops, as well as many of the endowments for poor Muslims, e.g., the town of Nestru, and others, taking it for themselves, their churches, and monasteries despite its being forbidden to transfer anything of that kind into their own hands. Whosoever, being able to do so, refrains from interfering, thus allowing them to continue to steal and to retain all that is in their power, he is responsible for it in this world, and will have to render account for it on the day of resurrection (pp. 846–47).

al-Asnawi (d. 1370) in M. Perlmann, *Notes on Anti-Christian Propaganda.*

27. Account of a Danish Traveler (1761)

In Cairo

In Cairo no Christian or Jew may appear on horseback. They ride only asses, and must alight, upon meeting even the most inconsiderable Egyptian lord. Those lords appear always on horseback, with an insolent servant before them who, with a great staff in his hand, warns the riders on asses to shew the due marks of respect to his master, crying out *ensil* [*sic;* i.e., *enzil*], get down. If the infidel fail to give instant obedience, he is beaten till he alight. A French merchant was drubbed on an occasion of this kind. Our physician, too, was insulted for being too tardy in alighting from his ass. For this reason, no European dares walk the streets without having a person to attend him who knows all those lords, and can give him notice when they approach. At first, when I went about in Cairo, I made my janissary go before, and my servant follow, both mounted on asses as well as myself. But, after having the mortification to see these two Mussulmans remain upon their beasts, while I was obliged to alight, I determined to walk on foot.

It is true, that in Egypt, these distinctions between the Mahometans and persons of other religions, are carried a greater length, than any where else through the East. Christians and Jews must alight even before the house of the chief Cadi; before more than a score of other houses in which the magistrates distribute justice; before the gate of the janissaries; and before several mosques in high veneration for their sanctity; or by the quarter *El-Karafe*, in which are a great many tombs and houses of prayer; they are obliged to turn out of their way, to avoid these places, as even the ground on which they stand, is so sacred in the eyes of the people, that they will not suffer it to be profaned by the feet of infidels (1:81–82).

The dress of the Christians in the East is nearly the same as that of the Turks. Only they are prohibited the use of bright-coloured stuffs. They may not wear boots of yellow leather. And they must use dark colours in painting their houses. European Christians are allowed to wear yellow leather, and clothes of any colour, except green, which, rather by custom than by law, is reserved for the peculiar use of Mussulmans (1:113–14).

In Yemen

I know not whether the Christians of the East have ever settled at Mokha. A good many Jews live here, in a separate village, as in the other cities of Yemen (1:400).

It will not be amiss to add one slight observation concerning the brokers of different nations. A stranger cannot be too much on his guard against Mahometan brokers. He will find his account in addressing himself rather to the Banians [Indians], among whom are many considerable merchants, very honest men. Through all the countries in the East, Mahometan merchants have the knavery to seek to irritate the Christians, when, after having duped them, they fear their resentment: And then, when any term of reproach is uttered by the strangers in the heat of passion, the rascally Mussulmans make a great noise, under pretence that their religion is abused, and threaten to complain to the magistrates. Several Europeans have been obliged to pay considerable sums by these arts of knaves who have previously cheated them (1:408).

These Jews of Arabia resemble those of Poland; only they have a more decent and less beggarly aspect. They dare not wear the turban, but are obliged to content themselves with a small bonnet. Neither are they suffered to dress in any colour but blue; all their clothes are of blue cloth. They are also forbidden the use of the *Jambea* [dagger] (2:239).

Linguistic Discrimination

Although the Arabian conquerors have introduced and established their language in the countries which they conquered, yet their subjects have not always left off the use of their mother tongue. In Syria and Palestine, indeed, no language is to be heard but the Arabic; and yet the Syriac is not absolutely a dead language, but is still spoken in several villages in the Pachalick of Damascus. In many places, in the neighbourhood of Merdin and Mosul, the Christians still speak the Chaldean language; and the inhabitants of the villages who do not frequent towns, never hear any other than their mother tongue. The Christians born in the cities of Merden and Mosul, although they speak Arabic; write in the Chaldean characters, just as the Maronites write their Arabic in Syriac letters, and the Greeks the Turkish in Greek letters.

Many people living under the dominion of the Arabians and Turks have lost the use of their mother tongue. The Greeks and Armenians settled in Egypt and Syria speak Arabic, and the services of their public worship are performed in two languages at once. In Natolia, these nations speak their own languages in several different dialects. The Turkish officers sometimes extend their despotism to the language of their subjects. A Pacha of *Kaysar,* who could not endure to hear the Greek language spoken, forbade the Greeks in his Pachalic[k], under pain of death, to use any language but the Turkish. Since that prohibition was issued, the Christians of *Kaysar* and *Angora* have continued to speak the Turkish, and at present do not even understand their original language.

The *Kurdes,* who are nearly independent, have preserved their ancient language, of which there are in *Kurdistan* three principal dialects. I was informed that the *Sabaeans,* who are commonly called Christians of St. John, still speak and write their ancient language. The most learned of the few of this sect, who are settled in Basra, was a farrier; him I prevailed with to write me out the characters of his language; but he wrote them so indistinctly, that I could form no idea of his alphabet (2:256–57).

*K. Niebuhr

*Karsten Niebuhr, one of five scientists sent in 1761 at their's sovereign's expense as explorers to Egypt and Arabia. He reached Bombay in 1763, the sole survivor of the group and later became captain of engineers to the King of Denmark.

28. Christians in Syria-Palestine (18th century)

Faithful to the spirit of the Koran, it [the government] treats the Christians with a severity which displays itself in varied forms. Mention has been sometimes made of the toleration of the Turks; the following is the price at which it is purchased:

All kind of public worship is prohibited the Christians, except in the

Kesraouan, where the government has not been able to prevent it. They cannot build any new churches; and if the old ones fall to decay, they are not allowed to repair them, unless by a permission which costs them very dear. A Christian cannot strike a Mahometan without risk of his life, but if a Mahometan kill a Christian, he escapes for a stipulated price. Christians must not mount on horseback in the towns; they are prohibited the use of yellow slippers, white shawls, and every sort of green colour. Red for the feet, and blue for the dress, are the colours assigned them. The Porte has just renewed its ordinances to re-establish the ancient form of their turbans; they must be of a coarse blue muslin, with a single white border. When they travel, they are perpetually stopped at different places to pay *Rafars* [i.e., *ghafar*], or tolls, from which the Mahometans are exempt: in judicial proceedings, the oath of two Christians is only reckoned for one; and such is the partiality of the Cadis, that it is almost impossible for a Christian to gain a suit; in short, they alone are subject to the Capitation, called *Karadji*, the ticket of which bears these remarkable words: *Djazz-el-ras*, that is (redemption) *from cutting off the head*—a clear proof of the title by which they are tolerated and governed.

These distinctions, so proper to ferment hatred and divisions, are disseminated among the people, and manifest themselves in all the intercourse of life. The meanest Mahometan will neither accept from a Christian, nor return the salute of *Salam-alai-k*, health to thee, on account of the affinity between the word *Salam* and *Eslam* (Islamism),[1] the proper name of their religion, and *Moslem*, (Mussulman) the name of the person who professes it: the usual salutation is only good morning, or good evening, and it is well too, if it be not accompanied with a *Djaour*, *Kafer*, *Kelb*, i.e. impious, infidel, dog, expressions to which the Christians are familiarized (2 : 398–400).

Rivalries between Communities

Jerusalem has from time to time had Governors of its own, with the title of Pachas; but it is in general, as at this day, a dependency of Damascus, from which is receives a *Motsallam*, or deputy Governor. This Motsallam farms it and receives the revenues arising from the Miri, the Customs, and especially from the follies of the Christian inhabitants. To conceive the nature of this last article, it must be understood, that the different communions of schismatic, and catholic Greeks; Armenians, Copts, Abyssinians and Franks, mutually envying each other the possession of the holy places, are continually endeavoring to outbid one another in the price they offer for them to

[1] The observation is correct, but not the motive. Cf. above, doc. 16, p. 197.

the Turkish Governors. They are constantly aiming to obtain some privilege for themselves, or to take it from their rivals: And each sect is perpetually informing against the other for irregularities. Has a church been clandestinely repaired; or a procession extended beyond the usual limits: has a Pilgrim entered by a different gate from that customary: all these are subjects of accusation to the Government, which never fails to profit by them, by fines and extortions. Hence those hatreds, and that eternal jangling, which prevail between the different convents; and the adherents of each communion. The Turks, to whom every dispute produces money, are, as we may imagine, far from wishing to put an end to them. They all, in whatever station, derive some advanatage from these quarrels: some sell their protection, others their interest. Hence a spirit of intrigue and cabal, which has diffused venality through every class; and hence perquisites for the Motsallam, which annually amount to upwards of one hundred thousand piasters. Every pilgrim pays him an entrance fee of ten piasters, and another for an escort for the journey to the Jordan, without reckoning the fines imposed in consequence of the imprudencies committed by these strangers during their stay. Each convent pays him so much for the privilege of processions, and so much for all repairs they undertake, besides presents on the accession of a new superior, or a new Motsallam; not to speak of private gratifications to obtain secret trifles they solicit: all which is carried to a great length among the Turks, who are as well versed in the art of squeezing money as the most able law practitioners in Europe. Besides all this, the Motsallam collects duties on the exportation of certain singular commodities from Jerusalem; I mean *beads, relics, sanctuaries, crosses, passions, agnus-dei's, scapularies, &c.* of which near three hundred chests are sent off annually (2:304–7).

The European Merchants of Cairo in 1785

[The protected merchants are] shut up in a confined place, they live among themselves, with scarcely any external communication; they even dread it, and go as little out as possible, to avoid the insults of the common people, who hate the very name of the Franks, and the insolence of the Mamlouks, who force them to dismount from their asses in the middle of the streets. In this kind of habitual imprisonment, they tremble every instant, lest the plague should oblige them entirely to shut themselves up in their houses, or some revolt expose their quarter to be plundered; lest the chief of some party should make a pecuniary demand (They have observed, that these extortions amount, annually, on an average, to sixty-three thousand livres—two thousand six hundred and twenty-five pounds.), or the Beys compel them to furnish them with what they want, which is always attended with no little danger (1 : 230).

Behavioral Distortions Resulting from Oppression

The Turks never speak of the people of Damascus without observing, that they are the most mischievous in the whole empire; the Arabs, by a play on words, have made this proverb: *Shami, shoumi,* The man of Damascus, wicked: on the contrary, they say of the people of Aleppo, *Halabi, tchelebi,* The Aleppo man, *a petit maître.* From a prejudice arising from the difference of religions, they also add, that the Christians there are more vile and knavish than elsewhere; doubtless, because the Mahometans are there more fanatic and more insolent. In this they resemble the inhabitants of Cairo, like them, they detest the Franks, nor is it possible to appear at Damascus in a European dress; our merchants have not been able to form any establishment there; we only meet with two Capuchin Missionaries and a physician who is not permitted to practise.

This hatred the people of Damascus bear the Christians, is maintained and increased by their communication with Mecca. Their city, say they, is a holy place, since it is one of the gates of the Caaba: for Damascus is the rendez-vous for all the pilgrims from the north of Asia, as Cairo is for those from Africa. Their number every year amounts from thirty to fifty thousand . . . (2 : 272–73).

It is remarkable, that, in consequence of the difference in religion, there exists between the Christians and Mahometans of Syria, and indeed of all Turkey, as marked a difference of character as if they were two distinct nations, living under different climates. Travellers, and our merchants, who on account of the habits of intimacy in which they live with both, are still better qualified to decide, agree that the Greek Christians are in general wicked and deceitful, abject in adversity, insolent in prosperity, and especially remarkable for levity and fickleness; the Mahometans, on the contrary, though haughty even to insolence, possess however a sort of goodness of heart, humanity, and justice; and above all, never fail to manifest great fortitude under misfortune, and much firmness of character. This contrast between men living under the same sky, may appear surprising; but the prejudices of their education, and the influence of the government under which they live, sufficiently account for it. The Greeks, treated by the Turks with all the haughtiness and contempt they shew to their slaves, cannot but at last assume the character perpetually ascribed to them: they have been obliged to practise deceit, to escape from violence by cunning, and they have recourse to the meanest flatteries, because the weak must ever court the strong; they are dissemblers and mischievous, because he who cannot openly revenge himself, disguises his hatred; cowardly and treacherous, since he who cannot attack in front, naturally strikes behind; and insolent in prosperity, because they who attain wealth or power unworthily, are eager to revenge themselves by returning all the contempt they have received in the pursuit (2:489–90).

*C. F. Volney

*Constantin-François Volney (né Chasseboeuf) (1757–1820), member of the French Academy. His *Voyage en Egypte et en Syrie* (1783–85), first published in 1787, brought him fame. His *Les Ruines, ou Méditations sur les Révolutions des Empires* appeared in 1791. He emigrated to the United States where he traveled extensively (1795–98) and wrote an uncompleted study of that country on his return to France.

29. On the Way to Jerusalem (1807)

Preceded by my guide, and followed by my servants at some distance, I walked absorbed in the contemplation of this fine spectacle, when on a sudden two old men presented themselves and stopped the guide. Their abrupt appearance produced upon me an effect which I cannot describe. My guide who knew them, told them immediately that we were Mussulmans; the old men replied, "No, they are Christians." My guide, raising his voice, repeated "they are all Mussulmans"; upon which one of them advanced, and seizing my horse's bridle, said, "Thou art a Christian"; the guide and servants cried out "He is a Mussulman, he is a faithful believer." I knew not what to do, for I was ignorant of their intention, and their conduct appeared to me very extravagant. The first old man resumed the conversation, and said, "By God, thou art a Christian"; I replied, "Man I am a Mussulman, I am the Scherif Abbassi; I have just performed my pilgrimage to Mecca." He then asked me my faith, which I repeated to satisfy him; after which they suffered us to continue our journey. But why should this old man so obstinately persist that I was a Christian, without having seen my face or heard my voice? It was because I wore a blue bournous, and in this country that colour is particularly worn by the Christian inhabitants. But why this attack in such a place at so unseasonable an hour? It was because the Christians and Jews who go to Jerusalem, pay at this place a tribute of fifteen piastres each, which is received for the Sultan of Constantinople. These old men farmed this tribute, and as this place, from which the village is at no great distance, is the only defile in the mountains by which travellers can pass, they are perpetually on the look-out to prevent any Christian or Jew eluding payment of the duty (2:212–13).

After a short visit to this Temple, I went to the Jews' synagogue.

MARONITE MONK AND PILGRIMS IN JERUSALEM
"Only Turks [Muslims] could wear a turban. . . , Christians being contented to wind round their bonnet a striped cloth in imitation of a turban."—J. Dandini (1685), p. 41
Engraving by L. Mayers (1804)

E. Rosenmüller

Poor people! a wretched building, or rather barrack composed of three or four rooms, the ceiling of which may be touched with the hand; a court-yard still smaller, the whole covered with cobwebs and filth, constitutes the present Temple of the children of Jacob, the heirs and descendants of Solomon! I found there some Jews who were reciting prayers in the different corners of this hovel, but the whole was so miserable, melancholy, dirty, and disgusting, that I hastily withdrew (2:23).

*Ali Bey

*Ali Bey (General Domingo Badia y Leblich), a Spanish scientist, carried out numerous political errands during his wide travels in the earlier nineteenth century. His account soon became a standard work.

30. Jews and Samaritans in Palestine (1816)

Previous to the invasion of Syria by Buonaparte, a law existed among the Turks that there should be no more than two thousand Jews in Jerusalem, on pain of death to those who exceeded that number. At that period, the Christians were all shut up in their convents, and the Jews in their quarter, and if Jerusalem had then been attacked by the French, it was intended by the Turks here to massacre all who were not Mohammedans without distinction of age or sex (p. 257).

The whole of our road from Nazareth to Sook-el-Khan had been more or less rugged and hilly, but on our departure from hence, we entered on a fertile plain. In our way across this, we met a party of Jews on asses, coming from Tiberias to the great public market, and conceiving me, from my Turkish dress and white turban, to be a Mohammedan, they all dismounted and passed by us on foot. These persecuted people are held in such opprobrium here, that it is forbidden to them to pass a mussulman mounted, while Christians are suffered to do so either on mules or asses, though to them it is also forbidden to ride on horseback without the express permission of the Pasha (p. 457).

Though Nablous is a place of considerable trade with Damascus and with the towns on the sea-coast, yet there were no Jews here who remained as permanent residents. As for the Samaritans, though a remnant of them existed so late as the time of Maundrell's journey [1697], or about a century ago, there were not, as I was informed, half a dozen families remaining, and these were so obscurely known, and remained in such privacy, that many who had passed all their days in this town did not know of the existence of such a sect. To so low a state are the people reduced, who once held this city as their metropolis,

SAMARITAN HIGH PRIEST, NAẞLUS
Engraving by A. Kohl from a drawing by E. Ronjat (after a photograph)
L. Lortet (1884), p. 199

and who established here the chief seat of their religious as well as of their temporal power! (p. 528).

In the year 1676, there was a correspondence between the chief priest of the Samaritans at Nablous, and the learned Scaliger,[1] on the differences between the Hebrew and Samaritan pentateuch; and in the year 1697, Mr. Maundrell had a personal conference with the then residing dignitary; but I was assured by all those who knew of the existence of this people at Nablous, though these were very few, that their numbers were more reduced now than at any former period, and that, at most, there were not more than a dozen families composing their church [community]; these, they said, never visited the summit of Mount Gerizim, but performed their religious rites in studied seclusion and obscurity, and were, if possible, more despised here than the Jews are in other Mohammedan cities (p. 538–39).

J. S. Buckingham

[1] Joseph Justus Scaliger (1540–1609), French philologist and Hebrew scholar. There seems to be some confusion in the date of this correspondence.

31. Visit to the Jews of Hebron (1836)

I followed the janissary, who conducted me around outside the walls and through the burying-ground, where the women were scattered in groups among the tombs, to a distant and separate quarter of the city. I had no idea where he was taking me; but I had not advanced a horse's length in the narrow streets before their peculiar costume and physiognomies told me that I was among the unhappy remnant of a fallen people, the persecuted and despised Israelites. They were removed from the Turkish quarter, as if the slightest contact with this once-favored people would contaminate the bigoted follower of the Prophet. The governor, in the haughty spirit of a Turk, probably thought that the house of a Jew was a fit place for the repose of a Christian;[1] and, following the janissary through a low range of narrow, dark, and filthy lanes, mountings, and turnings, of which it is impossible to give any idea, with the whole Jewish population turning out to review us, and the sheik[2] and all his attendants with their long swords clattering at my heels, I was conducted to the house of the chief Rabbi of Hebron.

[1] The author probably did not know that in all Muslim lands, travelers could be lodged only in the Jewish quarter (or Christian, if it existed) or in *khans*.

[2] The *sheik* and his attendants were Arabs paid to protect the security of the traveler. Every traveler, even if indigenous to the country, was obliged to place himself under the protection of an escort so as to escape the danger of being robbed or killed by the Bedouins.

If I had had my choice, these were the very persons I would have selected for my first acquaintances in the Holy Land. The descendants of Israel were fit persons to welcome a stranger to the ancient city of their fathers; and if they had been then sitting under the shadow of the throne of David, they could not have given me a warmer reception. It may be that, standing in the same relation to the Turks, alike the victims of persecution and contempt, they forgot the great cause which had torn us apart and made us a separate people, and felt only a sympathy for the object of mutual oppression. But, whatever was the cause, I shall never forget the kindness with which, as a stranger and Christian, I was received by the Jews in the capital of their ancient kingdom; and I look to my reception here and by the monks of Mount Sinai as among the few bright spots in my long and dreary pilgrimage through the desert. . . .

Judge, then, of my satisfaction at being welcomed from the desert by the friendly and hospitable Israelites. Returned once more to the occupation of our busy, money-making life, floating again upon the stream of business, and carried away from the cares and anxieties which agitate every portion of our stirring community, it is refreshing to turn to the few brief moments when far other thoughts occupied my mind; and my speculating, scheming friends and fellow-citizens would have smiled to see me that night, with a Syrian dress and long beard, sitting cross-legged on a divan, with the chief rabbi of the Jews at Hebron, and half the synagogue around us, talking of Abraham, Isaac, and Jacob as of old and mutual friends.

With the few moments of daylight that remained, my Jewish friends conducted me around their miserable quarter. They had few lions to show me, but they took me to their synagogue, in which an old white-bearded Israelite was teaching some prattling children to read the laws of Moses in the language of their fathers; and when the sun was setting in the west and the Muezzin from the top of the minaret was calling the sons of the faithful to evening prayers, the old rabbi and myself, a Jew and a Christian, were sitting on the roof of the little synagogue, looking out as by stealth upon the sacred mosque containing the hallowed ashes of their patriarch fathers. The Turk guards entered the door, and the Jew and the Christian are not permitted to enter; and the old rabbi was pointing to the different parts of the mosque, where, as he told me, under tombs adorned with carpets of silk and gold, rested the mortal remains of Abraham, Isaac, and Jacob (pp. 312–14).

*J. L. Stephens

---

*John Lloyd Stephens (1805–1852), the later discoverer of the Maya civilization, was highly praised by E. A. Poe and others for his successful *Incidents of Travel* (1837).

32. Improved Conditions in Syria-Palestine (1836)

The Mussulmans [of Syria-Palestine], whatever may be said of the diminution of their fanaticism, deeply deplore the loss of that sort of superiority which they all and individually exercised over and against the other sects. Pride, selfishness, and ignorance, may be said to be the characteristic of a Mussulman; and from the bottom of his heart he believes and maintains that a Christian, and still more so a Jew, is an inferior being to himself. With such principles, it is no matter of astonishment to remark, that the political equality to which the other sects have been raised by the present government of Syria [of Ibrahim Pasha], creates a sort of religious disaffection towards their rulers, which, I am inclined to believe, has more deep roots than all the other just motives of complaint which they possess. The Christians, as well as the other sects, who have been benefited by such change, are necessarily attached to the present system, and dread any change that would tend to restore to the Mussulmans that supremacy of which they would certainly make them feel the return into their hands. The condition of the Jews forms, perhaps, an exception, and cannot be said to have improved comparatively with that of other sects: this is owing to a personal feeling both of Mahomet Ali and Ibrahim Pasha, as also of all the Christians and other sects in Syria, against them: they are, however, protected in the open and full exercise of their religion, and have justice in all their civil cases; and Ibrahim Pacha has given permission for a synagogue to be built at Jerusalem, and in which public worship is now performed. An English Jew of Jamaica, residing in Jerusalem, told me that the Jews had every cause to be satisfied with Ibrahim Pacha (pp. 136–37).

Judiciary System

In every province a Chief Mufti, called Mufti, was yearly appointed by the Porte; and he, in his turn, had the appointment of the inferior "Cadis," or judges. The Mekemeh [tribunal] takes its decisions from the Koran, and Christians are only admitted as witnesses. The depravity and venaltiy of all these tribunals is beyond conception, and even at Constantinople there is a coffee-house known as the rendezvous of false witnesses, who can be bought at so much for the day. The Muftis generally make their fortunes in ten years, for the appointment of the cadis does not depend upon their fitness for this situation, but on the sum which they can pay for the same. (p. 132)

Colonel P. Campbell, in J. Bowring.

33. A Visit to Israel's Holy Places (1839)

We proceeded toward the Mosque [built upon the tombs of the
Hebrew patriarchs at Hebron], the Consul's janissary going before.
Several Jews joined in the train. As we passed through the streets, the
boys and girls cried *Nazarani,* teaching us that "the Nazarene" is still a
term of reproach in this land. . . . We were allowed to ascend the wide
massy staircase that leads into the interior of the building. The door
into the mosque was thrown open, but not a foot was allowed to cross
the marble threshold. We were shewn the window of the place which
contains the tombs of Abraham and Sarah, beneath which is understood to be the cave of Machpelah. There is none of the sacred places
over which the Moslems keep so jealous a watch as the tomb of Abraham. It was esteemed a very peculiar favour that we had been admitted thus far, travellers in general being forbidden to approach
even the door of the Mosque. A letter from the Governor of
Jerusalem, who had been with us on the evening before we set out,
gained us this privilege. . . .

The Jews at present are permitted only to look through a hole near
the entrance, and to pray with their face toward the grave of Abraham (pp. 180–81).

The same evening we visited all the synagogues of Jerusalem at the
time of evening prayer. They are six in number, all of them small and
poorly furnished, and four of them under one roof. The lamps are
the only handsome ornaments they contain. The reading-desk is little
else than an elevated part of the floor, enclosed with a wooden railing.
The ark has none of the rich embroidery that distinguishes it in
European synagogues. . . . We were much impressed with the melancholy aspect of the Jews in Jerusalem. The meanness of their dress,
their pale faces, and timid expression, all seem to betoken great
wretchedness. They are evidently much poorer than the Jews of Hebron. . . .

All Jews in Palestine speak Hebrew, but then they often attach a
meaning to the words that is not the true meaning or grammatical
sense, so that it is absolutely necessary to know the vernacular tongue,
in order to be sure that you and they understand the same thing by
the words employed (pp. 192–93).

We found all the Jews here [Safed] living in a state of great alarm.
The troops of the Pasha had been withdrawn, being engaged in the
war, and the Bedouins were every day threatening an attack to plunder the town. Only four soldiers had been left to defend them, and
these, along with ten Jews, used to patrole the town all night to give
alarm in case of an assault. We observed how poorly clad most of the

Jews seemed to be, and were told that they had buried under ground all their valuable clothes, their money, and other precious things. It was easy to read their deep anxiety in the very expression of their countenances: they were truly in the state foretold by Moses more than 3,000 years ago. . . . And all this in their own land! (p. 273).

The Chances of Evangelization in Palestine

But here let us for a moment review all that we have seen and heard in regard to the condition of Israel in their own land. We visited every city and village in Palestine where Jews are to be found (with the exception of Jaffa, and two small villages upon Mount Naphthali), and we have been led to the conclusion that the Holy Land presents the most important and interesting of all the fields of labour among the Jews.

I. The Jews are in affliction in the land of their fathers, and this makes them more friendly there than in other land[s]. In other countries, where they are wealthy and comfortable, or deeply engaged in worldly business, we found that they care little to attend to the words of the Christian missionary. But in Judea the plague, poverty, the oppression of their rabbis, and the insults of the heathen, have so humbled them, that they cling to any one who offers to shew them kindness, however adverse to the doctrine which he teaches.

II. They are strictly Rabbinical Jews, untainted by the infidelity of France or the neology of Germany. They hold the Old Testament to be indeed the Word of God. They have a real expectation of the coming of the Messiah; and this expectation is certainly greater now than it was formerly. The missionary has thus firm ground to stand upon, and with the Hebrew Bible in his hand, may expound to them, with intelligence and power, all that is written in the Law of Moses, and in the Prophets, and in the Psalms, concerning Jesus.

III. Moreover, Judea must be regarded as the centre of the Jewish world. Every Jew, in whatever country he sojourns, turns his face toward Jerusalem in prayer. It is the heart of the nation, and every impression made there is transmitted to all the scattered members. We afterwards met a poor Jew at Ibraila, a small town upon the Danube, who told us of conversions that had taken place at Jerusalem. In this way, whatever is done for the Jews in Palestine, will make a hundred-fold more impression than if it were done in any other land.

IV. Another important consideration is, that in Palestine the Jews look upon the English as friends. Three months before our arrival in Jerusalem, an English Consul [Vice-Consul W. T. Young] had been stationed there—a true and zealous friend of Israel, whose jurisdiction extended over the country once given to the twelve tribes, and whose instructions from the British Government were, that he should, to the utmost of his power, afford protection to the Jews. The recent changes in Syria [the return of Ottoman rule after Muhammed Ali of Egypt abandoned his claims on Syria under British pressure] have no doubt for a time interfered with these arrangements; but still, is not the hand of an overruling Providence visible in them? And is it not our duty to improve to the utmost the interest we have in the affections of the Jews, by being the friends of their never-dying souls? . . .

On these grounds, we rest our conviction that the Holy Land presents not only the most attractive, but the most important field for missionary operations among the Jews (pp. 320–22).

A. A. Bonar and R. M. M'Cheyne

34. The Prince of Wales Visits Hebron (1862)

The entrance [to the cave of Machpelah] is by a staircase, to which access is forbidden to Christians, though we succeeded in running up and peeping in at dawn, without being detected. But this is a rash and rather dangerous experiment. It is only within the last few years that two or three royal and princely parties have been permitted to enter (3 : 186).

The entrance to the mosque is most jealously forbidden by the Muhammedans to any but their fellow-worshippers; by special firman of the Sultan, an exception was made in favour of the Prince of Wales in 1862, the Marquis of Bute in 1866, the Crown Prince of Prussia in 1869, and the sons of the Prince of Wales in the present year, 1882.

Of these occasions the most noteworthy was the visit of the Prince of Wales. His Royal Highness was accompanied by the late Dean [of Westminster, Arthur Penrhyn] Stanley, who thus describes the event:—Before our arrival at Hebron, the Governor of Jerusalem, Sûraya Pasha, had made every preparation to ensure the safety of the experiment. Accordingly, as the protracted file wound through the narrow valley by which the town of Hebron is approached, the whole road on either side, for more than a mile, was lined with soldiers. The native population, which usually on the Prince's approach to a town streamed out to meet him, was invisible, it may be from compulsion, it may be from silent indignation. . . . We started on foot, two and two, between two files of soldiers, by the ancient pool of Hebron, up the narrow streets of the modern town, still lined with soldiers. Hardly a face was visible as we passed through; only here and there a solitary guard, stationed at a vacant window, or on the flat roof of a projecting house, evidently to guarantee the safety of the party from any chance missile. It was, in fact, a complete military occupation of the town. At length we reached the south-eastern corner of the massive wall of enclosure, the point at which enquiring travellers, from generation to generation, have been checked in their approach to this, the most ancient and the most authentic of all the Holy Places in the Holy Land (3 : 197–98).

The shrine of Abraham, after a momentary hesitation, was thrown open. The guardians groaned aloud. But their chief turned to us with the remark, "The Princes of any other nation should have passed over my dead body sooner than enter. But to the eldest son of the Queen of England we are willing to accord even this privilege." He stepped in before us, and offered an ejaculatory prayer to the dead patriarch: "O Friend of God, forgive this intrusion." We then entered. . . . It was impossible not to feel a thrill of unusual emotion at standing on such a spot—an emotion enhanced by the rare occasion which had opened the gates of that consecrated place, as the guardian of the mosque kept repeating to us as we stood around the tomb, "to no one less than the representative of England" (3 : 199).

C. Wilson

THE ERA OF EMANCIPATION

35. Nineteenth Century Ottoman Palestine

In times gone by these native Jews had their full share of suffering from the general tyrannical conduct of the Moslems, and, having no resources for maintenance in the Holy Land, they were sustained, though barely, by contributions from synagogues all over the world. This mode of supply being understood by the Moslems, they were subjected to exactions and plunder on its account from generation to generation (individuals among them, however, holding occasionally lucrative offices for a time). This oppression proved one of the causes which have entailed on the community a frightful incubus of debt, the payment of interest on which is a heavy charge upon the income derived from abroad.

In Jerusalem their synagogues are four, and all collected under one roof, so that they may pass from each into the others, and they are but meanly furnished (1 : 103).

Until the English Consulate was established in Jerusalem [1839], there was, of course, no other jurisprudence in the country than that of the old-fashioned corruption and self-will of the Mohammedans, and for many ages but very few (often none) of the European Jews ventured to make an abode in Palestine. . . .

The Egyptian Government [1831–1840], with its rigour and rough-handed justice, afforded much relief to all non-Moslem inhabitants of Jerusalem; and the institution of consulates in the Holy City proved a further blessing to non-Turkish subjects of all religions, but especially to the poor oppressed Israelites (1:105–6).

In 1847 it seemed probable that the Christian pilgrims, instigated by the Greek ecclesiastics, were about to reproduce the horrors enacted at Rhodes and Damascus in 1840 [against the Jews].

A Greek pilgrim boy, in a retired street, had thrown a stone at a poor little Jew boy, and, strange to say, the latter had the courage to retaliate by throwing one in return, which unfortunately hit its mark, and a bleeding ankle was the consequence. It being the season of the year when Jerusalem is always thronged with pilgrims (March), a tumult soon arose, and the direst vengeance was denounced against all Jews indiscriminately, for having stabbed (as they said) an innocent Christian child, with a knife, in order to get his blood, for mixing in their Passover biscuits. The police came up and both parties were taken down to the Seraglio for judgment; there the case was at once discharged as too trivial for notice.

The Convent Clergy, however, three days afterwards, stirred up the matter afresh, exaggerated the state of the wound inflicted, and en-gaged to prove to the Pasha from their ancient books that Jews are addicted to the above cannibal practice, either for purposes of necro-mancy, or out of hatred of Christians, on which His Excellency un-wisely suffered the charge of assault to be diverted into this different channel, which was one that did not concern him; and he commanded the Jews to answer for themselves on the second day afterwards. In the interval, both Greeks and Armenians went about the streets in-sulting and menacing the Jews, both men and women, sometimes drawing their hands across the throat, sometimes showing the knives which they generally carry about with them, and, among other in-stances brought to my notice, was that of a party of six catching hold of the son of the late Chief Rabbi of London (Herschell) and shaking him, elderly man as he was, by the collar, crying out, "Ah! Jew, have you got the knives ready for our blood?"

On the day of the Seraglio-hearing, the scene in the Mejlis was a most painful one. The Greek ecclesiastical party came down in great force, and read out of Church historians and controversial writings of old time the direct and frequent accusations levelled against the Jews for using Christian blood in Passover ceremonies. The Moslem dig-nitaries, being appealed to, stated that in their sacred books such

PALESTINIAN JEWISH BOY
Son of Rabbi Samuel Majha, 2nd Chief Rabbi of Jerusalem
W. J. Woodcock (1849)
no. 1982, in A. Rubens (1981), and pl. 60 (1973)

charges against the Jews are to be found indirectly mentioned, and therefore the crime may be inferred as true: it was possible to be true. The Rabbis deputed from the Chief Rabbi, pale and trembling, argued from the Old Testament, and all their legal authorities, the utter impossibility of the perpetration of such acts by their people, concluding with an appeal to the Sultan's Firman of 1841, which declares that thorough search having been made into this matter, both as to Jewish doctrine and practice, the people of Israel were entirely innocent of that crime advanced against them.

On this the Pasha required them to produce the Firman on the second day afterwards, the intervening day being Friday, the Moslem Sabbath. I then arranged with the Pasha that I should be present at the meeting, and early on Saturday went down to the Seraglio; but earlier still His Excellency was happy (he said) to acquaint me that the Firman had been produced, and on his asking the accusers and the Effendis in council if they could venture to fly in the face of that document, they had, with all loyalty, pronounced it impossible; he therefore had disposed of the case by awarding a trifling fine for medical treatment of wounded ankle (1 : 107–10).

About this time [1847] a Jew was set upon by the crowd of fanatic Christian pilgrims, and nearly killed, for having crossed the farthest side of the open square which is in front of the Church of the Holy Sepulchre; he, being newly arrived from Europe, was unaware of the city custom which restricts that passage to Christians, who, however, admit the Moslems because they dare not shut them out. Redress was sought through the English Consulate, although the man was a Russian or an Austrian subject, because he had no Consul of his own. I appealed to the Pasha. The Greek ecclesiastics pleaded before him that the passage was not a public thoroughfare, but part of the Sanctuary of Christianity, and only used for transit upon sufferance. They even dared to send me word that they were in possession of an ancient Firman which fixed the "Deeyeh," or blood-fine, to be paid by them if in beating a Jew in that vicinity for trespass they happened to kill him, at the sum of ten paras, about one half-penny English. However ridiculous or wicked such a message might be, it was nevertheless a duty to report it at Constantinople, with a view to an authoritative contradiction of the statement. As might have been expected, the official reply was that no such document ever existed. Thus that mischievous untruth was silenced, but the incident shows the disposition of the high convent authorities towards the Jews. It may be that they themselves believed there was such a Firman: if so, what degree of pity or liberality could one expect from the multitude of brutal pilgrims? The Pasha said that he knew of no such Firman as that referred to, but that Greeks, Latins, and Armenians, all believed a Jew might be killed with impunity under such circumstances (1:111–12).

At the early hour on that day [18 July 1855] the roads and fields were thronged with an unwonted Jewish population, for these were seldom to be met outside the city walls, except in small companies, and that but occasionally, in the opposite direction, going to Rachel's Sepulchre or to Hebron. It was a wonderful spectacle, never before witnessed. Sir Moses [Montefiore] and his lady were attended by the late Colonel Gawler, riding in brilliant scarlet uniform, white plumes, his Waterloo and several other medals, etc. Near the city gate the multitude, of all denominations of people, was immense, and the principal personages of the procession went at once to the Synagogue, while the tents were pitched on the Meidân outside the north-west corner of the wall.

Never before in modern times had there been a Jewish demonstration publicly made, for in former days of oppression and sorrow it would have been as impolitic as impossible (1:115).

Before concluding this sketch of Jewish affairs, we may take notice of two curious peculiarities of Jerusalem—both founded on the idea of the place being still their own—an idea which, although but a shadow at present in relation to other people, is not without weight among themselves. The customs are, of course, limited to the "Sephardim," or Israelites of the country.

One is the coining of money, or rather of an equivalent to that special prerogative of royalty (Matt. 22:19). The articles are small squares of brass foil, stamped with the Hebrew words בקור חולים [meaning *biqqur holim*], i.e., "Visiting the Sick." The practice seems to have originated in adopting a fictitious currency, on temporary occasions, as a means of almsgiving, in anticipation of real money coming to hand. In the Jewish bazaar these pieces are current for all purposes of trade, and are sometimes accepted and passed among other inhabitants of the city as paras, though inferior in value to even that small coin. The Turks disapprove of the practice, and now and then take the trouble to prohibit it. The Jews, however, are proud of their show of independent royalty, and even if willing to discontinue it, would find it difficult to call in these tokens, so long as their heavy debt remains, for they do actually represent a certain amount of metallic value.

The other custom is that of getting possession of the great keys of the city gates on the decease of each Sultan of Constantinople, and after a religious service of prayer, and anointing them with a mysterious preparation of oil and spices, allowing them to be returned to the civic authorities on behalf of the new monarch. For the exercise of this traditional custom they make heavy presents to the local governors, who allow of a harmless practice that has prescription to show on its behalf. It is a matter of "*bakhsheesh*" to them, and there is always a class of superstitious people to be found in Palestine who think that the benediction of the ancient "children of Israel" is worth having; the Jewish feelings are gratified, for their expectation of the future is refreshed, and the Jerusalem Rabbis are enabled to boast all the world over among their people that they suffer the Sultan of Turkey to keep possession of the Holy City (1:116–18).

Notwithstanding these glimpses of honorary distinction the Jews are humiliated by the payment, through the Chief Rabbi, of pensions to Moslem local exactors, for instance the sum of 300*l.* a year to the Effendi whose house adjoins the "wailing place," or fragment of the western wall of the Temple enclosure, for permission to pray there; 100*l.* a year to the villagers of Siloam for not disturbing the graves on the slope of the Mount of Olives; 50*l.* a year to the Ta'amara Arabs for not injuring the Sepulchre of Rachel near Bethlehem, and about 10*l.* a year to Shaikh Abu Gosh for not molesting their people on the high road to Jaffa, although he was highly paid by the Turkish Government as Warden of that road. All these are mere exactions made upon their excessive timidity, which it is disgraceful to the Turkish Government to allow to be practised. The figures are copied from their humble appeals occasionally made to the synagogues in Europe. Other minor impositions were laid upon them which they were afraid to discontinue to pay, such as, to one man (Moslem) for superintending the slaughtering of cattle by themselves for food, to see that it is performed by the Sephardi Rabbi who has purchased his licence to do it. Periodical presents likewise of sugar, etc., to the principal Moslems at their festivals.

One more observation upon the condition of the Jews in Jerusalem. At that time, and for many centuries previous, the common shambles of the city (called the Meslakh)[1] was kept in the midst of their quarter. The offal accumulated in a deep and wide pit, was never cleared out, and of course at all seasons, particularly in summer heat, was most prejudicial to health, and so it remained for a few years after the Russian war was over [1856]. It was there before the conquest by the Arabs, for, according to tradition of all classes of people, it was purposely left there after its existence being reported to Caliph Omar; and it is mentioned as being there later by a Norman writer in the time of the Crusades (see Williams' 'Holy City') (1:118–20).

It was distressing to behold the timidity which long ages of oppression had engendered. Many times a poor Jew would come for redress against a native (Moslem) and when he had substantiated his case and it had been brought by the Consulate before the Turkish authorities,

[1] Abattoirs.

he would, in mere terror of future possible vengeance, withdraw
from the prosecution, and even deny that any harm had been done
him; or if that was too manifest, declare that he could not identify the
criminal, or that the witnesses could not be produced. Still, even then,
the bare fact that some notice had been taken had a deterrent effect
upon criminals who had hitherto regarded the defenceless Jews as
their special prey (1 : 127).

With regard to pure Hebrew, the learned world in Europe is greatly
mistaken in designating this a dead language. In Jerusalem it is a
living tongue of everyday utility—necessarily so, for in what else could
Jewish strangers from the opposite ends of the earth converse together? In our Consular office Hebrew was often heard spoken—on
one occasion by a Jew from Cabool [Kabul], who had to enter into
explanations with one from California: of course in Hebrew. That
language was a medium of transacting business in the English Consulate (1 : 127–28).

Obstacles to Dhimmi Emancipation in Palestine

A great change had, as has been already stated, passed over the
land, as well as over Jerusalem, with respect to toleration of religion in
the existing generation, not only caused by the Hatti-Shereef of
Gulhaneh in 1838 [1839], but also by the surviving effects of previous
Egyptian dominion between 1832 and 1840, which had swept away
much of the bigotry and tyranny of former ages.

There had even been, since 1845, a profession of equality for all
religions in the administration of local government, and certainly less
of injury and insult from the Moslem populace to the Christians.
Their functionaries were no longer endured as intruders into Christian houses for food, lodging, and money, remaining there till their
demands were satisfied. Christian women were not now dishonoured
with impunity of the offenders. "Avanias," or levies of money, at any
irregular time or place, without reason assigned, were no more suffered. Christians were not now pushed into the gutters of the streets
by every Moslem taking up the best part of the pavement, and with a
scowl crying out, "Shemmel-ni ya kelb" (turn to my left, thou dog);
neither were Christians debarred from riding horses or wearing
cheerful colours.[2]

---

[2] As specimens of old times, see Journal of Rev. P. Fisk who was in Jerusalem in 1823.
He was seated with two friends on the Mount of Olives, and while singing a hymn, an
armed Moslem came up and commanded them to be silent, threatening Mr. Fisk to
strike him with his gun.

The same day (it seems) the President of the Greek Convent of Mar Elias was bastinadoed to a fearful extent, under the idea that he could be made to discover hidden
treasure. And some of the villages around having refused to pay the excessive and

Legal commentary-books of the detestable old bigotry were indeed still in existence, and even acted upon in small or remote places, but it was at length known by experience that in towns where European Consuls had cognizance, reports might be made to higher stations still, and then not merely written rebukes for illegal acts, but displacement from office could be obtained from Constantinople.

Christians had felt in 1852 much more secure in life and goods than their fathers had been, yet the actual generation, even when elected to be members of the Civic Council, dared not venture so far in acting upon their privileges as to refuse giving their seals to notoriously false documents. They took their places humbly in the lowest part of the Divan, thankful for the comparative honours they enjoyed (1 : 201–2).

The Russian[s] were regarded as protectors and champions of Eastern Christianity—hence the ignorant Moslems, and these were by no means confined to the poorer classes, even in Jerusalem, considered the war now imminent as a Holy war, in which Islam was to be ranged against Christianity. Among such every Moslem was to consider as his enemy every native Christian, or at least all those who had any relations with Russia (Greeks, and even Armenians).

The timorous and panic-stricken Christians helped forward this idea by the very excess of their fears. They had not the sense to conceal their dread of a probable approaching massacre, in which scenes of horror and bloodshed were to be enacted, such as their fathers had endured in consequence of the war of Greek independence about thirty years before.

The condition of these poor people was distressing: neither reason nor argument made any impression upon them. Fear had been sucked in with their mothers' milk, in days gone by, and now it overpowered them.

If this was the case in Jerusalem where the Convents, and Patriarchs, and Consuls, were ready protectors, it was tenfold worse in all distant towns and villages. There incidents occurred which would have been simply ludicrous but for the intolerance backed by power on one side, and abject alarm on the other, which they revealed (1 : 202–3).

In Palestine, besides the usual mosques, there were two places of especial fanaticism reserved:—

1. The Hharam of Jerusalem, site of the ancient Temple of Israel,

---

arbitrary taxation laid upon them, the soldiers caught hold of an infirm old peasant of the Christian village of Bait Jala, shot him, cut off his head, and stuck it up inside the Jaffa gate of Jerusalem, where it was pelted and spit upon by boys of the street for three days. Christians passing by were melted into tears, but dared not give expression to their feelings (note in Finn's text).

called the "noble sanctuary," and by Europeans, incorrectly, the Mosque of 'Omar.

2. The Hharam of Hebron, which is Machpelah.

From access to these all but Mohammedans were excluded, and the former was guarded by a police of ferocious Africans called Takarni (plural of Takroori), a people from Darfoor.

Who has not heard of the former impossibility of getting access to the Mosque of 'Omar, and what traveller to Jerusalem of that or earlier periods has not gazed with wistful eyes at a distance, either from Olivet, or from the roof of the barracks when admitted there by special favour, upon those sacred precincts, which of old contained the one temple of the one God, and where prophets, priests, kings, apostles, and the Saviour himself, have certainly walked: now presenting so Oriental an appearance, a spacious area with green grass, olive and cypress trees, around an edifice of remarkable beauty?

Many mistakes, and consequence insults or injuries, having arisen from strangers imagining that place to be one of public promenade, as they peered through the open gateways, it became necessary to represent these instances to the Embassy. Our people were sometimes beaten by the Africans with clubs and pelted with stones when approaching in that direction or merely passing at some distance within view of the gates (1:205–6).

The following incident of July, 1851, will show what sort of occurrences were to be apprehended. A Moslem in Nizâm (military) uniform was praying within the Hharam enclosure, with a book before him and according to proper ritual, his shoes off, and his unbuckled sword laid by his side, when one of the old school of devotees came up, and accusing him of being a Christian, bade him repeat the Confession of Faith. This he did, but in a manner more deliberate than is usual with Moslems of the country, on which the other snatched up the sword, and cut him deeply across the face.

The man died of the wound the next day.

Now, it may have been that the victim was not a born Moslem, but a renegade serving in the Turkish army, and therefore not yet versed in traditional observances prescribed for prayer; or he may have been a born Moslem from some distant land, not sufficiently familiar with the Arabic language to be able to recite the formulated verses without a book.

No enquiry was made on the subject, but the event showed the peril of any non-Moslem entering within the Hharem-esh-Shereef of Jerusalem. I never heard of any punishment reaching the religious murderer. The crime had not even the specious excuse of being an infliction by the appointed police.

The town of Nabloos (Shechem) has been commonly held in bad

repute for its intolerance of Christianity. Very few Christians resided there, but they had constant reason to complain of gross injustice on the part of the local authorities. European travellers, too, were hooted through the streets; the men kept themselves from detection, but their children were taught to run along the flat roofs of the houses, singing disgusting rhymes to a simple air, and as these juvenile offenders could not be got at, the men in the streets or bazaars, in reply to remonstrances, merely shrugged their shoulders and said that the children were ill-behaved. Happily few of the travellers understood what was going on, and the poor creatures representing police acted as well as they could under the lax rule of the period.

In the village of Sebustieh, occupying part of the ground of the ancient metropolis Samaria, less than two hours from Nabloos, the people have even a worse character, and are distinguishable by a vile scowling demeanor towards Europeans (1:206–7).

We were surprised to find that at the same period the peasantry even in the district about, and to the south of Nabloos, understanding better than before the real condition of our alliance with their rulers, adopted the practice of saluting us Europeans on the highways with the greeting of "Salâm 'aleikom" (peace be upon you!) which had always been strictly reserved for Mohammedans only; and the Kâdi of Caifa [Haifa] declared to me that the reservation was merely a matter of custom and not the result of any law or tradition, appealing to his friends around him for confirmation. It is, however, most probable that this was but a flattering untruth, adapted to time and circumstance[3] (1:209).

In Palestine, we had to deal with three principal types—the pure Arabs, the Syrian races on whom Islam had been imposed by conquest, and the Turks, now dominant as conquerors and rulers over both.

But we had also foreigners—Turkomâns, Kurds, Indians, Afghans, Tartars, Egyptians, and Africans, more or less in daily intercourse with us.

These all were of the Sunnee or orthodox sect.

The Shiahs were represented among us by Persian pilgrims and by the whole population in the Metâwilah district of the Belâd Bashâra.

To have confounded these together, or to have treated them all alike, must have led to perhaps even fatal consequences.

The so-called Arab Moslem settled population of Palestine is separ-

[3] This Moslem exclusion of Christians from the benefits of Salâm, which belongs to the world to come as well as to this world, prevails in most Mohammedan countries; but I am told that in India that salutation is freely given to the English, partly because we are masters of the country, and partly because amid the vast nations of idolaters they look upon us almost as co-religionists (note in Finn's text).

able into two classes: first, the mere (almost brutal) peasantry, the *Fellahheen* and, secondly, those somewhat more civilised, the inhabitants of towns, the *Belladeen*.

The first, who form the bulk of the population, have been indiscriminately called Arabs by Europeans, without any consideration as to whether they come from Arabia or not. They do not call themselves so, but simply *Fellahheen* (i.e. tillers of the soil, ploughmen).

The second, the *Belladeen*, or dwellers in towns, are a mixed race of various origins, but there are among them families entitled to the name Arab, their ancestors having been immigrants from Arabia at the time of the Mohammedan conquest. This class forms but a small proportion of the population, but these people are proud of their descent: they know, even the ignorant among them, something of their system of religion, and look back to its Arabian source (1:214–15).

While these things [riots] were going on in Nabloos, the formal reading of the Sultan's gracious Hatt-i-Humayoon had taken place in Jerusalem. . . .

Indeed there were indications that the uproar had been stirred up by people furious at the idea of this edict being granted by the Sultan, as popular report had already informed them. All the leading inhabitants of the country, Moslems as well as Christians, had by this time a general knowledge of its intent.

The Pasha announced, on the day after the admission of the great party of travellers and Europeans to the Temple Sanctuary, that on the morrow—April 7 [1856]—the formal reading of the Sultan's decree would take place at the Seraglio.

That document was justly regarded at the time, and, indeed it ought to be so still, as one of extreme importance—especially by the Rayahs or non-Moslem subjects of the Sultan.

His Excellency invited the heads of the various religious communities and the foreign Consuls to be present. . . .

I arrived first, in semi-uniform, assigning the reason to the Pasha that it seemed to me best not to make more show lest it should seem that we intended to exhibit a triumph over the Moslem population—thus causing irritation instead of soothing and allaying differences and excitement (2:441–42).

It was evident that the Turks had not wished to make a conspicuous parade of the affair, but that some of the Christian authorities did.

And the latter were in the right in requiring that there should be full publicity with all necessary formality, after the trickery in 1853, about the Vizerial letter respecting the Holy Places. It was well to take all precautions against this publication of solemn *Hatt* [edict] becoming a mere hole-and-corner reading—and to make sure that it was read at all.

There can be no doubt of this charter of religious toleration and equality having been eminently distasteful to the old Mohammedan population, and distressing to their ancient feelings. It is usually believed, as we afterwards learned, that formal indignities were cast upon it by some Moslems in Constantinople, when it was read in the presence of the Shaikhu'l Islâm, the Christian Patriarchs, and the Jewish Rabbi—indignities offered, intelligible only to those versed in state formalities and the Arabic language, by people making outside show of submission and reverence.

This remarkable decree confirmed all the guarantees previously given by the Hatt of Gul-Hane[4] and by the Tanzimât[5] to all subjects of the Ottoman Empire, without distinction of classes or of religion, for the security of their persons and property, and the preservation of their honour. All privileges and spiritual immunities granted of old to all Christian communities, or other non-Musulman persuasions, were confirmed. These privileges were very great and had always included self-government, according to their own customs, under their own patriarchs or spiritual chiefs, who after election by their own people received a patent from the Sultan. . . .

Perfect accuracy of expression was of course essential, especially in paragraphs such as the following:—

"Every distinction or designation tending to make any class whatever of the subjects of my Empire inferior to another class, on account of their religion, language, or race, shall be for ever effaced from the administrative protocol. The laws shall be put in force against the use of any injurious or offensive term, either among private individuals, or on the part of the authorities.

"As all forms of religion are and shall be freely professed in my dominions, no subject of my Empire shall be hindered in the exercise of the religion that he professes, nor shall be in any way annoyed on this account.

"No one shall be compelled to change their religion."

Further, all subjects of the Empire were made admissible for public offices as appointed by the Sultan; all were to be admissible to the civil and military schools. Christians were to be no longer brought before purely Moslem courts of justice. Mixed tribunals were to be established, before which the testimony of every one was to be received on oath taken according to the religious law of each sect. Everything that

[4] Rescript of the Rose Chamber, legal reform improving the position of non-Muslims, promulgated by Sultan Abd al-Majid I, on November 3, 1839.
[5] Turkish reform laws, including the Hatt-i Humayun of 18 February 1856.

resembles torture was entirely abolished. Christians were to be equally taxed and equally liable for recruitment into the army; and the principle of purchasing exemption was admitted. And finally, it was stated that it should be lawful for foreigners to possess landed property, conforming themselves to the laws and police regulations, and bearing the same charges as the native inhabitants, and after arrangements had been come to with the foreign Powers.

These are the most important of the provisions contained in the Hatt-i-Humayoon, or Edict of Toleration (2:442–45).

Henceforward, if the laws of Turkey were only enforced, there would be neither necessity nor pretext for any protection of Christians in the East.

A few words must be said on the subject of religious equality before the law in Turkey, as connected with the administration of government, *extra* the Korân code with its commentaries. These latter, which are deeply engraved in the hearts and customs of their adherents, are undoubtedly adverse *in principle* to such notions of equality, and cannot be made to fall into harmony with them. How can unbelievers be put on an equality with believers in theory or in practice?

Consequently the Hatti Shereef of Gulhaneh, in 1838 [1839], and the rules known as "Tanzimât" or "Canoon Nameh," for carrying out that charter, were only accepted by the bigoted part of the Moslem population as temporary regulations of the Turks, in their mistaken system dictated by the exacting Europeans. The same of course with the still greater document, the Hatt-i-Humayoon of 1856.

Under the conviction that this persuasion underlay the universal sentiment of the old-school people in the provinces, I must say that I was slow to join in the cry of breach of faith made against the Turks, for not carrying out to the full from the very beginning all the liberal provisions of those charters. They ran so strongly counter to the recorded principles of old that are held so sacred, and to the inveterate habits of many generations, appealing only to the light of human conscience as it was before that light became darkness, that it really did require patience, together with firmness, for putting the new charters and edicts into execution. . . .

At a distance from Jerusalem the Proclamation of Toleration had less effect, as at Gaza, Nabloos, and in Galilee; but there the Christians were few and dared not look their masters in the face; they had no Consuls to ask after their welfare or to note the tyranny of their Moslem fellow-subjects or rulers, who, however, were not Turks, but Arabs.

This appears to have also been the case in other regions of the empire, as testified by Parliamentary and other reports that have been published in Europe.

It appears that obstructions to the carrying out of the reforms were not so much created in Constantinople as by ill-disciplined governors in their several departments at a distance, or that they arose from the ancient prejudices of the dominant class; and it must be added that something was also due to the acknowledged timidity, which appeared like apathy, of those intended to be benefited (2:446–49).

J. Finn

36. Abduction of Christian Children; Weakness of Governor (Aleppo, 1842)

I have the honor to remark to your Lordship that there exists a strong tendency in this part of Syria to return to ancient fanatical usages, and the highest public functionaries, if they partake not [in] the feeling itself, consider it politic to affect to do so.

The provisions of the Hatti Sheriff [of Gülhane, 1839] for securing an equality of privileges in judicial proceedings to the Rayahs of the Porte, have not been enforced at Aleppo, on account of Mahometan prejudices, and no christian is admitted as a Member of the Shawra, or Municipal council, altho' christian interests are decided by that Tribunal.

A similar feeling is evinced in all other matters. A few days ago the mother of a Boy from eight to nine years of age came to intreat me to use my influence for the release of her child, whom she said had been decoyed away by a Turk, and made a Mahometan.

On enquiry, the facts proved to be as stated, but I found that any intervention on my part with the Pacha would be useless, as His Excellency dared not, even if so inclined restore the child to its parent, lest he should array against himself the whole Mussulman population.

The poor woman told me that she had been repulsed in every attempt to get a hearing from the Pacha.

Proselytism to Mahometanism has taken place to a considerable extent since the return of the Turks to Syria.[1]

I have been informed of twenty-five cases in Aleppo, five of which are children from seven to twelve years of age.

F.O. 78/500, Moore (Aleppo) to Aberdeen (London), 27 Jan. 1842, no. 5.

---

[1] Muhammad Ali of Egypt controlled Syria from 1831–1840.

37. Riots and Massacres in Aleppo (1850)

Mr. Consul Werry has already reported to your Excellency the deplorable events at Aleppo, and a mass of statements which I have received on the same subject, place in still darker relief those occurrences. I shall state a few facts which will prove, that, only for the impardonable misconduct of the Turkish Civil and Military Authorities, the revolt might easily have been put down.

There are two Mussulman parties at Aleppo, the Moderate and the Fanatical, which latter includes the "Ayans," or Notables. The first treat the Christians well, and many of them, during the late troubles, guarded the houses of the Europeans, and even defended with arms the Christians against their Mussulman enemies.

There is a garrison of 1,400 men, cavalry and infantry with three guns at Aleppo. With this force and the Moderate Party, the two Pashas might easily, as will be shown, have crushed an Aleppo mob, and wild Bedouins armed only with bad matchlocks. But the two Pashas at Aleppo, instead of acting with the resolution of men, or the sense of duty, of responsible authorities, abandoned the City, and its stronghold, the Castle, full of warlike stores, where they only left 30 native Artillery men of doubtful fidelity, and retired to the Barracks where they remained the whole night in pretended consultation with the "Ayans," whose fanaticism and bad example had, mainly, caused the outrage on their Christian neighbours.

Having allowed the Insurgents full scope to commit, during the night, every sort of atrocity in the Christian Quarter, Kerim Pasha, in the morning makes what he calls "a military demonstration," that is, he marches his troops and guns, the band playing, round the Quarter where the rioters, in broad day, were burning and pillaging the Churches, murdering the Clergy and laity, and violating Christian women in the very presence of their nearest and dearest relatives. The Insurgents well understood the nature of this pusillanimous parade, for Mr. Werry reports "that, during it and after it, the horrors in 'Guedidah' were continued."

Eventually, after 24 hours uninterrupted outrage, a few troops were sent with Abdalla Bey, a Civilian and some orderly Mussulmans, into the Christian Quarter, and [they] reestablished order there. This fact proves how easy it would have been, as I have stated, for the authorities to have restored order. . . .

The events at Aleppo have caused amongst all classes of all nationalities a sensation such as I never witnessed here before. The population of Aleppo is the wealthiest, best conducted community in Syria. That such a body of people, in a time of profound peace, living under the protection of an organized Government, of two Pashas, and a garrison of regular troops of all arms should find themselves, without the slightest provocation on their part or a moment's warning, the victims of atrocities which are rarely practised on a town taken by storm, is a consideration which has, I regret to say, produced a feeling most unfavorable to the responsible Government. The Christians of Syria, even those under the protection of regular troops and Authorities, tremble lest the fate of their coreligionists of Aleppo should be their own. The fears of those where there are no regular troops and Government are of course more intense.

The only means of restoring confidence in Syria, and of preventing a recurrence of events as hurtful to the Porte's political interests as to those of humanity, is that the Porte should, for the future, grant equal justice, before the laws, to Christians and Mussulmans, view the catastrophe of Aleppo in all its painful gravity, and punish the authors of it with unshrinking justice and severity; that is, punishment of the two Pashas of Aleppo; capital punishment, or banishment for life of the perpetrators of murder, and violation; and indemnity for the sufferers by the confiscation of the properties of those inhabitants, who have, directly or indirectly, been concerned in depriving their unoffending fellow townsmen of all that men hold dear.

But if the Porte adopts, or is misled by the short sighted views of its Agents in Syria, who already endeavour to find unworthy excuses for the culprits, and causes of blame for the sufferers, to cloak the cruel fanatacism which caused, and the irresolution of treachery of the Pashas which literally encouraged the commission of Aleppo, and Maloula[1] atrocities, then, I have the honor to say, that the Porte will never regain the confidence of its Christian subjects in Syria, who will unceasingly seek for foreign protection and sigh for foreign rule; nor will the Porte be able to prevent the recurrence of the tragedy of Aleppo, nor keep in subjection its Mussulman subjects who will be confirmed in the unfortunate impression which they now have, that, notwithstanding all ostensible declarations, the Porte, in reality, looks on its Christian subjects with mistrust, if not aversion, and on its Mussulman subjects as the only faithful guardians of its rule; and further, that if left to itself, the Porte never would punish, with substantial justice, any oppression which Mussulmans might exercise on their Christian countrymen. And here, however delicate the subject, I cannot, from a sense of duty, fail to report a cause, which, only one of many, confirms such dangerous impressions. I allude to the present, which the Sultan, when dispensing favors, this summer, during his Royal progress, made to Bedr Khan Bey, actually under punishment

---

[1] The homes of the Christians in Maloula were plundered, the clergy killed, and their women dishonored by the regular troops. (*FO* 78/836, Rose to Canning, 31 Oct. 1850, no. 48).

for having committed one of the most unprovoked and sanguinary massacres of Christians on record. It is impossible that the provincial Pasha, the fanatical Ayans of a Country town, an Aleppo mob, or wild Bedouins, can view such an act but as a mark of Royal favour to a Mussulman, who had done to Christians all the wrong that fanatical inhumanity could do. And however willing I am to do justice to the good intentions of the present Turkish Ministers, yet I must state that there is one general complaint among Syrian Christians, those of the Lebanon excepted, and unfortunately only too true an one, that Mussulmans and their laws oppress them, and that it is almost useless to ask for justice either from the Turkish Authorities, or Tribunals of justice.

I have frequently had the honor in my despatches, and lately in my military report, to foretell two evils which have mainly brought about the disaster at Aleppo. I mean the lawless and menacing state of the Arab tribes on the desert Line from Aleppo to the Dead Sea, and the inability of the troops to keep in subjection those tribes.

Mr. Calvert's report, No. 29, to Her Majesty's Embassy gives a further proof of the inability of the Turkish troops to enforce the Pasha's order on the Desert Line. . . .

F.O. 78/836 Rose (Beirut) to Canning (Constantinople), 31 Oct. 1850, no. 47.

38. Muslims, Orthodox Christians, and Protestants in Nablus (1853)

I have the honor to report that on the 3rd. Instant [November] His Lordship our Bishop sent me an official complaint that his school house at Nablus had been entered by persons of the Greek religion in that town, who beat the native Protestants assembled there for prayers, and drove them out of the premises.

I sent my Dragoman together with the Dragoman of His Lordship to our Pasha to represent the case and we obtained a letter for the Governor of Nablus. The former of the two rode off that night to see the case properly investigated.

On arriving there, he found the Osmanli Governor who has been recently established utterly helpless for he has only 19 of the petty police with him for governing that turbulent mountain district which of late years could scarcely be kept quiet, by a ruthless military Pasha with a regiment of cavalry, half a dozen pieces of artillery, and a large number of irregular horse.

On that day the Medjlis (Council) was fully occupied with the business of the Sultan's conscription. Next day came an Agent of the Greek Convent named Nxyphon who immediately spent 10,000 Piasters (or £ 100) among the members of the Council, and the Governor refused to summon a meeting that day under the pretext of its being Friday, or Public prayer day.

When they met on Saturday, the Mufti silenced all discussion and on his giving a signal the room was quickly surrounded by a riotous mob, who for the most part far from knowing why they were called together thought it was to get up an excitement against the Greek Church in the town, and accordingly vociferated as to the necessity of destroying Christian Churches, or at least of diminishing their privileges and lowering their doors and windows. They shouted out "Look at the Dragoman sitting on a chair—kill him, kill him. Did you ever see a Christian like that before?" And the Mufti drew up a Fetwah, or a legal decree that it is against the honor of the Moslem religion to permit Christian Churches to be erected, but only to tolerate such as were found in the country at the time of the Mohhammedan Conquest—he also reiterated orally, that the Protestants should not be allowed to worship in any place of general meeting, and even in their own houses not above three together, and then in a subdued voice.

The next day being Sunday, the Dragoman (himself a native Protestant from Damascus but educated in England and France) attended public prayers with the rest in the house of one of the Protestants—not in the school room—then returned on the morrow to Jersualem.

On learning the tidings I proceeded to the Pasha whom I found very ill, chiefly from the infirmities of his advanced age. I complained of the violence of the Mufti, the threats of the crowd to kill my official Dragoman requested a copy of the Fetwah and demanded that the Mufti with a certain Sheikh Shehadeh be brought to Jerusalem to answer for their resistance to the gracious Firmans of His Majesty the Sultan in favor of his Protestant subjects.

The Pasha refused to do any thing till he should receive an answer to the letter which the Dragoman had taken to Nablus about the original beating. There had been already an abundance of time for that answer to be received here, but still His Governance persisted in the refusal and I have not yet heard that an answer has arrived. . . .

The Vice Consul by a long forced march reached Nablus in one day, viz Saturday.

The next morning he sent notice to the Governor, that the native Protestants were about to hold Divine Service in the School room. The Governor advised them not to do so, and sent for the headman of that community to whom he read a letter from the Pasha of Jerusalem warning him not to allow the Protestants to have a special room for worship without a vizirial Order from Constantinople.

Divine Service was however performed in the School room, and also in the afternoon in a private house where the rite of baptism was administered to an infant.

Next day a Council was held—The Governor refused to produce the Pasha's order, but the Vice Consul has been informed by persons of the town that it is dated several days after the first riot.

And so the matter stands at present. The Protestants of Nablus have been advised by Mr. Sandreczki not to meet again for prayer in the School room until a Vizirial order be obtained, in compliance with the Sultan's Firman, which fully allows them to have stated places of worship. . . .

F.O. 195/369. Finn (Jerusalem) to Clarendon (London), 18 Nov. 1853, no. 28.

39. Expulsion of Protestants from Nablus (1856)

The humble petition of the Protestants of Nablous showeth:

That your humble petitioners on account of their afflicted and calamitous state, humbly represents to your Excellency the injuries inflicted on them, the loss of their freedom, the violation of the law which they have suffered, the distruction [sic] of their peace, the insecurity of their lives, property, and families, all which they at present endure, through the proceeding of the Ulamah Council at Nablous, which was held five months ago; and we humbly petition that your Excellency may be moved with compassion, to deliver us from those obstinate and factious men, who are violently opposing the will of his Imperial Majesty, by robbing Christians of their liberty in the way which your humble petitioners now state.

Since the issue of the Firman [Hatt-i Hümayun, Feb. 1856] declaring religious liberty, the Mohammedans of Nablous have been filled with rage against the Christians, insulting his Majesty the Sultan, and crying "No obedience to a creature, who causes disobedience to the Creator." On Friday, April 4th, at 10 o'clock before noon, most of the Ulamahs of Nablous including about twenty of the most influential, assembled in one of the Mosques, and deliberated together. After this, one of them sallied forth, going through the streets and markets crying aloud, Allah Akbar! God is great! Oh religion of Mohammed, attack the Christians; at the same time all the Mohammedans being assembled in the Mosques for prayer, the Ulamahs stopped the Muazzins and made them come down from the Minarets, saying there shall be no prayers for the religion of Mohammed is dead; and they con-

tinued to excite the populace, arousing them to fury, that they might
fall upon the Christians.

The Christians hearing all this, were filled with fear, and endeavoured to hide themselves, but in vain, for the Mohammedans
rushed furiously upon them shouting, the Mufty-Al-Shek-Ahmed-Al-
Khaniahshi and Shek Salha-Al-Bakaney, one of the chief of the
Ulamahs, led on the people against the Christians. The first house
they entered was that of the French Consular Agent Mohammed
Ameen Effendi-Al-Kasim, and broke both the French and Turkish
flagstaffs and dragged the flags through the streets which had been
hoisted two days before, in honour of the birth of the son of the
Emperor Napolion 3ᵈ [sic], thence they proceeded to the school of
Bishop Gobat, pulled part of it down destroyed the furniture tore up
and burned the books, and did the same to the room set apart for
Divine Service breaking in pieces the bell, which the Bishop had
caused to be fixed there two days before; afterwards they despoiled
the Greek Church and the house of the Wakkeel of the Greek Convent, then they assaulted the house of Ouda-Azzam (the Agent of
J. Finn Esqr. H. M. Consul) seeking to kill him and to plunder his
house, providentially he had left the town two days before, accompanying the Bishop to Nazareth, (they sought also for some of your
humble petitioners to kill them; viz. the Revd. Mr. Zeller, Michal
Kawar, and Saeed-Kawar the Prussian Consular Agents;) as the door
of the house was very strong, they broke it with axes, they entered in,
plundered whatever they found, and destroyed what they could not
carry away, broke the British flagstaff, dragging the flag in the streets,
which also had been hoisted two days before, in honour of the birth of
Napolion [sic] the third's son, they found in the house the servant of
Revd. Mr. Zeller wounded him severely and left him for dead; they
found another influential Christian named Samaan Kawar, father of
one of your humble servants Saeed Kawar and killed him stabbing
him with twenty-eight wounds; thence they went to the house of the
Revd. Mr. Zeller a Clergyman sent out to your humble petitioners by
the English Church Missionary Society, and plundered it, together
with the property of the Revd. Mr. Bowen, an English Clergyman
formerly resident in the same house, stoling [sic] whatever they could
carry away and destroying that which they could not; thence they
went to the house of Saeed Kawar, but it was protected by some of his
compassionate (Mohammedan) neighbours, who feared lest, they
should seize the widow of the man, already murdered, and treat them
[sic] in like manner. Also meeting with five other Christians they
wounded them, and mercilessly tormented and burned a poor boy by
burying him in lime; their shouts were frightful, together with those

of the females who shrieked on the terraces to excite and encourage them, and from the terror, thus occasioned 12 Christian women suffered mis-carriages; the rebels then rushed to the Governer's house, to seize the Revd. Mr. Lyde (who had had [*sic*] accidentally shot a dumb man that day) but they could not enter the house, on account of the Kayim Makam and some of the soldiers; and after this, finding they could not seize Mr. Lyde, and that the others whom they sought for, were absent from town, their rage somewhat abated. Should your humble servants have reported to your Excellency all the sad and lamentable things which took place, they would not have been contained in this brief petition; the Greeks [Orthodox] from fear, have appeared outwardly satisfied with the Mohammedans and have made no claim [of] satisfaction for the injuries done.

They have continued since that time regarding your humble petitioners, the Protestants with an evil eye, with frequent threats of revenge and murder, so that all those of your humble servants who were able to do so, have fled from persecution, leaving Nablous and thereby losing our business and means of subsistence, and those who could not leave, threw themselves upon the Greeks in the hope of protection, because their chief rap [*sic*] was against your humble petitioners, for they in their ignorance regard Protestants in general as English, on account of the unity of religion, therefore they treat your humble servants answerable for the calamity that happened with the Revd. Mr Lyde, because he is an Englishman; the Mohammedans make no distinction between the Christian nations, in their general hatred and enmity against that religion.

The truth of Christianity will alone suffice to move your Excellency to plead our case and protect us, for your humble petitioners know the benevolent disposition of the British Government to assist every one unjustly injured like themselves. The injury is not a small one, five months have now elapsed, and your humble petitioners are waiting to obtain redress through your Excellency, hoping for the just punishment of the guilty and the satisfaction of those who have suffered unjustly.

We believe that some official personages connected with other Governments, may have reported to their respective Government that the disturbances of Nablous were a trifling affair, unworthy of their interference, but enough has been already stated for your Excellency to perceive that it is a very serious matter which demands your consideration, the injury done is not to your humble servants alone, it is a contempt of the higher power, as well as of truth and justice of the Supreme; your humble petitioners have become a proverb and taunt to all who are round abount [*sic*] them, everywhere now if a Christian disagrees with a Mohammedan, the latter say to him we will do to you as it has been done at Nablous, and therefore in numerous places Christians have been maltreated since this disturbance at Nablous.

Your humble petitioners have thought it no trifling matter, which they have left bound in conscience to lay before your Excellency, praying you to deliver them from their present state of oppression, and hoping from the known humanity of your Excellency for a speedy redress, for if this be longer delayed your humble petitioners will be reduced to nothings.

And as they and their children are in duty bound, your petitioners ever pray.

Your obedient humble servants

Ouda-Azzam. Saeed Kawar. Michal-Kawar. Yakoub El Mousah. Dahoud-Tannous. Gerges-Tannous. Michal-Dourzey. Mousah-Dourzey; and all the native Protestants of Nablous.

F.O. 195/524. Petition (English and Arabic) to Canning (Constantinople), 13 Sept. 1856.

Appeal of Jerusalem Protestants

We, Members of the Congregation of Protestant Christians in Jerusalem, beg respectfully to call your Excellency's attention to the present distressed condition of our brethren the native protestants of Nablous who have been obliged to fly their homes and seek refuge in Jerusalem from the outrages of Mohammedan persecution.

Your Excellency, we presume, has already been officially furnished with a detailed account, through the British Consul at Jerusalem, as well as through Christian friends in Constantinople, of the fearful riot which took place among the Mohammedan population of Nablous in the month of April last, of which the death of a Dervish, in a casual rencontre with an English subject, was the accidental origin. That event, which is universally acknowledged to have been the result of accident, and which at any other time would have produced only a partial sensation, was on this occasion made the pretext of a general and furious outbreak of Mohammedan fanaticism, which vented itself in acts of violence against the persons and property of the Christian inhabitants without discrimination. The Protestants, however, suffered more severely than the other Christians: One of them, the father of the Prussian Agent, was murdered, another, the servant of the Revd. Mr. Zeller of the Church Missionary Society, was dangerously wounded, and all were placed in imminent peril of their lives. The School room of the Mission was broken into and nearly destroyed, and a large stock of Bibles and school books, torn and scattered. The house of the Missionary was plundered, and valuable

books, furniture and wearing apparel either destroyed or carried off
by the rioters. The sufferers seeing that they could expect no security
for themselves in Nablous, had no other alternative than to seek a
temporary asylum in Jerusalem, where they have been kindly received and lodged by the Bishop.

Five months have now elapsed, since they have been driven from
their homes and deprived of the ordinary means of gaining their
livelihood in their respective callings, and as yet no legal measures
have been taken to bring the rioters to Justice and to indemnify the
sufferers for the losses and injuries they have sustained.

It is but justice towards our persecuted brethren to repell the unfair
attempt which has been made by an Ultramontane [Roman Catholic]
journal of Paris, to prejudice their cause, by giving a false colour to
their disturbances of Nablous, as having been provoked by the impru-
dent demonstrations of the Protestants, and that the hostility of the
Moslems was particularly directed against them; whereas it is notorious that the Moslems, whose prejudices had been previously inflamed
by the promulgation of the Hatti Scheriff [Hümayun, Feb. 1856] were
actually ripe for an outbreak before the accidental death of the Dervish had occurred, and that the fury of the rioters was indiscrimately
directed against all Christians without distinction. The houses of the
French, English and Prussian Agents were all forced and plundered;
and their national Flags, which had been there hoisted for the first
time to signalize the birth of an heir to the Imperial throne of France,
were also torn down and trampled under foot by the mob. The Greek
Church together with the house of the Greek priest, were at the same
time broken into, ransacked and damaged. The priest was obliged to
make his escape and save his life by flight.

It is with feelings of deep sympathy with our suffering brethren of
Nablous, not unmixed with apprehension for our own personal
safety, as well as that of the protestant communities existing in other
parts of Palestine and Syria, that we turn with confidence to your
Excellency for protection in these perilous times and circumstances.
We are fully sensible of the necessity of the greatest caution, forbearance and prudence on our part towards the Moslems in avoiding
every demonstration that would needlessly irritate their pride, prejudices and jealousy. Such, we are persuaded, is the sentiment that
pervades the protestants of these countries; but we cannot be answerable for the conduct of Christians of other communions, who
may be disposed to make an ostentatious and offensive display of
their newly acquired liberties, and which may at any time provoke a
repetition of the riotous scenes of Nablous: for the excitement is not
confined to that place, but extends widely throughout the Moslem

population, which seems determined to resist the execution of the Hatti Scheriff.

The measures to be adopted for restoring the poor outcasts of Nablous to their homes, and indemnifying them for the losses and cruel treatment they have suffered, we confidently leave to your Excellency's superior wisdom and experience. But we respectfully suggest that a tardy Justice would both weaken the effect of a vindication of the law on the offenders, and encourage impunity for a repetition of similar outrages in other quarters. . . .

F.O. 195/524. Nicolayson (Jerusalem) and nineteen other Protestant signatories. Encl. in Finn (Jerusalem) to Canning (Constantinople), Sept. 1856. See identical copy—encl. in Finn (Jerusalem) to Clarendon (London), Sept. 1856 (F.O. 78/1217)

40. Impunity of the Ulama in Palestine

I have the honor to report that the Pasha is still absent at Nablus, collecting taxes.

Some time ago he requested a visit of my Dragoman, and while recapitulating with him the events of the riot of April 1856 [in Nablus] His Excellency expressed the best will in the world to do justice, but stated that he had no power to do any thing—only to make a report of his investigation of the matter.

He was as unwilling as any other Governor to punish any offender— talked of his being officially instructed to act with prudence, and not to risk a disturbance of the public peace, and he expressed his opinion just as all others do, of the danger there is in attempting to punish any of the learned class—the Ulema. This is exactly the language held to me whenever I wish to punish the Mufti at Gaza.

Hence it appears that notwithstanding the paper Reforms of the Turkish Empire, there remains a class of persons who may excite to sedition, burglary and murder with impunity—they must not be touched, because they are of the Ulema.

But I must state further that this immunity was not so grossly boasted of, or so much really in force, between the epoch of the restoration of the Sultans' authority here in 1841 and the conclusion of the late war [the Crimean War], when the insolence of Mohammedanism took a spring upward in consequence of Turkey being politically courted and being told that she is now adopted into the family of European nations.

We hear such expressions triumphantly quoted by the Moslems

from Turkish and Arabic journals, while the ancient corruptions are scarcely even modified in practice.

I can positively affirm that among the Christians a strong feeling of discontent is on the increase, and many an aspiration is uttered in favor of Russian intervention.

The Christians complain that they are insulted by language in the streets—that they are not placed in equal rank at public Courts with Moslem fellow subjects—are ousted from almost every office of government employment—are not allowed the honor of military service, but instead of it, have the old Kharaj tax doubled upon them under the name of Mal-a anek—and during the absence of the Pasha, the old Colonel appointed to act as his deputy, has behaved in a manner peculiarly irritating to Christians—his ignorance too of business has led me, and after me, some other Consuls to refuse accepting military rule in treatment of public affairs.

F.O. 195/524. Finn (Jerusalem) to Canning (Constantinople), 22 July 1857, no. 29.

41. Christians in Jerusalem (1858)

In continuing to report concerning the apprehensions of Christians from revival of fanaticism on the part of the Mahometans, I have the honour to state that daily accounts are given me of insults in the streets offered to Christians and Jews, accompanied by acts of violence.

The latter, though generally petty cases, are of frequent occurrence, and the sufferers are afraid, if natives, to report them to Turkish authorities, inasmuch as, notwithstanding the hatti-humayoon, as far as I have learned, there is no clear case yet known of a Christian's evidence being accepted in a court of justice, or in a civil tribunal (Medjlis) against a Moslem. There have been some instances of Moslems being punished for offending Christians, but only in a summary method, without the formality of a trial or the Christian's evidence being placed on record. Of such justice we may read instances in the "Arabian Night's Entertainments," as existing previous to the hatti-humayoon.

But even in matters of important personages the same evils occur. Only a few days ago his Beatitude the Greek Patriarch was returning through the streets from the Cadi's Court of Judgment (having perhaps paid a visit to the new Cadi), preceded by his cavasses and dragoman, but had to pass through a gauntlet of curses hurled at his religion, his prayers, his fathers, &c.

This in Jerusalem, where Christian Consuls have flags flying, including the Russian: but can this state of things be expected to last long?

The occurrence is rather one of indicating the tone of public mind, than one to be dealt with by punishment of offenders, which could scarcely be done. But it could not have happened in the time of Kiamil Pasha, though he was a patron of Latin interest.

The present Pasha piques himself upon not believing too readily the complaints of Christians, and he has recently, in an unguarded moment, avowed to my dragoman that his mission here, especially over and above common work, is not to depress Christianity so much as to abate or bring down European influence.

I beg leave to express my opinion on this point, that among the few patriotic Turks, such a desire may, under certain limitations of feeling rather than of action, be excusable, but unfortunately these persons think they have to arrive at their object only by crippling of progress among their own people. Public works are not only not undertaken, but are by authority hindered. The feeblest commencement of a public-press opinion is stifled, and because Europeans are Christians, and Europeans are to be checked, the independence of the Turkish Empire is made to consist in the independence of Mahommetanism (pp. 500–501).

Finn (Jerusalem) to Malmesbury (London), 8 Nov. 1858, no. 67, in P.P. 1860 [2734] LXIX. (Extract)

42. Expulsion of Christian Villagers near Nablus (1858)

I have the honour to enclose copy of my despatch of the 27th ultimo to Mr. Moore, Her Majesty's Consul-General, and to report that, whereas many villages in the district of Nablous have a few Christian families located in each, such families were subjected in every direction to plunder and insults at the approach of Tahir, the Military Pasha, shortly before his arrival.

But the two villages of Zebabdeh and Likfair (where all the inhabitants are Christian, and in the former of which is a humble chapel) were utterly sacked, men and women stripped even to their shirts and turned adrift. This was done by the people of Tubaz and Kabâtieh, always a violent people, and no redress or punishment has yet been given by the military force. I need not say that none is afforded by the civil authority, himself a factious leader.

But on the arrival of Tahir Pasha in the city, and demanding a house to serve for a barrack, instead of encamping in tents at this beautiful season, the house of the Christian priest (Greek) was taken in his absence and his stores of grain and oil for household use during the winter were taken, not to be consumed by the soldiers (for that would entitle the owner to a claim on the Government) but were mixed into one heap, wheat, barley, lentils, and oil, by the Moslems of the city, and thrown into the street.

I feel myself more and more to be warranted in attributing the riots of Nablous, in 1856, to an anti-Christian feeling.

At this present period it may be that the Military Pasha has not been informed of what was done in the process of appropriating the priest's house to his use. But why does he not know it when I do? Simply because I am a Christian, and they fear to tell him who is not one, and who is himself afraid to coerce the inhabitants.

In conclusion, I have the honour to quote the perpetual expression of Christians in Palestine, that their lot is become far worse since the termination of the Russian War than it was before that period, extending back to 1831 (p. 501).

Finn (Jerusalem) to Malmesbury (London), 8 Nov. 1858, no. 68, in *P.P.* 1860 [2734] LXIX.

43. Report on the Christians in Aleppo (1859)

The Christian subjects of the Sultan at Aleppo still live in a state of terror. It is difficult to explain this otherwise than as a reflex of the panic they received nine years ago, for I cannot see that their condition is in any way worse than that of the Christian population in other Turkish cities where no such dread exists.

But events like those of 1850 are not easily forgotten. Houses were plundered, men of distinction amongst them were murdered, and women violated. It is therefore hardly to be wondered at that the eye witnesses of such horrors should conceal their wealth and prevent their families from appearing in the streets beyond the limits of the Christian quarter. Before the Egyptian occupation in 1832 they had grounds of complaint which cannot now be adduced. They were not allowed to ride in the town, not even to walk in the gardens. Rich merchants were fain to dress in the humblest garb to escape notice; when they failed in this they were often forced to sweep the streets or act as porters in order to give proofs of their patience and obedience; and they were never addressed by a Mussulman without expressions of contempt. The Egyptians treated them differently, and nothing of the kind has been outwardly renewed by the Mussulman population since the cessation of their occupation [1840]. In heart, however, I believe in little or no change. The Christians say that none has taken place excepting most superficially, and they constantly talk of pillage and massacre as imminent on every occasion when fanaticism is roused by Mahometan festivals.

The Bedelieh Askerieh or Tax in lieu of military service is one of the grievances of the Christians who admit that the principle is just but find fault with the mode of its application. They say, for instance, that they should not be called upon to pay the tax when the conscription is not in activity,—that if the Turks give men, it is fair to take money from the Christians,—but that, by levying the tax without enlisting recruits, the Government relieves the mussulman population at the expense of the Christians, whom it professed to favour by abolishing the Kharadj [poll tax],—and that the distribution of the tax is unequal in as much as it has been collected in some towns and not in others. The Kharadj of Aleppo amounted to 100,000 Piastres per annum while the sum of 240,000 Piastres is claimed for the Bedelieh payable by 15,000 Christians and 4,000 Jews, in lieu of 48 soldiers at 5,000 Piastres each. This falls heavily on them, and it appears the more onerous because the change was represented as a boon which the Sultan granted to his Christian subjects when yielding to pressure from abroad in their behalf. The Verghi, or personal tax, is taken unequally from the different classes of the population of Edlib, a town of this Pashalik, 25 Piastres from the Mahometans and 40 Piastres from the Christians, who complain bitterly of this injustice. Their Bishops have brought the matter before the Governor, who, strange to say, admitted that the division was unfair by consenting to reduce the amount paid by the Christians, but took upon himself to fix an arbitrary ratio which diminished the disproportion without removing it altogether. He offered to receive as a favour the quota of 38 Piastres, which favour the Christians declined to accept. The other assessments furnish no subject of dissatisfaction. . . .

In another part of this Consular District there seems to have been little change from the old times of rapine and bloodshed in Turkey. I allude to the Ansaireh mountains, stretching from the valley of the Orontes to Mount Lebanon. On a late occasion a member of the Medjlis of Tripoli, passing through a Christian village in pursuit of the revolted Ansaireh, set fire to it, and, where the inhabitants conveyed their moveable property of value into their Church which they hoped would be respected, it was broken open and plundered. This case, with many others equally abominable, of simultaneous occurence, was laid before Her Majesty's Consul General for Syria, the perpetrators of the outrages being under the jurisdiction of the Pasha of Beyrouth, and will thus have already come under Your Excellency's notice.

F.O. 78/1452, Skene (Aleppo) to Bulwer (Constantinople), 31 March 1859, no. 11. (Extract)

MARONITE MAN AND WOMAN
Engraving by Lally from a drawing by A. Bida
E. A. Spoll (1859), p. 1, in *Le Tour du Monde* (1st sem. 1861)

44. Slaughter of Christians at Hasbeya and Rasheya
(June 1860)

On the 6th and 7th August such bad Accounts were given me by certain natives of Hasbeya and Rasheya of the condition of the Christians in that district, that I determined upon visiting without delay both those Towns, so recently the scene of horrible massacres. On the 8th I had an interview with His Excellency Fuad Pasha and announced to Him my intention, at the same time asking authority for removing, if necessary, the Christians from that country, or for making the best possible arrangements for their safety. The Pasha seemed delighted with my proposal for he said he was extremely anxious to obtain accurate information of what was going on in that quarter, and hitherto he had been able to obtain no authentic accounts whatever. He immediately ordered me an escort, promised to be guided by my reports, in his future measures for the security of the country about Hermon, and placed at my disposal the sum of twenty thousand piastres for distribution among the unfortunate Christians of the country I was about to visit.

I left Damascus that same evening, Wednesday August 8th, and reached Rasheya the next morning. On arriving there I went to the house of the Druze Chief Khazâi el Ariân, and immediately began my enquiries as to the number of Christians at that moment in the place, and as to the condition in which they were. I soon found that they were indeed in a miserable state; they had nothing to eat except what they owed to the bounty of the Druzes, and that was little enough! The population amounted to 1,100 souls whereof only 76 were men, all the remaining males having been killed, and some few having fled to Damascus and Beyrout. In order to distribute the funds committed to my case, I had all the women and children mustered, and then separated in divisions according to the quarters of the Town they occupied, each division again was shut up in a house and then one by one the women and children were admitted through the door at which I stood and placed in their hands money, so that I had an opportunity of ascertaining almost to an accuracy the number of the population at that moment in Rasheya. The Druzes however soon became very jealous of this and came in numbers to ask what I was doing in their town and what my object was in coming.

. . . That night I started for Hasbeya, and passing through Kfeir and Mimis, two villages in which almost all the Christian houses had been burned and some 110 Christians killed, I reached the other large town belonging to the district of Hermon,—Hasbeya, Here I repeated my enquiries, numbered the women and children, distributed money, and received visits from the principal inhabitants. The whole number of Christians at that moment was 1,430, there having been only three months ago, no less than 3,200[;] some few are in Beyrout and Damascus but I fear that fully 1,300 were slaughtered. Here the Christians were in the same state of suffering as those whom I found at Rasheya, and in both places they were hourly in terror of a massacre, so excited had the Druzes again become. I visited the Serai, which was full of the Corpses of the Christians, none had been buried and strange to say the bodies were well preserved, having been parched by the burning Syrian sun. The sight was dreadful, bodies lying in every attitude on the paved court of the Palace, the stones naturally white being stained a deep brown; but the upper rooms presented even a more horrible spectacle; in almost all of them, the bodies were piled one upon another to the hight [*sic*] of 5 or 6 feet, and lay just as they had fallen; to add to the horror of this frightful scene the poor women followed me in, and began to howl and mourn over their dead; they led me from corpse to corpse, telling me how they had seen their brothers, fathers, husbands, sons, slaughtered before their eyes, and calling me to witness and to avenge their wrongs. The Druzes who accompanied me made their jokes on the bodies, and one fellow showed me a pair of pistols set in silver, one of which had been broken in dashing the brains out of the Christians' heads. He lamented over his pistol and said "Oh that it should have been spoiled against their cursed hard skulls." Here again the Druzes were more bold and insolent than I had ever seen them anywhere before. I have travelled over all their country and even visited them in their strongholds in the Haurân, and have never met with anything but courtesy; Now however they speak with great insolence, boast of the number of Christians they have killed, and assert that they will cut to pieces any force which shall be brought against them. The Emir Saad ed Dîn who had been most obnoxious to the Druzes had his head cut off during the massacre, and his body thrown out under the walls of the Castle. It is said that the Druzes on first entering the Serai began to cut the Christians to pieces, but some of them remarked, "If we do this we shall spoil their clothes" let us strip them and then kill them. So accordingly after that, they stripped them and slaughtered them in cold blood. I made enquiries about the gun, which the commander of the troops had with him in the Serai at Hasbeya, how often it had been fired &c. The Christians told me it had been fired twenty-seven times, but all the balls had struck the houses of the Christian quarter, this was certainly the case; and on asking the Druzes, they said "Yes it is true Osmân Bey intended to fire upon us but he did not elevate his gun enough, so that it destroyed the Christians instead of us." Osman Bey had the doors of the Serai opened and in rushed the Druzes and commenced their slaughter.

In the evening the Druzes here again threatened my life, on which one of my escort had some words with them, two Druzes thereupon fell upon him, and there would have been bloodshed, had not some others interfered. I then returned through some of the other burned villages, where a few Christians were still struggling for their existence, coming back to Rasheya, where I visited the Serai in which a second scene like that at Hasbeya presented itself, I again mounted and rode down to Damascus where I arrived early on the morning of the 12th.

The result of my journey and of my enquiries was, that I ascertained the Christians to be in a state of great danger. No man dare go out of the towns. Each week several persons were maltreated and even killed. The Druzes threaten to exterminate them altogether should any attempt be made to remove them to Beyrout. . . .

F.O. 78/1520, Extracts from "Report of Cyril Graham Esq. on the Conditions of the Christians in the districts of Hasbeya and Rasheya", encl. in Brant (Damascus) to Russell (London), 13 August 1860, no. 13.

45. Massacre of Christians in Damascus (July 1860)

I have the honour to transmit to your Lordship a copy of a narrative I have requested Mr. Robson to draw up for your Lordship's information of the circumstances under which the massacres of Damascus have occurred.

Mr. Robson is an Irish Presbyterian Missionary. He is a person of sober judgment and great intelligence. He has been a resident at Damascus for eighteen years; he speaks Arabic perfectly; and is naturally in a position to speak with very considerable authority on everything connected with the country.

His narrative, combined with that of Mr. Graham's, a copy of which I have already had the honour of transmitting to your Lordship, will form a trustworthy and connected history of the deplorable events which have deluged this province with human blood.

Memorandum

From the commencement of the war between the Christians and the Druses in Lebanon, the Christians of Damascus were in the greatest alarm, for their Moslem fellow-citizens indulged constantly in very threatening and very insulting language towards them. Whenever they went into the bazaars or streets in the Moslem quarter of the city,

MARONITES AT MAR-ANTUN CONVENT
Engraving by F.-J. Gauchard from a drawing by J.-P. Grandsire (after a sketch
by N. Enault)
E. A. Spoll (1859), p. 8, in *Le Tour du Monde* (1st sem. 1861)

men and boys applied offensive and degrading epithets to them and their religion, cursed them, and often spoke of a rising against them. The repeated successes of the Druses increased the insolence of the one party and the terror of the other. The murders of the Christians in Kinakir, known in the city on the 11th of June; the massacres in Hasbeya and Rasheya; the outrages committed by the Moslems and Druses in villages in every direction in the surrounding country, and the sight of the wretched fugitives who flocked to the city for safety and food, to the number of 5,000 or 6,000, excited and emboldened the Moslems, and intensified the terrors of the Christians.

The impression began to prevail among all sects and classes that the Government itself desired and intended the destruction of the Christians. They were retained in the city only by the impossibility of escaping to any safe place. The fall of Zahleh, and the massacre in Deir-el-Kamar, added to the exultation of the Moslems, and rendered the panic of the Christians extreme and universal.

During all this time the Moslems became more assuming, insolent, and threatening; the insults heaped on the Christians more numerous, shameful, and alarming; while the Christians became more terrified, subdued, and cringing. They seemed to yield up at once all the rights and liberties which they had gained during the last twenty-seven years. They did not venture to ride any animal in the city; they ceased to resent any insult, or complain of any injury; they abstained from demanding payment of debts or enforcing claims against Moslems; they submitted in silence to impositions, and sometimes to assaults. To avoid the abuse to which they were exposed they ceased to frequent the cafés, the walks in the gardens, and other places of public resort, and almost abandoned their shops and business in the city. Few of them hoped that the approaching feast of the Kurban Beiram would pass without an attack on their quarter; and during the four days of the feast they confined themselves almost entirely to their houses and their own quarter.

The festival began on the 29th of June. On that day troops were stationed in the Christian quarter, and gave some encouragement to them. But they knew that the Imperial troops had been present at all the massacres of their brethren in the mountains, and that some of the officers and many of the men sent to their quarter had been themselves at those of Hasbeya and Rasheya; and the more they talked of these circumstances and reflected on them, the greater became their anxiety and their distrust of the soldiers.

The Beiram passed over, and they breathed a little more freely; but as the bearing of the Moslems did not become less insolent and hostile, and as Christians and Christianity were as much insulted as before, great anxiety and terror were still felt.

However, by Monday, 9th July, as nothing serious had happened in the city, and as there had been no further massacres elsewhere, the Christians had generally persuaded themselves that the danger which had distressed and terrified them so much and so long was nearly over.

It appears that some Moslems took pains to reassure them. On the previous evening, the now infamous Mustafa Bey-el-Hawasaly called on several of the principal Christians to persuade them that there was no longer any reason to fear, and that they might go to sleep with their doors open, and he would guarantee their perfect safety. On the 9th July, therefore, the poor Christians congratulated one another that they had escaped, and they generally returned, after a long inter-mission, to their usual occupations. The Government Clerks went to the Seraglio; the shopkeepers resumed their business; the tradesmen went to their work; the children were sent to school.

On that day the Pasha ordered two young Moslems to be put in irons for insulting Christians, and about 2 o'clock P.M. they were sent to sweep the streets. Immediately, as if this had been a preconcerted signal, the people in the principal bazars began to shut their shops, call on the religion of Mahommed, curse infidels, excite one another to arm and attack the Christians, and run together to the Christian quarter. Almost at the same moment, the mob began to collect, arm, and run from the streets adjacent to the Christian quarter, the Shagur, a suburb on the south of the city, the Medân, a large suburb on the south-west, and a mile and a-half to two miles from the Christian quarter, and from Salehîyeh, a large suburban village two miles off. They encouraged and excited one another by calling on their religion and Prophet, by imprecations on the infidels, and by crying, "Arm, arm! kill, plunder, burn; the time of slaughter has come, the sun of slaughter has arisen!" and by similar expressions.

The women also stimulated the men by their cries and curses, and their prayers of success and victory. At first they were afraid of the troops, and avoided the places where they were stationed, but they soon found that they had nothing to fear from them. The Bashi-Bozouks [irregular troops] of Salim Agha-el-Muhaïneh, Mustafa Bey-el-Hawasaly, and others, the Kurdish Irregulars under Muhammed Said Agha, and the Zaptiehs or police, were among the earliest and the most active in the work of murder and plunder. Many of the Bashi-Bozouks, as those under Hawâsaly, had been specially enrolled to preserve the peace of the city during the excitement. The people of the city were gradually joined during Monday evening and Tuesday by Druses from The Medân and from Jermana, a Druse village two miles from the city, and by Moslem peasants from several of the surrounding villages. But no Druse Chief nor any regular Druse force from a distance took part in the affair.

The mob, with the exception of the Bashi-Bozouks, were very ill armed. Only a few had muskets, some had pistols, some had swords, a great number had battle-axes or daggers, but the great majority had only clubs or sticks. Perhaps not more than one in twenty had a gun, and many of the guns were of little value.

If the Bashi-Bozouks and Zaptiehs had done their duty, the insurrection would have been put down at once; if they had only abstained from interfering no great effort would have been necessary to quell the mob. As it was, the troops, if they acted with any vigour, would probably have encountered little opposition even from the Bashi-Bozouks.

The Christians made no defence. It is said that a Greek fired some shots on the mob, and that shots were fired from two houses by natives. With these exceptions no resistance was offered to the murderers. The Christians were almost without arms. A few young men had fowling-pieces, and some few had pistols, but there was perhaps not a sword or axe among them.

The Russian Consulate, in the centre of the Christian quarter, was one of the first houses attacked, plundered, and set on fire. His dragoman was killed. Two of his servants escaped by hiding in a cellar, where, though the house was burned over them, they remained four days without food or drink. Among the houses first broken into were those of the Dutch and Belgian Vice-Consul, the United States' Vice-Consul, and Mr. Frazier, an American missionary. The first of these had escaped with his family before the house was attacked. Mr. Frazier and his family had gone from the city before the outbreak. The American Vice-Consul was very severely wounded, and escaped with great difficulty. His two eldest sons were not in the house; his whole family were scattered, and it was several days before they were reunited. The houses of the richer Christians were all early assaulted; the mob being attracted by the prospect of rich plunder. Then the houses adjoining them were attacked, and so the plundering, murder, conflagration and ruin spread more and more. The Greek Church and Patriarchate afforded plunder of great value in church ornament and plate, the rich dresses of the clergy, the patriarch's plate, and the money in the treasury.

It was guarded by soldiers on the day of the outbreak till after sunset, when it was broken into, rifled, and burned, and a large number of persons were murdered in it.

The course of proceeding was generally the same. The mob broke the door of the house with axes, rushed in, sought first for the men, murdered any they could find with clubs, sticks, axes, daggers, swords, and using sometimes fire-arms also. Then they plundered the house of furniture, clothes, stores for food, the materials of trades, and everything in it, searching carefully for money or valuables which might be concealed, and threatening and terrifying the women and children to make them tell where the men were, and if anything was hidden. They searched the women lest they might have ornaments or money concealed in their clothes, and they generally took away any articles of dress of any value which the women or children happened to have on. They very generally seized the young girls and the younger women in the house, and often took them off and kept them for a time. Finally the house was set on fire.

The better armed, the more respectable, and the more bold and violent of the murderers generally appropriated to themselves the more valuable articles in the house, and then left it for another. But they were followed by successive parties of the lower rabble, the un-armed, the poor, the weak, the women, and even children, and they stripped the house of all that remained. Not only the contents of the house, but doors, windows, window-shutters, and the panelling on the walls, were carried off. Even firewood, charcoal, the marble of the floors, and the timber of the roofs, were in many cases taken away. Besides what men, women, and children carried away, camels, horses, mules, and donkeys were employed to remove plunder.

At the moment of the outbreak a great number of merchants, shop-keepers, Government Clerks, the clerks of the Moslem merchants, and some tradesmen, as stone-cutters, and masons, were at their business in the Moslem part of the city. When the mob began to collect a part of these attempted to reach their houses, some with a feeble hope of assisting their families, and some because they knew of no other place of safety: some succeeded in getting to their homes, and some were killed in the streets. Another part fled to the English, French, and Prussian Consulates, to the house of the Emir Abd-el-Kader,[1] or to the houses of Moslem partners or acquaintances, often, in their terror and despair, forcing themselves into houses where they were little welcome. Others concealed themselves in the khans in which or near to which they happened to be at the moment, and they were generally conducted to the old citadel the next day by the troops. Had all the men been in the Christian quarter and in their own houses, as they were during the Beiram, the slaughter of the Christians would have been greater than it was, perhaps much greater.

Of the men who were in the houses or in the Christian quarter some fled to the churches, to the Austrian Consulate, or to the houses

---

[1] 'Abd al-Qadir al-Hajj (1808–1883), leader in Algeria of the war against the French. Imprisoned in France and later exiled to Damascus.

of their richer neighbours; but none of these places afforded safety. Many hid in closets, necessaries, or cellars, or on the roofs of the houses, and they were almost all discovered and most of them murdered. A number of them went down into the wells, and though a deep and narrow well was a difficult, unpleasant, and dangerous hiding-place, nearly all those who went down into them were saved, and were taken out after remaining three, four or five days, without food, and enduring all the inconveniences of such a retreat. A few escaped by passing over the roofs from house to house, and hiding at last among the ruins of houses already plundered and burned. A few got out of the city, but of these the peasants afterwards killed some and compelled others to become Moslems. Every possible expedient for concealment or flight was adopted. A few disguised themselves as women, but they were generally detected. A few also took off their outer clothes, assumed the appearance of rioters, and went off carrying furniture as if they were plunderers. Some fled from one Moslem house to another by day and by night, and though many perished in doing so, a good many finally reached a place of safety. In such perplexity, terror, and danger, and amid such scenes of plunder, outrage, murder and fire, did those saved make their escape. To the fears which every one had for himself was added anxiety about the fate of his family and friends. Of the 2,000 families of Damascenes involved in the massacre hardly one family escaped all together and reached a place of safety without being separated. Generally one member of the family did not know what had happened to the others, and days passed before the survivors all met again.

From about 2 o'clock P.M. on the 9th of July, the plundering and burning of houses, the murders, and the outrages committed on women, went on incessantly till about two hours after sunset. During most of that time several thousands of rioters were actively engaged. The most valuable part of the plunder was secured and the murders were very numerous. Most of the mob retired from the Christian quarter during the night, but many remained, and the work of destruction never entirely ceased. The fire was by that time extensively spread, and several hundred houses must have been in flames. At daylight the next morning the Moslems returned to the Christian quarter in as great numbers as on the previous afternoon, and the plundering, burning, and murder went on throughout the day, diminishing, however, towards the evening, because little remained to be attacked. On this day almost all the shops of the Christians in the principal bazaars were broken, open and plundered. By sunset there was nothing left to the Christians but the stones and fragments of the timber of burning houses, and a few houses and rooms which the flames had not yet reached, and there remained no Christians in the quarter except those who were effectually concealed in the wells or amid the ruins of the houses.

On Wednesday morning a false and very improbable report was spread, that some Christians had fired from a Moslem's house on Moslems in the street, and killed two of them. The object of this report was soon evident from what followed. A mob of Moslems from Salehîyeh brought, it is said, by Sheik Abdullah-el-Haleby, under pretence of putting out the fire, commenced a new and very horrid work, in which others soon joined them. They went round the different quarters in which Christians had taken refuge, demanded that they should be given up, and either killed them as soon as they appeared in the streets, and dragged their bodies to the Christian quarter, or first conducted them alive to the ruins, and killed them there. The number massacred in this brutal and shocking way, after their property and houses were destroyed, and after that they had hoped that the bitterness of death was passed, it is impossible to ascertain with any exactness unless the Government were to institute a *bonâ fide* and rigid investigation in the districts of the city which were the scenes of these horrible murders. But it is certain that several hundred of those who vainly hoped that they had found a refuge, perished on that day, and that very few of those in private houses escaped, except such as consented to embrace Mahometanism.

After that day, Wednesday, the 11th July, there were only a few murders because no Christians remained within reach of the murderers. Doors, timber, and marble were carried off from the ruins, but not to any great extent. The fire continued till the beginning of the following week, when it almost ceased for want of materials, though for some ten days longer it was partially maintained by setting on fire any portions of houses which here and there remained. The houses in Damascus, and especially the poor houses, owing to the way in which they are built, do not readily burn. Accidental fires are very rare, and almost all originate in the establishments of cooks or bakers—seldom in private houses. As there was a perfect calm during the massacre, the fire would have gone out of itself without spreading far if it had not been constantly kept up by setting fire to additional houses.

The work of the plunderers was complete. Nothing to be found in the Christian quarter was left if it seemed worth carrying away. Many had concealed some of their more valuable effects under the floors or in secret recesses, closets, presses, or holes in the wall, or by throwing them into wells; most of what was thrown into wells was preserved, but almost everything else was discovered and taken away. The shops in the bazaars were plundered, but the khans were not attacked, and the property which Christians had in them was not disturbed. The Consulates of England, France, and Prussia, owing to their situation in the Moslem quarter, to their being guarded, and to other special circumstances, were not plundered. Besides, these, a house in the Moslem quarter in which an Englishman lived, escaped.

About 1,500 houses were robbed; one private and unguarded house was left untouched. Some 200 houses adjacent to or among Moslem houses were plundered and greatly injured, but not burned. All the rest of the quarter to the number of 1,200 or 1,300 houses, with all the churches, schools, convents, workshops, and khans, is now heaps of ruins. In many places, in pulling down walls and cutting down ornamental trees, there are traces of laborious efforts to destroy even what the first spared. The lowest and perhaps the most accurate estimate of the loss of property is between 300,000 and 400,000 purses, equivalent to 1,250,000£ to 1,500,000£. To this might well be added the loss resulting from the compulsory idleness of the whole Christian population while the settlement of affairs is pending.

The number of persons murdered will never be exactly ascertained. Of hundreds, it is only known that they disappeared. The survivors are so scattered, and so occupied with other cares and anxieties, that it would be almost impossible to make an accurate list of the missing. An estimate may be made of the number of males in Damascus on the day of the insurrection, and of the probable proportion which the murdered bore to the survivors. The number of Christian males resident in the city were about 8,000 to 9,000, and of refugees from the surrounding country from 2,000 to 3,000. Thus the whole number of males would be between 10,000 and 12,000, and of this one third may be deducted for children under fourteen years of age. Of the remaining 7,500 to 8,000, probably more than a third, or about 3,000 were murdered. This is the lowest estimate yet given, but it is perhaps within a few hundreds of the truth.

But it is difficult to speak with confidence, for there was great diversity in the fate of families and sects. The proportion of murders was greater among the members of the Greek Church than among those of any other sects, for their houses were exposed to the first attack of the mob. Many families did not lose a member; many lost every adult male. In the house next to the Russian Consulate on the north, the father and his three sons were murdered, the women were abused, and the house was, as usual, plundered and burned. Four brothers who lived together abandoned their house before it was attacked, and were separated in the streets; the two elder were murdered, the two younger escaped. Two men lived in one house; one went down into the well and was saved, the other hid on the roof and was killed. In another house, where four unmarried working men lived, two of them were killed, and the other two were badly wounded and left for dead. In the Protestant Church four men and several women took refuge. One of the men was disguised as a woman and escaped from the Church, but was wounded in the street; the other three concealed themselves, but were discovered, and two of them were killed. Some thirty men were murdered in the house of a Greek priest. In the house of a working man, who was in Beyrout at that time, eleven of his neighbours were killed in the presence of his wife. In the premises of the Greek Church and Patriarchate there were several hundred refugees from Rasheya, and many Christians from the adjoining houses. The mob broke in after sunset of the first day of the insurrection, and the slaughter, both of citizens and strangers, was very great. There was a large number of the refugees in houses connected with the Armenian convent, and there also a great number were murdered. In the streets and houses near the house of Mustufa Bey el-Hawasaly, a great many dead bodies were left. The Franciscan monks were all killed. The Lazarists were saved by the Emir Abd-el-Kader. About thirty ministers of religion, including the Franciscan and a Protestant missionary, were killed. Of the native priests only five or six escaped.

It was not out of pity that the murderers spared the children. Had it been so they would, probably, not have butchered old feeble men as helpless as children. It is a doctrine of Mahometanism, founded on a saying of the Prophet, and held by all Sunnites, that every child is from birth a believer in Islam, the true religion, and that unbelieving parents make it, as it grows up, a Jew or a Christian, or an idolater, as the case may be.[2] Children, therefore, being Moslems, it is unlawful to kill them; but it was doubtless intended to take possession of them and bring them up as Moslems. Several children who have been restored to their parents were circumcised.

Unlike the Druses, who generally respected the women, the Mahometans of Damascus acted most brutally towards them. The number of young girls, and of married women and mothers, abused by them, was, perhaps, greater than that of the men murdered. A great number were taken to houses in the town, or to the villages, and even to remote villages, and were kept, some for days and some for weeks, before they were allowed to return to their families. There was great diversity in the treatment to which those taken away were subjected.

Hundreds professed Mahometanism, during the massacre, in the hope of saving their lives, but hardly any of them were spared by the mob. Many, however, of those who found a precarious refuge in the houses of Moslems, and became Mahometans to avoid being killed or

[2] *Hadith.* See Bokhari, vol. 1, t. 23, chap. 93.

delivered up to the mob, were spared. Most of these involuntary apostates were only inspired with a greater dread and abhorrence of the persecutors and their religion, and took the first opportunity of leaving Damascus to seek a place where they might venture to abjure their forced conversion.

Only a very few remain in the city and seem disposed to adhere to their new profession. In the villages of the surrounding country also a very considerable number have been forced to abjure Christianity and embrace Mahometanism.

It is manifest that the design of the rioters was to exterminate the adult male population, take possession of the women and compel them to apostatize, bring up the children as Mahometans, and destroy the Christian quarter utterly and for ever.

The mob believed that all this was sanctioned by the views of the officers of Government, the chief men of the city, and the heads of religion, and that it was permitted, if not [unreadable], by their religion. As long as Jews and Christians submit to the Moslem authorities, and pay their taxes, they are entitled to protection for their lives, their women and children, and their property, even if they resist or rebel against their Sovereign. Recent authorities teach that a Frank, even if not submitting to the authority of the Moslem Sovereign, nor paying the taxes imposed on infidels, yet, if allowed to live peaceably among Moslems for a time, becomes thereby virtually entitled to protection; and it is unlawful and contrary to the Mahometan religion to kill him, or seize his property, or take away his wife or children. Yet, in opposition to these principles, the Mahometans of Damascus had come to believe that the Christians, by taking advantage of the privileges and liberties conceded to them during the last thirty years, had placed them[selves] in a state of disobedience and rebellion, and forfeited their right to security and protection; and that it was, therefore, lawful to kill and rob them and carry off their women and children.[3]

This belief that what they did was according to their law and religion, and agreeable to the wishes of their superiors, palliates, so far, the monstrous crimes of the mob, but casts a weightier responsibility and guilt on the influential teachers and guides who disseminated such ideas among the common people, and on the Government, which did nothing to correct the erroneous impressions as to its views and designs, which were so widely circulated and believed.

The Emir Abd-el-Kader did his utmost, from the commencement of the excitement, to inculcate right views; and it is said that one Sheik earnestly adopted a similar course. But it is not known that the Mufti

[3] According to the laws of *jihad,* see "Jurists' texts".

or Sheik Abdullah-el-Haleby, the most venerated of the Ulema, or any others of that body, or of the influential people, assisted them. Rumour ascribes to them a very different course of conduct.

On the day of the outbreak, Colonel Ali Bey was in command of the troops in the Christian quarter, and actually refused to act against the mob. Another officer, Colonel Salish Ziky, without orders, made some of the troops fire on the rioters, and he also fired a gun, once or oftener. One or two persons were killed, and some wounded. When the troops fired, the mob fell back, and not the slightest symptom of resistance to the troops was shown.

This partial and feeble effort soon ceased. After sunset the troops were collected in one place, and remained till 1 or 2 o'clock on Tuesday morning, when they marched to the barracks. Not a sentinel was left in the Christian quarter. On subsequent days, a few of the troops were employed to conduct some Christians from khans and other hiding-places to the citadel (pp. 173–79).

Dufferin (Beirut) to Russell (London), 23 September 1860, no. 146 & encl. in *P.P.* 1861 [2800] LXVIII.

46. Situation of the Christians throughout Syria (1860)

I have the honor to inform Your Excellency that by last evening's Beyrout post we learned the departure of the Seraskier with two battalions on Sunday the 22nd. Inst [July]: and the promised departure of His Excellency Fuad Pasha with two other battalions; thus the arrival of necessary succours is deferred from day to day and in the same degree the restoration of confidence. The Jews who had taken refuge in Turkish houses were beginning to return to their own, but they are persecuted by people demanding money under threats of violence. It is reported that many Druzes are walking about the Town today which occasions apprehension, and shows weakness in the Government. We learned by the post that a strong message had been sent through the French Ambassador to the Porte, that seeing the inability of the Sultans Government to protect its Christian subjects, France would consult with her allies as to the means of preventing the massacres which have been disgracing Syria. If an armed intervention were resolved on without protection to the Christians being in some way secured, not one would escape, for before foreign aid could reach those in the interior, they would to the last soul be murdered, unless it were those who embraced Islamism. The Porte therefore should be urged to send adequate forces, and active and energetic employés to restore order for the time, but if it could not be permanently ensured,

then the momentary security should be availed of to withdraw the
Christians to the coast before foreign troops were sent into the interior. I would beg Your Excellency to consider what is to be done with
regard to the men and boys who have become Mussulmans under
threats of death, and what with regard to the women who have been
taken by Moslems as wives and concubines and made to conform to
Islamism.

I have come to an end of my pecuniary resources, and know not
how to obtain supplies; nobody in the actual state of insecurity will
cash private bills, nor have I funds to draw upon if they would. I have
managed to give sustenence to those under my roof; many have departed, but I still have about 30, and I know not when I shall be able
to get them off my hands, for many are widows and orphans, and
have neither houses to go to, nor friends to help them, and all are
without resources of any kind, for providing food clothing or lodging.

F.O. 78/1520, Brant (Damascus) to Bulwer (Constantinople), 25 July
1860, no. 28.

47. Refusal to Condemn Murderers

Property of great bulk has been restored, but I fear of small value.
About 750 persons, accused of murder and robbing or of robbing
alone, are under arrest, some have been proved guilty of murder.
Only one as yet has been executed, and in the Christian Quarter the
very same day a Christian was massacred, and the report was spread
about the City that the inhabitants were determined to murder a
Christian for every Mussulman executed. This report has renewed a
panic and increased the desire of the Christians to quit the City, many
of whom were beginning to think that they might be able to remain.

The Criminal Commission cannot get any witnesses to swear to a
man being a murderer, many will testify that people have been guilty
of plundering, but as to murder, one might almost believe that none
had been committed, and although it is certain that above 5,000 persons have been massacred in broad daylight or by the light of blazing
houses, yet nobody will testify to having witnessed a murder committed, or will recognise a single man guilty of such a crime. If the
ordinary forms of Turkish law cannot reach such criminals, extraordinary proceedings must be resorted to, and people proved guilty of
plundering must be treated as having at the same time committed
murder. Atrocities such as have been committed cannot go unpunished by such subterfuges as are attempted to turn aside the sword of
justice. If other means cannot be devised a Hat-i-Sheriff should be

published condemning to death every one guilty of arson or robbery in the late outbreak at Damascus, giving to the Court power to recommend to a less penalty than death such persons in whose favor strong extenuating circumstances can be adduced.

F.O. 78/1520, Brant (Damascus) to Bulwer (Constantinople), 9 Aug. 1860, no. 31. (Extract)

After Some Criminals Were Arrested

I anticipate that Fuad Pasha will immediately commence executing some of the Criminals condemned, and I have no doubt his doing so will strike terror into the population. The Mussulmans will not yet believe that any executions can result from the murder of infidels[;] when that is made clear to their mind, many will change their tone and conduct and make revelations which they at present withhold.

F.O. 78/1520, Brant (Damascus) to Bulwer (Constantinople), 16 Aug. 1860, no. 34. (Extract)

48. Causes of the Massacres (Syria, 1860)

. . . I observed to Ahmet Pasha [governor of Damascus] that when the Mussulman boys were set to sweep the streets of the Christian Quarter in chains, precautions should have been taken to repress a possible outbreak; he replied that it would have been useless as the plot was prepared, and had not this pretext been found some other would have served the purpose. I then asked him what was then done by the secret police, of whose activity and intelligence he had boasted, that he was not informed of the plot; to this he gave no answer. At one time however, he pretended that there was a plot, at another that no such existed. I have not yet seen any distinct evidence that an organised plot was formed. The disposition to plunder and murder the Christians no doubt was very strong, but the exhibition of vigour on the part of the Government, it is universally acknowledged, would have repressed it. The soldiers recruited in Syria were not to be depended on, as was evident from their conduct at Hasbeya and Rasheya, and these very men were those selected to guard the Christian Quarter on the occasion of the Beiram, and to repress the outbreak, this certainly looked suspicious, but I believe the real reason was that the Mushir [Ahmet Pasha] was afraid of them, and wished to remove them from the Serai, and preserve for his own protection,— which alone seemed to occupy his thoughts—the well-disposed men. The Ex-Mushir is now on his trial [sic] and must justify his conduct and explain his motives as best he can. . . . For such neglect of duty and incapacity in an Employé of his high rank and for such arrant cowardice in a general Officer, by which the lives of probably 10,000 Christians were sacrificed, besides the intense misery occasioned to twice as many, by wounds and sufferings, by loss of parents and relations and of property, by the disgrace brought on his Sovereign, by the ruin on his country, and the indelible stain on his religious faith, supposing even nothing but incapacity for his high functions and cowardice as an officer be proved, the punishment of a disgraceful death has been merited.

It would indeed produce most lamentable consequences were this contest to degenerate into a religious conflict, but such a result is not improbable, unless very great discretion and forbearance be enforced on the Christians of the Lebanon. Their conduct for some years past has been marked by an intolerant and irritating spirit, and at Beyrout now they have taken courage at the presence of French troops, they have directly become insolent and provoking towards the Mussulmans, and if such behaviour be not severely repressed by their religious chiefs, great inconvenience will result.

The incidents of the war, in which Druzes and Maronites were alone concerned must be considered apart from the massacres of Hasbeya, Rasheya and Deir-el-Kamer, which were perpetrated in cold blood after the Christians had surrendered their arms on their safety being guaranteed by the Turkish Officers commanding the garrisons. It might have been impossible for the Authorities to have hindered or arrested the war, but it was in their power to have prevented the massacres, and therefore they may be charged with having allowed them. This gives to these massacres a character of enormity independent of the war. The massacre of Damascus was no further connected with the war than as that [it] afforded a good pretext for the outbursting [sic] of a long pent up hatred of Christians, and that the passions of lawless men once excited, they were ready to join in any acts of murder and plunder. With respect to the causes which produced the fanatical feelings of the Damascenes, it is of long standing and is only an old wound reopened. Up to the period of the Egyptian occupation [1831–1840], fanaticism reigned unchecked in Damascus. It then received a severe blow, beneath which it was crushed temporarily, and was not allowed to revive while the province was attached to Egypt. Since the restoration of Syria to the Sultan, the local Government has been yearly becoming more lax, and fanaticism has been gradually reviving. Since the close of the Russian war [Crimean War, 1853–1856], it has made a more marked advance, and the Porte itself has used it as one of the means of diminishing European influence; this was of course done secretly, but it was pretty evident to superficial observers even, for the disguise was too transparent not to allow the purpose to be seen through it. In the last two years it was remarked that abuse of Christians and terms of reproach towards their faith were more frequently used than formerly. Boys threw stones at Christians and Europeans in the streets, and respectable Mussulmans passing and witnessing these outrages did not reprove the authors of them. When the war between the Druzes and Christians broke out these impertinences were more frequent but the authorities did not increase in vigilance, and the ill-disposed became more bold. The respectable inhabitants did not to my knowledge encourage these acts, neither did I hear they discouraged them; they seemed to treat them with indifference. A large bell lately placed in the Maronite Church gave great umbrage. The magnificent Lazarist Convent was not seen with pleasure. The splendid houses built by the rich class of Christians excited jealousy, and their general prosperity tended to create in the Mussulmans feelings of envy. The persons who managed the affairs of the Pashalik were Christians; they kept the Public Accounts and grew rich in the employment. The Christian traders were more prosperous than the Mussulmans; in short, the intelligence and industry of the former bore its natural fruits, but the pride of the latter was all the more deeply wounded. All these circumstances annoyed the Mussulmans and they felt their inferiority as well in influence as in riches, and it rankled in their breasts, no doubt therefore these people were not sorry to see the Christians humbled. Perhaps Your Excellency will consider the foregoing,—added to the impotence of the local authorities in representing the misconduct of the Mussulmans towards their Christian neighbours—as sufficiently accounting for an outbreak without the existence of an organised plot, when the ill-timed exercise of severity by the Infenkgee Bashi produced the explosion. The Arab portion of the troops were excited by the desire of seizing the Christian women, and were greedy of booty, having tasted both at Hasbeya and Rasheya, and they were therefore eager to promote, rather than suppress, a movement which would gratify their lustful passions and their love of plunder. I have already stated that no conduct on the part of my colleagues would have altered the course of events. . . .

F.O. 78/1520, Brant (Damascus) to Bulwer (Constantinople), 30 Aug. 1860, no. 40.

49. Responsibility of Muslim Notables

. . . The position of Syria is certainly different from that of other parts of Turkey, in as much as a war between the hostile sects of

Maronites and Druzes has been raging, and an outbreak of fanaticism
has occurred, of which recent ages do not afford a parallel. The two
cases, as Your Excellency pointed out, in their origin were distinct, but
they ultimately became blended together, and will probably be submitted to one treatment. . . .

It is, I am well aware, the object of the Sultan's allies to sustain His
Majesty's Government, but the means of doing this are not very obvious; that Fuad Pasha will establish the authority of the Porte I have no
doubt, but if afterwards the same mode of governing be continued, by
agents of the same stamp as formerly, no better result is probable.

In my various reports on the state of this Pashalik, I have often
made suggestions for the improvement of the administration and for
the better security of the inhabitants in their property and rights, but
since the outbreak matters are so changed that it is not merely the
introduction of improvements that will reestablish the Government
on a solid basis. A complete change of system is required which must
be the result of the serious consideration and enquiry of the Commis-
sioners. As to the financial system, there was none that I could ever
discover, except that as much should be extracted from the people as
they had to give, and that as much as possible of these exactions
should remain in the hands of the employés in its passage to the
Treasury. Such a system—if it can be so called—is not susceptible of
improvement [and] it must be totally changed.

Fuad Pasha is considered by many not to have been prompt enough
in executing criminals and thus to have diminished the effect which
would otherwise have been produced. A prompt punishment would
have struck a degree of terror into the people which would have made
a permanent and deep impression; the gradual executions have engendered rather a sulky feeling of wrong—a stronger enmity towards
the Christians—and a fixed desire to avenge themselves; and thus the
Mohamedans and Christians are more inimical to each other than
they were before. There is also a strong feeling that the Ulema have
been too leniently dealt with. Fuad Pasha says he cannot get positive
evidence against some who are in [under] arrest, but most people
think the evidence would have sufficed to have hanged any other
persons. The Sheikh Abdallah el Halebee—The Mufti—and Ghuzzee
Effendi, are believed to have pushed on the Mussulmans to the excesses they committed, the first in particular is known to have been the
chief instigator in the murder of the Christians. By common report I
learn that evidence enough of guilt has been given against this man,
his residence was full of plunder, but was not searched—he was assailed in his house by Moslem women wailing the execution of their
husbands, and charging him with having caused their fate by his
counsels. Everybody believes that sufficient evidence could be found

if it be wanted, and that to allow these men to escape the punishment of death will be a great wrong and do more harm than the executions have done good. There is no doubt that Mussulman fanaticism has been the occasion of all the troubles, and that to crush it is the best chance of future security. One great means would be to prevent the Mecca Caravan from assembling at Damascus as the point of departure and from its being made the point of separation on the return of the Pilgrims. . . . The Hadj from Damascus once peremptorily abolished, fanaticism would gradually diminish and perhaps die out. I mentioned the subject to Fuad Pasha and he seemed to think the suggestion a good one.

It would be desirable to reorganise the Grand Council, to select— not members of the Ulema—but men of business habits, and to pay them for the time they devoted to their work; they hitherto have paid themselves by keeping back from the Treasury large balances, and by taking bribes from applicants for justice to obtain decisions in their favor. . . .

Further suggestions do not occur to me at the present moment, but should any strike me I will not fail to bring them to Your Excellency's attention. After Fuad Pasha has reestablished the Sultan's authority, a strong honest, impartial administration must replace that which has been so long bringing on the ruin of the country, and of which the massacres have been the natural consummation.

F.O. 78/1520, Brant (Damascus) to Bulwer (Constantinople), 25 Sept. 1860, no. 48.

50. Exodus of Christians from Damascus

I have the honor to report to Your Lordship that since my despatch No. 30 of the 5th Instant matters here have not improved, but on the contrary the panic has gained a great hold on the Christians. Some of the principal [Christians] who wished to quit the City, were refused permission by the Government and left clandestinely on the 6th Instant.

The military Commander Khaled Pasha for some nights past has patrolled the streets and last night ordered lanterns to be hung up before the houses at short distances. He has also ordered the gates separating the different quarters to be repaired, and the entrances of the City are carefully closed and guarded. Only half the troops pass the night in bed, the other half patrolling from sunset to sunrise. The guards are supplied with ball-cartridge and are ordered—on the least symptom of a rising—to fire on the mob. The Artillery are always in readiness for action, and Colonel Gessler—a Prussian instructor of Artillery in the Turkish Service—admits that no officer could do his duty better than Khaled Pasha. Last night however houses inhabited by Christians were again marked with crosses and this—with the measures of precaution taken—have renewed the panic to such an extent that a number of Christians came to the Consulate this morning to beg me to procure from the Government mules for them to quit, stating that their fears were so overwhelming that they may be said to be dying of them daily, for they cannot sleep or take any repose, being always harassed by the dread of a new massacre. I used every argument I could to give them courage but it was in vain; they said the men and women could walk, but the children could not; they required animals only for them. Finally, they declared that if nothing could be obtained, the men would go, leaving the women and children—the old and the sick—behind. People who even under the worst circumstances can decide on such a resolve deserve but little consideration. I believe that there is no immediate danger. I am informed that Sheikh Abdallah el Halebee is allowed to receive any visitors he pleases in the room where he is detained, and consequently can carry on his machinations as well as if he were at liberty. His execution I consider to be a measure indispensable to the public security.

The conduct of Ibrahim Bey Karami—a Christian employé left here by Fuad Pasha to superintend the affairs of the Christians, but who pretends to be His Excellency's representative—is most infamous, and he should be immediately removed; he will not be controlled by the Vallee Pasha [governor], and liberates prisoners on his own responsability [sic]. He is known to receive money as bribes to a large extent, and without a bribe justice cannot be obtained. . . .

The Jewish Rabbis have applied to me in respect to some Jews arrested on suspicion, and who have been detained in prison for nearly two months, one having already died there. The Rabbis demand that they should be brought to trial, and the chief Rabbi offered to Ibrahim Karami his testimony that one of the prisoners was all the time of the outbreak in his house, to which Ibrahim Bey replied "Your testimony is valueless as they will all be condemned to death."

It is said that the cause of the present panic is mainly owing to the manner in which the Turks are dealing with the Druzes. The Mushir marches about and as fast as he moves from one place the Druzes return.

It is pretended that he expressly allows them a passage and does not attempt to cut off their retreat to the Haurân. The impression made by this conduct on the public is the conviction that the Turks do not mean to punish the Druzes, but leave them to act as they like—or rather—that there is an understanding between them; so that people believe that the troops would not act hostilely against the Druzes even in the case of an attack made by them on the City.

F.O. 78/1520, Brant (Damascus) to Russell (London), 8 Oct. 1860, no. 31.

Abduction of Christian Women by Warring Bedouin

I had the honor of reporting to Your Lordship on the 8th of October 1860 that the nomadic Arabs were at war amongst themselves.

A tribe, now, has appeared from the south to take the part of the Anezi against the Shammar. This tribe was near Damascus during the massacre, and I have just learnt that many of the 800 Christian women, then carried off to the desert, are with them.

The Turkish Authorities, possessing neither influence to persuade nor power to coerce, can do nothing to rescue them. By going to the tribe I might perhaps be able to bring back some, if not all, of them, and I therefore proceed immediately to make the attempt, having arranged for the efficient transaction of the Consular business, during my absence, which will I trust be approved by Your Lordship.

F.O. 78/1538, Skene (Aleppo) to Russell (London), 20 Oct. 1860, no. 62.

51. Frustrated Christians Seek Revenge against Damascus Jews (1860)

With painful reluctance I submit to your Lordship the accompanying translation of a letter from the Heads of the Jewish community at Damascus.

There can be no doubt whatever that the Jewish body of that city is guiltless of any participation in the recent outbreak, and I venture to believe that your Lordship requires no argument to satisfy your mind on this point. May I entreat your Lordship, as heretofore, to exercise the powerful influence of Her Majesty's Government to protect and save the Jews of Damascus from the perils to which they are so imminently exposed? As the affair is urgent, I venture personally to attend your Lordship with this letter and its inclosure (p. 193).

*Montefiore (Ramsgate) to Russell (London), 16 Oct. 1860, no. 157, in *P.P.* 1861 [2800] LXVIII.

*Sir Moses Montefiore (1784–1885). Renowned Jewish philanthropist. Sheriff of London (1837–1838). He engaged in many humanitarian efforts on behalf of Jewish communities in various countries.

The Heads of the Jewish Community at Damascus to Sir Moses Montefiore

. . . We had the honour to address you a letter in the course of last month, in which we spoke of the enmity of the Christians towards the Jews in Damascus, which has risen up in addition to all former hatred. Now a great, bitter, and intense jealousy fills hearts, by reasons that they have been murdered, plundered, and maltreated, whereas the children of Israel were left uninjured.

Our hearts were then moved by the apprehension lest, by reason of this bitter hatred and jealousy, false accusations should be brought against us. We therefore besought you to aid us by obtaining instructions from the English Government to the Consuls, Generals, and Commanders who come to Syria, also from the Turkish Government to his Highness Fuad Pasha, that he shall stand by us, and not be ready to receive malicious reports against the Jews, for his Excellency is a just and upright man.

Now we have to inform you that since the commencement of the month of Ellul (August) the Christians have been plotting against us and setting up false accusations against us; many have been thrown into prison and wrongly accused of having participated in the massacre. The Christians are believed in their statements: when they say "so and so killed some one," that person is immediately brought before the Tribunal. Testimony of honourable men among the Turks is not received, when they declare that the accused was in their house during the tumult. Even the evidence of Christians is not received when they bear witness to the Jews having been hidden with themselves, and not parted from each other during the whole time of the outbreak. Even should the accuser himself testify anything in favour of an accused Israelite, it is not attended to. A woman accused a certain Jew, who she thought had killed her husband; she was asked to swear according to her own faith that the accused was the man; she refused to swear, and she asked the Jew to swear by the law of Moses that he had not done it, so that he might go free. But the tribunal would not listen thereto. Even the testimony of our Chief Rabbi has been rejected. The Jews still are in prison, and one has since died in his dungeon from the effects of terror.

Oh, Sir! consider, only for a moment, how innocent and pious Jews, without sin, are being thrown into prison with murderers; and how all testimony and proof that they may bring forward will not aid them in their deliverance. We know not, therefore, what is to become of the people of Israel when the Christians see there is no hope for them, but their false accusations are listened to from the judgment-seat; but to the voice of Israel there is none to give ear, to reply—none to pity or to compassionate.

Those who rose against the Christians and killed them are not judged according to the ordinary laws of the land, nor is evidence taken in the usual manner; but there is established what is termed an "extraordinary tribunal."

Now it appears that it is intended to judge the Jews also by this tribunal, and to condemn them to death upon the mere word of the Christians. This is, indeed, a great and bitter sorrow. How is it possible to compare the condition of the Jews with that of those who rose up against the Christians? Were the Jews themselves during that terrible time not in the greatest fear and danger? Surely there was "but a step betwixt us and death." Most of the Jews hid themselves in the houses of respectable Turks, in cellars, and in caves, and in company with Christians. Is it possible to suppose that one who was in momentary fear for his own life should rise up to kill another? Reason and common sense testify against it. God forbid that such a thought could enter into the mind of Her Most Gracious Majesty the Queen of England, or her Government, for whose prosperity, honor, and glory we, the congregation of Damascus, have prayed these twenty years.

In this trouble do we lay our supplications before her, beseeching her to have pity and compassion upon poor afflicted Israel in Damascus, who only desire her aid, support, and all-powerful influence, so that the captive Jews may have a fair trial before the ordinary tribunals, in accordance with the well-known custom of the country. For Israel, both young and old, are wholly guiltless in this matter, and free from the crime of shedding blood.

Truly, this is a time of great trouble, and distress; for every Israelite dwelling in Damascus is in great dread lest he should be falsely accused: for there is none to say unto the Christians, Why do ye thus? It has been openly declared by some of them that they will grant Israel neither peace nor rest. Even already have they begun to conspire against the best, the most honourable, and esteemed of our community—the well-known Jacob Aboulaffia, and Solomon Farchi, son of Isaac Hyam Farchi (of whose hospitality you partook on your visit to Damascus), a youth 14 years of age, an only son of his father's house. A certain Christian declared that his father was killed between the two houses of the above-named parties. Were not the Lord on our side, what would become of us? The accused being under French protection, the French and Greek Consuls prevented this case being brought before the tribunal, but had it heard before the two Consuls. The Lord brought innocence to light.

And on what was the whole accusation based? If a man was found slain in the highway at the time of the rising of the mob, when all the streets of the Christians, as well as the streets of the Jews and Turks, which are near each other, were filled with the slain, was it in the power of man to prevent a murder being committed before his own house? Would the ruffians have had any disregard? Who should tell them not to murder all who stood in their way? Were the Jews, then, secure of their own lifes [sic]?

Wherefore, we beseech you to have compassion upon us, to hear our prayer, and to exert yourself to obtain the influence of the English Government, as well as that of the French and Turkish, with His Highness Fuad Pasha, who is an upright Judge; and that instructions may be sent to the English Consul in Damascus, so that the Jews may not be confounded with those who rose up in rebellion, and not be judged in the same tribunal.

You are our father! Hasten to help us! As you have been our former deliverer,[1] so save us now, and be the instrument of terminating our endless troubles.

Attached are the signatures of the Rabbins, the Elders, and most worthy of the Congregation of Damascus, who anxiously await your answer (pp. 194–95).

Hyam Romano, David Harpi, Menahem Farchi, Jacob Halevi, Jacob Peretz, Raphael Halevi, Isaac Maimon, Aaron Jacob (Damascus) to Sir Moses Montefiore (Ramsgate), 7 *Tishri*, 5621 (23 September 1860), no. 157 & encl. in *P.P.* 1861 [2800] LXVIII.

[1] In 1840 the Jewish Community of Damascus, menaced by a false accusation of ritual murder, was saved by Sir Moses Montefiore, who obtained a special *firman* from the sultan. See above, pt. one, chap. 3, notes 11 and 12, p. 96.

52. Armenians in Armenia (1869)

The Kochers and Koords are under very imperfect subjection, and it is only by satisfying all demands, however outrageous, that the Christian agriculturists can maintain their position. One unbearable custom, that of Kishlak, has done more than anything else to contribute to their present paucity and decay. That custom, originating some years ago in the weakness of the Government and growing power of the Koords, enabled the latter to exercise the extraordinary right of quartering themselves and flocks during winter in and about the Christian villages, entailing upon the inhabitants large expenses, not only for their animals, but also food and fuel for themselves, during at least four months.

Repeated complaints to Government have done little to remedy this evil, and, consequently, to escape the intolerable burden, 750 families have, within the last six years, emigrated to Russia, while 500 more have this year sent representatives to Erivan to negotiate a similar step. The few peasants still unwilling, from old associations and attachment to the soil, to remove, in order to get rid at least of part of the great expense the Kishlak custom entails upon them, have entirely abandoned the culture of any other grain than wheat, as all others being in some form or other useless as food for cattle, their stocks would certainly be laid under heavy contributions by the Koords for that purpose. But the Koords do not confine themselves simply to plunder. The slightest complaint to Government on the part of the Christians against them is followed by night attacks, or open assaults in the day upon them. In this manner, during the last year, no less than ten have been killed and forty wounded, because they—the Christians—had the temerity to complain to the authorities of the oppression they suffered at the hands of the Koords.

These marauders are aided and abetted by a society of so-called holy men, styled Sheiks, living in the Boolanik district of Moosh. They preach their conduct to be lawful and even meritorious, when practiced against Giaours [Infidels]. The influence of such teaching instigated their mureeds or disciples last autumn to satisfy their fanaticism and avarice at the same time. They stormed and completely plundered the venerable church and convent—dating from the time of the Illuminator—of Surb Ohann, not ten miles from Moosh itself. In the mêlée, two of the highest ecclesiastics were severely wounded, all the church plate, ornaments and embroidered robes carried off; but the most irreparable loss consisted in the complete destruction of the valuable MS. library by these miscreants. For these, and other cases alluded to, no redress has been given, no punishment awarded. Several Koords and mureeds have indeed been put into prison, and a species of inquiry instituted; but the venality or partiality of the Moosh Medjliss, and indifference or sympathy of the Mutessarif, assured them from any further inconvenience.

Lately a new Commissioner, Osman Bey, a native of Erzeroum, has been sent to undertake a fresh inquiry, with a view of bringing the guilty parties to justice, but public opinion places no faith in the native selected for this purpose, or his desire to institute a searching inquiry. The immunity the Koords seem to enjoy disinclines the Christians from making complaints, or following them up if they do so, for, as stated before, should they do so and the guilty parties be punished, sooner or later they would, both in person and property, suffer more, endure infinitely greater calamities than those they originally complained of. It is thus that great crimes always unpunished, grievous oppressions unredressed, are perpetrated, and merge into what the Koords and Sheikhs consider, as warranted by custom, permissible. An active, upright Governor, really desirous of putting a stop to such practices, and punishing the criminals, is thus, from the popular Moslems clamour, unable to hold his post a month, while the time-server becomes a tool in their hands (pp. 638–39).

Extinction of the Dhimmi Peasantry

It was dispiriting, on my onward route to Kaghizman through Shuragel, the ancient Shiraj, formerly the richest and most populous district in Armenia, to pass so many spots marking the sites of towns and villages, some of them only recently deserted, but now encumbered with their ruins or the mean huts of the indigent population that remained. On many of these deserted sites the massive fabrics of early Armenian churches had successfully resisted the ravages of time and the efforts of man, urged by an implacable hostility to everything Christian, to destroy them. Round several, in spite of decreasing numbers, poverty, and oppression, the Armenians still cling with affectionate pertinacity, dragging on an existence, as well as they are able, under the tolerance of the Turkish Aghas or Beys who, either as the descendants of the Timariots or in consequence of the poverty of former owners, have in the course of time dispossessed the Christians of the lands and villages about. But the Aghas, though deriving their income from the industry of the Christian fellahs, are unable to protect them or their crops from the rapacity of the Koords, the causes of most of the distress the Armenians labour under. It is hardly possible to enumerate the different methods they pursue to satisfy their wants at the expense of the peaceable sedentary agricultural classes. They are however, without reckoning forced contributions and "corvée", so various and onerous as to curtail agriculture and stifle industry, reducing both to the smallest minimum compatible with existence. Thus, they have been driven from most of their ancestral lands by the increasing numbers and unpunished licence of the Koords; the crops on lands still in their hands are, when yet green, partially grazed by the flocks of the intruders, who, after what remains is ripened and cut, will not allow the owners to re-sow for autumn crops, as at that time, on their return from the hills, they turn their flocks into the aftergrass that then springs up.

An original course a Koord adopts to extort money is to extract one of his teeth, and then purposely engage in a quarrel with a Christian, during which blows are of course exchanged. The Koord then makes a complaint to his Chief, producing the extracted tooth in evidence, which he swears was knocked out by the Christian during the quarrel. The Chief inflicts in every case, unless he is bribed by the Christian, a fine in money, varying with the reputed wealth of the falsely-accused aggressor, who has no remedy whatever against his accuser. The "pièce de conviction," that is, the old tooth, never in any case being impounded, serves for many similar charges, and is sometimes lent to a friend for the like purpose. This custom is so common that a provincial proverb says "A Koord carries his teeth in his pocket" (p. 642).

Government orders remain dead letters there [in the Hakkaree mountainous district south of Van]; it is the Alsatia for all the brigands and miscreants in the land. Murder, robbery, and brigandage are every-day crimes, and when practised against the Christians receive the sanction and support of the so-called holy men, styled Sheikhs, who infest that country, and who, in fact, are as forward as the Koords in every act that fanaticism or avarice can dictate. The principal sufferers, although sedentary agricultural Turks must be included in the category, are the Nestorians, Armenians and Jews.

Within the last two years several have been murdered, others plundered of their property, forced to become Moslems, or emigrate for safety to Persia; while during the same period seven Christian churches have been destroyed, more than thirty human beings killed, virgins and married women abducted, whole villages devastated and plundered, without (in spite of repeated orders from Constantinople) the slightest notice on the part of the Van and subordinate authorities, or an attempt being made by them to check proceedings that promised ultimately to drive all peaceable people over the borders into Persia and Russia. The chief instigators, Sheikh Obeyd Ullah of Katoona and his mureeds (disciples) in the mean time enjoy the favour of the Kaïmakams and Mudirs, and the former the adoration of ignorant Koords (blind instruments of his will), as they regard him as little short of the Deity (p. 644).

A few of the wealthier Christians [of Ikhlat], whose position with respect to Government or means enable them to hold on to their estates—if they do not from their influence—suffer openly, constantly sustain serious damage and loss from their secret malice. Their hay and corn ricks are burnt at night or their outstanding crops devoured by the Koords' sheep. It is the aim and policy of those people to drive the industrious population out of the country, or by their system of usury to reduce them to the level of serfs, as then they think they will be able to secure the pasture grounds still remaining to them, and take possession of their fields, for lands forsaken during a certain term lapse to the State, which grants new titles on the payment of small sums for purchase and fees.

The Koords will thus, by a legal process, become the owners of lands their unceasing persecution has robbed from the real owners, at the expense ultimately of the State, which must suffer in consequence of the substitution of a mixed agricultural, pastoral ownership for one of purely sedentary agriculturalists. Turks here, equally with Christians, suffer from similar causes, and their complaints were even louder than those of the Christians.

From Ikhlat I reached Erzeroom, viâ Boolarick, already noticed, and Khunnus.

On my way I stopped at the miserable village of Pirran, on the Boolanik Lake, containing only fourteen houses, or rather hovels, although a few years back it had a population of 500 souls, owning amongst them more than 1,000 head of horned cattle; now I had the greatest difficulty in obtaining the necessary milk for tea.

The evening before, a Koord in the service of the Boolanik Kaïmakam, a notorious character, only lately released from prison, aided by six other miscreants of his tribe, the Hassananlee, had broken into the house of the village priest, and after beating him and his son so as to leave them half dead, abducted the young bride of the latter. She was recovered some ten days after, and delivered up to her friends, but in a most pitiable state. It proves the abject terror the Koords have drilled into the Christians by the system they pursue towards them, that, although this assault and abduction took place at an early hour, and the villagers heard the cries of the victims, none of them ventured to their rescue (pp. 646–47).

Armenians [of the Erzeroum Vilayet: 295,300 persons]—The advice and ostentatious leaning towards Russia of the Armenian clergy in my district, headed by the Catholicas residing at Etchmiazin in Russia, and his bishops in these parts, have naturally enough inclined the more ignorant members of their flocks—rich and poor—to adopt the same views; and considering also that a whole Christian house of ten souls in Russia pays only, for all taxes, 9 roubles (1£.10s.) annually as against three times the sum here, if there has not been a general emigration, it is simply owing to the fact that disposable arable lands in Russian Armenia are scarce, while the reverse prevails in Turkey.

Everywhere throughout these districts I found the Armenians bitter in their complaints against the Turkish Government, at the same time that they were unreserved in their praises of Russia, openly avowing their determination to emigrate. This bias is owing, as already stated, to the constant hostile teaching of their clergy; at the same time ample cause for discontent, as has already been shown further back, is afforded by the really wretched system of Turkish provincial administration, the unequal imposition of taxes, scandalous method of levying them and the tithes, persistent denial or miscarriage of justice, and practical disavowal of the Christians' claim to be treated with the same consideration and respect as their equals among Moslems. But experience has taught me that which candour and strict impartiality compel me to state, that the subordinate officers of the local Government are aided and abetted in their disgraceful proceedings or encouraged in persistent indifference to crying wrongs, as well by the criminal assistance as [by the] wilful apathy or silence of the Armenian Medjliss members, ostensibly elected by the suffrages of their co-religionists to guard their interests. Unfortunately, then, as the evil lies as much with the Christians as the Turks, under existing regulations there is no remedy for it, and there can be none till the local authorities really see for themselves that the Porte's orders are really carried out and to open the way for the introduction of a higher class of people for such employments. As it is, no man of wealth, influence, or character will accept a seat in any one of the Councils; he will not waste time in attending to official duties in a place where he has to put up with the contumely and impertinent insults of the Moslem members, all which are patiently borne by the fawning and obsequious Christians whose living depends upon this appointment. And even were a man of character and ability to accept a nomination at the hands of his community, the Pasha, with whom in fact the fate of such elections lie, as he has the power of rejection, would always prefer a needy, pliant member to one whose riches and position would place him beyond the reach of his menaces or influence. The interests of the community are consequently intrusted to speculators accustomed to the atmosphere of the Serai in their capacity of revenue farmers or Serafis, who in such positions have, in addition to their own disgusting servility, all the chicanery and vices of Turkish officials,—acquired a dangerous influence, either as the partners or creditors of the chief provincial officers. Such an influence might be meritorious and useful if exercised in the interests of justice and duty, but it becomes a downright evil when practised, as it always is, for their own benefit or that of their partners in corruption, and scarcely ever for their brethren. The claims of the poor are either neglected or betrayed, and those of the rich depend upon the amount of their presents or degrees of their sycophancy. The Armenian clergy and head men, on their part, purposely ignoring the villainous conduct of their Medjliss members, representing the repeated failures of justice that inevitably result as due to the fanaticism or imbecility of a Government determined to ignore all just claims, exaggerate actual facts; the more readily to induce their dependants to adopt the disloyal views they propagate. As they pursue such intrigues, apparently unchecked and with the secret approval of Russian agents, wavering members, formerly content with or resigned to their lot, openly express disaffection and traitorous ideas.

Some of the reasons educated Armenians give to account for this Russian feeling among their countrymen are well expressed in a letter I lately received from one of the most intelligent Armenians in the capital. I am obliged to state that, as far as my experience goes, his views are not groundless. While English and French Agents support by all legitimate means the efforts, of their missionaries and complaints of proselytes, the Armenians are left to fight their battles through the interested elders or corrupt Medjliss members of their creed, and are thus perforce driven to seek protection from a Power that does everything to gain their sympathy. The inhabitants of the Erzeroum Vilayet, as being closer to and more in contact with Russia, more especially the borderers, partake in a greater degree of this feeling than those living in the remoter districts of Diarbekr and Kharpoot, where it is comparatively confined to the Armenian agriculturalists; but, here in Erzeroum, I do not believe that one of the members of the higher moneyed classes does not in a greater or lesser degree heartily share such sentiments, while most of them, though Turkish subjects, are supplied with Russian passports. The traffic in such documents, carried on as secretly as possible, is well known, and widely disseminated; no large town in my district being free from these pseudo-Russians.

The exaggerated pretensions, overbearing conduct, and ostentatious display of the Russian Consul in his relations with the local authorities, in which it is needless to say other Consuls do not indulge, coupled with the unaccountable servility of the Turkish officials here in their intercourse with him, tends, among an ignorant people, to give a false value to his particular importance or rather to that of the country he represents, which by still further strengthening their belief that no other power than Russia is so able or willing to help them, makes them eager to apply to him in their differences and to acquire documents that to them appear claims to the interference of a foreign Power in their behalf. That the intriguing meddling conduct of the Russian Consul is approved, I may state that, although in disfavour with the Embassy at Constantinople, he is supported by the authorities in the Caucasus, to whose diplomatic Chancery at Tiflis he is directly subordinate. It is the policy of The Russian Government, and, therefore, of its Agents, to encourage such ideas, as also to exaggerate real existing evils, or trump up imaginary complaints, in order to keep up that chronic disaffection so suitable to the line of conduct it has always pursued in limitrophe Eastern countries. As suited to its interests, such conduct perhaps is excusable; but what can excuse the forbearing attitude of the Turks here, who by their indifference, indulgence, or fear permit a foreign Agent to address them officially in the insulting manner he does, and conduct himself otherwise in a manner towards them that only serves to convince the Rayas of the weakness of their rulers and inability, in consequence of the overwhelming influence of Russia, to prevent such conduct.

I have ventured this far to intrude my opinions of what I believe to be the predominant feeling among the Armenians in this province, because they form in their numbers, position, and occupations the most influential class, and as being the one most favourable under present circumstances to Russian interests, the most dangerous in an underhand way to the State. The only efficient panacea for such hostile feeling rests entirely with the Government. Were it to take efficient measures to insure the content of the people by radically redressing their wrongs, inflicting severe and impartial justice on their oppressors, remodel its system of tithe assessment, that under which at present the other taxes are divided and collected, and really carry out the spirit of its numerous Firmans in favour of Christians, it would, I am confident, remove existing disaffection and promote the present and progressive loyalty of its subjects. Without such a pro- gramme they will be forced into bankruptcy; that sooner or later must give rise to emigration or open downright rebellion. I cannot exag- gerate the gravity of the situation, nor urge too emphatically that the measure alluded to be recommended to the authorities (pp. 651–52).

Although I have scrupulously endeavoured to record impartially all I saw or that was brought to my notice, for good or for evil, during my tour, the tenor of this report would make it appear, I have confined myself to reciting Christian wrongs without at the same time noticing improvements in their condition, consequent upon late Firmans or orders. I have certainly dwelt principally upon the serious oppression the Christians suffer from the Koords, not because, however, I would make it be believed they are the only sufferers, or that I purposely shut my eyes to the grave injuries sustained also by the agricultural Turks; for personal observation showed me all industrious Moslems, having the misfortune to live in localities partly inhabited by Koords, are under their influence, and, therefore, losers, accordingly; but because the Christians, in addition to deprivation of property, daily jeopardise their lives, and what is more terrible, the honour of their females, in daily struggles for existence; trials from which the Mos- lems are exempt.

Agricultural Turks, too, in these northern districts form both in numbers and industry an insignificant class as compared with the Christians. Other means of subsistence closed to the latter are open to them. . . . Personal security at the same time is unknown. Many of the local Mudirs and Kaïmakams—generally local Koords or Turks— either from fear, relationship, or pecuniary motives, siding with the robbers, and sharing their spoil; and the miserable police, employed for the public protection, being the worst characters in the place, are far more frequently the partners than deterrers of criminals. (p. 655).

Taylor (Erzeroum) to Elliot (Constantinople), 18 March 1869, no. 13, in *P.P.* 1877 [C. 1739] XCII.

53. Obstacles to Christian Emancipation (1870)

The Austrian Chancellor professed much friendliness towards Turkey, and disclaimed all wish to interfere in the internal affairs of the Empire.

At the same time, he said, it was impossible to allow Russia to monopolise the whole appearance of interest in the Christian subjects of the Sultan, and if the Russian Government brought their grievances forward, other Governments durst not lag behind.

In his opinion the general protection of Europe over the Christians would be better for Turkey than the sole protection of Russia, and the true way for the Porte to render it harmless was to remove the grievances complained of by the Christians (p. 662).

I took the opportunity of this conversation [with Aali Pasha, the Grand Vizier], to press the Grand Vizier to lose no opportunity of raising the Christian element in the country, and of proving the reality of the equality professed between the two religions.

Aali Pasha seemed to consider the friendly Governments rather unreasonable in complaining that more progress had not been made, which, for his part, he looked upon as being greater than could possibly have been anticipated.

Who, for instance, would have believed a very few years ago that Christians would be found, not only sitting in the Council, but holding the position of Ministers of the Sultan? It was he repeated, the intention of the Porte that all distinctions should cease, but in what country in the world had it been found practicable to efface in a day the effects of the habits and traditions of ages by a simple change of the law or in the disposition of the Government? . . ,

I said I did not question the wish of the Government to act liberally by the Christians, but, as a matter of fact, they were still in many places by no means treated as the equals of the Mussulmans, and it was this state of things which required remedying.

Aali Pasha frankly admitted that it had in many cases been impossible to make the authorities second the views of the Porte; some of them could not understand the full adoption of a new system, which was repugnant to all their old prejudices, and it was only by degrees that these could be overcome.

It does not seem to me that his Highness overstated the difficulties that have to be contended with, and the progress in toleration and liberalism has certainly, within the last few years, been very marked and far more real than at times when there was greater ostentation of it shown, for it was easier to issue a Firman of a Hatti Sheriff proclaiming the equality than to take the smallest step to realise it.

There are various considerations connected with the relative positions of the Mussulmans and Christians which are too often lost sight of when it is assumed to be within the power of the Government to establish their equality by the simple scratch of a pen.

The Turks [Muslims] have been so long accustomed to regard themselves as the superiors, and the Christians are so much used to recognize them as such, that it can only be by slow degrees that they will learn to look upon each other as equals, and there is still one circumstance which prevents, and will continue to prevent, a real assimilation.

The whole of the military force is still drawn from the Ottoman population, and heavily as this falls upon them, and much as it contributes to advance the comparative wealth and population of the Christians, as long as every person in authority from the general to the policeman is a Mussulman, the feeling of his being of a dominant race must be kept alive, on both sides.

The question is one which is attracting the attention of the Government, and they hope before long to be able gradually to attempt to introduce Christians into the army; but the abrupt application to them of the general rule of recruitment would, even if it were practicable, be looked upon as an act of hardship and oppression (p. 663).

Elliot (Therapia) to Granville (London), 1 November 1870, no. 18 in *P.P.* 1877 [C. 1739] XCII. (Extract)

54. Disturbances on Mt. Carmel (1877)

I have the honour to report to you that last Monday the 9th instant a fatal quarrel took place at Hader of Mount Carmel, between the Bedouins of the neighbourhood of Caiffa, the Jews, and the Christians of Caiffa [Haifa].

The quarrel began between the Bedouins and the Jews at Hader, and then the Christians interfered to protect the Jews.

They attacked each other with stones, and two Christians were wounded and one Bedouin dangerously so.

Afterwards the Mussulmans of Caiffa are said to have intended to make a demonstration against the Christians of Caiffa, but the presence of the "Torch" and a German frigate kept them quiet, and the matter was peaceably checked.

Yesterday evening news from Beyrout was circulated to the effect that war has been declared between Russia and Turkey.

Up to now the local Government is well disposed to maintain good order, but if the said news is true I am of opinion that the presence of some European ship-of-war would be necessary to protect the tranquility of the Christians and Europeans residing in this country (p. 143).

Finzi (Acre) to Eldridge (Beirut), 15 April 1877, no. 185, in *P.P.* 1877 [C. 1806] XCII.

MAGHREB

55. Jews and Converts in Morocco (ca. 1790)

The Jews in general are obliged to pay to the emperor [sultan] a certain annual sum, in proportion to their numbers, which is a considerable income, independent of his arbitrary exactions. Those of Morocco were exempted by Sidi Mahomet [1757–1790] from this tax, and in its room he compelled them to take goods of him, of which they were to dispose in the best manner they could, and pay him five times their value; by which means they were far greater sufferers than if they paid the annual tax (p. 198).

Discrimination after Conversion

When a Jew or a Christian is converted to the Mahometan faith, he is immediately dressed in a Moorish habit, and paraded round the streets on horseback, accompanied with music and a great concourse of people. He then chuses himself a Moorish name, and fixes on a person who adopts him as a child, and is ever afterwards called his father. This adoption, however, is only nominal, for he is by no means bound to support him. The new convert is not allowed to marry any other woman than a Negro, or the daughter of a renegado; and his descendants are not considered as genuine Moors till the fourth generation (p. 342).

W. Lemprière

56. Sultan's Agents and Courtiers (ca. 1790)

These people, whether Jews or Gentiles, are nothing but the King's tools. So long as the King uses them, they are precious vessels which nobody dare touch lest he come to harm; but if the King hides his face from them for a moment they perish for ever like their own dung— they who have seen them will say: where are they? They are feared and not loved, they are ready to do evil and do not know how to do good. They grow rich by ruining others; they say to their father and

mother: I have not seen you; they do not recognise brothers nor do
they know their children. One talks smoothly to another and his in-
nermost heart offers an offering to him, and he returns from his
plotting to prepare instruments of death for him. They pull the
mighty by the strings of hope and drag the young by intimidation.
Hell has expanded over the heights of their greatness; the same is
under their feet. The word but issues from the King's mouth, and
they are no more. When they govern, the people groan, and when
they perish, the city rejoices. Most of them do not die natural deaths.
None of them are visited after the visitation of all men. They will
suffer death, castration, forfeiture of property, or imprisonment, or
they will be cut in pieces and their houses will be made a dunghill. I
have found one among all these who lasted until his end. It is they
who are called *sahab al-sultan* (friend of the King). Therefore, when
you are told that so-and-so stands high in the King's favour, pity him;
pray for him or for yourself: he presently puts his feet in the stocks,
presently sets out to destroy. When you hear that so-and-so is one of
the country's noblemen, of the people's notables, of the seed of the
princes, do not believe it; truly as the Lord lives, these are words
intended to flatter him because he is feared; he is but one block of the
hope of rubbish that serves [as] a cornerstone until the King obtains
his wish. The King's servants are not securely established in high
places; the King's wish kills and lets live, impoverishes and enriches,
abases and exalts. Therefore at one moment they mount up to the
heaven[s] at another they go down to the depths, and always, in bad
and good times, their soul is melted. Had I known all this when I first
set foot in the Maghreb, such things would not happen to me today.
But who reads us the signs? (2:290–91).

*S. Romanelli, *Massa Ba'arav*, in H. Z. Hirschberg.

*Samuel Romanelli (1757–1817), Italian Jewish poet and traveler. While stranded in
Morocco (1787–90) he wrote a description of Jewish life there.

57. Dehumanization of the Dhimmi in Tunisia (1800)

The Jews are the only subjects of the Regency who pay a personal
tax to the bey. However, although this payment is claimed for their
protection, nothing is more common than to see them being molested
and even struck by the Moors. Moreover, they accept these mistreatments and blows with astonishing resignation. However, should one
of them dare to reply to his aggressors, he would most certainly run
the risk of becoming involved in serious proceedings from which he

could extricate himself only at the cost of a large sum of money. Often these insults have no other aim but this abusive and tyrannical extortion.

Certain Jews wear European clothes and this costume is adopted more particularly by those originating from Leghorn. Others wear Oriental dress, donning the bonnet and the grey or blue shawl, for the latter color is imposed upon them so that they cannot be confused with Muslims, whose dress does not otherwise differ from theirs.

Despite these humiliations and the state of disgrace to which they have been reduced, they are allowed to ride on horses and mules, which they are forbidden to do in Egypt and in the majority of other countries under Muslim rule (p. 95).

Quite a number of Jews and Jewesses roam the city peddling their wares, which these hawkers sell in houses and harems. It is remarkable that the Moorish women do not feel obliged to veil themselves before a Jew, whom they consider to be no more than a vile animal and who they are far from believing belongs to the human race.

As it has often transpired that Jews of both sexes have been murdered in those houses after their goods were stolen, the bey decreed that in future the hawkers of either sex should travel in pairs and that one should remain at the entrance while his companion would enter with his wares. Since this decree, as simple as it was wise, no Jew has fallen victim to the greed and treachery of murderous robbers (p. 96).

*L. Frank

*Louis Frank, Belgium-born doctor, accompanied General Bonaparte on his Egyptian campaign. He became the private physician to the Bey of Tunis in 1806 and finished his study on the Regency of Tunis in 1816.

58. Sack of the Jewish Quarter of Fez (1820)

In Fez, the Udaya invaded the Jewish quarter next door to their own in Fez al-Jadid. They began to pillage and steal everything they found. They ran off with canvas, silk, silver, and gold, which was deposited with the Jews and which belonged to the merchants of Fez for whom the Jews worked, employed in tailoring and other manual occupations. Thus enormous sums were lost, the value of which cannot be estimated. Next, the Udaya stripped men and women, carrying off the latter and raping the virgins among them. They murdered the menfolk and drank alcoholic drinks while it was the month of Ramadan. They killed several children who were suffocated in the crush of the pillage. Not satisfied with these acts, they dug under the houses in order to discover what was hidden beneath and found much money.

Upon seeing this, they seized the Jewish notables and shopkeepers, showered them with blows and tortured them in order to force them to disclose where they had hidden their money. If one of them had a beautiful Jewess, they stole her from her husband to force him to pay the ransom. These serious incidents took place on the 13th of Ramadan 1235 H (1820). When they had finished with the Jews, the Udaya turned on the other inhabitants of Fez (1:65).

an-Nasiri, (d.1897) (part 4, p. 156, Arabic). See trans. E. Fumey

59. The Dhimma in Algeria and Morocco
(early 19th century)

They [the Jews] are not allowed to inhabit the same town with the Mohammedans, but are assigned a quarter for themselves, outside the walls, where they are locked in every night at nine o'clock, and not permitted to stir out, under any pretence, until the following morning at sunrise. . . .

In Algiers, a Janissary, if so inclined, would stop and beat the first Jew he met in the street, without the latter daring to return, or even ward off the blows. His only resource was to run as fast as he could, until he had made his escape: complaint was worse than useless, for the cady always summoned the Janissary before him, and asked why he had beaten the Jew? The answer was, "because he has spoken ill of our holy religion"; upon which the Janissary was dismissed, and the Jew put to death. It is true the testimony of two Mussulmans was required to the fact of the Jew having abused their religion; but on such occasions witnesses were never wanting.

All the most humiliating offices the Jews are required to perform: they execute criminals, and afterwards inter their bodies; they are obliged to carry the Moors on their shoulders, when disembarking in shoal water; they are employed to cleanse the streets, to feed the animals in the menageries of the seraglio; "in short," says Keatinge [traveling in 1785], "whenever power has a call for a scavenger, that office devolves upon a Jew." . . . In passing along the street, the Jew was always obliged to yield the wall to a Mussulman, and further to salute him by bowing to the ground; if he failed in this, he was severely beaten, and perhaps got a stab of a yataghan. This inequality between the followers of the different creeds commences from the very cradle; the youngest Turk [i.e., Muslim] may trample on the most aged Jew; and as a melancholy proof how early degradation begins on one side, and tyranny on the other, a Jewish child will submit to be beaten by a Moor of its own age, without lifting a hand in its own

defense. The Jews are further obliged to wear a distinguishing costume, to take off their slippers on passing a mosque, or the house of
the cady, or even of some of the principal Mussulmans, though in
some cities, such as Fez, and particularly at Saffy, where there are
numerous sanctuaries, they are compelled to go altogether barefoot.
They are in no place permitted to ride on a horse, that being considered too noble an animal for so unworthy a purpose; but they are
permitted to mount an ass, or, as a particular favour, a mule; being
required, however, to alight and assume an attitude of respect,
whenever a true believer meets them on the road. Should a Jew come
to a fountain, he is obliged to wait until all the Mohammedans, even
those who may come much after him, have left it, before he can
attempt to draw water. Death is his punishment, if he should ascend
the roof of his own house, from whence he might see the Moorish
maidens; and death is his punishment, should he intrigue against
government, strike a true believer, or look accidentally into a mosque
while the faithful are at prayers. They are all considered as slaves of
the Dey or Emperor in whose dominions they live, and cannot depart
without obtaining his permission, and giving large security that they
will return. Any Turk might enter the Jews' town, walk into a house,
eat, drink, insult the owner, and ill-treat the women, without opposition or complaint; the Jew was too happy if he escaped being beaten
or stabbed. In Morocco, no Moor could be put to death for killing a
Jew, though killing a Christian might be a capital offence; in fact, it
not unfrequently happened, that a Jew complaining of the death of
his friend or relative, was himself the person punished, while the
murderer was let go free. The consequence of this is, that the Jew
seldom thinks of an appeal to justice, or an attempt at obtaining
satisfaction. He cringes to receive the blow, or fawns on the hand
uplifted to strike (2:80–84).

Revolt of the dhimmis

A little previous to the arrival of the British embassy (Mr. Payne's) in
1785, a Moor at Morocco had murdered a Jewish merchant, cut his
body in pieces, and thrown them into the shafts of the aqueduct in the
plain outside the town. The murder was attended with circumstances
of uncommon treachery and atrocity, insomuch that the whole body
of the Jews, throwing aside their apathy and cowardice, set to work,
and with indefatigable diligence, in spite of power and contrivance,
discovered the murderer, who was seized and thrown into prison,
when it was intended some punishment should be inflicted on him—
not a capital one, that being forbidden by the law before alluded to,
but perhaps a bastinado, which on occasions can be so managed as to

produce the same effect. Some delay, however, occurring, the Jews, under a strong sense of the wrongs they had received, collected in crowds round the palace, and clamoured for justice. The Emperor, though originally inclined toward granting it, soon lost every other feeling in that of astonishment at this new and unexpected noise; then suddenly becoming indignant that these infidels should dare to raise their voice around the precincts of royalty, he ordered his guards to drive them all back to their quarter,—an order which they readily and with much pleasure obeyed, while to prevent a repetition of similar offences, a large fine was levied on the Jews' town, and not a single individual permitted to pass the gates until it was paid (2:84–85).

The Dhimma and the Payment of the Jizya in 1815

In fact, the Jews seem principally to be tolerated on account of their affording a ready resource whenever money is required. . . . Their only mode of obtaining protection is by attaching themselves to some person of high rank; and by yielding him a share of their profits, and devoting themselves entirely to his service, they are preserved from molestation, and even ensured a certain degree of outward respect; a great man's Jew, like a great man's dog, is not to be trampled on with impunity.

The Jews are subject to a yearly impost, regulated by the Emperor, and occasionally called for somewhat in advance. This is particularly apt to happen when there has been a change of governors, the new ruler generally requiring some money to begin with. On such occasions, he send a *chaoux,* or king's messenger, with orders for the instant payment of a certain sum; the miserable privilege being left to the Jews of apportioning the tribute amongst them as they please. Meantime, however, their quarter is closed up by a guard, and no one suffered to leave it, until they declare themselves ready to pay the sum required. The mode in which this is done was witnessed by Mr. Riley at Mogodore [in 1815], as during his stay there an order came from the Emperor for the immediate levying of three thousand five hundred dollars. The Jews then did not amount to more than six thousand, and the greater number were very poor. They were assembled by their priests [rabbis] in the synagogues, and divided into four different classes, each obliged to furnish a certain portion of the tax. Four Jew merchants [Ben Guidalla, Macnin, Abitbol and Zagury], of some wealth, and chief in rank amongst them, formed the first class, and were rated at more than half the entire sum; the petty traders formed the second, the mechanics the third, and the lowest order of miserable labourers the fourth. The priests and Levites, who formed a great part of the number, were exempt, as they always are on such occasions, the other classes contributing to their support. Not a Jew, man, woman, or child, was allowed to pass the gate for three days, during which they were preparing their several rates, except they were wanted by the Moors to work, and not then without an order from the Kaid.

"During this period," says Mr. Riley, "I visited the Jews town several times, but never without seeing more or less of these miserable wretches knocked down like bullocks by the gate-keepers, with their large canes, as they attempted to rush past them, when the gates were opened, to procure a little food or water for their hungry and thirsty families. On the fourth day, when the arrangements had been made by the priests and elders, they sent word to the governor, and the three first classes were ordered before him to pay their appointment. I wished to see the operation, and went to the house of the Kaid for the purpose. The Jews soon appeared by classes: as they approached they put off their slippers, took their money in both hands, and holding them alongside each other, as high as the breast, came slowly forward to the talb, or Mohammedan priest, appointed to receive it. He took it from them, hitting each one a smart blow with his fist, on the bare forehead, by way of receipt for his money, at which the Jew said "Nahma Sidi,"[1] and retired to give place to his companion.

"Thus they proceeded through the three first classes without much difficulty, when the fourth class was forced up with big sticks: this class was very numerous, as well as miserable. They approached very unwillingly, and were asked one by one if they were ready to pay their gazier [jizya]; when one said 'yes', he approached as the others had done, paid his money, took a similar receipt, and went about his business; he that said 'no, he could not,' or was not ready, was seized instantly by the Moors, who, throwing him flat on his face to the ground, gave him about fifty blows with a thick stick upon his back and posteriors, after which he was conducted away to a dungeon, under the fortifications of the city, from which he was not released until his friends had made up the money; and if this had not been done within three days, he was brought out and again bastinadoed" (2:85–89).

Discriminatory Dress

The dress of the Jews nearly resembles that of the Moors, but they are strictly forbidden to have it of any other colour than a black, or a very dark green or blue, shades which are held in abhorrence by the Mohammedans. The privilege of wearing an European dress was

---

[1] I.e., *na'm yà sayydi*, Arabic for, "At your service, Master."

formerly allowed to any Jews who might happen to be only sojourn-
ing for a time, on mercantile affairs in Africa; but in consequence of
the native Jews' attempting to imitate them, a general prohibition was
issued. The occasion of the restriction was as follows. One day the
Emperor of Morocco, as he was giving public audience, saw at a
considerable distance a person in a very sumptuous European dress.
Supposing him to be one of the European ambassadors, whom at the
time he was anxious to conciliate, he sent one of the courtiers in
waiting to inquire what nation he represented, and to bear him a
complimentary message requesting his presence; but when the cour-
tier returned and reported that he was only a Morocco Jew, the Emperor, enraged at having wasted so much civility on a being so utterly
unworthy his imperial notice, flew into a violent passion, ordered the
scarlet and gold dress to be torn off in his presence, and the offender
to be clothed in a coarse black burnoose, after which he was to be spit
upon, and buffeted, and kicked out of the place of audience (2:98–
99).

Messianism

The Jews still retain all that strength of affection for their native
land which has caused them such an amount of misery and suffering;
and wretched, degraded, oppressed though they be, they still send
every year a considerable sum to maintain the priests and elders of
their nation, who are suffered to reside within the holy city on paying
a certain tribute to the Sultan (2:115–16).

Christians Reside in Jewish Quarter

Several of them [the Jews] are to be found capable of conversing in
the tongues of these several countries [Spain, France, Italy, England],
and possessed of considerable information on general topics. For this
reason they are in constant communication with all foreigners who
may visit the country, and as, according to Mohammedan institutions,
all Christians who have not their own tents or houses are obliged to
lodge in the Jew quarter, a new bond of connection, and a new source
of emolument, are thus opened (2:136).

Collective Reprisals During a Rebellion at Algiers (1804)[2]

No where in Barbary was the Hebrew nation more free and better
considered than they were at Algiers about the year 1804. At that

---

[2]Extract from a letter of Dr. Naudi to the Rev. C. S. Hawtrey, dated 15 Oct. 1816
(reproduced by Barton Lord).

epoch, very remarkable for the Algerine Jews, a tumultuous rebellion rose up in the neighbourhood of the town, and the Jews were unjustly charged with the crime. The traitorous promoters were persons in the government, and nearly intimate with the Dey too; but as some of these gentlemen borrowed money from a merchant Jew, the Jews were considered as the perpetrators, notwithstanding they were not concerned at all in the affair. The Sultan's reasons were, that had it not been for the Jewish money the riot in all probability would not have taken place; *ergo*, the Jews should be considered as the true revolutionists: *causa causae est causa causati*, which, I am sure, in the case of the Jews, in 1804, was a very unjust induction. They were, therefore taken away, tortured, and racked in a variety of barbarous ways, and made to suffer every kind of torment, particularly that most terrible one, of being suspended alive by a long rope on the outside of the tower walls, having hooked-nails thrust into different parts of the body, often under the chin bone, so as to suspend the body perpendicularly. Several hundreds lost their lives in this desperate way; others were punished by burning, some by stripes; and the greater part, by confiscation of their goods and properties, were reduced to a state of poverty. Those who had something to lose suffered by this latter means; and bastinados, gibbets, and impalings, as is generally the case in all despotic countries, were administered to those who had nothing to lose. This contingency was the cause of great migrations of the Jewish people from Algiers to other parts of Barbary, particularly to Tunis. Numbers of the more religious among them, imputing the general persecution to an advice, or warning from Heaven, to leave distant countries, and concentrate in the Levantine parts, *resorted to Palestine and to the neighbourhood of Jerusalem, as if the time of their restoration was at hand* [sic]. The state of the Jews at this present time in Algiers is as follows:—There are about nine thousand; and several synagogues . . . (2 : 138–39).

P. Barton Lord

60. Change of Reign in Algiers (early 19th Century)

Whenever it was seen to promise success, a revolt was heartily joined by all the rest of the Turkish soldiery, who, always, when a new master mounted his *trone sanglant*, received from his hands no stinted bounty; and during the brief period of an interreign, had by dire *usanza*, the lawful, lawless right of pillaging the whole Jewish population; unless they could be prevailed upon to accept an extravagant compensation which was levied by the king [chief] of the Jews, upon each member of his persecuted race.

This arrangement was, at least whilst we were at Algiers, always

entered into betwixt the leaders of the revolution and the wretched
Israelites. The former were influenced to it by dread of the consequent ruin of all the commercial interests of the country,-and their
followers were prompted by the conviction, that it was more advantageous to make such a bargain, than to run the chance of seeking out
where were the hidden treasures of the wary *Judeos,* who, whatever
Golcondan mines they may be owners of, both in their dress and in
the furniture of their residences, ever affect an appearance of a fortune below mediocrity; the Jewesses, of whatever rank, never having
other than silver salmas, and but few ornaments of value.

   Never did I behold grief so demonstrative as that of the Jewish
women, which we witnessed from the terrace of our house in town, on
the occasion of the murder of the old Ali Pacha. The terrace of every
house inhabited by these wretched people, was covered by women
and children, who evinced the most frantic distress, beating their
breasts, tearing their hair, and invoking protection from on high, on
their bended knees. It was most heart-rending to behold. By the
mercy of God, the hearts of their oppressors were softened, and the
usual compromise was accepted (pp. 352–53).

E. Broughton

61. Jews of Algiers before the French Conquest (1825)

   The Jews, of whom there are about five thousand in this city, have
the free exercise of their religion secured; they are governed by their
own laws in civil cases, administered by a chief of their own nation,
who is appointed by the Bashaw; as Algerine subjects they may circu-
late freely, establish themselves where they please, and exercise any
lawful calling throughout the kingdom; and they cannot be reduced
to slavery. They pay a capitation tax, and double duties on every
species of merchandise imported from abroad; as elsewhere, they
practise trade in all its branches, and are here the only brokers, and
dealers in money and exchanges; there are many gold and silver-
smiths amongst them, and they are the only artificers employed in the
mint.

   Independent of the legal disabilities of the Jews, they are in Algiers
a most oppressed people; they are not permitted to resist any personal violence of whatever nature, from a Mussulman; they are compelled to wear clothing of a black or dark colour; they cannot ride on
horseback, or wear arms of any sort, not even a cane; they are permitted only on Saturdays and Wednesdays to pass out of the gates of
the city without permission; and on any unexpected call for hard
labour, the Jews are turned out to execute it. In the summer of 1815,

this country was visited by incredible swarms of locusts, which destroyed every green thing before them; when several hundred Jews were ordered out to protect the Bashaw's gardens, where they were obliged to watch and toil day and night, as long as these insects continued to infest the country.

On several occasions of sedition amongst the Janissaries, the Jews have been indiscriminately plundered, and they lived in the perpetual fear of a renewal of such scenes; they are pelted in the streets even by children, and in short, the whole course of their existence here, is a state of the most abject oppression and contumely. The children of Jacob bear these indignities with wonderful patience; they learn submission from infancy, and practise it throughout their lives, without ever daring to murmur at their hard lot. Notwithstanding these discouraging circumstances in their condition, the Jews, who through their correspondence with foreign countries are the only class of Algerine society possessing any accurate knowledge of external affairs, meddle with all sorts of intrigue, even at the risk of their lives, which are not unfrequently forfeited in consequence. The post of chief of the Jews is procured and held through bribery and intrigue, and is exercised with a tyranny and oppression corresponding to the tenure by which it is retained. During the times of prosperity of the Regency, several Jewish houses of trade rose here to great opulence, but of late years, through the intolerable oppression under which they live, many wealthy individuals have been ruined, others have found means to emigrate, and the Moors, who have a singular aptness for trade, are daily supplanting them in the different branches of commerce practicable in this country; so that they appear now to be on a rapid decline even as to their numbers. It appears to me that the Jews at this day in Algiers, constitute one of the least fortunate remnants of Israel existing.

In respect of manners, habits, and modes of living, with the above exceptions, the Jews in Algiers differ so little from the other corresponding classes of society that they are not worth describing. The Jews of Algiers are a fine robust race, with good complexions, but the effects of the abject state in which they are born and live, are imprinted on their countenances; nothing is more rare than to discover a distinguished trait in the physiognomy of an Algerine Jew, whether male or female. There is a very affecting practice here with these people, which cannot be contemplated without feelings of respect, and even of tenderness, for this miraculous race. Many aged and infirm Jews, sensible that all their temporal concerns are drawing to a close, die as it were a civil death, investing their heirs with all their worldly substance, with the reserve of only the small pittance necessary to support the lingering remnant of their days in Jerusalem,

YOUNG JEWISH GIRL OF ALGIERS
ca. 1840–50

no. 45, in A. Rubens (1981)

where they go to die. In the year 1816, I witnessed the embarkation of a number of ancient Hebrews, on this last earthly pilgrimage, on board of a vessel chartered expressly for the purpose of transporting them to the coast of Syria. The number of Jews in the kingdom of Algiers is computed at about thirty thousand (pp. 65-68).

*W. Shaler

*William Shaler, American Consul General in Algiers (1816–1828).

62. Emancipation in Algeria and Dhimmi Notables

Under the Turkish dominion, it is certain that the Jews were most oppressively treated. Their injuries were aggravated by insults. They durst not wear any habiliment but of a darkish colour. When the Dey issued an order that neither Musulman nor Christian was to walk the streets at night without a lighted lantern, the light was enjoined on the Jews, but it was to be carried without a lantern; and if they could not keep it from being blown out by the shelter of their fingers, it was a nice joke for the police to bastinado or fine poor Moses for going about without a light. A Jew that was struck by a Moor or Turk durst not, but at the peril of his life, lift his hand to defend himself. A person still living in Algiers tells me that he has seen an aged Jew flying through the streets, pursued and pelted with stones by Mussulman boys. The usual capital punishment of the hapless race was, to be burnt alive (1 : 154).

If you ask me what is the use of conjuring up the remembrance of such horrors as these, that are almost enough to make us wish our species had never existed, I will answer you by a counter-question. Are the horrors I advert to fiction or truth? Alas! they are too true. They are passed, it is true; but what has happened before may happen again, unless we appeal to the human heart against such atrocities.

From the fact of the Jews having been so ill used in this country, I inferred that I should find them at Algiers embittered against the late Turkish government, and enthusiastically attached to the French. But the case is otherwise. The Jews of better condition, and it is only among these that I can find persons who can talk French, seem to wince at the mention of their by-gone oppression, and to shun the subject as something that hurts their pride. Conversing with one of their richest and most respectable men, I taxed him with this foible, and he laughed, half confessing it. The burning and the pelting of his brethren he could not deny: "But," he said, "we were not so entirely wretched as you seem to imagine. We had an arbitrator, or king, as we still call him, of our own, who settled all differences amongst us. Commerce and the exchange of money were almost exclusively in our hands before the French came; though, alas, it is not so now. Every rich Jew had his Turkish patron for a reasonable sum, who protected not only *him,* but poorer Jews that were *his protégés.*" I pushed him no further in the argument. What he said reminded me that, in the worst circumstances of man, custom and nature always seek and find out *some* means, more or less, to alleviate his misery (1 : 155–57).

T. Campbell

63. The Sultan of Morocco Defines Jewish Rights (1841)

The Jews of Our auspicious Country were granted certain guarantees from which they benefit in exchange for their carrying out the conditions imposed by our religious law on those enjoying its protection: these conditions have been and still are observed by Our coreligionists. If the Jews respect these conditions, our Law prohibits the spilling of their blood and enjoins the protection of their belongings, but if they break so much as a single condition then our blessed Law allows their blood to be spilt and their belongings to be appropriated. Our glorious faith only allows them the marks of lowliness and degradation, thus the sole fact that a Jew raises his voice against a Muslim constitutes a violation of the conditions of protection. If in your country they are your equals in all matters, if they are assimilated to you, this is all well and good for your land, but not for Ours. Your status with Us is different from theirs: you are considered as [having the status of] the "reconciled," whereas they are the "protected."

Consequently, if one of them ventures into Our blessed empire in order to engage in commerce, he must conform to the same obligations as the "protected [peoples]" in our midst and adopt the same external signs [of discrimination]. He who does not desire to observe these obligations would be wiser to stay in his own country, for we have no need of his commerce, if the latter is to be conducted in circumstances contrary to Our blessed law . . . (pp. 14–16).

Ended the 20th of the holy month of dhu 1-Hijja, of the year 1257 (1841).

Letter from the Moroccan Sultan, Mulay Abd al-Rahman (1822–1859), to the French consulate at Tangiers, in E. Fumey.

64. Vestmental Discrimination in Morocco (1850)

They [the Jews] were first permitted the usage of this kerchief in Morocco [Marrakesh] and Meknez, as a means of covering their ears. They really wanted to elude the customary insult of Moorish children, who delighted in knocking off their bonnets, which were a sign of servitude. They are not allowed to fasten the kerchief with a double knot below the chin; this knot must be a simple one and the kerchief removed in the presence of Muslim dignitaries. . . . They are obliged always to wear the black or dark blue cloak *(ya'lak)*; it is only as a concession that they wear the white *slam*, a small coat, useful against the hot sun. The coat's hood, made of blue cloth, must not fold over the head, lest the Jew be mistaken from afar for a Moor; for the Moor sometimes wears a hood of the same color, except with a different rim.

Moreover, the black bonnet must always be visible. Furthermore, the coat must have a little opening on the right, and the hood must fall over the left shoulder in order to trouble the movement of the arm as another sign of servitude (pp. 27–28).

L. Godard (p. 35) in J. Goulven.

65. Defenseless Dhimmis of Morocco (19th century)

The Barbary Jews are, in every sense of the word, complete slaves to the Moors. They are obliged to wear a particular costume to distinguish them from the Mahometans, and can on no account wear a red cap or yellow slippers, the same as the Moors. If they should be bold enough to do so, a very severe punishment would be the consequence. Neither are they permitted to adopt the European costume without especial leave from the sultan himself, which is sometimes granted as a matter of very great favour. The Jews wear a black skull-cap on their head, and black slippers: the latter they are compelled to take off when they come within ten yards of a mosque or sanctuary, and to proceed barefooted by it. No exception is made to this regulation, whatever may be the wealth and consequence of the individual, or the state of the weather and streets. The Jews throughout the country are held in the greatest contempt by all classes of the Mahometans. The Moorish boys, who are usually extremely insolent, even to Christians, treat the unfortunate Israelites with the greatest effrontery and wanton cruelty, sensible as they are that they will not be punished, and being encouraged in this behaviour by their parents. I have, on more

JEWS FROM DEBDOU, MOROCCO
Wearing traditional garments
Collection Z. Schulmann (1955)

than one occasion, seen a Moorish boy about ten years of age step up to a Jew in the street, and, having stopped him, kick, and slap him in the face, without his venturing to lift up a hand and defend himself. Should he dare to do so, his hand would be cut off, as being raised against one of their true believers. The poor man was obliged to content himself with crying out, addressing his little persecutor at the same time by the title of sidi, or master, and supplicating him to let him pass. As to the unfortunate Jew boys, they make their appearance with fear and trembling where any Moorish children may chance to be playing, being considered as fair game, much in the same light as a dog, and are sure to be well thumped and pelted. It is in consequence of this system of persecution that the Jews of Tetuan and some other towns—Fez, for instance—have a separate quarter or town to themselves, the only communication with the Moorish town being by gates, which are shut at night. By these means they are very much protected from the ill-treatment and insults of the Moors, particularly on the sabbath, when they do more as they please than on any other day, as no Moor is then allowed to enter their quarter and molest them. Sometimes they depend so much on the security they enjoy on their sabbath, that they venture now and then to put on a hat of European make, although subject to the risk of being reported to the governor, and either heavily fined or receiving the bastinado for their infringement of the general regulation on this head (1:338–39).

A Jew or a Christian is esteemed no valid evidence against a Moor, particularly the former, and it may easily be imagined how wide a door is left open to corruption, injustice, and persecution. The poor unprotected Jews are greatly exposed to imprisonment and fines (the principal object always of Moorish justice), especially under an iniquitous governor, which too often is the case, and who then neglects no opportunity for the purpose of squeezing the poor wretches, namely, extracting from them every farthing they possess in the world (1:424).

A. de C. Brooke (1831)

Although the Jews are subject to the general laws of the country, they are allowed to settle their civil disputes according to their own *shraa,* which accords with the Mosaic law. In this they possess a great advantage; for, according to Mohammedan law, neither Christian nor Jew has, in legal matters, any *locus standi.* In taking evidence their oath is not received, and the presumption is always in favour of the true believer (p. 254).

A. Leared (1876)

If a Moor murders a true believer the family of the murdered man have a right to his life, and very rarely fail to obtain it, unless they choose to condone the offence, and surreptitiously accept blood-money from the murderer or his family. But the life of a murderer of a Jew is never in danger from the Moorish law, as, of course, according to their creed the life of a true believer is not to be compared in value with the life of a Jewish dog. So if a Jew becomes obnoxious to a Moor, he generally has him murdered. If any fuss is made, or if the Jew is protected by a foreign power, or has friends protected by a foreign power, the investigator of the murder generally pays about ten pounds blood-money, and the whole matter is hushed up (pp. 326–27).

S. Bonsal (1891)

66. Restrictions of Movement and Residence

Morocco (1789)

The Jewdry [of Tarudant] is a miserable place, situated about a quarter of a mile from the town. The inhabitants are in the most abject state of poverty and subjection, and when they enter the Moorish town are obliged to go barefooted (pp. 160–61).

The Jews, who are at this place [Marrakesh] pretty numerous, have a separate town to themselves, walled in, and under the charge of an Alcaide, appointed by the emperor. It has two large gates, which are regularly shut every evening about nine o'clock, after which time no person whatever is permitted to enter or go out of the Jewdry, till they are opened again the following morning. The Jews have a market of their own, and, as at Tarudant, when they enter the Moorish town, castle, or palace, they are always compelled to be barefooted (p. 197).

The Jews of Barbary shave their heads close, and wear their beards long; their dress indeed, altogether, differs very little from that of the Moors (which I shall hereafter describe) except in their being obliged to appear externally in black. For which purpose they wear a black cap, black slippers, and instead of the *haick*[1] worn by the Moors, substitute the *alberoce*,[2] a cloak made of black wool, which covers the whole of the under dress. The Jews are not permitted to go out of the country, but by an express order from the emperor; nor are they allowed to wear a sword, or ride a horse, though they are indulged in the use of mules. This arises from an opinion prevalent among the Moors, that a horse is too noble an animal to be employed in the service of such infidels as Jews (p. 202).

W. Lemprière

---

[1] A large cloak like a blanket.
[2] I.e., *al-burnus*, or hooded cloak.

Christians Are No Longer Insulted in Tunis (1835)

Thirty years ago, a Christian could scarcely walk through the streets, much less the country, without being insulted. This, says M. Blaquière, seldom occurs now; and although the hatred of the natives towards Jews and Nazarenes has not subsided in the least, the fear of punishment is a certain bar to their insolence (p. 284).

M. Russell

67. Impurity of Infidels in Morocco (1789 and 1889)

The Moors will not allow Christians or Jews to pass over their places of interment; as they have a superstitious idea, which is perhaps more prevalent among the lower class of people than those who are better informed, that the dead suffer pain from having their graves trodden upon by infidels; and I recollect when at Tangier I received a very severe rebuke from a Moor, for accidentally having passed through one of their burying grounds (p. 341).

W. Lemprière

We passed the tomb of a Moorish saint. It was a small, white-washed, but ruinous square enclosure, surmounted by a white flag. These places, although as in this case close to the road, may not be approached by Christians or Jews without risk of giving deadly offence (p. 41).

A. Leared

68. Purity of Arab Land

At Kerwan: An infidel, whether Jew or Christian, is not allowed under any circumstances to enter this town, which is strongly walled in, and the fanaticism of the populace goes so far, that even the highest and most influential travellers can enter only in disguise, and furnished by an official order from the Bey to the Caid of the town (p. 237).

At Sfax: The exclusiveness of Sfax is so great that an Arabian immigrant, whether he comes from Tunis or from the Oases, may not remain long in the town. . . . Of course Christians are hated: not one lives in the town; they and the Jews—2,000 in number—occupy a separate quarter on the sea-shore, which is lower than the town, and called Rabat (p. 278).

E. von Hesse-Wartegg

At Shellah (Morocco) in 1890: Several years ago the place was guarded, and no Christian or Jew was permitted to enter within the precincts of its sacred walls. The first who entered on scientific researches did so under an escort of soldiers; but now Christians not only freely walk about, but even enter and inspect the ruins of the sacred mosque (p. 51).

At Fez: Fez has two principal mosques. . . . Christians and Jews are not allowed to pass the streets in which its doors open (p. 139).

On our return from the Mellah our soldier informed me that I ought no longer to entertain the idea of going to Sifroo, as the Kaids both of Old and of New Fez refused to give me a letter. Sifroo is under the jurisdiction of the Governor of New Fez, but he refused to give a letter, on the ground that Christians are not permitted to go there except they have a permit from the Sultan (p. 153).

Dr. R. Kerr

In Yemen: The Jews run most of the better shops in Sanaa proper, but have to clear out before night and go back to their quarter, as no Jew is allowed to live in sacred Sanaa (p. 257).

G. Wyman Bury (1915)

69. Economic Importance of the Dhimmis and their Exploitation

In every country where they reside, these unfortunate people [the Jews] are treated as another class of beings; but in no part of the world are they so severely and undeservedly oppressed as in Barbary, where the whole country depends upon their industry and ingenuity, and could scarcely subsist as a nation without their assistance. They are the only mechanics in this part of the world, and have the whole management of all pecuniary and commercial matters except the collecting of customs. They are, however, intrusted in the coinage of money, as I myself witnessed.

The Moors display more humanity to their beasts than to the Jews. I have seen frequent instances where individuals of this unhappy people were beaten so severely, as to be left almost lifeless on the ground, and that without being able to obtain the least redress whatever, as the magistrates always act with the most culpable partiality when a Moor and Jew are the parties in a suit (pp. 198–99).

W. Lemprière (1790)

From their wretched appearance and the degraded state of slavery in which they exist, one would little suppose them to be so necessary to the very existence of the Moors as they are; yet such is the case; and this indolent, cruel, and helpless race could no more dispense with the aid and assistance of the Jew, than the Arab could with the services of the camel. Beaten, taunted, unprotected by the laws, a by-word of reproach and contempt, with the hand of every urchin lifted against them without [their] daring even to complain, it is the Jew, nevertheless, that does every thing, and the whole commerce of the country is carried on through his means. To the European consuls the assistance of a Jew is indispensable, both in diplomatic affairs and in every kind of business. Even the sultan himself cannot do without Jews, and their services are requisite in a variety of ways connected with the highest offices. In short, the Jew of Morocco, abject as his state is, has succeeded by his address in ruling the Moor himself (1 : 249).

From what has been said, it will be seen that the character of the Barbary Jews appears little altered by their enslaved condition, and is the same as is observed all over the world. They are industrious, active, lively, patient, willing; and possessing as much honesty in their dealings as the Moors, and not more than their European brethren. They excel in gold and silk embroidery, are good tailors, shoemakers, and engage in a variety of little trades and occupations with which the Moors are unacquainted both from ignorance and idleness. Eternally scheming and having some speculation in their head, which is usually some little adventure of goods from Gibraltar, they generally succeed in their plans if they happen to have a little capital. The greater part, however, are miserably poor; and if they were not so humble and unwearied in their endeavours to earn something, and the necessaries of life were not to be procured on such moderate terms, they would find it very difficult to exist among a race from whom they can expect no relief or commiseration (1 : 255–56).

A. de C. Brooke (1831)

In the southern province of Sus the Jew is regarded as so indispensable to the prosperity of the country that he is not allowed to leave it. If he gets permission to go to Mogador to trade, it is only on condition that he leaves his wife and family, or some relation to whom he is known to be attached, as surety for his return (p. 217).

A. Leared (1876)

In Egypt

The bureaucracy engaged in the collection of the revenue were of two sorts—Moslems and Copts. . . . The Copts did all the mechanical details of calculation in the actual collection of the revenue, as well as in the expenditure of the government, and were most expert arithmeticians. . . . The Copts were a well-behaved, inoffensive people, but being a miserable minority of the population, and professing the Christian religion, their position was a subordinate one. (1 : 79–80).

A. A. Paton (1870)

70. Servitudes in the Maghreb (1870)

The oppressions to which those latter [the Jews] are exposed, even to this day, are almost incredible. In Algiers The French Government emancipated them some forty years ago, but in Tunis, Morocco, and Tripolis they only got certain liberties during the last few years. Till then they had to live in a certain quarter, and were not allowed to appear in the streets after sunset. If they were compelled to go out at night they had to provide themselves with a sort of cat-o'-nine-tails at the next guard-house of the "Zaptieh," which served as a kind of passport to the patrols going round at night. If it was a dark night, they were not allowed to carry a lantern like the Moors and Turks, but a candle, which the wind extinguished every minute. They were neither allowed to ride on horseback nor on a mule, and even to ride on a donkey was forbidden them except outside the town; they had then to dismount at the gates, and walk in the middle of the streets, so as not to be in the way of Arabs. If they had to pass the "Kasba," they had first to fall on their knees as a sign of submission, and then to walk on with lowered head; before coming to a mosque they were obliged to take the slippers off their feet, and had to pass the holy edifice without looking at it. As Tunis possesses no less than five hundred mosques, it will be seen that Jews did not wear out many shoes at that time. It was even worse in their intercourse with Mussulmans. If one of these fancied himself insulted by a Jew, he stabbed him at once, and had only to pay a fine to the State, by way of punishment. As late as 1868 seventeen Jews were murdered in Tunis without the offenders having been punished for it; often a Minister or General was in the plot, to enrich himself with the money of the murdered ones. Nor was that all. The Jews—probably to show their gratefulness for being allowed to live in the town, or to live at all—had to pay 50,000 piastres monthly to the State as a tax! (pp. 118–19).

E. von Hesse-Wartegg

71. Wages in Marrakesh (1876)

Needless to say it is primarily the working classes and the petty shopkeepers who are the most exposed to the arbitrary measures of the authorities. The Jewish craftsman who brings his work to the Morrocan official is paid with blows of a staff if he is not satisfied with half the price originally agreed upon. The heaviest tasks are continuously imposed upon the working population, women and children not excepted. While roaming through the bazaar in the Arab quarter, I saw long lines of young Jewish girls, bareheaded and barefooted, working in the manufacture of military uniforms, earning but 10 or 15 centimes per day. But the bodily sufferings are nothing in comparison to the moral vexations to which these sensitive and modest creatures are constantly exposed. In a country where no decent woman would be seen in the street without a veil, these Jewish women and girls are obliged to work unveiled in the middle of the bazaar and thereby exhibit themselves to the impudent stares of the Arab crowds.

A Muslim himself admitted to me that this humiliating exposure has no other purpose than to force these Jewish women to convert as the only means of escaping from such intolerable treatment. Indeed, must not their spirit be exceptionally noble in order to withstand such a life of misery and untold suffering, when conversion can offer them the most precious advantages, freedom, wealth, and honors?

The petty shopkeepers in the Mellah are not treated any better, for retail transactions are often the cause of arguments between Arabs and Jews, from which the former are certain in advance to triumph. A Muslim who buys some commodity from a Jewish shop comes back some hours later accusing the vendor of having cheated him on the weight or quantity. Since, on the one hand, the testimony of a Jew is worthless and, on the other, it is impossible to find Arab witnesses in the Mellah, the Muslim's word is taken and the ghetto overseer (muhtasib) sees no harm in punishing the presumed offender with a round of thrashes from his staff, which leaves him unconscious on the ground or maimed for the rest of his life. With my own eyes I saw a great number of these victims, mostly butchers, woefully dragging themselves along the ground, unable to walk upright, their backs horribly hacked to pieces and looking like one gaping wound. Black decayed flesh hung at their ankles and their feet, crooked and swollen by the violent blows, ended in a hideous blue blister which hid the atrocious remains of toenails that had been smashed by the staff. It was hideous and heartbreaking to see, and yet these wounds were already ten or fifteen days old. What had the state of these wretched people been on the day when this treatment had been inflicted upon them?

MOROCCAN JEWISH GIRL
Engraving by Giles from a painting by G. Beauclerk (1828)
no. 1903, in A. Rubens (1981)

Sometimes the cruelest punishments are meted out on these poor Jews without the slightest pretext, if only to remind them that they have masters who can do what they want with them. The main idea of the Morrocan authorities is that the Jew must not undertake nor initiate a commercial transaction without their mediation, the aim of which obviously is to receive a handsome commission. Consequently, their anger knows no bounds when such an opportunity escapes their greediness (*BAIU:* 52–54).

Dhimmi Notables—Instruments of the Rulers—and the Oppressed

The Arab system has always aimed at dominating the mass of the people by a small number of privileged individuals dependent on the government. This tendency has brought about within the population of the Mellah the formation of quite a powerful oligarchy, which the authorities quite openly favor and which, through fear or gratitude, always collaborates with the administration in order to stifle the voice and complaints of the population. This group of *gebirim* (notables) is made up of ten families who have become rich by trading with the money that the sultan lent them some years ago. They reside in spacious houses that are sumptuously furnished; their table is well garnished with meats and even wines from Europe, but upon leaving their houses they are assimilated with the others and subjected to the same discriminatory laws as the least commoner. They are accused of scheming with the authorities in order to hoard the grains and the best meat from the butchers for their own daily needs. I think there is much exaggeration in these claims, but it certainly does not contribute to the happiness of the wealthy, who are continuously faced with the antipathy of the population. Caught between the fear of the Arabs and the hardly disguised animosity of their fellow Jews, the *gebirim* of the Mellah appear to me rather to be pitied than envied. Their life is torn between the need to survive and remorse, so much so that they have little time left to enjoy their riches (*BAIU:* 54–55).

*J. Halévy, Report, in Archives, *AIU* (FRANCE IX A 73), and *BAIU* (1st Sem. 1877): 44–70. See also Littman, "Quelques Aspects", in *Yod* 2, no. 1 (1976): 39–42.

---

*Joseph Halévy (1827–1917), born in Adrianople, Turkey. French orientalist and writer. Traveled to Ethiopia in 1868 (Falashas), Southern Arabia in 1872 (Sabean inscriptions) and to Morocco in 1876. Professor in Ethiopic at the *Ecole Pratique des Hautes Etudes* (Paris) from 1879. He founded the *Revue Sémitique d'Epigraphie et d'Histoire Ancienne* in 1893.

RABBI WEARING DISTINCTIVE SPOTTED KERCHIEF
Ifrane Synagogue, Morocco
Collection Z. Schulmann (1955)

72. Oppressors and Dhimmis in Marrakesh (1876)

On entering the town, I was not able to distinguish the different
groups of the population in the midst of the crowd that gathered
through curiosity around my little caravan; but as I advanced the
crowd divided itself into two parts, each recognizable from their attire. On one side, men of an aggressive expression, clad in
magnificent burnooses with rich edgings, their heads covered with
large turbans neatly folded and their feet shod with beautiful yellow
sandals, largely embroidered with gold and silver filigrane; on the
other side a shy and shoddy crowd, whose only headgear was a blue
kerchief with black spots, carelessly knotted around their necks, carrying in their hands rustic sandals while continuing to walk barefoot,
despite the sharp stones in the road. Need it be said that the latter
were the Jews, for whom it is prohibited to wear a turban, which is the
only sure protection for the head against the rays of the tropical sun,
and who cannot, thanks to a cruel refinement, even wear shoes out-

side of their quarter, the Mellah. It is impossible to imagine the sufferings of these wretches, who, amid the jeerings of the Muslim population along the road, jump and cringe with pain, their feet torn and their nails crushed by the stones (*BAIU:* 50–51).

J. Halévy

73. Refusal to Emancipate the Dhimmis in Morocco

Formerly the Jews were compelled to walk barefoot when they ventured into the Medinah or Moorish quarter, and always when passing a mosque. They were not allowed to mount on horseback (the horse being considered too noble an animal) or to sit cross-legged in the presence of a Moor. The meanest Moslem might insult or maltreat them with impunity, so much so that it was quite a common occurence to see boys beat, spit upon, and pull by the beard any Jew, however respectable, they might meet in the streets. The Jews were also obliged to wear a peculiar dress, in order to mark their degradation.

These oppressive enactments and usages were somewhat modified at the instance of the benevolent Sir Moses Montefiore, who paid a visit to the late Sultan Sidi Mohammed in 1864,[1] but the edict then issued has been enforced at the seaports only. The Jews are still compelled to walk barefoot in all the towns in the interior, and to wear a distinctive dress. The present Sultan, on being reminded of his father's edict, replied that all Jews who, being under foreign protection, wished to wear their shoes, must also dress as Europeans. This, the Sultan and his ministers knew very well, no Jew at Fez, or any other town in the interior could do, without running great risk if recognised by the populace. The usual dress of the Jews at the seaports consists of a tunic and vest of dark cloth, closely buttoned up to the throat with a double row of silk buttons; a wide sash round the waist; a dark fez, and black shoes or slippers. In the interior their costume is simply a dark coloured caftan, belted at the waist, and a head dress consisting of a blue or dark coloured cotton kerchief, tied under the chin. They are prohibited from wearing any but black shoes or slippers, as black is a colour despised by the Moors (pp. 11–12).

J. V. Crawford (1889)

---

[1] D. G. Littman, "Mission to Morocco (1863–1864)," in Sonia and V. D. Lipman (ed.) *The Century of Moses Montefiore* (Oxford University Press, 1985).

The disqualifications and indignities to which the Jews are subjected in the city of Morocco [Marrakesh], so far as they came under my own observation, were as follows:

1. They are never allowed to wear the turban.

2. In the presence of a governor, or when passing a mosque, they are obliged to remove the blue handkerchief with which the head is at other times bound.

3. They must wear black instead of the yellow shoes always worn by the Moors.

4. When they go from their own quarter into the Moorish town, both men and women are compelled to take off their shoes and walk barefooted; and this degradation appeared especially painful when one had occasion to walk with a Jewish friend through the filthy streets of the Moorish quarters.

5. A Jew, meeting a Moor, must always pass to the left.

6. Jews are not allowed to ride through the city.

7. They are not permitted to carry arms.

8. The use of the Moorish bath is forbidden to the Jews.

9. In the exercise of their religion they are restricted to private houses; hence there are no public buildings used as synagogues. This restriction applies equally to other parts of the empire, except Tangier.

No doubt there are other more or less annoying interferences with personal liberty which do not meet the eye. But the list given is enough to show that the grievances of the Jewish community are far from being merely sentimental. They live under the yoke of an iron despotism, and, as might be expected, betray this in their manner and appearance. The men are in general of medium height, but slender, long-visaged, and sallow. It is sad to see them walk with bowed heads and slow steps through the streets of their mother city; rather, indeed, a hard step-mother, who, while acknowledging their right to a harsh protection, subjects them to the taunts and ill-treatment of her more favoured progeny. Even the horse-play and practical jokes of the Moors are highly inconvenient to the Jew. Here is one instance:—In some seasons the gardens in and about the city are so productive that oranges are absolutely of no value except for pelting the Jews. It is, indeed, regarded as seasonable sport, like that of throwing snowballs in England, for which oranges are no bad substitutes. Woe to the unhappy Israelite who is seen in the streets, or on a housetop, during this saturnalia of the Moorish youth. Assailed by shouts and jeers, he is, unless saved by hasty flight, ridiculously besmeared; and, from the violence of the blows, he also runs the risk of receiving more serious injury. On this account the authorities have, of late, made efforts to suppress this curiously liberal kind of "Orange riots" (pp. 175–77).

A. Leared

74. Unpunished Crime (1880)

During the evening of the 15th of January [1880], some Jewish children were, as usual, at play in a public thoroughfare near the Jewish quarter at Fez, when they were attacked by a Mahomedan, one of them being seriously injured. A Jew, a naturalized French subject, who happened to be passing at the time, seeing the injured child, and wishing to have the Mussulman punished for his cruelty, seized him with a view of bringing him before the authorities. On arriving at the Palace of Justice he found the gates closed, in accordance with the custom which prevails when the sultan passes the place. Whilst awaiting the re-opening of the gate, the crowd of Mussulmans became more and more numerous. The Jew still kept a tenacious hold of his prisoner, but the latter, emboldened by the presence of his coreligionists, complained that his custodian had ill-treated him, and that the behaviour of the Jews had become unbearable. The Mahomedans thereupon precipitated themselves upon the Jew, whom they struck with sticks and stones. He only escaped certain death by giving some money to a Mahomedan, who covered him with his person, and thus enabled him to escape. He had barely time to rush into the first open door which he espied; it was that of the prison.

The Mahomedans, who were furious at seeing the Jew escape from their clutches, followed after the Jews, who, at the close of their daily occupations, were about to enter their quarter. Several of them reached their homes seriously injured and were compelled to take to their beds. Others escaped unhurt only through having been able to outstrip their pursuers in the general stampede. But a poor Jew, seventy years old, named Abraham Elalouf, a highly respected member of the community at Fez, was unable to run on account of his advanced age. He was attacked by the Mussulmans, who soon killed him by the force of their blows; they then trampled his body under their feet, so that his bowels protruded. But even then the miscreants were not satisfied with their work. They collected a quantity of combustible materials, whilst the shopkeepers in the neighbourhood brought mats and wood. Others then poured petroleum on the corpse and set it on fire.

Meanwhile the Jews, expecting every moment to see the Mussulmans arriving in their Ghetto in order to make it a prey for massacre and pillage, hastened to close the gates. So great was the terror that about thirty Jewish women, who were in a state of pregnancy, miscarried. During the whole of the night, no one dared go into the street in order to ascertain what had become of the unfortunate old man, and it was only in the morning that they found his body, half burnt and half devoured by dogs. An influential Jew presented himself on the following day before the Palace of the Sultan, and demanded justice.

He only received a derisive answer, and was told that as far as he was personally concerned, he had nothing to fear.

The Jews of Fez are in an extremely critical condition; they fear an invasion of their quarter, accompanied by massacre and pillage. The Mahomedans, on their part, have not ceased from tormenting the Jews, and their attitude is the more provoking since their crimes have as yet remained unpunished.

This outrage is a sample of what may be expected, should the threatened withdrawal of European protection in Morocco be carried into effect. The Spanish Government has already withdrawn its protection from the Jews, who had hitherto enjoyed this privilege, and it is believed that the outrages at Fez are the first fruits of this withdrawal.

The Jewish Chronicle, London, 6 February 1880.

The family of the late Abraham al-'Aluf, who was murdered and then burned at Fez, requested from the government a document certifying the murder of their unfortunate relative. (It is the custom in Morocco, among the Muslims, to request such a document in such circumstances, which serves as evidence against the murderers.) The vizier told them that before he could reply he would have to consult his master. His Majesty replied that no such document could be delivered either for the murder of a Jew, a Christian, or a slave and He recommended that the Jews forgive the murderers and that there should be no further mention of the matter. Those Muslims arrested by the government, so we are informed, have been released. You can understand to what our unfortunate brethren in Morocco, victims of Muslim hatred, will now be exposed. Our brethren are threatened at every moment, and people even shout in the streets: *"Give us the paraffin, give us the fire, here comes the Jew!"*

We will not be surprised to learn one day that the Muslims have entered the ghetto, either in Fez or Meknes, or another city of the Moroccan interior, and that they have there murdered men, women, and children.

Letter of 3 February 1880 from Dr. Miguerez, vice-president, regional committee of the *AIU* in Tangiers, to the secretary *AIU,* Paris, Archives, *AIU* (MAROC IV C 11). See also Littman, *"Quelques Aspects,"* in *Yod* 2, no. 1 (1976): 42–43.

75. The Dhimmi as Parasite

There are said to be over ten thousand Jews in Fez, all of whom are obliged to live in the Melha, or Jews' quarter—the Ghetto, in fact, of

Fez. They are particularly odious to the Moor, being held in greater contempt even than Christians; and the interest taken in them by foreign societies tends to make them insolent and independent, increasing thereby the Mussulman aversion to them. A few days ago a deputation of Israelites, with a grave and reverend rabbi at their head, waited upon His Excellency to thank him for past favours (he is one of the committee for their protection), and to beg for more. Among other things was a request that he would interest himself in their behalf to get permission from the Sultan for them to wear their shoes in the town. "We are old, Bashador," they said, "and our limbs are weak; our women, too, are delicately nurtured, and this law presses heavily upon us." Though I can quite sympathise with the poor Hebrew in his non-appreciation of having to walk over such streets as these barefooted, yet I was glad they were dissuaded from pressing their request, the granting of which would exasperate the populace, and might lead to consequences too terrible to contemplate. This argument has already been put forward by His Majesty, when pressed on a former occasion to remove the disabilities of the Jews, together with the pertinent one that the admission of their ancestors into Marocco as refugees was made conditional on the observance of this practice; so, if the contract is broken on one side, it might with equal justice be annulled on the other. I do not know what other suggestions they made, as the conversation was all in Arabic; but their excited gestures, and their bending forward across each other's back to get as near as possible, and not lose a word of the Envoy's advice to them, looked as if they put great faith in His Excellency's power of pleading their cause with the Sultan. This chosen people are at present the subject of much discussion, as at the Madrid Conference one of the chief topics under consideration is that of their protection by foreign powers. No doubt some change in the treatment they now meet with is desirable, but that their account of the hardships and injustice under which they labour is exaggerated, is also beyond dispute. The story of the slaying and burning of a Jew here, a few months ago [see document 74], though an act of undoubted barbarism and ferocity, was much garbled and made capital of by the societies for their protection; and it would be well for such associations to inculcate, among their *protégés*, principles of chastity towards women, it having been an attempt on the part of an inebriated Jew to outrage a Moorish woman which excited the feelings of the mob on this occasion. Melh', or Melha, signifies "salt," and the place is so called from the old custom of giving the heads of criminals, when executed, to the Jews, who were compelled to *salt* them before they were distributed over the gates of cities as a warning to others (pp. 176–78).

SALTED HEADS OF MOROCCAN REBELS
On Bab-al-Maroc (Marrakesh) Gate at Fez
Engraving from a drawing by C. Biseo
E. de Amici (1882), p. 243

In many respects the Jews in Marocco are better off than the Mahommedans, especially in this matter of enquiry into acts of violence against them; for whereas one Moor may kill another, and very little be said, if a Jew is the victim, there are a dozen advocates to take up his cause. They are exempt, too, from military service, which in a country like this is no small boon; and though their evidence is not accepted before any tribunal, neither is that of a Christian (p. 179).

The Jews, of whom the place [Arzila] is full, are all in their Saturday's best, and, luxuriating in the twofold comfort of wearing shoes and riding mules, present a great contrast to their barefooted and black-robed compatriots in Fez and Mequinez. One or two Moors who have taken advantage of our escort to travel this way for the first time, are much astonished at this licence, and young Hassan, the khalifa's new valet, has already assaulted two Israelitish boys, to the effusion of blood, for presuming to appear in coloured garments and slippers near our camp (p. 278).

P. D. Trotter (1880)

76. The Dhimmi as Scapegoat

The Mellah [of Wazan], or Ghetto, is not very large, though the Jews are less bullied here than in most cities [of Morocco]. They are, of course, confined to their own quarter after sundown, and have to wear a distinctive dress and go about bare-footed, but otherwise they have a fairly good time, and struck us as presenting a less miserable and dejected appearance than elsewhere (p. 57).

They are confined strictly to their own quarter after sundown, the gates which lead into it being locked and barred, they cannot at any time go outside except barefoot, and certain streets are forbidden them altogether; they must wear the black cap and a distinctive dress; no synagogues or public places of worship are allowed them; they must address Mohammedans as Sidi (my lord), and pay them other marks of respect; and they cannot ride on either horse or mule. Besides these, a thousand other petty indignities help to make their lives a burden, and they also run the risk at times of more serious ill-treatment. Some few years ago [1880] the Fezians got hold of a Hebrew who had made himself particularly obnoxious, and roasted him alive, an event which caused a great sensation, and had the effect of bettering their condition to some extent, owing to pressure on the Government from abroad. My readers will doubtless recall the exclamation of King Alphonso of Spain in the Ingoldsby legends, "Pooh! pooh! burn a Jew, burn two, burn two!" when that monarch was at a loss for other means to procure an heir to the throne. So in Marocco, if anything goes wrong, the Jews are apt to be made the scapegoats, or, at any rate, to suffer in some way or another. Some of them, however, manage to put themselves beyond the reach of Moorish ill-treatment. We had letters of credit to one such, a rich merchant, who struck us as a very favourable specimen of his race. He enjoyed American protection, which might have freed him from many of the restraints imposed on his countrymen, but, to his credit, he refused to avail himself of his privileges, for fear of exciting the mob against his poorer co-religionists, and walked the dirty, ill-paved streets barefooted like the rest. America, by the way, appears to throw the aegis of the Stars and Stripes over a surprising number of Jews in Marocco. The cause of this gratifying solicitude for their welfare is, no doubt, true republican sympathy for an oppressed nationality (pp. 96–97).

Of the disabilities under which the Jews in Marocco labour, and their persecution by the Moors, I have already spoken, but without alluding to the causes thereof. When first in Marocco, I expended much pity on these unfortunate Hebrews which, however, gradually evaporated as I became more acquainted with their character and conduct. I came to the country somewhat of an upholder and admirer of the Jews; I went back, I had nearly said a confirmed Anti-Semite (p. 136).

Apologists for the Jews have always tried to represent them as being the victims of religious persecution. This is only natural, as nothing is more gratifying to human nature than the distinction of martyrdom. The position, however, is quite an untenable one, and has been de-molished by Professor Goldwin Smith, among others, in the pages of the *Nineteenth Century* [November 1882]. He there showed conclu-sively that it is *not* fanaticism that prompts outrage, but "economical and social" causes; "the unhappy relation of a wandering and para-sitic race, retaining its tribal exclusiveness, to the races among whom it sojourns, and on the produce of whose labour it feeds" (p. 137).

H. E. M. Stutfield (1886)

77. Influence of International Opinion

During the last decade, thanks chiefly to the vigilance of several European ministers in Tangier and the agents of the Anglo-Jewish Association throughout the Empire, the number of outrages to which the Jews in Morocco have been subjected has greatly diminished. The cases of barbarous cruelty, some of which I have related in the forego-ing pages, that have come to light have given the Moors so much bother that happily an opinion is growing up in official circles and making itself manifest throughout the land, that Jew-baiting is not worth the subsequent trouble and expense it almost invariably entails, and as the neighbourhood in which an outrage against a Jew's life or property is committed is directly responsible for the blood-money, a strong feeling has shown itself, at least near the coast towns, against the commission of any injury to Jews, at least where there is the slightest chance of its being found out. The outrages against Jews that one hears of most often now are not really the evidences of racial feeling and religious hatred, though both certainly do still exist to a very large extent in Morocco. . . . Of course it should be added that this amelioration of the condition of the Jew is not owing to any spontaneous outburst of humanity and brotherly love on the part of the Moors. It is due entirely to diplomatic pressure from without, to which the Moors have always yielded with the very worst grace in the world (pp. 323–24).

The lawlessness of the country, the oppression of the Sultan and his officers, and the fact that only by courtesy can Morocco be considered a civilized country, has given rise to the system of *protégés*, so absolutely necessary in a country misgoverned like Morocco. It has prevented much cruelty, shielded thousands of innocent people from oppression, and made commerce with Morocco possible during the last hundred years. Of course the provisions of the protection system have been abused. The most flagrant instances of this have come within my personal knowledge, but after everything has been said, and after passing in review the evidence for and against this system, I for one would be very sorry to have it removed (pp. 334–35).

S. Bonsal (1891)

78. The Sultan of Morocco Protects the Jews

Edict Forbidding the Persecution of the Jews at Damnat (Sept. 1884)

By the present edict, we make it publicly known that we have suppressed all vexations to which the Jews of Damnat have been subjected by their governor, to wit:

(1) Forcing them to work on the days that their religion requires them to rest;
(2) Employing them in the cleaning of latrines;
(3) Compelling them to carry heavy loads;
(4) Forcing them to work without wages;
(5) Forcing their wives to work without their husbands' consent;
(6) Forcing them to sell their merchandise at half its value;

(7) Obliging them to purchase products, such as oil, when their price is low and demanding payment only after the price has risen.

(8) Using their beasts of burden against their will and without compensation;

(9) Forcing them to take counterfeit money instead of legal tender;

(10) Obliging them to accept dirhams at thirteen ducats per duro;

(11) Later, to pay fifteen ducats per duro;

(12) Taking from them tanned hides without payment;

(13) Giving them tanned hides in exchange for fresh ones;

(14) Obliging them to relinquish the wool of their flocks against their will;

(15) Obliging them to put their beds and furniture at the disposal of the governor;

(16) Imposing other officials [*sic*] on their fellow Jews of Tesmit;

(17) Violating customary rights by imposing upon them taxes and imposts.

We hereby order their governor, our servant Hajj al-Jilani-al-Damnati to suppress the foregoing [abuses], to be considerate toward them, to put an end to oppression and injustice, and to treat them in all respects as the Jews of other cities [are treated].

We also order the Jews not to exceed the limits that are assigned to them and to strictly observe their obligations.

Peace, Written on the 25th day of Qa'ada 1301 (1884) (1:342–43)

N. Leven

Letter to the Caid of Marrakesh (1892)

It has come to the knowledge of Our Sherifian Majesty that you do not maintain a proper attitude toward the Jews under your jurisdiction; that you mistreat them, that you beat them and load them with chains, without respect either for children or the aged.

These facts, which are notorious, have caused us surprise; for you are well aware of the punishment which, on the Day of Judgment, awaits those who mistreat a servant of God. The Prophet has said: "*He who commits an injustice against a Jew shall be my enemy on the Day of Judgment.*"

Therefore commit this fault no longer; maintain good government in respect of the Jews. Behave yourself towards them in the same way as towards the Muslims whom you govern; do them justice in civil cases, and leave the burden of deciding religious cases absolutely to their rabbis.

As to Jews protected by foreign powers, act towards them in accordance with the provisions of the treaties and conventions in force. However, if one of these people refuses to submit to fair treatment, record his conduct in a declaration, which you shall then send to Our Majesty in order that We may settle the matter with the foreign government which protects him.

Sultan Mulay Hassan (1873–1895) to the Caid Uwida of Marrakesh, Arabic letter (7th Djumada 1310 = Dec. 27, 1892) with French translation, in Archives, *AIU* (MAROC IV. C. 11). English translation in Littman, *WLB* (1975): 74–75.

79. Payment of the Jizya in Marrakesh (1894)

I wish to bring to your attention the mistreatments of which I was today the victim on the part of a soldier belonging to the cadi of our city, Mawlay Mustafa.

The Caid Uwida and the Cadi Mawlay Mustafa had mounted their tent today near the Mellah gate and had summoned the Jews in order to collect from them the poll tax (*jizya*), which they are obliged to pay the sultan.

They had me summoned also. I first inquired whether those who were European-protected subjects had to pay this tax. Having learned that a great many of them had already paid it, I wished to do likewise. After having remitted the amount of the tax to the two officials, I received from the cadi's guard two blows in the back of the neck. Addressing the cadi and the caid, I said: "Know that I am an Italian-protected subject." Whereupon the cadi said to his guard: "Remove the kerchief covering his head and strike him strongly; he can then go and complain wherever he wants."

The guard hastily obeyed and struck me once again more violently. These public mistreatments of an European-protected subject demonstrate to all the Arabs that they can, without punishment, mistreat the [European-protected] Jews.

Letter dated 25 February 1894 from a Jew of Marrakesh (Italian-protected subject). *BAIU* (Monthly), Jan.– Feb., 1894. See also Littman, "Quelques Aspects", in *Yod* (1976): 45.

80. A Court Dhimmi in Morocco (1906)

Near the castle of the Kaid lies the Mellah of Imanin [Great Atlas]. Here lives Hazzan Moshe el Drai, intendant to the Kaid and Sheik of the Jews. He is the only Jew who possesses a beautiful house with a garden, for gardens are a forbidden luxury to the rest of the Jews. R. Moshe is a type of the court Jew which Samuel Romanelli knew in Morocco in the eighteenth century (in his book *Massa Ba-Arab*). A clever Talmudist, he has a cunning and subtle mind. He plays up to every caprice of the Kaid, and knows the art of making himself indispensable to the courtiers. He is very friendly with the black eunuchs, who are so influential in Mussulman courts, and he is even admitted to the Harem. Thanks to the place he has won for himself at court, he has been able to monopolize all the export trade, dividing the profits with the Berber chiefs, and he often comes into conflict with other Jewish merchants, who fear and detest him. An undying feud exists between him and his rivals, who only wait for the moment when he will fall from grace to exact their revenge and take his place. Reb Moshe persuaded me to turn to account my little medicine chest, and I played the court physician with considerable success. The Kaid and many of the nobles availed themselves of my elementary medical knowledge.

Yet, not all his influence was able to shield Reb Moshe from the jealousy of the Berber nobles. I asked him: "Why are your children dressed so poorly, when you yourself wear such good clothes?" "I do not want to give my Berber neighbors any cause for jealousy," he replied. "They do not believe that Jewish children ought to be well dressed" (pp. 464–65).

N. Slouschz, *Travels*

81. Jews, Berbers, and Arabs (Libya, 1906)

The relationship between Jew and Berber is better than that between Jew and Arab. Until the middle of the last century, the Jews were treated as the serfs of the Berber lords. While abolishing this humiliating institution, Turkey has not yet had the time to curb the moral vexations that the Muslims inflict on their Jewish neighbors. One example out of a hundred: the rabbi of the region [Djebel Nefussi], having journeyed to Nalut, was attacked by local inhabitants who ordered him to get down from his mule, since a Jew may not straddle a mount in the presence of Muslims. Should he dare to complain, he would run the risk of seeing his family massacred by the Arabs.

The most venerated places of worship, the most ancient cemeteries are desecrated by the Muslims and as for agriculture, their Arab neighbors have no qualms in seizing the products of the Jews' harvest. In spite of the goodwill of the ruling authorities [the Turks], these matters often escape their control.

For example, is it known in Tripoli that the Jewish inhabitants of a village called Al Qsar, who possess about fifty acres of arable land and several hundred olive trees, were forced last year to pay 1,600 francs for their tithe and, moreover, that many a Jew, after having been molested by the local inhabitants, would not dare to lodge a complaint for justice with the authorities? (pp. 107–8).

N. Slouschz, *Israélites*

82. Expropriation in Tripolitania (Libya, 1908)

Yehud Beni-Abbes is on the very margin of the desert which lies between the oasis and Tripoli; the village comprises two hundred and forty inhabitants, who take up six underground courts. At one time the Jews were very numerous in this country, holding most of the land and defending it successfully against all invaders. We were shown the fertile ravine, which ends in a well-watered valley and which commands the approach of the region towards Tripoli. Here, on the slopes, we found grottoes and traces of mines of an ancient civilization.

We were led across spaced-out fields, and were told that all of this splendid country belonged at one time to the Jews. But towards 1840 the plague ravaged the Jewish population; the only survivors were four families of Beni-Abbes, while many of the neighboring villages were completely wiped out.

The Ulad Beni-Abbes Arabs took advantage of the unhappy plight of the Jews to deprive them of their lands; the rightful owners kept on struggling against the invaders, but to no purpose; besides this, the Arabs, with that meanness characteristic of the servile *fellah*, took possession of the cemetery, the resting place of a whole line of ancestors, and ploughed it up. They could not have conceived a more malignant act, nor one which would have wounded so deeply the "infidels," who now, with tears in their eyes, led us across this field which contained the desecrated remains of their ancestors and their rabbis.

The Arabs, however, had not dared to dispossess the last native Jews entirely; they managed, instead, to force them into a collective ownership of the whole village, so that the Jews, having no distinctive property of their own, are yet forced to till fields and cultivate fruit trees belonging exclusively to the Mussulmans, and at a distance from their homes. The outcome is that the Jewish farmer must look on, without daring to protest, while his Arab neighbour appropriates the first-fruits of his olive-groves and the best produce of his own plot of land, which is swallowed up in the vast Arab fields.

Even this did not satisfy the oppressors. There is in the village an ancient synagogue, a sanctuary held in deep veneration. It is situated in a hollow surrounded by an open court, and its roof is colored like the soil in order to conceal it from view. This spot affords them the only moral gratification they have; it is the one meeting place where they can offer up their prayers or pour out the plaints of the *Piyyutim* [liturgical compositions], which mourn the sorrows and proclaim the hopes of Israel.

The fanatic Mussulmans, jealous of this sanctuary, planned, after the desecration of the cemetery, the ruin of the synagogue, on the pretext that the neighboring mosque would, according to Mohammedan law, be profaned by its proximity.

Fortunately, there were judges in Tripoli and money in the hands of the Jews. By a happy chance the Jews have in their possession a document which proves that the synagogue was in existence on its present site five hundred years before the foundations of the mosque were laid, that is to say, seven or eight centuries ago. The administration, basing its decision on the right of priority, was able to rescue the synagogue, to the unbounded joy of the Jews. Looking through the Geniza of this sanctuary we found, among other things, a tablet dating from 5359—that is, 348 years old. Surely these Jews, swallowed up in the Sahara, have deserved a better fate (pp. 127–29).

N. Slouschz, *Travels*

PERSIA

83. Forced Conversions of Greek Christians and Jews (1843–1845)

Trebizond is inhabited by Armenian and Greek Christians, beside Turks, and some European Christians. And around Trebizond are great numbers of villages inhabited by Greeks, who outwardly profess the Muhammedan religion, but in secret they practise the Christian religion. This they have carried on since the establishment of Muhammedanism at Constantinople. They have their priests, who, in secret, are ordained by the patriarch of Constantinople, and by the bishop of the Greek church at Trebizond (p. 47).

At Mowr [Merv], all those Jews who have been constrained to embrace Muhammedanism in other parts of Persia, are permitted to return to their ancient usages and religion. But it is a remarkable fact, that there are some Jews at Mowr who have professed the Muhammedan religion and become Turkomauns; and that there are Jews at

Khiva, of whom I was told at Mowr, that, though remaining Jews, they
have intermarried with the Usbecks. And is it not striking that Jews
have received the most powerful protection among the wild inhabitants of the desert? Thus Jews, who are tyrannised over at Bokhara
and Persia, fly to the inhabitants of the desert, at Mowr, Sarakhs,
Akhaul, and to the Hazarah in Affghanistaun. And this is even the
case in Morocco, where they often fly from the tyranny of the emperor to the inhabitants of the desert at Tafilla-Leth. And in
Mesopotamia they escape from Bagdad and Mosul to the wild
Yeseede, in the mountains of Sunjar (pp. 120–21).

J. Wolff, *Narrative*

84. Forced Converts and the Condition of Jews (1850)

Only about twenty years since, nearly 3000 Jews lived in this once
magnificent and flourishing city. By persecutions, oppressions, and
odium of all kinds more than 2500 of them were compelled to go over
to the Mussulman sect of Ali [Shi'ism]. Although outwardly apostate,
a great number of these families still preserve in their hearts the faith
of their fathers, and even find means of having their children circumcised in secret. Nine synagogues in the town testify the former
greatness of the Jewish community; now unfortunately, they are almost all laid waste. The Jews of Shiraz speak the Hebrew language,
almost like the Askenasim (German Jews).

On my arrival I found the town in a state of ferment and revolt in
consequence of a change of government in Teheran. Fierce combats
took place in the streets, and it was not until the evening that the
tumult was calmed. The vice-consul received me into his house, and
gave me a safe escort to the Nassi [head of the Jewish community],
Mullah Israel. This Nassi, a venerable old man, received me with the
greatest kindness, and according to Eastern custom, gave me an hospitable shelter, and I lodged with his son Isaac.

My presence had quickly become known among the brethren of the
faith, and I was soon visited by the leading members. From morning
until night I was in request, my advice and help asked in many matters, and my opinions regarded as oracles. One day my room became
gradually filled by women all wearing white veils, who, one after
another, introduced themselves to me. As the Jewish women are allowed only to wear black veils, in order to distinguish them from
others, this visit desquieted me, for I imagined the house might be
attacked by insurgents. I was, however, pacified when they told me
that all these women belonged to the families who had been compelled to embrace the faith of Islam, but who in secret adhered to the

JEWISH WOMAN OF SAMARKAND, UZBEKISTAN, ca. 1900
pl. 68c, in A. Rubens (1973)

faith of their fathers. My visitors lifted their veils, and kissed my forehead and hand. I addressed some words to them on their apostacy, whereupon the women wept bitterly. One of the men present came forward and said: "Our brethren know under what fearful circumstances we were compelled to apostatise: we did it to save ourselves from tyranny and death. We acknowledge, however, that, notwithstanding our apparent apostacy, we still cling with all our hearts to the faith of our fathers, and this we testify by our presence here this day; for if it were known, we should all certainly be lost!" These words much affected me; I tried to console them . . . (pp. 184–86).

The Situation of Persian Jews

Among the Persian Jews are some who are very rich, and this wealth is the source of so many dangers, that they are obliged to conceal their treasures like crimes. – I comprise their oppressions under the following heads:
(1) Throughout Persia the Jews are obliged to live in a part of the town separated from the other inhabitants; for they are considered as unclean creatures, who bring contamination with their intercourse and presence.
(2) They have no right to carry on trade in stuff goods [textiles].
(3) Even in the streets of their own quarter of the town they are not allowed to keep any open shop. – They may only sell there spices and drugs, or carry on the trade of a jeweller, in which they have attained great perfection.
(4) Under the pretext of their being unclean, they are treated with the greatest severity, and should they enter a street, inhabited by Mussulmans, they are pelted by the boys and mob with stones and dirt.
(5) For the same reason they are forbidden to go out when it rains; for it is said the rain would wash dirt off them, which would sully the feet of the Mussulmans.
(6) If a Jew is recognised as such in the streets, he is subjected to the greatest insults. The passers-by spit in his face, and sometimes beat him so unmercifully, that he falls to the ground, and is obliged to be carried home.
(7) If a Persian kills a Jew, and the family of the deceased can bring forward two Mussulmans as witnesses to the fact, the murderer is punished by a fine of 12 tumauns (600 piastres): but if two such witnesses cannot be produced, the crime remains unpunished, even though it has been publicly committed, and is well known.

PERSIAN JEWISH BRIDEGROOM
Ben Shlomo playing the tar
Oil on canvas (ca. 1840)
no. 2013 and pl. 65, in A. Rubens (1981)

(8) The flesh of the animals slaughtered according to Hebrew custom, but as Trefe declared [forbidden by Mosaic law], must not
be sold to any Mussulmans. The slaughterers are compelled to
bury the meat, for even the Christians do not venture to buy it,
fearing the mockery and insult of the Persians.

(9) If a Jew enters a shop to buy anything, he is forbidden to inspect
the goods, but must stand at a respectful distance and ask the
price. Should his hand incautiously touch the goods, he must
take them at any price the seller chooses to ask for them.

(10) Sometimes the Persians intrude into the dwellings of the Jews
and take possession of whatever pleases them. Should the owner
make the least opposition in defence of his property, he incurs
the danger of atoning for it with his life.

(11) Upon the least dispute between a Jew and a Persian, the former
is immediately dragged before the Achund [al-hukum = judges]
and, if the complainant can bring forward two witnesses, the Jew
is condemned to pay a heavy fine. Is he too poor to pay this
penalty in money, he must pay it in his person. He is stripped to
the waist, bound to a stake, and receives forty blows with a stick.
Should the sufferer utter the least cry of pain during this proceeding, the blows already given are not counted, and the punishment is begun afresh.

(12) In the same manner the Jewish children, when they get into a
quarrel with those of the Mussulmans, are immediately led before the Achund, and punished with blows.

(13) A Jew who travels in Persia is taxed in every inn and every
caravanserai he enters. If he hesitates to satisfy any demands
that may happen to be made on him, they fall upon him, and
maltreat him until he yields to their terms.

(14) If, as already mentioned, a Jew shows himself in the street during the three days of the Katel (feast of mourning for the death
of the Persian founder of the religion of Ali) he is sure to be
murdered.

(15) Daily and hourly new suspicions are raised against the Jews, in
order to obtain excuses for fresh extortions; the desire of gain is
always the chief incitement to fanaticism.

These points give a clear insight into the wretched condition in
which the Jews languish in a country where, not so very long since
[sic], a woman of their people [Esther] was wife of the ruler, and one
of her brethren [Mordechai] was first minister (pp. 211–13).

*I. J. Benjamin

*Israel Joseph Benjamin (1818–64), known as "Benjamin II" was born in Rumania
and died miserably in London while preparing a second long voyage to the Orient. He
also published (1862) a volume on his three years of travels to the United States.

85. Servitudes in Persia

At Hamadan in 1890, Shah Nasr-ad-Din (1848–1896) renewed his 1880 edict, which forbade advantages in inheritance for a Jewish convert to Islam to the detriment of the other Jewish heirs. This royal edict incited the mollahs and the mob to force the Jews of Hamadan in 1892 to conform to the following obligations, under threat of death or conversion:

1. The Jews are forbidden to leave their houses when it rains or snows [to prevent the impurity of the Jews being transmitted to the Shiite Muslims].
2. Jewish women are obliged to expose their faces in public [like prostitutes].
3. They must cover themselves with a two-coloured izar (an izar is a big piece of material with which Eastern women are obliged to cover themselves when leaving their houses).
4. The men must not wear fine clothes, the only material permitted them being a blue cotton fabric.
5. They are forbidden to wear matching shoes.
6. Every Jew is obliged to wear a piece of red cloth on his chest.
7. A Jew must never overtake a Muslim on a public street.
8. He is forbidden to talk loudly to a Muslim.
9. A Jewish creditor of a Muslim must claim his debt in a quavering and respectful manner.
10. If a Muslim insults a Jew, the latter must drop his head and remain silent.
11. A Jew who buys meat must wrap and conceal it carefully from Muslims.
12. It is forbidden to build fine edifices.
13. It is forbidden for him to have a house higher than that of his Muslim neighbour.
14. Neither must he use plaster for white-washing.
15. The entrance of his house must be low.
16. The Jew cannot put on his coat; he must be satisfied to carry it rolled under his arm.
17. It is forbidden for him to cut his beard, or even to trim it slightly with scissors.
18. It is forbidden for Jews to leave the town or enjoy the fresh air of the countryside.
19. It is forbidden for Jewish doctors to ride on horseback [this right was generally forbidden to all non-Muslims, except doctors].
20. A Jew suspected of drinking spirits must not appear in the street; if he does, he should be put to death immediately.
21. Weddings must be celebrated in the greatest secrecy.
22. Jews must not consume good fruit (1 : 377).

N. Leven. English translation in Littman, *WLB* 32 (1979): 7–8

86. Official Edicts of Protection (1875 and 1897)

In Hamadan in 1875, a Jew accused of blasphemy was murdered by a mob and burned. This event marked the beginning of a riot against the Jews, accompanied by looting. The grand vizier sent the governor the following dispatch:

To the great Prince 'Izz ad-Dawla: Received telegram informing us of the uprising in Hamadan, that a Jew was burned there after having been daubed in pitch and that others have been beaten, their homes looted, and several Jews are besieged in their homes and are unable to go out. His Majesty was most disturbed by this news. It is surprising that the authorities did not take the necessary steps to check the uprising during the three hours that transpired from its outset until the murder of the Jew. Even if you were absent from the city, the other government representatives were not. How could this act of cruelty have taken place in their presence? Consequently, when this dispatch reaches you, endeavor to arrest the culprits. A special commission is about to leave Teheran. While awaiting its arrival, you will keep in prison all those you know to have been guilty of having taken part or only to have had an interest in this disturbance (1:263).

N. Leven

In May 1897, the Jews of Teheran were forced to wear a special badge of discrimination and to cut their hair. The Shah published the following decree:

H. M. the Shah, to whom we all owe allegiance and whose laws are obeyed by all the governors of the provinces of Iran, makes public his supreme will by this order.

So that the different nations subject to the sceptre of H. M. should live in peace one with the other, Muslims are required to cease their persecutions of Jews and refrain from imposing on them a distinctive badge. Those who continue to mistreat our non-Muslim subjects or who attempt to establish a discrimination between them and others [i.e., Muslims] will be severely punished.

All the governors are obliged to publish this order, which emanates from the supreme authority so that everyone will know where lie the limits of the law. May everyone submit gladly to the Shah's sovereign will.

Shah Muzaffereddin (1896–1907), in Archives, *AIU* (IRAQ I.C.2.), 9 June 1897, and *BAIU* (1st. Sem, 1897):78–79. English translation in Littman, *WLB* 32 (1979): 11.

87. The Descendants of Forced Converts (1929)

We made our way to the Jewish quarter, situated lower down in the vicinity of the Matsha Djuma mosque. The small, low houses thus escape the attention of the Muslims. We had to descend several steps to enter the main synagogue, whose large arches rested on thick pillars. The women, mixed with the men, chattered loudly. Silence was called for and I addressed them in Hebrew, while the rabbi translated. A member of the community replied and insisted that the *Alliance* [*Israélite Universelle*] set up a school for girls as soon as possible. . . . Emotion reigned in their hearts; we were from different backgrounds, but we were able to share a common admiration for knowledge, and a remembrance of the past.

Yezd had something of an intellectual life; their "mollahs" [rabbis] were obeyed throughout Persia; the name of Mollah Agha Baba is still venerated and the present incumbent, Mollah Hillel, is consulted in connection with legal problems. This is why Yezd receives help from everywhere and in particular from the crypto-Jews of Meshed.

The life of these Mesedis reminds one of the Marranos. Although converted, they are said to be the best Persian Jews. In the past they were watched and were forced to practise Islam. Today it is enough for them to say they are Muslims. They open their shops on Saturdays, but they are kept by children and no transactions are carried out. They no longer frequent the mosques and have their own secret synagogues. They marry among their own, carry out circumcision, observe Passover, and teach their children Hebrew. When they travel they act as Jews when among Jews.

Apparently, Muslim fanatacism in Yezd was less violent [than elsewhere]: the last remnants of the fire-worshippers have taken refuge here. They were known and tolerated and the Jews also took advantage of this tolerance. Moreover, in this very poor center, the hardworking Jew who was a good craftsman worked for Muslim industrialists. [Jewish] men and women are still employed in the streets to empty the spindles of silk and cast the rows for weaving; others make belts and ribbons on posts planted in the wall (p. 25).

Y. D. Sémach, *A travers*

ARABIA

88. Expulsion of the Jews from San'a (Yemen, 1666)[1]

Were we to suppose that this pact had taken place in the past, it would be invalid, since the Imam Yahya and a host of jurisconsults declared that they [the Jews] cannot be valid parties to an everlasting pact unless they were, at that time, people of a Book that had not been modified or falsified. Since, however, this pact was made after [their Scriptures] had been modified and falsified, it is therefore invalid, for they are not people of a Divine and eternal book, for the Koran testifies to their having falsified their Scriptures. Furthermore, we have come to realize recently that they have an idea that their time [of subservience] is ended[2] and they are seeking to leave the Yemen for other regions, in order to gain domination there over the Muslims, to destroy their mosques, to rule over the nation of Muhammed, and reduce their children to slavery, thereby showing disbelief in the word of Allah, which declares: "For they have no dominion until the day of Resurection." Therefore did the Imam al-Mutawakkil [Isma'il b. Qasim] declare that they were to be afforded no protection and he forbade them to be called *dhimmis* and wrote in his noble hand that their presence [in the Yemen] was unlawful . . . this would [even] apply to those who were faithful to the conditions of the *dhimma*. However, today we see that they [the Jews] ignore the *dhimma* and criticize Islam and its great men. They discuss their own religion and its supremacy in public and allow themselves even that which a Muslim would dare not do. . . . All this has transpired because of the enmity they bear us for having put to death their Chief Rabbi,[3] who was executed by al-Mutawakkil in San'a. I heard it said that their leaders swore to recover from the possessions of the Muslims the money that the Imam confiscated from them. . . . It is proper to know these people and their hatred toward our beloved Prophet . . . for they curse him and mock him and were it not that the Prophet had initially allowed them to stay here, the faithful would not have suffered them to remain near the face of the earth, especially since the Koran states that: "Thou wilt surely find the most hostile of men to the believers are the Jews . . ." (Koran 5:85). If he [the Imam] allows them to remain, we must humiliate and belittle them in accordance with the edict of Umar ibn al-Khattab, who is the ultimate authority in

---

[1] See doc. 99 for the same event.

[2] The author refers to the aspirations of the Jews to emigrate to the Land of Israel on the news that the Messianic era was approaching (1666).

[3] The reference is to the beheading of the Chief Rabbi of San'a by the Imam al-Mutawakkil Isma'il b. Qasim in 1666, in the wake of a Messianic uprising.

this matter. But if the Jews ignore these conditions and conduct their funeral processions in broad daylight and embellish and beautify their synagogues to make them look like wedding canopies, outshining our mosques, whereas the pact between our ancestors and theirs forbade that they do any of this outwardly, then they must be humiliated by the destruction of their synagogues. Does our religion not recommend the destruction of a dilapidated mosque? How much more so a synagogue, in which the Lord of all flesh is cursed? Indeed, it is a principle to destroy synagogues, so that the only trace of them is to be found in their books of history (p. 146).

Ibn ar-Rijal (d. 1681)

89. Toleration at Maskat (1828)

There are a few Jews in Maskat, who mostly arrived there in 1828, being driven from Baghdad, as we have before stated, by the cruelties and extortions of the Pacha Daud. Nearly the whole of this race were compelled to fly. Some took refuge in Persia, while others, in their passage towards India, remained here. The same toleration exercised towards all other persuasions is extended to the Beni Israel, no badge or mark, as in Egypt or Syria, being insisted on. They are not, as in the towns of Yemen, compelled to occupy a distant and separate part of the town, nor is the observance, so strictly adhered to in Persia, of compelling them to pass to the left of Mussulmans when meeting in the streets, here insisted on. Their avocations in Maskat are various, many being employed in the fabrication of silver ornaments, others in shroffing money [evaluating coin], and some few retail intoxicating liquors (1:21–22).

J. R. Wellsted

90. Edict Promulgated by the Imam Yahya of Yemen (1905)

In the name of Allah, the all-merciful and clement.

This is the regulation that I ordain for all the Jews who must remain subjected to my laws and pay the [poll] tax without any change.

I recall to mind the ancient words and their meaning; I recall to mind the obligations that the Turks have forgotten and that were observed in the time of the pious imams, before the triumph of people ignorant of the law.

The Jews can remain untroubled and be assured of their existence if they regularly pay the *jizya*.

Every male having reached the age of thirteen years is subject to this tax . . . and by this their life will be preserved under our domination.

No one can avoid paying this tax before the end of the year . . . for it is written in the Koran, the book received from Allah. . . .

Businessmen and shopkeepers must also pay five percent of their profits if they reach the recognized amount; otherwise they are not liable, like those who are engaged in other trades.

The Jews must not:
(1) Raise their voices in front of Muslims,
(2) Build houses higher than the houses of Muslims,
(3) Brush against Muslims while passing them in the street,
(4) Carry on the same trade as the Arabs,
(5) Say that Muslim law can have a defect,
(6) Insult the prophets,
(7) Discuss religion with Muslims,
(8) Ride animals astraddle,
(9) Screw up their eyes on perceiving the nudity of Muslims,
(10) Carry on their religious devotions outside their places of worship,
(11) Raise their voices during prayers,
(12) Sound the *shofar* [ram's horn] with much noise,
(13) Lend money at interest, which can bring about the destruction of the world,
(14) They must always rise in front of Muslims and honor them in all circumstances (pp. 38–40).

Y. D. Sémach, Une Mission.

91. Behavioral Distortions Resulting from Oppression (Yemen 1910)

Here is a handsome robust fellow, his face well defined, a pointed nose, an intelligent countenance: Aaron Hayyim Uzayri from Malhan. . . . I tell him that I intend visiting him in his workshop in Malhan. What a look of terror appears on his face upon hearing my words: "Don't do that, Rabbi" he trembles, pleadingly, "they will kill you"; and he throws himself down at my knees and starts kissing my feet, so that I promise him I will not go to Malhan. "But you," I ask him, "how do you live there?—We are in *jalut* [exile], we are accustomed to suffering, we are not humans, we are beasts." It was said in

YEMENITE JEWS (ca. 1910)
Israel Museum (Jerusalem)

such a tone of despair that I was deeply overcome with emotion. This
human being, whom I saw for the first time, so different from myself
by his dress, his thoughts, his manners, I felt to be a brother, a Jew like
myself. He bowed his head before an unavoidable fate, but one
sensed within him a great courage, a suppressed energy, a tenacious
hope for the end of the *jalut,* the future redemption; and I thought to
myself that, whatever the cost, this man must be delivered from his
misery, his disgrace, as well as his brethren, who are as wretched as he
(p. 13).

Everyone is happy to see the representative of the *Alliance,* and all
bid me welcome, voicing their hopes that I will improve their situation
and that a new era is about to commence for them. They keep repeating to me; "We are ignorant and know nothing, we are uncivilized and
want to become men. We have written so much, prayed so much and
cried so much, but our voice has not been heard. Now at last God has
had pity upon us." In fact, no, on the contrary, despite their miserable
appearance, I do not find them so uncivilized; in discussion they make
an excellent impression. They are ignorant of many things, which is
not their fault, but they have an intelligent air about them; what they

need is order, method, and manners. They lack confidence in themselves, and beneath the weight of Arab oppression they cower and
crawl in the dust. They are despised and they seem despicable. Yet
their spirit is not destroyed . . . they have had the time to devote
themselves to intellectual pursuits. A large part of the day and night is
devoted to prayer and pious reading, and their eyes sparkle with the
light of wisdom. When conversing with them, I do not perceive their
ludicrous appearance; rather, I reflect on the vivacity of intellect,
which has been preserved despite ten centuries of ignorance and
degradation (pp. 31–32).

The Jew is not allowed to wear white or colored garments outside
his quarter . . . he must wear a ridiculously short garment that does
not cover his legs, and he must walk barefooted and wear on his head
a little black cap. . . . The Jew cannot ride within the town on a donkey
and morning and evening he must walk on foot the two miles that
separate his quarter from the marketplace. Recently, the chief Arab
sheikh said to the chief rabbi "It is rumored that you would like to
ride on a donkey, even on a horse. Beware." The rabbi hasn't forgotten this warning and whenever I invite him to ride with me in the
carriage he always refuses and sadly replies: "Do you want me to be
stoned? if I were not in your company, I would never have ventured
down the main street on a Friday." So we went on foot and his dragging steps raised clouds of dust that whitened his thin legs. Last year a
Jew from Tiberias, on a fund-raising mission, was nearly knocked
unconscious because he had walked through the town clad in a long
cloak. The Arab children spat at him and covered him with garbage
and he was saved only by the arrival of a *mullah* who knew him from
Palestine. Every day young Arabs found amusement in throwing
stones at passing Jews while they, pretending not to notice, would
hasten their stride. If one spits in their face, they turn their heads. A
high-ranking [Turkish] officer described to me a scene that he had
witnessed more than once: some youths had caught hold of an elderly
Jew and amused themselves by pulling his sidelocks, while their victim
grinned and simpered stupidly. Constantly obliged to bear these insults, the Jew has lost all sense of dignity, and has come to accept his
fate; instead of fighting back, he smiles. What else can he do? A revolt
would bring even more trouble. Every day our coreligionists suffer all
kinds of humiliations and violence. They do not even complain: for
them there is no justice, there cannot be. The Yemenite courts are all
religious courts and the testimony of Jews is not accepted. A Muslim
can knock down a Jew in front of fifty witnesses, yet he need only
deny it to be acquitted; no Muslim would want to lodge a complaint
against a brother for the sake of an infidel (pp. 72–73).

Y. D. Sémach, Une Mission

92. Yemen (1914)

In the towns of central Yamen, Jews occur in large numbers, living in their own quarter and noted as craftsmen. Turkish rule has secured them tolerance, for they are recognized as an important economic factor in the development of the country. At Menakha, the best smiths and carpenters are Jews, and they are even allowed to hold garden-land—a striking concession in Arabia. Still, their's is rather a harried existence and, now that the Islamic code is rigidly enforced and the Immam's influence is to the fore, their position in Yamen may yet be one of jeopardy.

They are not allowed to have schools or synagogues, but they assemble for worship at private houses unmolested, and I was much impressed, on passing a Jew cobbler's shop in a hamlet near Menakha, to see him teaching his children to read the Hebrew Scriptures. I understand that this practice is general; it denotes a laudable standard of education and considerable stiffness of mental fibre in a difficult environment (pp. 30–31).

C. Wyman Bury

93. On the Arabian Coast (1947)

Lodar had some stone-built houses, two mosques and a Jews' quarter. Most of the dwellings were made of dry branches of bushes tied together. The Jews, of whom there were thirteen families, all lived together, narrowly hemmed in by the Arabs. Their houses were the same as Arab houses except perhaps that they were a little cleaner inside. We entered the workshop of a silversmith where two Jews were working at a woman's belt. With the submissive kindness peculiar to this suppressed people they made us welcome. They had no objection to our ascending the outer staircase to have a look at the sitting-room. We asked this so as to be, for a moment at least, free of our escort of noisy youth. The upper room was indeed much cleaner and better kept than in an Arab house of the same type. But the women we found here were not given the rough outdoor tasks in the fields and with the cattle that are allotted to their Arab sisters. They were dressed and had their hair made up in exactly the same way as the Arab women and even their faces were also painted yellow. The men and the boys were at once and everywhere distinguishable from Arabs by the ringlets they wore in front of their ears, by skull-caps they wore instead of turbans or head-cloths and by the absence of belts to their long gowns. According to the Arab saying they were too weak for work on the fields or to carry arms. Is it not more probable that they

were denied landed property and so had no chance of doing agricultural work and that the carrying of arms had been forbidden them
from earliest times? They had good intellectual qualities that were
continually cultivated thanks to their marvellous faithfulness to the
religion and traditions of their forefathers. They studied the Hebrew
language; they read the Books of the Old Testament; they raised their
spirit from scorn and oppression by recourse to their election as God's
chosen people, by holding on, in unshakable belief to the promise of a
national restoration and of a reconciliation with the Lord of Israel. In
this way they had been able to endure twenty centuries of oppression
and no contempt had been able to break them spiritually.

The thirteen families in Lodar, narrowly ringed in by the dominant
Moslems, had kept faith with Judaism. They made no marriages with
the Arabs and no acceptance of their religion. The tiny group, cut
adrift from its fellows and its native land, kept itself pure. They could
only live by enduring in silence but they could survive by clinging to
their great traditions and to a belief that was more abiding than the
centuries. Moslems rulers had forced upon them outward distinctions
to single them out and keep them apart but these were not really
necessary. The Jew although cut off from the mass of his nation for
nearly twenty centuries, the lonely and oppressed Jew of South
Arabia, carries his own distinguishing marks. They shine from the
soul that has clung to a great tradition and has been ennobled by
Jehovah's promises to His people (pp. 40–41).

                                                    D. van der Meulen

III
Aspects of the Dhimmis' Existence
As experienced

94. Forced Conversions and Degradation (12th century)

Under the Almohads (Spain and the Maghreb)[1]

Our hearts are disquieted and our souls are affrighted at every moment that passes, for we have no security or stability. On account of our numerous sins it was said of us, "And among these nations shalt thou find no ease, neither shall the sole of thy foot have rest: but the Lord shall give thee a trembling heart, and failing of eyes, and sorrow of mind: And thy life shall hang in doubt before thee; and thou shalt fear day and night . . ." (Deut. 28:65–66), and because of our constant fear and despair we say, "In the morning . . . would God it were even!" (Deut. 28:67).

Past persecutions and former decrees were directed against those who remained faithful to the Law of Israel and kept them tenaciously so that they would even die for the sake of Heaven. In the event that they submitted to their demands, [our enemies] would extol and honor them. . . . But in the present persecutions, on the contrary, however much we appear to obey their instructions to embrace their religion and forsake our own, they burden our yoke and render our travail more arduous. . . . Behold the hardships of the apostates of our land who completely abandoned the faith and changed their attire on account of these persecutions. But their conversion has been of no avail to them whatsoever, for they are subjected to the same vexations as those who have remained faithful to their creed. Indeed, even the conversion of their fathers or grandfathers a hundred years ago has been of no advantage to them, as it is said, ". . . visiting the iniquity of the fathers upon the children, and upon the children's children . . ."

[1] The Almohad persecutions had started in 1140, whereas Ibn Aqnin was writing at the time of Abu Yusuf al-Mansur (1184–99), by which time the Jews, forcibly converted to Islam, were third-generation Muslims. Even so, al-Mansur imposed several restrictions on them, which are described in this text.

346

(Exod. 34:7). Was it not written. "But in the fourth generation they shall come hither again . . ." (Gen. 15:16)? Indeed, this treatment has induced many converts to return to their former faith, for "Lo, thou trustest in the staff of this broken reed . . . whereon if a man lean, it will go into his hand . . ." (Isa. 36:6) [143a]. Had the Lord not provided first a healing before the blow of adversity, then we would surely have perished and our eyes have become dim in trying to comprehend the gravity of the great misfortune that had befallen us. Indeed, we would speedily have waned away with no regard for survival or descendants. We would have ceased to have offspring and remained childless, since we would have become as fools and drunkards who are unaware of their condition. God's healing has prevented us from giving up on account of our great worry and anxiety . . . (143b).

If we were to consider the persecutions that have befallen us in recent years, we would not find anything comparable recorded by our ancestors in their annals. We are made the object of inquisitions; great and small testify against us and judgments are pronounced, the least of which render lawful the spilling of our blood, the confiscation of our property, and the dishonor of our wives. But thanks to the grace of God, who has taken pity on the faithful remnant, their testimonies have proved contradictory, for the nobles pleaded in our favor while the common folk testified against us, and the custom of the land would not allow the testimony of the vulgar to supersede that of the gentry. These measures were renewed repeatedly and God took pity twice and thrice. Then a new decree was issued, more bitter than the first, which annulled our right to inheritance and to the custody of our children, placing them in the hands of the Muslims, fulfilling that which is written, "Thy sons and thy daughters shall be given unto another people . . ." (Deut. 28:32). They intended thereby to dissipate our belongings and make us assimilate with the Muslims. For the [Muslim] custodians are able to dispose of our young children and their belongings as they see fit. If they were given to an individual who feared Allah, then he would endeavor to educate the children in his religion, for one of their principles is that all children are originally born as Muslims and only their parents bring them up as Jews, Christians, or Magians.[2] Thus, if this individual educates them in [what they state is] their original religion [i.e., Islam] and does not leave the children with those [i.e., the Jews] that will abduct them therefrom, he will obtain a considerable reward from Allah [144a]. If however, the tutor be a wicked person, then his only concern will be to

[2] Islamic theology holds that all men are born Muslims but non-Muslim parents educate them as Jews or Christians, etc. See doc. 45, n. 2.

SYNAGOGUE IN FEZ
Engraving from a drawing by C. Biseo
E. de Amici (1884), p. 276

extort money and God will show mercy [i.e., in permitting the ransom of the children].

. . . Then another misfortune and terrible trial fell to our lot, ". . . such as never was since there was a nation *even* to that same time . . ." (Dan. 12:1). We were prohibited to practice commerce, which is our livelihood, for there is no life without the food to sustain our bodies and clothes to protect them from the heat and cold. The latter can only be obtained through trade for this is their source and cause, without which its effect, namely our existence, would disappear. In so doing their design was to weaken our strong and annihilate our weak. . . . If you consider these persecutions [144b], you will find them to be worse than those suffered during our servitude in Egypt, for there we were able to retain our belongings, none of which were confiscated. . . . Then we were obliged to dismiss our servants and were forbidden to employ others in accordance with the word of God, ". . . secretly in the siege and straitness, wherewith thine enemy shall distress thee in thy gates" (Deut. 28:56), for he who is deprived of aid finds himself in dire straits.

Then they imposed upon us distinctive garments as it was foretold in the Holy Scriptures, "And thou shalt become an astonishment [a repulsion], a proverb, and a byword, among all nations whither the Lord shall lead thee" (Deut. 28:37). The word *repulsion* signifies "desolation" on account of the scorn of the nations at our state of humiliation, abasement, and contempt. For no other nation can be compared unto us, no matter how persecuted they be. Indeed, our scorn of ourselves is greater than that of the nations toward us. We have become a repulsion and an example so that when they desire to exaggerate a state of contempt or humiliation that has befallen any of them or their fellows they say, "My humiliation was like that of the Jews." Similarly, if they wish to offend or insult their neighbor, after having exhausted all other insults, or if they are in anger against their son or a slave, they will say, "O you Jew." Likewise if they want to curse someone in the worst possible manner, they say, "May Allah make you like them and count you among their number." If they want to describe a distasteful deed or a blemish they say, "Even a Jew, with his detestable ways, would not be content with such a thing." Thus we have become a proverb wherefrom they derive instruction and reproach. . . . A "byword" refers to our outward appearance, which is distinguishable from members of other groups. The Hebrew word is a diminutive meaning "*dishonour*," for the garments that have been imposed upon us are the vilest, the most degrading, and the most humiliating attire. . . , as the Prophet Ezekiel foretold, "So it shall be a reproach and a taunt, an instruction and an astonishment unto the nations that *are* round about thee, when I shall execute judgments in thee in anger and in fury and in furious rebukes . . ." (Ezek. 5:15) (145a). Thus he foretold that we should become a subject of repulsion for the surrounding nations, so much so that should one of them take a Jewish girl captive and have a child by her, he is belittled by them for so doing. Moreover, his children are despised and he does not find it easy to marry them off, for they are spurned and none, even the meanest of them, will contract an alliance with him, as it says in the verse, "*Those that be* near *and those that be* far from thee shall mock thee, *which art* infamous and much vexed" (Ezek. 22:5), ". . . Remove the diadem and take off the crown . . ." (Ezek. 21:26) refers to the decree enforced against our wearing turbans . . . and obliging us to wear black, which is the color of mourning, as it is said, ". . . Feign thyself to be a mourner and put on now mourning apparel . . ." (2 Sam. 14:2). As for the decree enforcing the wearing of long sleeves, its purpose was to make us resemble the inferior state of women, who are without strength.[3] They were intended by their length to make us unsightly, whereas their color was to make us loathsome. . . . The ugly bonnets they have placed upon our heads are meant to contradict ". . . and bonnets shalt thou make for them, for glory and for beauty" (Exod. 28:40) (145b). . . . The purpose of these distinctive garments is to differentiate us from among them so that we should be recognized in our dealings with them without any doubt, in order that they might treat us with disparagement and humiliation. . . . Moreover it allows our blood to be spilled with impunity. For whenever we travel on the wayside from town to town, we are waylaid by robbers and brigands and are murdered secretly at night or killed in broad daylight as it is said, "Let not mine hand be upon him, but let the hand of the Philistines be upon him" (1 Sam. 18:17). And we cry out against ourselves on account of these garments saying, "And the leper in whom the plague is . . . unclean, unclean" (Lev. 13:15). . . ; but there is no plague worse than the sins on account of which these persecutions have befallen us. . . : "My confusion is continually before me, and the shame of my face hath covered me" (Ps. 44:15) . . . and yet we hear and remain silent. Even their slaves, beggars, and lepers have dominion over us and afflict us as best they can [146a] . . . and they treat us as unclean, as it is said, "They cried unto them, Depart ye; it is unclean; depart, depart, touch not . . ." (Lam. 4:15).

It is clear from what I have explained that we have deserved all these persecutions that we have suffered, for they bare not even a fraction of the sins that we have committed against God and the great punishment we deserve for having sinned whether deliberately or

---

[3] It is significant that the author here compares the status of the *dhimmis* to that of women in Islam, who were always in a state of inferiority.

unwittingly when we were forced to forsake our faith. For of a truth, we should have suffered martyrdom rather than convert, since our Law requires that if the sin demanded of us is not for the benefit of our enemy . . . but only in order to convert us, then we must die rather than transgress, . . . Now, the purpose of the persecution of Ishmael, whether they require us to renounce our religion in public or in private is only to annihilate the faith of Israel and consequently one is bound to accept death rather than commit the slightest sin . . . as did the martyrs of Fez, Sijilmasa,[4] and Dar'a. But since we have remained sinful, having taken pity on ourselves, and have profaned the Name of the Lord, though not willfully. . . , these terrible calamities have befallen us.

*Ibn Aqnin (d. 1220)

In Yemen (ca. 1200)

You write that the rebel leader in Yemen decreed compulsory apostasy for the Jews by forcing the Jewish inhabitants of all the places he had subdued to desert the Jewish religion just as the Berbers had compelled them to do in Maghreb. Verily, this news has broken our backs and has astounded and dumbfounded the whole of our community. And rightly so. For these are evil tidings. . . . Indeed our hearts are weakened, our minds are confused, and the powers of the body wasted because of the dire misfortunes which brought religious persecutions upon us from the two ends of the world, the East and the West (p. ii).

Remember, my coreligionists, that on account of the vast number of our sins, God has hurled us in the midst of this people, the Arabs, who have persecuted us severely, and passed baneful and discriminatory legislation against us. . . . Never did a nation molest, degrade, debase and hate us as much as they. . . . Although we were dishonored by them beyond human endurance, and had to put [up] with their fabrications, yet we behave like him who is depicted by the inspired writer, "But I am as a deaf man, I hear not, and I am as a dumb man that openeth not his mouth" (Psalm 38 : 14). Similarly our sages instructed

[4]When Sijilmasa was taken by the Almohades in 1146, the Jews of the town were given the choice of conversion to Islam or death. Some 150 Jews preferred death while some others—led by the *dayyan* Joseph b. Amram, who later returned to Judaism—converted to Islam. Dar'a shared a similar fate. Both cities are mentioned in Abraham Ibn Ezra's moving elegy on the Almohad destruction of the Spanish and North African Jewish communities, *ahah yarad al sefarad.*

*Ibn Aqnin (1150–1220), born in Barcelona, was an outstanding philosopher and commentator. He and his family fled to Fez in order to escape the Almohad persecutions. There he lived as a crypto-Jew, met Maimonides, and wrote a sad couplet when the latter left for the Holy Land.

us to bear the prevarications and preposterousness of Ishmael in silence. . . . We have acquiesced, both old and young, to inure ourselves to humiliation, as Isaiah instructed us, "I gave my back to the smiters, and my cheeks to them that plucked off the hair" (50:6). All this notwithstanding, we do not escape this continued maltreatment which well nigh crushes us. No matter how we suffer and elect to remain at peace with them, they stir up strife and sedition, as David predicted. "I am all peace, but when I speak, they are for war" (Ps. 120:7) (p. xviii).

May God, Who created the world with the attributes of mercy, grant us the privilege to behold the return of the exiles to the portion of His inheritance, to contemplate the graciousness of the Lord and to visit early in His Temple. May He take us out from the Valley of the Shadow of Death wherein He put us. May He remove darkness from our eyes, and gloom from our hearts. May He fulfill in our days as well as yours the prophecy contained in the verse, "The people that walked in darkness have seen a great light" (Isaiah 9:1). . . . Peace, peace, as the light that shines and much peace until the moon be no more. Amen (p. xx).

*Moses b. Maimon (Maimonides)

*Maimonides (1135–1204); was born in Cordoba, Spain. He fled with his family to Fez (1160), from there to the Land of Israel, finally settling in Egypt where he became court physician to the Sultan's vizier. Renowned philosopher, he is universally recognized as one of the most illustrious figures in Judaism.

95. Palestinian Jew Seeks Refuge in Christian Spain (1291)

In the verse ". . . the wild beast *(ziz)* of the field doth devour it" (Ps. 80:13), the term *ziz* refers to Ishmael, for he is to be compared to a "wild man" (Gen. 16:12) who dwells in the wilderness and in the desert. Moreover, he is called a "field" *(saday)* as in "every beast of the field" (Ps. 104:11), for he has his own tent in the desert where he resides, like the beasts. The word *ziz* in Arabic is derogatory, for when they wish to say in that tongue, "Strike him upon the head," "Give him a blow upon the neck," they say *zazzhu* ("hit him"). Furthermore, the term for robbery in Arabic is *bazaz*. Indeed, on account of our sins they strike upon the head the children of Israel who dwell in their lands and they thus extort money from them by force. For they say in their tongue, *mal al-yahudi mubah*, "it is lawful to take money of the Jews."[1] For, in the eyes of the Muslims, the children of Israel are as open to abuse as an unprotected field. Even in their law and statutes they rule that the testimony of a Muslim is always to be believed

[1] The author is alluding to the customary blow the Muslim official would deal the Jew upon payment of the latter's poll tax. See above, docs. 3, 4, 5, 11, 13, 18, 19, 59, 79.

THE PROPHECY FULFILLED
Yemenite Jew of Jerusalem (ca. 1910)
Israel Museum (Jerusalem)

against that of a Jew. For this reason our rabbis of blessed memory have said, "Rather beneath the yoke of Edom [Christendom] than that of Ishmael." They plead for mercy before the Holy One, Blessed be He, saying, "Master of the World, either let us live beneath Thy shadow or else beneath that of the children of Edom" (Talmud, Gittin 17a).

*Isaac b. Samuel

*Isaac ben Samuel of Acre (c. 1270–1350) was one of the most outstanding Kabbalists of his time. Although Isaac was conversant with Islamic theology and often uses Arabic in his exegesis, he believed that it was preferable to live under the yoke of Christendom rather than that of Islam. Thus when Acre was taken from the Crusaders by the Mamelukes in 1291, despite the precept to dwell in the Holy Land, he fled to Italy and thence to Christian Spain.

96. The Bread of Tears (circa 1600)

In his commentary on The Lamentations of Jeremiah, *the master Kabbalist of Safed, Samuel b. Ishaq Uceda, refers to the situation of the Jews in the Land of Israel toward the end of the sixteenth century.*

"The princess among the provinces, how is she become tributary!" (Lam. 1:1).

Perhaps this is an allusion to the situation that prevails in our times, for there is no town in the [Ottoman] empire in which the Jews are subjected to such heavy taxes and dues as in the Land of Israel, and particularly in Jerusalem. Were it not for the funds sent by the communities in Exile, no Jew could survive here on account of the numerous taxes, as the prophet said in connection with the "princess of the provinces" (fol. 3a): "They hunt our steps, that we cannot go into our own streets" (Lam. 4:18).

The nations humiliate us to such an extent that we are not allowed to walk in the streets. The Jew is obliged to step aside in order to let the Gentile [Muslim] pass first. And if the Jew does not turn aside of his own will, he is forced to do so. This law is particularly enforced in Jerusalem, more so than in other localities. For this reason the text specifies ". . . in our own streets," that is, those of Jerusalem (fol. 101a).

Samuel b. Ishaq Uceda

97. Life in the Mellah of Fez (1610–1613)

. . . On the holy Sabbath in the year 5371, our eyes were full of tears. Woe to me for my hurt, Mulay Zaidan[1] under whose shadow we thought we would live, threw out all his wrath at us. On the 8th of Tishri [15/25 September 1610],[2] there came the minister, the oppressor Barihan, may his name and memory be blotted out, and said that the Jews were to pay 10,000 okias, by order of the King because he had saved them from the Gentiles, who had come to pillage the *mellah* of the Jews; he said that if they did not pay before night, they would have to pay twice as much the next day. They began to collect, but the day did not suffice. The next day, he came and said that they must give him 20,000 okias. And there was a great cry, and all the city was moved, on the night of the Day of Atonement and on the Day of Atonement itself, and, for our many sins, the holy Day of Atonement was desecrated; all day and all night was the tax collected. And the rabbis wept and wailed, a cry in the morning and a shout at noon, and the voice of mirth and the voice of gladness ceased out of them, and to this were added sore sicknesses, and of long continuance. Woe is us now, for we have sinned.

On the 11th day of Tishri, the two kings, Mulay Zaidan and Mulay 'Abdala ibn Mulay al-Shaykh,[3] joined battle near the city. And Mulay Zaidan was defeated, and most of his men were killed, including the aforementioned enemy and oppressor, Barihan, may his name and memory be blotted out. And Mulay 'Abdallah entered the city, and the Nagid, R. Jacob Rute,[4] with the community, went to meet the King, but he did not receive them. He said to them: You rejoiced in Zaidan, and he vexed you. And the next day, he sent to us evil messengers to say that the Jews were to pay him 20,000 okias, as they had done to Zaidan. Woe is to the eyes that see such things. And some of the Jews and the rabbis did severe penance, and I, Saul, was the least of them. And we all had difficulty in raising the money and, for our great sins, the Feast of Tabernacles was also desecrated. Therefore I mourn and wail, for a strange and horrible thing was committed in the land. There is no strength in me to tell even the thousandth part, for some of the Jews were seized and lost all their property, and some caravans were plundered. [And in addition, the Lord afflicted us with an epidemic by which four hundred innocent children perished.] Woe (is us) on every side and in every corner. May the Lord, blessed be He, lead us out into the light. Amen, so be it. . . .

[1] Zaydan b. Muhammed, ruler of Marrakesh (1603–28).
[2] According to the Julian calendar.
[3] Abdallah b. Muhammed, Zaydan's brother, was ruler of Fez from 1603–13.
[4] Scion of the aristocratic family of *Negidim* of Fez, 17th century.

And the aforesaid Mulay al-Shaykh went to Tetuan may the Most High establish it firmly, amen—and mulcted the Gentile [Muslim] residents 100,000 okias, the Spaniards 150,000 okias, and the Jews 10,000 okias; even the scrolls [of the Law] were stripped bare [of their silver ornaments].

And on the New Moon of Tebet of the said year [one week after the preceding date], Mulay 'Abdallah mulcted us 10,000 okias, in addition to the fixed tax imposed on us. And on the New Moon of Adar [two months later] he burdened us with another eight thousand okias.

Alas for the news that arrived on the 3rd of Adar of the year concerning the city of Tadla, which was entered by Arab Gentiles who destroyed the house and burnt fifty Tora scrolls and two thousand Pentateuchs and many books. We appointed a fast like the Ninth of Ab [date of the destruction of the Temple by the Romans in 70].

[The 2nd of Iyar of the same year (5/15 April 1611) the community paid another contribution of 4,000 okias.] And on the 15th of Iyar we gave another 3,000 okias to the Qa'id Muhammad Gharni and the Qa'id Muhammad al-Senussi.

Tell it in Judah that on the Eve of Pentecost Mulay al-Shaykh sent the Qa'id Gharni to collect 25,000 okias from the Nagid, our honoured teacher, Rabbi Jacob Rute, but we were unable to pay. Now he had a written and signed pledge from the community, may God protect them and keep them alive, that they would fully compensate him for any damage he might incur in consequence of his nagid-hood; and the community paid the 25,000 okias for the Nagid. If all the heavens were parchment and all the seas ink and all the reeds calami, they would not be sufficient to record our troubles. Another 5,000 were levied from us, making a total of 87,000 from Tishri to Sivan, in addition to the fixed tax. And another 4,000 on the 5th of Ab. And there were so many battles that we cannot record them all.

On the 13th Tishri, 5372 [11/20 September] (1611), we were mulcted another 6,000, and this was a heavy blow for us, because the people were all poor; wheat cost 40 okias a *sahfa*, [5] and the city was tightly enclosed.

On Monday, the 23rd Heshvan of the said year [20/30 October 1611], while we were keeping a fast, we heard that the King was collecting Arabs to fight with the people of Fez-al-Bali. (This fighting lasted) until the 4th Kisleb. We were under siege and in great distress. There was fighting every day, and the Jews paid 100 okias to the guardians of the wall [of the *mellah?*], for the King had so ordered.

On the night of [Saturday to] Sunday, the 7th of Kisleb [3/13 November], of the said year there was a great cry, and terror [in the

---

[5] 1 *sahfa* = 60 *mudd-s* or bushels.

Mellah], for the Sharagha troops[6] had departed and the King had
gone with them, and the people of al-Bali [Old-Fez] came to the gates
of the city and wished to break them. And we recited penitential
prayers, and we assembled all the children of the Tora school, the
little ones and the older ones, in front of Tora scrolls which we had
brought out into the street of the city, and all the rabbis surrounded
the children. And we wailed, weeping sorely, and said: Our brethren,
House of Israel, know ye that we have no right and no standing to
beseech the Lord, blessed be He, because of this trouble, save on
account of these little ones. And the little ones read *"Wa-ya'avor"*
(Exod. 34:6–7)[7] aloud, and the little ones and the older ones wept
sorely. And aged people, octogenarians, who were there, testified that
they had never seen more weeping and penitential prayers as the little
ones said, among the penitential prayers: "We have no father and
mother but the Tora of Moses our teacher, peace be upon him, who
will hear the sound of our weeping and make supplication for us to
our Creator." And when the congregation heard their voices and their
weeping, they all wailed, weeping sorely, and recited *Wa-ya'avor* thirteen times. And anon the Holy One, blessed be He, Who did won-
drously for us, granted our prayer, and the people of Fez al-Bali [Old-
Fez] made peace and opened the portals. This was the Lord's doing.

Until the 12th of Kisleb of the said year, no Jew went to Fez al-Bali
because it was said that it was in the hands of the Sharagha, their
enemies. And there was growing hatred against the Jews, and we
appointed three fast days. And on the third day—praise be to God,
may His name be praised and exalted, for He saved us from all
trouble and distress—messengers came and reported that the great
ones had assembled and said that the Jews were guiltless, and that
they had said many good things about the Jews, especially the Qadi.
And the Jews went to Fez al-Bali, and no one was allowed to harm
them.

Who can write the story of our sorrow? There are taxes every day—
it cannot all be told. For the King's decrees concern only the Jews.

And on the night of the New Moon of Shebat of the said year (5372
[26 December 1611–5 January 1612], thieves came to the synagogue
of R. Joseph Almosnino[8] and stole all that there was in the synagogue.
They stole two Tora scrolls and threw them into the Street of the New
Park. There we sat down, yea, we wept, and we read several lamentations and rent our garment; and on the next day we fasted. And

---

[6] Arab tribe forming the army of al-Shaykh al-Ma'mûn.

[7] Supplications for forgiveness, containing Exod. 34:6–7. See D. Obadyah, *Fas we-
Hakhameha* (Hebrew) (Jerusalem, 1979) 2:459–66.

[8] Joseph b. Abraham al-Musnino (ca. 1530–1600), famous rabbi and physician who
became *Nagid* of the Fez community.

JEWISH CHILDREN LEARNING HEBREW IN FEZ
J. Bouhsira, Fez (early 20th century), in G. Silvain (ed.)

although the thieves were well known they were not brought to trial, for the hand of the princes was in this trespass. May the Lord avenge us.

And on the 24th of Shebat of the said year, the King mulcted us another three thousand. And the price of wheat was sixty okias a *sahfa*. . . .

. . . And on the New Moon of Elul [19/29 August 1612] of the said year the Nagid was seized through the action of an informer—he and eleven others. And they lost six hundred shekels, and the next day the community assembled in the street between the synagogues, and we read *"Wa-Ya'avor;* and we excommunicated the man who had informed, although he was a well-known person. And there was not a week in which not 400 okias was paid, and every 15 days the King was given 1000 okias, in addition to the fixed tax imposed on us . . . (2:197–200).

From the chronicle of *Saul b. David Serero, *Dibrey ha-Yamin shel Fez (Chronicle of Fez),* in H. Z. Hirschberg. Texts in square brackets, from G. Vajda, *Un Recueil*

*Saul b. David Serero (1575–1655), most prominent rabbi of Fez, wrote a chronology of the events of the period.

98. Elegy of a Persian Jewish Poet (17th century)

During the Forced Conversions under Abbas II (1641–1666)

O thou our Lord, thou art one and none is to be compared unto thee; bring upon our heads an end to our troubled faith.
O Lord who giveth sustenance to all, who art the Creator of all creatures, do not suffer this troubled faith to endure!
O Lord who art the Most-compassionate, who commandeth the heavenly spheres, heal us from our troubled faith!
O Musa [Moses], you are his messenger, whose dust is greater than fire,
O deliver us from this troubled faith!
We are all weary of waiting for the benevolence of Aaron's brother,
O deliver us from this troubled faith!
We are the nation of Musa, demented and become mad because of our troubled faith!
We are devoid of glory and of the Torah;
We are deprived of festivals and we lament as a willow;
We are without peace of mind, without a name, devastated and in a pit;

We are without houses of study and mollahs [rabbis];
We are indeed not worthy of our Lord;
We have all become infidels because of our troubled faith.
We are without precepts or beliefs, we have fallen into disgrace, egoists;
We are called the new faithful in our troubled faith.
We are without fastday or New Year, day and night we are consumed in lamentations;
It is said that we do not learn this Muslim faith.
We are without guide or master, without dignity and guidance.
We are all joyless infidels because of our troubled faith;
We are like pagans without a faith, without strength or endurance,
We dissolve into tears as rainclouds, because of the violence of Islam.
We are without protection and decency, like a rose devoid of perfume;
We weep without pause because of our troubled faith.
We are without signs and roots, empty like the wind;
We wear upon our head the turban of Islam;
We are without heart or soul, we are deprived of our Law;
What availeth our life to us in this troubled faith?
We are as hares without eyes or ears;
We have the stings but no honey because of our troubled faith.
We are without a guide and without the Law;
We are all divested of our faith; broken in heart and spirit because of our troubled faith.
Although we are apparently Muslims, within our hearts we are Jews.
Verily we do not resemble in any way the Muslims;
Outwardly we practice Islam, but we do not tremble in fasting [at Ramadan].
We all feign to believe when we act as Muslims,
We are moulds with no soul; we are similar to the helpless ants.
We all wail without exception because of our troubled faith;
We are helpless and ailing, we have fallen upon misfortune;
It is on account of oppression that we have delivered our souls to the faith of the Muslims.
Our bodies are in chains and we are afflicted;
We have wandered from the path of the Lord;
We are without Torah and light because of our troubled faith;
O, Almighty take pity on us!
It is time to free us from the Muslim faith.
We are full of excesses and agitation and would like to burn ourselves;
We would like to throw ourselves into the abyss because of our troubled faith.
We are immersed to our necks in debt and have not a penny.
We are kept busy like a hunting dog, continually running, because of

our troubled faith;

We are as a tree without leaves, without protection, enveloped in gloom;

We are in quest of death because of our troubled faith. . . .

A thousand times, at every moment, we curse Islam.

Our heart and soul delight not, when we must act as Muslims. . . .

They expelled us from the town [probably Isfahan] and acted toward us with violence;

They have made us Muslims through violence. . . .

We have become completely ignorant; there is no one amongst us who is not now a fool.

We say: this is surely because of the Muslim Koran. . . .

I am called Hizkiya, the slave, and am presently sheikh of the idolators;

I feel dispair because of my troubled faith.

Cup after cup, I drink poison from the hand of Islam;

O that I might drink cup upon cup of wine from the hand of Judaism! (pp. 94–101).

Rabbi Hizkiya

99. Trials and Sufferings in Yemen (1666)[1]
Two Versions of History

The Version of the Victims

Messengers arrived in San'a from Jerusalem announcing that the Messiah of Israel had arisen. . . . The people burst into tears and through their great longing they believed in perfect faith . . . and they cried: such and such a day we shall be redeemed and then we shall fly away and in a moment be transported to our land. . . .

Now the power at their time lay in the hands of King Ishmael [b. Qasim, Imam al-Mutawakkil]. When the latter heard this from his ministers and nobles and from his Muslim subjects, he sent for the leaders of the Jews in San'a and Hemda[2] and their [community] heads and asked them, "What is this that ye are about?" They could not conceal the facts, since there were numerous witnesses, and so the king detained them in his [fortress] in the place known as as-Sawda,[3] until the situation could be clarified. He was then filled with anger against them and all the Jews and he decreed among those of his

---

[1] See doc. 88 for the same event.
[2] A town seventy miles north of San'a.
[3] A large town north-west of San'a.

religion and his people that officers should be appointed in every city in every province and in every locality where Jews lived, in order to punish them and deal with them however they wished. And many soldiers and horsemen attacked the Jews and afflicted them with many sufferings. It was decreed that their houses, fields, and belongings were to revert to the [king] and his successors until the end of time and that Jews could no longer have a portion or inheritance in his land. Subsequently it was decreed that the Jews were to remove their headgear and that they were no longer permitted to wear turbans. When the Muslims heard this they made fun of the Jews by knocking off their turbans. The Jews were thus greatly humiliated and at [the approach of a Muslim] they would cover their heads in shame beneath their garments. The Muslims would then pull them down shouting, "Take off your clothes and go bare-headed." The Muslims would then boast among themselves, saying, "Today I did whatever I wanted with so and so the Jew, and I smote him and cursed him and threw down his turban from his head." Thus all would make fun of whomsoever they wanted, whether great or small.

Then the heads of the community were imprisoned in the fortress of King Isma'il, after which they were taken out and brought to the torture chamber, where they were to be exposed in the hot sun. Thereupon they were stripped naked and hung up in the sun at the entrance to the palace in front of all the [Muslims] who passed by. These cried out, "Forsake your faith; of what use is it to you!" The Jews suffered in silence for they could not speak but addressed their hearts to their Father in Heaven that He should deliver them. The rest of the Jews who had been arrested with the community heads had iron chains put round their necks and were led stark naked to the dungeons where they were imprisoned in darkness and in the shadow of death. The head of the community of San'a was led naked in iron chains to the place called Kamran,[4] where he was imprisoned and where no Jew had ever been. He suffered all kinds of torture and affliction, which had been decreed by God against him and his people, and he sat and cried with grief, but there was none to deliver him save God Almighty.

Now there was another rabbi of San'a by the name of Sulayman al-Aqta who was a great scholar in the knowledge of the Torah, the Law, and above all the Qabbalah. Having received a divine sign he decided to go to the king on the intermediate days of the festival of Passover. No one knows what transpired between him and the king, except that the latter stated that he claimed that God meant to try him. Until this day no one knows what his intentions were, except that he was heard

---

[4] An island in the Red Sea off the coast of Hudayda, used as a prison even today.

to have cried out in the synagogue, "Happy are you, O Israel, for that which awaits you," and then he went up to the fortress. After his meeting with the king he was arrested, tortured, and imprisoned in an underground cell. Then he was taken before one of the king's ministers who was responsible for gathering the *jizya,* who had him incarcerated in a pit full of snakes and scorpions. It was decreed in the name of Isma'il, the great king, that he was to be beheaded in the market place in the center of the city on the following Friday following their prayers. After they had paraded him through the streets of the city, he was beheaded there, as it had been decreed. Then they tied him upright and ordered the Jews to drag him to the city gate, where they hung him naked on the ramparts for all to see during three days and agreed to his burial only after the Jews had paid heavily to ransom his corpse. Then the Lord appeased the heart of the king, who agreed to release the other Jewish dignitaries, after they had been tortured and after much money had been paid for their ransom.

. . . On this occasion, nearly five hundred Jews abandoned their faith and this generation was likened to those of the periods of great persecutions that led to conversions as a result of misery (pp. 51–52).

Se'adyah ha-Levi (1667), in Tobi, ed.

The Version of the Oppressors

In the month of Rajab of the year 1077 [1666] the Jews were over-come by the utmost depravity, for they were making preparation to leave the Yemen and join their brethren in the Holy Land and Jerusalem. They claimed that their king, the Messiah, son of David, had arisen and had restored their kingdom.[1] They sold their belong-ings at a ridiculous price and prepared to depart in the path of the devil. They claimed that they would be transported there miracu-lously without effort. . . . They said that their Messiah had arrived but in reality he is the antichrist [*addajjal*] . . . and Allah calleth this arrogance and he hath withheld from them their desire. . . .

Now the Qadi Shihab ad-Din Ahmad b. Sa'ad ad-Din [d. 1669] addressed an inquiry [concerning this state of affairs] to the Imam,

[1] In May 1665, Sabbatai Sevi, a Jew from Smyrna suffering from manic depressions, announced in Gaza that he was the Messiah sent to end Israel's exile. Although many of the rabbis initially opposed his pretensions, he was supported by devoted disciples and friends. Legendary stories about him awakened Messianic dreams throughout the Jew-ish communities in the Ottoman Empire, Europe, Yemen, and Persia. This Messianic enthusiasm, nourished within a context of misery and persecutions, ran high, disturb-ing the Muslim authorities. In 1666 the Grand Vizier imprisoned Sevi in Constantino-ple and, to save his life, Sevi converted to Islam.

who, in his reply laid down that the nonsubmission of the Jews to the condition of the *dhimma* was tantamount to its annulment. When this decision reached [Mount] Kawkaban and Shibair,[2] the inhabitants attacked the womenfolk of the local Jewish community and they appropriated their belongings, jewels, and money. When the news broke out that what had transpired at Shibair had been with the Imam's blessing, the inhabitants of Haz and Gharza lost no time in pillaging their Jewish neighbors. . . .

When the stupidity of the Jews waxed strong and their irresponsibility was at its height, they took hold of one of their kind and adorned him with handsome garments and gave him much drink. When his heart was merry with wine, he ascended to the royal palace and asked to be placed upon the throne, demanding that his request be obeyed. He addressed Prince Jamal ad-Din in the Hebrew tongue, saying that his rule had come to an end, his house had been condemned, and that he was to surrender and quit the palace. The courtiers present hurried to strike him down and pelted him with the blows of their shoes in return for this disgraceful act.

They then carried him off to the Bustan prison and degraded him by every means, stripping him of his silken garments and transforming his pretended kingship into torture, just as his brethren had been changed into apes and pigs [see doc. 9]. Then they inquired of the Imam what should be done to him and it was replied that he should be punished for his evil and he should pay dearly for his disobedience. So he was taken to the marketplace and beheaded, and thereafter he was hung for several days on the city gate as one crucified, during which time the Imam meted out a severe punishment to all the Jews. Their turbans were knocked off their heads and their notables were imprisoned.

Ibn al-Wazir, *Tabaq al-Halwa* (Br. Mus. London, Arabic Ms) Entry for 1115 H. (1703)

[2] Mountain villages, a day's march from San'a.

100. Description of the Status of Non-Muslims in Palestine (1700)

We [Jews] were obliged to give a large sum of money to the Muslim authorities in Jerusalem in order to be allowed to build a new synagogue. Although the old synagogue was small and we only wanted to enlarge it very slightly, it was forbidden under Islamic law to modify the least part. . . . In addition to the expenses in bribes destined to win the favor of the Muslims, each male was obliged to pay an annual poll tax of two pieces of gold to the sultan. The rich man was not obliged to give more, but the poor man could not give less. Every year, generally during the festival of the Passover, an official from Constantinople would arrive in Jerusalem. He who did not have the means to pay the tax was thrown into prison and the Jewish community was obliged to redeem him. The official remained in Jerusalem for about two months and consequently, during that period, the poor people would hide wherever they could, but if ever they were caught, they would be redeemed by community funds.[1] The official sent his soldiers throughout the streets to control the papers of the passers-by, for a certificate was provided to those who had already paid the tax. If anyone was found without his certificate, he had to present himself before the official with the required sum, otherwise he was imprisoned until such time as he could be redeemed (fols. 3a–b).

The Christians are also obliged to pay the poll-tax. . . . The Muslims, however, are not permitted to exact payment of the tax on the Sabbath or Holy days, and consequently we could walk in the streets unmolested on those days. However, during the week, the paupers dared not show themselves outside. Likewise, the soldiers are not allowed to carry out their controls to collect the tax from door to door, and all the less so in prayer houses. But in their wickedness, the soldiers would go to the synagogues, waiting by the doors, requesting the certificate of payment from the congregants who emerged. . . .

No Jew or Christian is allowed to ride a horse, but a donkey is permitted, for [in the eyes of Muslims] Christians and Jews are inferior beings [fol. 7b).

The Muslims do not allow any member of another faith—unless he converts to their religion—entry to the Temple area, for they claim that no other religion is sufficiently pure to enter this holy spot. They never weary of claiming that, although God had originally chosen the people of Israel, He had since abandoned them on account of their iniquity in order to choose the Muslims (fols. 8b–9a).

In the Land of Israel, no member of any other religion besides Islam may wear the color green, even if it is a thread [of cotton] like that with which we decorate our prayer shawls. If a Muslim percieves it, that could bring trouble. Similarly, it is not permitted to wear a green or white turban. On the Sabbath, however, we wear white turbans, on the crown of which we place a piece of cloth of another color as a distinguishing mark (fols. 13a–b).

---

[1] This is the concept of ransom paid for the life of the *dhimmis*. There is an interesting parallel between the situation of the *dhimmis* and that of contemporary hostages, whose survival depends on the requirements of their kidnappers. In both cases life and liberty are not considered as natural and inalienable human rights, but as assets to be exploited or exchanged.

The Christians are not allowed to wear a turban, but they wear a hat instead, as is customary in Poland. Moreover, the Muslim law requires that each religious denomination wear its specific garment so that each people may be distinguished from another. This distinction also applies to footwear. Indeed, the Jews wear shoes of a dark blue color, whereas Christians wear red shoes. No one can use green, for this color is worn solely by Muslims. The latter are very hostile toward Jews and inflict upon them vexations in the streets of the city. It is rare, however, for the Turkish or even the Arab notables to harm the Jews when passing them [in the street], but the common folk persecute the Jews, for we are forbidden to defend ourselves against the Turks or the Arabs. If an Arab strikes a Jew, he [the Jew] must appease him but dare not rebuke him, for fear that he may be struck even harder, which they [the Arabs] do without the slightest scruple. This is the way the Oriental Jews react, for they are accustomed to this treatment, whereas the European Jews, who are not yet accustomed to suffer being assaulted by the Arabs, insult them in return.[2]

Even the Christians are subjected to these vexations. If a Jew offends a Muslim, the latter strikes him a brutal blow with his shoe in order to demean him, without anyone's being able to prevent him from doing it. The Christians fall victim to the same treatment and they suffer as much as the Jews, except that the former are very rich by reason of the subsidies that they receive from abroad, and they use this money to bribe the Arabs. As for the Jews, they do not possess much money with which to oil the palms of the Muslims, and consequently they are subject to much greater suffering.

*Gedaliah of Siemiatyce

[2] The difference in the mentality of the European Jew and the *dhimmi,* alienated by daily oppression, could not have been better described.
*Gedaliah (d. 1716), braving numerous perils, came to Jerusalem in 1700. However, appalling conditions, which he described in his book, forced him to return to Europe in order to raise funds for the Jews of Jerusalem, oppressed by heavy taxation.

101. Reign of Terror in Fez (1790–1792)

Thereafter the Malicious One [Mulay Yazid] came to Fez, and the whole community went forth from al-Harumat,[1] where they were, with presents in their hands in order to receive him. But he paid no attention and did not accept the presents from them, and they returned disappointed. And the Malicious One asked the Chief whether

[1] Possibly the name of a district within the city.

the Jews had paid the tax, and he told him that they had given only twelve talents. And on Sunday, the 24th Sivan of the year [26 May–6 June 1790], in the early morning, the Malicious One sent a man, and he came to us and assembled the Jews and said to them: Give me a note for one thousand mithqals, for the Malicious One has forgiven you. And they gave him their hand-writing, and he at once told them: The forgiveness he grants them relates to your persons and money, that you will not be hurt, but he had decreed that you shall leave the city [Mellah] and dwell in al-Qasba de-Zirara [Shrarda].[2] And when we heard this, we were seized with trembling, with pangs as a woman in travail, for the King's [Sultan's] order required haste, saying: Arise, depart from this place; and at once some chiefs and slaves came and urged us to depart from the city, and we began to depart. And if I said: I will report all the occurrences and happenings that happened to us, time would run out but they would not run out, for on that day we were very hot, because the sun had come out of its sheath in the Tammuz season, and we walked barefoot to the said al-Qasba with the donkey drivers and porters who carried our belongings and put them in the street there. And the way was long, and on the same day the slaves who were among us went to live in Meknes, they and their wives and children, and the Wadaya[3] who lived in Meknes, about 3,000 came to live here in Fez, they and their wives and children; the former left and we left and the latter came in. And there was a great throng and much dust and an intense heat, so that we were bathed in sweat; and we kissed the walls of the synagogues, as it is written: For their servants take pleasure in their stones (Ps. 102:15), and we wept and wept for others, because of all the tribulation that had befallen us. And he decreed that if anyone remained until evening his blood would be upon his head. And there were many thieves and robbers on the way, and they despoiled us until nothing was left us; several householders, poor people, rabbis, and invalids had left all their possessions in the city for fear. And there was fulfilled in us the passage: I will send a faintness into their hearts (Lev. 26:36).

. . . And the Gentiles entered our houses and took away all the locks and doors of the houses and courtyards. And they entered all the synagogues and houses of study and took from them all the benches and arks and lecterns, and several Tora scrolls were stolen and it was just like the Destruction of the Temple; and the meeting-house was converted into a place of idolatry and prostitution. And they devastated them and distilled liquor in them, and all the majesty of the community of Fez departed from it.

[2] A fort on the northern wall of the city between Fas Jadid and the Medina.

[3] An Arab tribe, part of which was encamped in Fez as a police force, formed by Mulay Isma'il.

. . . And our faces became like the under side of a pot because the
sun looked upon us; and we lived in tents like the sons of Kedar and
Arabia and we were left without knowledge and understanding, without worship, prayer, and Tora, because our minds had become disor-
dered with sorrow and grief. We found no rest, for there was so much
dirt that we did not even find a place wherein to put the Tora scrolls;
everybody voided or threw his excrement in the streets of al-Qasba,
and an evil stench pervaded the whole of that locality. And we were in
great trouble concerning the times of the sanctification of the Sabbath, and of prayer, for every place was full of excrement so that there
was no room. And dainty women drew water, and we paid money for
the water we drank, and poor Jews bought water every week at the
price of one-and-a-half okiya. And that summer, there were many
flies, fleas, vermin, scorpions, mice, and snakes, and we did not sleep,
until we were tired of life; and a number of little children died of the
heat. And every day, a strong wind came, rending mountains, breaking rocks, and upsetting all the tents, so that our eyes and ears filled
with dust and sand, and it put out all the candles at night, so that we
sat in darkness as they that be dead of old (Lam. 3:6). And on every
Sabbath night we ate in the dark, and the Malicious One decreed that
the whole of our cemetery be dug up and that the dust of the dead
and the stones on the graves be taken and a *jami'a* mosque (great with
a minaret) be built in the *Mellah* with the said dust and stones, and also
places in Fez al-Bali, viz. Buta'a[4] and Buzlud,[5] and a *jami'a* in a place
called Arsif;[6] for the graveyard was very large, and gangs of Gentiles
dug in all its different corners, and a number of beasts and donkeys
carried the dust and stones to build also the new wall of Asluqiya.[7]
And they dug up the old graves, of the past three centuries, bottom
layer, second layer and third layer, and they found courtyards and
wells and walls—a world of former generations. And the workers
took the shrouds of the dead in which there was silver and gold, and
some became rich thereby. And they also dug up the cave of the
Castilian rabbis, may their memory be blessed in heaven, and, may the
Lord cause their light to shine, and the graves of a number of just
men and of countless pious men, and our eyes saw it and failed, but
we were powerless, for our sins were too many, and we went to the
cemetery, with the chief of al-Qasba who sat at the gate, every second
week and every month, and we gathered the bones, skulls, arms, and
legs of the dead which were scattered there, and we dug a great ditch

[4] Perhaps a deformation of Tala, the central avenue of Fas al-Bali.
[5] Bu Jalud, area between the Medina and Fas Jadid.
[6] "The pavement" in the Kairuwan quarter.
[7] Unknown.

at the place called al-Gisa[8] and buried those bones there; and they threw stones and sticks at us and said to us: Get you out of our city! The Malicious One has taken it from you and given it to us. And they gnashed upon us with their teeth. And we recognised the justice of the judgment inflicted upon us. . . .

. . . And the Malicious One decreed that no Jew or Jewess was to wear vetch green at all or a vetch green garment, and the chief came to al-Qasba and they issued a proclamation to this effect in the name of the Malicious One. And he enacted the same decree in all the cities of the Maghreb, and the Jews lost much money and the scarlet garments they had. Most of them put them into a dye vat to dye them a different colour, and the garment was eaten away. And after a year, they had no festive clothes left because they were all spoilt, and they had to buy new ones. . . . And that King resolved that he would not see or talk to any Jew, and everyone that was called Hebrew was utterly despised. And all the Jews who had served his father—may God have mercy upon him—in high positions were killed by him either by the sword or by hanging. And His Honour, our teacher, Rabbi Mas'ud ben Zikri and others, were hanged by their feet at the gate of the city Meknes, and remained hanging there alive for about fifteen days and then died. . . .

It so befell that we stayed in exile at al-Qasba for twenty-two months—representing the twenty-two letters of the Tora—to make expiation (2 : 296–99).

*Yehudah b. Obed Ibn Attar (1725–1812), *Zikkaron li-benei Yisrael* (*In Memory of the Sons of Israel*), in Hirschberg

---

[8] Bab Gisa, entrance to the Medina, which led to the city's cemetery.
*Ibn Attar (1725–1812) was *dayyan* (rabbinical judge) at Fez. On one occasion he and the scholars of the city were incarcerated by Mulay Yazid for many days in an underground prison.

102. Jews of Afghanistan and the Forced Conversions in Meshed (1839)

In the year 1839, in the wake of a false libel, the Muslims rose up against our forefathers on Thursday the 13th of Nissan and threatened to kill and annihilate all the Jews [of Meshed] and plunder their belongings unless they converted to Islam. Thirty-one Jews were murdered and had it not been for the mercy of Heaven, we would all have perished. . . . Some time afterward those who wished to remain faithful to the word of God departed from the city of Meshed and journeyed to Herat and, from 1840 onward, they dwelled there in peace and tranquillity for fifteen years. . . . However, in the year 1856, on account of our numerous sins, the army of Nasr ad-Din Shah Qajar attacked and besieged the city of Herat for nine months. At the end of the month of Tishri, 1857, the city fell through trickery, without a fight. Thenceforth, [the assailants] started to humiliate us with accusations and threaten us, saying, you have perpetrated this and therefore we will punish you with that. They calumniated us with lies before our king and his princes and persuaded him to banish us from the city and to send us into exile in the city of Meshed. Thus on the 15th of Sebat, 1857, the assailants fell upon us with mortal blows, saying "Get out of your houses by the order of the king." They threw out everybody, men, women, and children from their homes, without sparing the old or the infants, without mercy or compassion. The whole city echoed with the wailing of the poor and the orphans. We had no time even to gather our belongings and prepare provisions, for within three days all the Jews had been expelled from the city and assembled at a place called Musalla. On the 19th of Sebat they marched us away, and for nearly 30 days we walked by the way, surrounded by Muslim soldiers. It was cold; snow and hail fell from the heavens and several people perished on the road on account of the extreme cold, lack of food, and other innumerable misfortunes. We reached the city of Meshed in the month of Adar. We were not allowed into the city but were parked in animal pens in the fort known as Bab Qudrat, which was no more than a prison, the narrowness of which added to our shame and humiliation. Because of the great suffering a few of our brethren converted to Islam. It could have been said of us "The sword without and terror within . . ." (Deut. 32:25), for our captors beat us daily most savagely and exacted from us payment for the hire of the camels that had brought us . . . and moreover we were plagued with disease and pestilence and several people died. Other misfortunes befell us which it would be wearisome to recount, as it is said: "Captivity is worse than the sword of death" (TB *Baba Bathra,* 8b). We remained there for two whole years until such time as our sins had been forgiven in heaven and the king decided to allow us to return to our homes. In Kislev 1859 we set forth from Meshed and arrived in Herat on Monday the 13th of Tebet, and each man returned to his household (pp. 12–13).

*Rabbi M. Gorgi (b. 1845)

---

*Gorgi (1845–1918), born in Herat, was a scholar and communal leader. He settled in Palestine in 1908.

103. Jews of Palestine before 1847

O brothers of Israel, how can I convey to you the harshness of the yoke of exile that our brethren living in Palestine suffered prior to the year 1847?[1] Even were I to relate everything, would it be credible? Verily have our rabbis said: "The Holy One, blessed be he, hath granted three things to Israel after much suffering: the Torah, the land of Israel and the World to come" (TB *Berakhot*, 5a). . . . I shall recount some of the suffering of our brethren in Hebron, Jerusalem, Safed, and Tiberias, which my ancestors have related to me or which I have seen with my own eyes and which has remained in my memory to this day. . . .

It was a great danger for Jews to venture even a few yards outside the gates of Jerusalem because of Arab brigands. Alas, woe to him that fell into their hands for he would be [as one] struck dead. They were accustomed to say *Ashlah Yahudi*, that is: "Strip yourself, Jew," and any Jew caught in such a predicament, seeing their aggressiveness and weapons, would strip, while they divided the spoil between them and sent him away naked and barefoot. They call this spoil: *kasb Allah*, that is, Allah's reward. Moreover, the seven-hour journey from Jerusalem to Hebron was fraught with danger even with a large caravan, and all the more so was a trip to smaller towns. To this day it is customary to recite a thanksgiving prayer when arriving safely at a town from another. If a Jew encounters a Muslim in the [narrow] street and passes on the latter's right, the Muslim says *ishmal*, that is, "pass on my left side." If he touches him or bumps into him, and especially if he stains his clothing or shoes, then the Muslim attacks him and strikes him cruelly and finds witnesses to the effect that the Jew insulted him, his religion, and his prophet Muhammed, with the result that a numerous crowd of Muslims descend upon him and leave the Jew practically unconscious. Then they carry him off to jail, where he is subjected to terrible chastisement. When a Jew passes through their market, stones are thrown at him, his beard and earlocks are pulled, he is spat upon and jeered at, and his hat is thrown to the ground. The poor Jew is so in fear of his life that he dares not question their conduct lest they murder him, and so he runs for his life as one would from wild animals or from the lion's claws and thanks God that at least his soul is saved, and all these tribulations he is ready to suffer for love of the Holy Land. When a Jew buys anything from a Muslim and inquires its price, if the Jew tries to barter, as is the custom among traders, they attack him and spit in his face and

---

[1] The year in which the Ottoman reforms, known as the *Tanzimat*, were confirmed by the Grand Vizier, Mustapha Rashid Pasha.

give him fierce blows until he is obliged to buy the object for the original price. One of the present-day Muslim families known by the name of Abu Sha'ati is among their aristocracy; they are wicked haters of Jews. When they need to have something carried from the market to their house they wait around until by chance they see a Jew, even an elderly man. Indeed, they make no difference between a rich man or a scholar, but they strike him to their merriment until he is forced to carry the burden on his shoulders to their house. On one occasion they happened upon the saintly Rabbi Isaiah Bardaki,[2] who day and night was engaged in study and good deeds and had been a devout person since his youth. When they saw him they forced him with their blows to carry a heavy load on his back to their house. If they see a Jew dressed in green they take hold of him violently and strip him of his garments and have him imprisoned, claiming that he had mocked their religion, for according to their faith only their religious dignitaries may wear green. Likewise it is impossible for Jewish women to venture into the streets because of the lewdness of the Muslims.

There are many more such sufferings that the pen would weary to describe. These occur particularly when we go to visit the cemetery [on the Mount of Olives] and when we pray at the Wall of Lamentations, when stones are thrown at us and we are jeered at (chap. 4).

*M. Reischer

[2] Isaiah Bardaki (1790–1862) was the Chief Rabbi of the Ashkenazi community of Jerusalem and vice-consul of Russia and Austria in the 1840s, in which capacity he played an important role in the organization of the Capitulations.
*Moses b. Menahem Mendel Reischer, nineteenth century Polish traveler.

104. Jews of Baghdad (1877)

... The anguish of our hearts has brought us to make our suffering public to our people. Indeed, our brethren in Baghdad still dwell in humiliation and turn their cheek to the hand of those that smite them. They are satiated with scorn and the oppression of the Muslims who inhabit the city and continue to accost us with the words "turn aside, you impure (one)"; and they greet us with reproach and spit in our faces. Whenever a Jew passes in the street, "wolves" gather around him to hail him with pieces of refuse and cover his head with dirt. If he be an important person wearing a smart turban, then they scheme in their jealousy to downgrade his elegance and knock off his headgear so that it rolls in the mud and dirt. Once this happened to one of our most distinguished merchants while he was sitting among other [Muslim] traders. They threw his turban onto the ground. He, however, remained as silent as one who is dumb in order not to attract attention to his humiliation in public, so that he should not become the subject of scorn and derision. Were I to recount all the many and terrible tribulations that daily fall to our lot, all my paper would be used up and I still would not have related enough. So I will recount only one incident that is indicative of all the rest, that you may grasp the situation that we have to endure from the inhabitants of this country. It happened that one of our brethren had lent some money to a Muslim. When the appointed date was due he went to claim his loan. The Muslim impudently replied that he could not return the money at present and that the Jew was not the Angel of Death to claim money from him immediately. In his great disappointment the Jew cursed the Angel of Death, at which the Muslim rejoiced exceedingly as one who had found a great booty. For, in order to evade his debt he began to shout out to the Muslim bystanders: "Did you not hear how the Jew has cursed our faith and is deserving of the death penalty in accordance with Islamic law?" The Muslim passers-by surrounded the Jew on all sides and began to smite him until blood poured from him. Everyone passing by, seeing them hitting him so, joined in to strike the unfortunate Jew. Their anger was not appeased until they had dragged him to the prison house known as the *Saray*, where he was remanded into custody impending the decision as to what was to be done with him according to Islamic law. So we beseech our brethren, guardians of our deliverance, especially the representatives of the Alliance Israélite, to watch over their brethren in Baghdad and to inform their honorable governments of the terrible sufferings that have befallen us and to plead on behalf of their brethren that they should look kindly upon us to put an end to the beatings and persecutions from these savages, for we have heard that your government protects all those who seek refuge beneath its wings. The Master of retribution will surely reward your kindness.

*S. Bekhor

*Rabbi Solomon Bekhor-Husayn (1842–1892) was a celebrated printer, community leader, and journalist of Baghdad.

105. Jews of Morocco (1888)

Alas, I was not to experience only joy during my sojourn in this town [Fez], for the sun of my delight was to be eclipsed by a sinister cloud and my repose was to be disturbed. To be sure I was to behold there an outlandish spectacle and understand that which I had never imagined. The pen trembles between my fingers, and the paper is humid with my tears when I recall the atrocious sight that my eyes beheld the first of the month of Nisan (April), 1888—this first day of spring, when the living pray for the peace of those who sleep in the dust, may they rest in peace on their eternal couch. However, in this city, the contrary was to prove true, for here the departed are tormented and their remains are reviled as an abominable object. The departed, who during their lives were pursued by the government's persecutions, to which death alone put an end, were now to be chased even beyond the tomb and their resting places beneath the earth were to be pillaged. Upon emerging from the synagogue, the first of Nisan, I beheld my fellow Jews who reside in the Mellah. Suddenly an eerie atmosphere had enveloped the city; men, women, and children began to run in the direction of the cemetery. I thought that perhaps this was a day reserved for prayers in memory of the departed, as is the eve of the New Moon with us in Jerusalem. So I accompanied them in order to pray and prostrate myself on the tombs of the saints. However, upon arriving at the cemetery, my heart ceased to beat, my blood stopped in my veins and I was frozen in my steps by the frightful sight that met my eyes and that will remain forever engraved in my memory. The whole place was filled with lamentations. The noise of weeping and crying was heard from all directions. Some were wailing, others sobbing, while others still were sewing sacks of jute or little caskets, all this in a desperate haste that defies description. Nervous hands undertook the task, and eyes were full of tears, whereas everywhere clouds of dust arose and obscured the light of day. What did this sorrow signify? At daybreak, the royal guard, armed with picks, had descended on the Jewish cemetery and smashed all the tombstones in order to extend the sultan's[1] lands, for the latter wished to enlarge his palace, which gave onto the cemetery. He had now judged insufficient the land of the old adjacent cemetery, which had been emptied on his orders three years earlier. Who could hold themselves back from trembling and crying upon seeing the violation of these saintly tombs, and the people, like chalk-gatherers, filling the sacks that they held in their hands with the bones of their parents and dear ones, in order to bury them elsewhere? A watery marsh was allotted as a new cemetery by the authorities, in exchange for the present one. Throughout this spring day, the sound of wailing and tears was to be heard in this violated sanctuary. I also stood there right until nightful like a withered tree, the tears pouring from my eyes. From that day forth all the beauty of the city seemed to me like the

---

[1] Mulay Hasan (1873–1895).

poison of a snake. I felt as though I were in an evil valley whence mercy had been banished. Full of bitterness, I lamented over the plight of my brethren, who suffered such affronts in this miserable land. For the Jew is considered here as an object of disgust. If he is molested, his very hair being pulled out from his scalp or if he is struck a mortal blow, even though he is supposedly protected by the authorities, his assailant is no more rebuked than if he had struck a dumb animal. Long afterward I remained despondent and the memory of this cruel sight never left my mind, even at night time, when I lay upon my pillow. My heart was more afflicted than theirs, for they were resigned to their fate. . . . Such is the plight of my brethren in this savage land. I can only beseech the Rock of Israel [God] that He deliver them from their prison, and that He redeem them from the darkness, so that they can go up to Zion, their heads at last crowned with joy and light (pp.xi–xii).

*R. A. Ben Shimon

*Rabbi Raphael Aaron Ben Shimon (1848–1928) was born in Rabat, Morocco, and came to Palestine as a young boy. In 1887 he was sent to Fez to inquire after the welfare of the local Jews. In 1891 he became Chief Rabbi of Cairo. He was a prolific writer and edited ancient manuscripts. It was he who urged Solomon Schechter to bring the Cairo Genizah to Cambridge, where it would be preserved. Toward the end of his life he returned to Palestine and settled in Tel Aviv.

106. Jews of Tunis (1888)

A whole book would be necessary to describe the situation of the Jews here in relation to their [Muslim] neighbors, and I have not the time to do it satisfactorily. Nevertheless, I shall mention it, so as not to leave this matter out of my account. In the past,[1] there were Muslims who esteemed Jews as faithful neighbors, others who would consider them as no more than slaves, while still others behaved most disgustingly toward them. It is a fact that religious fanaticism obliges Muslims to act unpleasantly toward non-Muslims, for it is a principle with them that the latter must be considered as infidels. Our brethren have thus suffered great tribulations, which the Muslims have heaped upon them, so much so that many were converted to Islam, or have been driven out of their minds. Then there are all those who have disappeared outside the city or in the wilderness, while others have been assassinated in broad daylight. Some have been executed by the government as a result of false accusations. One individual was re-

[1] Before the beginning of the French protectorate in 1881.

cently killed in connection with an immoral affair, and another was
done to death for having insulted the Islamic faith (the Europeans
have made great endeavors in this respect to obtain greater freedom
and conditions of life that are more civilised, and have nearly succeeded). The Jew is prohibited in this country to wear the same
clothes as a Muslim and may not wear a red tarbush. He can be seen to
bow down with his whole body to a Muslim child and permit him the
traditional privilege of striking him in the face, a gesture that can
prove to be of the gravest consequence. Indeed, the present writer
has received such blows. In such matters the offenders act with complete impunity, for this has been the custom from time immemorial.
Indeed, our coreligionists suffer many such hardships: "I gave my
back to the smiter and my cheeks to them that plucked off the hair; I
hid not my face from shame and spitting" (Isaiah, 60:6). Consequently, the Jew is the target for all manner of vexation, for this has
been the lot of the wandering Jew in the lands of his exile.

Fellah

107. Return of the Exiles to Zion

Dhimmis from Yemen (1881–1910)

And they celebrated the festival [of Tabernacles] with great rejoic-
ing. And throughout the whole festival, day and night, men and
women spoke only of the subject of Eretz [the Land of] Israel. And all
the Jews who were in Sana'a and all the Jews of Yemen agreed together to sell all their houses and all their goods in order to use the
money to journey to their country. And almost all of them neither
slumbered nor slept at night, out of their longing and desire and the
burning enthusiasm of their love for Eretz Israel. And so strongly did
this love break out in their heart, that they cast away all their money,
selling all their houses and possessions at an eighth of the value, in
order to find money for the expenses of the journey by land and by
sea.

The Exodus from Yemen, Tel Aviv, (n.d.)

A first caravan of [Yemenite] Jews was fortunate enough to arrive [in
Jerusalem]. . . . This second caravan, and a third one recently arrived
from Sana'a and its surrounding mountains, are blocked at Hudayda.
The Turkish authorities have forbidden their departure for
Jerusalem. This order is most iniquitous, for it was only after these
poor people had sold to the Muslims the little that they possessed that
the Governor-General of Yemen decided to hinder their departure.

Unfortunately, I can do nothing for them without a ministerial order from Constantinople. It is also of the utmost urgency that these poor people leave Hudayda, where there is no possibility for them to earn their living. One of these poor unfortunate creatures, in order to avoid dying from hunger, was recently obliged to convert to Islam. Unfortunately, I was only informed of his apostasy after he had become a Muslim; I still hope to save him by sending him to Jerusalem as soon as the quarantine is terminated and the steamships will take passengers. . . .

There are at present at Hudayda 100 families of these poor people comprising 300 persons, men, women, and children (p. 21).

Letter (29 Nov. 1881) from Alexandre Lucciana, French Vice-Consul at Hudayda, Yemen, to President, *AIU* (Paris). Archives, *AIU* (FRANCE VIII D 49). See also G. Weill.

By making their way westward, the Yemenite Jews reached the Red Sea and aboard *sambuks* they traveled to Jedda, to Hudayda, and to Aden, where they boarded steamships leaving for Egypt, Palestine, and European Turkey. The last caravan to have left Haydan, a day's journey from Sa'ada, took three years to arrive at Jaffa. Once these poor folk had reached the coast, they found themselves penniless and made their way northward on foot, crossing the whole of Assyr, working for the Arabs, the women sewing and the men doing jeweler's work. When they arrived in Jedda they had thus gathered together enough money to pay their boat ticket to Jaffa. (p 109).

Y. Sémach, *Une Mission.*

Arrivals from Urfa, in the region of Upper Mesopotamia (1896)

Toward the middle of October, ten Jewish Chaldean families arrived in our town [Jerusalem] from Urfa—in Hebrew, *Ur Kasdim,* the homeland of Abraham.[1]

We are accustomed to see groups of Jews (always poor) flocking into the Holy Land from Russia, Rumania, Aleppo, Baghdad, Yemen, etc. Whereas in general, the latter are small, feeble, and puny-looking, those from Urfa struck us by the beauty of their looks. The men are tall, strong and superb; the women are white with fine features, some of them quite beautiful. From every side I was approached on their behalf, and soon they arrived themselves. I couldn't resist the temptation to take their picture.

I asked them why they had left their country.

---

[1] *Ur Kasdim* ("Ur of the Chaldeans", situated in southern Mesopotamia—modern Iraq) is here confused with Urfa (ancient Edessa), situated in Turkey, seventy-five miles northeast of Aleppo (Syria).

JEWS FROM THE HARRAN REGION (SOUTHERN TURKEY)
N. Behar (1896), *AIU*, Paris (ISRAEL I.C.5)

"We were very well there, they replied. We cultivated the fields of the Muslims which are very fertile. We gave an eighth to the owner and an eighth in taxes. But we lost our tranquility since the troubles in Armenia,[2] for the Muslims became very violent and when they began to massacre they sometimes confused us with the Armenians. A family lost a daughter whose throat was cut, another a sister likewise or a son, so that we were obliged to leave and seek refuge here. We want to work; in our country no-one is poor and everyone works."

Meanwhile, I urged a benevolent organization of young people, "B'nai Israel", to make an appeal for these men—to pay for their housing and to procure them flour, rice, and a little oil, etc.

As jobs are unavailable at this moment, I bought water skins for them and they started selling water. I had them employed with us at all kinds of work, even emptying the cesspools. But once again work is lacking and we are obliged to give them some assistance.

As a result of the reform measures announced by His Majesty the Sultan, the local authorities had decided to choose ten policemen from among the Jews. The chief of police sought to enrol them, but they refused on account of the Sabbath, and also because they prefer agricultural work.

These Chaldeans are not perfect. Like all our coreligionists—like all men—they have their faults. However, aside from their superb physical appearance (judge from the photograph), they are unaware of the name "America", or "Transvaal" and, above all, their almost primitive kind of life makes them very suitable to develop a country and attach themselves to the land that they cultivate. They are also more docile and easier to handle than our European coreligionists. I enclose a list of these families [the list comprises ten families, numbering forty-two persons, aged two to fifty].

N.B. With regard to the simplicity of their customs, our coreligionists from Persia and Yemen may be compared with those from Urfa, who are all Ottoman subjects, subsisting on very little, with no other ambition than to earn their livelihood and to observe in security the religion of our ancestors. It seems that the Jews of Kurdistan are similar [to those from Urfa]. This kind of people could provide the elements for a stable, economic and promising development of the Hauran [northeastern Transjordan, today part of Syria].

Letter of 13 December 1896 from [Nissim Behar (?), director of] the *AIU,* Jerusalem, to the Chief Rabbi [of Paris and France, Zadoc Kahn]. Archives, *AIU* (ISRAEL, I.C.5).[3]

---

[2] The first massacre of the Armenians of Urfa occurred on 28 Oct. 1895, the second on 28–29 Dec. 1895 (see above, chap. 3, n.9).

[3] Author's acknowledgment to David Littman for this letter and photograph.

RETURN OF THE DHIMMIS TO ZION
Yemenite Jews on the way to Israel via Aden (1948)
J. Schechtman, p. 256

Daily life in Yemen, ca. 1945

Until our departure from Yemen in 1949, it was forbidden for a
Jew to write in Arabic, to possess arms, or to ride on a horse or camel.
The Jews could only ride on donkeys, both legs on one side [side-
saddle] and were obliged to jump to the ground when passing a
Muslim, and had to make detours. Pedestrians went on the left of
Muslims. It was forbidden for Jews to enter mosques, but the Muslims
couldn't enter synagogues either. The Arabs forbade us to wear shoes,
so that we hid them when, as children, we went searching for wood
for cooking. When we were far enough away, we put on our shoes; on
returning, we took them off and hid them in the branches. The Arabs
frequently searched us, and if they found them, they punished us and

forbade us to collect wood. We had to lower our head, accepting insults and humiliations. The Arabs called us "stinking dogs."

Jewish children who became orphans before they were fifteen were forcibly converted to Islam. The families tried to save them by hiding them in bundles of hay. Afterward, the children were sent to other villages where they hid with another family and were given other names. Sometimes the children were put into coffins and the Arabs were told that they had died with their parents. Then they were helped to escape.

One of my brothers [Hannah is speaking] went to work as usual at the house of Arabs, friends of my mother. One day we heard a lot of noise. My brother had been dressed in a fine costume and had been put on a horse. He was happy . . . he was five years old. An Arab woman came secretly to inform us that they wanted to make him a Muslim. My mother was working outside of the village, my father was dead. My uncle went and took my brother, locked him up, and punished him severely.

One of my uncles worked for Arabs. Although he was quite young,

YEMENITE JEWISH GIRLS (ca. 1910)
Israel Museum (Jerusalem)

he was married and a father of four children. One day the Arabs wanted to convert him and locked him in a room; they tied him up and wanted to force him to swallow a soup with meat, which is forbidden in our religion [probably camel meat]. They beat him terribly, then they went to sleep. My uncle was able to free himself from his bonds and escape. He returned home and cried continuously and didn't speak a word. He was questioned, but didn't reply, and tears flowed all the time. He refused to eat or drink. He died two days later. When he had been prepared for burial, one saw that his body was covered with wounds. We learned the whole story later because the Arabs told it to us secretly.

I had cousins who became orphans. One of my uncles escaped with them from the village. He hid them for five years. The Arabs searched for him everywhere. Finally, they found him. The head of the village told him, "If I didn't know you as well as I do, I would have killed you for what you have done."

The Jews worked in all occupations except agriculture. They made shoes for the Arabs, but they themselves were not allowed to wear them. We liked the Imam Yahya [assassinated on 17 Feb. 1948]; he was good to us. He protected us, he was just. . . . [This statement has been made frequently to the author by many Jews from Yemen. Yahya was succeeded by his son, Ahmad, who allowed 44,000 Jews to emigrate to Israel in 1949–1950.].

Author's interview (8 October 1982) with Hannah [Lolou] and Sa'adya b. Shelomo Akiva [Aqua], born respectively at Dhamar and Menakha (Yemen). Since 1949 they have been citizens of Israel and live in Nes Ziyyona.

108. Expulsion of Jews from the Holy Land (1892/1896)

Jerusalem

Last Tuesday at 3 P.M. there was a large crowd of Jews and others before the new Stores, or shops, on the Jaffa road, in front of Fiel's Hotel, and in coming near I heard piteous female cries issuing from one of those stores. Those inside were trying hard to force the doors open, while police and a set of Moslem roughs were piling big stones against the doors, the police striking any who succeeded in putting head or hands out. I at once realised what the violent scene meant.

As you know several groups of Persian Jews, driven away, it is avowed by persecution [see document 85], have, within the last two months arrived in Jerusalem, via Jaffa. They are computed at 50, 80 and 100 families but I have found no evidence to warrant an estimate exceeding 50 to 60 [families] at most, or of over 150 individuals, children included.

The Jewish Community offered these exiles a plot of land near Siloam to settle upon, but not satisfied with it, they had an altercation with one of the Acting Rabbis, who imprudently called the police to quell the tumult. This came to the knowledge of the Pasha [governor] who thereupon telegraphed to the Porte [Turkish government in Constantinople], and received orders to expel them from the Country.

Accordingly, the police all day had been and were still hunting for the Persian Jews on every side and driving them by blows into that extemporised store-prison, to be kept penned up like wild beasts till all could be collected and marched away back to Jaffa to be shipped off.

I was told of a woman caught in the street and marched off by brute force, and she was shrieking piteously for the baby she left in her miserable hovel. Another, I was assured, being "enceinte" was taken with pains under the blows which hurried her to the prison store. The scene was heart-rending and outrageous to all humane feelings.

I remonstrated with the police against this inhuman, cruel treatment of these poor exiles, particularly the women and girls, but they were too excited and infuriated, and replied roughly that they were acting by superior orders. To the question "Had they committed any crime" there was no reply except that it was no business of mine.

Feeling sure you would generously interpose your good offices to mitigate their sufferings, I decided to call on you at once; but on the way I learnt that you had already sought an interview with the Pasha, who put you off with the plea that it was a matter of internal administration; as also that you were [away] from home.

I therefore called on Mr. Nessim Bachar [Behar], superintendent of the "Alliance Israélite's" Schools and Industrial Manufactories, a Hebrew gentleman of great influence and sound judgment. I found three of the leading Rabbis waiting to see him on the same distressing subject. He came soon, and fully an hour was spent in Conference and consultation. It was decided to seek to obtain a respite, that they might not be marched off on foot, in a cold night, men, women and young children, goaded on by mounted soldiers; to provide them with lodging and food; and to arrange to send them off in batches on carts. It was understood that over 80 had already been collected forcibly in the prison-store. I offered to shelter them in my house, at least that night, till some other accommodation could be found, as also to supply their immediate wants; but it was judged best to lodge them in the precincts of the principal Synagogue.[1] As the Pasha was known to

[1] The Rev. A. Ben Oliel, a converted Jew, was a Protestant missionary.

be irritated with solicitations for these persecuted exiles, efforts were made to communicate with the Chief of the Police, who, however, was found to be away at Jaffa. By my advice two Rabbis were sent to the prison-store to try and stop the shrieks and bitter crying of the distressed women with the tranquilizing assurance that efforts would be made to alleviate their hardships; and this had the desired effect.

Night came on and nothing had been accomplished and so Mr. Nessim and some Rabbis summoned courage and called on the Pasha, and they happily succeeded in obtaining the requisite respite and delay by becoming guarantees for the execution of the Porte's orders, pledging themselves to send the exiles out of the Country. Yesterday some 30 were sent off in carts, and the remainder will be sent off on Sunday or Monday. They go under the guardianship of a Rabbi and accompanied by an interpreter.

One aggravating circumstance is that these Jews speak Persian and not Arabic; another that they are mostly poor, having spent their little all in defraying the expenses of their long journey by sea and land. They are a robust, and hardy set, these Persian exiles, and even the women are remarkably muscular. They would therefore have proved an acquisition in this land of slothful and lazy people.

Mr. R. Scott-Moncrieff,[2] the philanthropic friend of the Russian refugee Jews, and the poor generally at Jaffa, here, etc., very generously provided these distressed people with food during the day (2:478–80).

Letter of 11 Feb. 1892 from the Rev. A. Ben Oliel, of the "Presbyterian Alliance Mission," to John Dickson, British Consul in Jerusalem, in A. M. Hyamson.

   [2] Agent in Jerusalem of Mrs. Elizabeth Finn's society for the assistance of local Jews, "Abraham's Vineyard," afterward known as "The Society for the Relief of Persecuted Jews."

The Hauran

You are no doubt aware that the Jews of the small sephardi settlement of "Artouy" (?), as well as from another settlement of the Hauran,[1] are threatened with expulsion by the local authorities. It would be a real disaster for our Palestinian communities if these expulsions are carried out. Already the situation of the Jews in the Holy Land is most deplorable. In seeing how those in authority treat us, the Arab population is itself becoming accustomed to treating our

   [1] For the Ottoman policy of Islamization in the Middle East (including the Hauran) during the nineteenth and the early twentieth century, see Planhol, pp. 259–60, and Karpat. Also, chap. 4, n.5, above.

coreligionists in the most humiliating manner. A Jew hardly has any standing here; the meanest Muslim insults and mistreats him without his daring even to reply, for at the least word he is immediately accused of having cursed the Muslim religion and this leads to serious complications.

Letter from M. Angel, director of the *AIU* (Jaffa) to the president of the *AIU* (Paris), dated 15 Sept. 1896. Archives. *AIU* (ISRAEL, I.C.5.).[2]

109. Muslim Colonization of Palestine (1875–1885)

Meantime it is a singular fact that the strip of coast from Haifa to Caesarea seems to have become a center of influx of colonists and strangers of the most diverse races. The new immigrants to Caesarea are Slavs. Some of them speak a little Turkish. Arabic is an unknown tongue to them, which they are learning. Their own language is a Slav dialect. When the troubles in the provinces of Bosnia and Herzegovina first broke out [1875], which led to Russo-Turkish war, a howl of indignation went up from the philanthropists. . . . When it [the agrarian question] was settled by handing over the provinces to Austria, the Slav-Moslem aristocracy, finding themselves in their turn persecuted by their former peasants and the Christian power which protected them, migrated to the more congenial rule of the sultan. So the curious spectacle is presented of a Slav population migrating from Austrian rule to Asia, in order to be under a Moslem government.

Close beside the new Bosnian colony there are planted in the plain of Sharon two or three colonies of Circassians. These are the people who committed the Bulgarian atrocities. The irony of fate has now placed them within three or four miles of colonists belonging to the very race they massacred. They, too, fleeing from government by Christians [Austria], have sought refuge under the sheltering wing of the sultan, where, I regret to say, as I described in a former letter, they still indulge in their predatory propensities. In immediate proximity to them are the black tents of a tribe of Turcomans. They belong to the old Seljuk stock, and the cradle of their tribe gave birth to the present rulers of the Turkish Empire. They have been here for about three hundred years, and have forgotten the Turkish language, but a few months ago a new migration arrived from the mountains of Mesopotamia. These nomads spoke nothing but Turkish, and hoped to find a warm welcome from their old tribesmen on the plain of Sharon. In this they were disappointed, and they have now, to my

[2] Author's acknowledgment to David Littman for this extract.

BOSNIAN MUSLIM NOBLEMAN
Engraving by A.B., from a drawing by
T. Valerio (1851–52)
G. Perrot (1868), p. 291, in *Le Tour du Monde* (1st sem. 1870)

BOSNIAN CHRISTIAN PEASANT
Engraving by A.B., from a drawing by
T. Valerio (1851–52)
G. Perrot (1868), p. 279, in *Le Tour du Monde* (1st sem. 1870)

disgust, pitched their tents on some of the spurs of Carmel, where their great hairy camels and their own baggy breeches contrast curiously with the camels and costumes of the Bedouins with whom we are familiar (pp. 238–39).

L. Oliphant, *Haifa*

IV
Modern Period

110. The Mufti of Jerusalem and the Nazis (1943–1944)

The German radio announcer describes a meeting in Berlin on 2 November 1943:

We are in the Luftwaffe building in Berlin, where Arab leaders are gathered to protest against the Balfour Declaration. The Hall is festooned with Arab flags and poster portraits of Arab patriots. Arabs and Moslems from every land pour into the hall. Among them are Moroccans, Palestinians, Lebanese, Yemenites, men from the Hedjaz, Indians, Iranians and Moslem representatives from all over Europe. Among the latter are a great many Germans friendly to the Arabs, high government officials, civilian and military, one of the S.S. chiefs, representatives of foreign embassies and at their head representatives of the Japanese Embassy. The audience runs into hundreds, and here now I see the Mufti of Jerusalem making his way into the hall. He is shaking hands with a number of notables and mounts the steps to the stage to deliver his address (p. 19).

After several anti-Jewish quotations from the Koran, Haj Amin el Husseini, head of the Higher Arab Committee (Palestinian Arab National Movement) declares:

Moslems throughout the Arab lands are united against the enemy which faces them today in Palestine and elsewhere—namely the British.

The Treaty of Versailles was a disaster for the Germans as well as for the Arabs. But the Germans know how to get rid of the Jews. That which brings us close to the Germans and sets us in their camp is that up to today, the Germans have never harmed any Moslem, and they are again fighting our common enemy (applause) who persecuted Arabs and Moslems. But most of all they have definitely solved the Jewish problem. These ties, and especially the last, make our friendship with Germany not a provisional one, dependent on conditions, but a permanent and lasting friendship based on mutual interest (p. 49).

Congratulations by telegram from Heinrich Himmler, Head of the S.S.

The Grand Mufti. The National Socialist Party has inscribed on its flag "the extermination of World Jewry." Our party sympathises with the fight of the Arabs, especially the Arabs of Palestine, against the foreign Jew. Today, on this memorial day of the Balfour Declaration, I send my greetings and wishes for success in your fight (p. 50).

On 1 March 1944 at 12:30 P.M., *speaking on Radio Berlin, the Mufti, after vilifying Jews, Britain, and America, called on the Arabs "to rise and fight."*

Arabs, rise as one man and fight for your sacred rights. Kill the Jews wherever you find them. This pleases God, history and religion. This saves your honour. God is with you (p. 51).

M. Pearlman

111. The Palestinian Dhimma

". . . Our revolution, which believes in the freedom and dignity of man, therefore gives priority to the consolidation of bases through which it can uproot racialism and end all forms of occupation by Zionist settlers. At the same time it is drafting a humanitarian plan which allows the Jews to live in dignity, as they have always lived, under the aegis of an Arab state and within the framework of an Arab society" (p. 454).

Fatah declaration of 19 October 1968. (See Fatah Annual 1968 for Arabic text.) Official English translation in Zuhair Diab, ed., *International Documents on Palestine (1968)* (Institute of Palestine Studies, Beirut, 1971).

112. Jihad in Modern Times (1968)[1]

The Definition of Jihad

The word "Jihad" means exerting all efforts. It means also struggling hard till you feel exhausted.

---

[1] Except for typographical errors, which have been corrected, the texts here reprinted from the 1970 Cairo publication have been left in their original form. No attempt has been made to improve the English.

To strive against the enemy is to fight him.

Jihad—from the view-point of religion means exerting all efforts in repelling the enemies and in fighting them.

Jihad is an Islamic word which other Nations use in the meaning of "War" (p. 182).

The Cause for Which Jihad is Legislated

Scholars have disputed about the reason for which Jihad is legislated.

Some of them said: Jihad is legislated in order to be one of the means of propagating Islam. Consequently Non-Muslims ought to embrace Islam either willingly or through wisdom and good advice or unwillingly through fight and Jihad. According to the above reasons, those scholars lay the foundation of the foreign policy of the Islamic state on the following bases:

I. It is unlawful to give up Jihad and adopt peace and weakness instead of it, unless the purpose of giving up Jihad is for preparation, whenever there is something weak among Muslims, and their opponents are, on the other hand, strong.

If anyone attacks Muslims, Jihad will become an enjoinment in person upon every Muslim qualified for Jihad.

Otherwise, it is an enjoinment by proxy, namely, when any party of Muslims carry out Jihad, the obligation is no longer binding upon the rest.

If Jihad is not carried out by any party of the nation, all the nation will become sinful.

II. War is the basis of the relationship between Muslims and their opponents unless there are justifiable reasons for peace, such as adopting Islam or making an agreement with them to keep peaceful.

III. The abode of Islam [dar al-Islam] is the homeland which is subject to the rules of Islam, and which guarantees the security of its inhabitants, whether they are Muslims or people of Scriptures.

The abode of war [dar al-Harb] is the homeland which is not subject to the rules of Islam, and its inhabitants are not as secure as Muslims (p. 184).

Islam has brought the ideal manners and the human principles which the Muslims should follow and must not ignore in the time of war. Islam is Allah's religion upon Earth to the Last Day.

These Laws which Islam has legislated and which the Muslims must consider before and during fighting, are the best laws ever known of mercy and humanity. . . .

The first one of these laws is the prohibition of the Sudden attack in fighting. This preliminary law necessitates calling the unbelievers to embrace Islam. If they refuse this item, then they are to keep their own religion and pay Jizia for their defence and protection. All these steps should be taken before fighting them (p. 231).

The Muslims are also free to break their covenant with the enemies if they are uneasy lest the enemies should betray them. . . .

Treachery was the business of Jews throughout their ages and times as it was their instinct to break their covenant with others and resort to treachery as soon as they had any chance to betray others. Allah, the Almighty, enjoined upon Muslims to keep their covenant with their enemies and to deal with them justly and openly. This enjoinment was imposed upon Muslims not out of weakness or inability but it was out of strength and heavenly support. Allah backed Muslims until they gained Victory throughout all incursions and battles against the treacherous hypocritic Jews (pp. 239–40).

Al Tabarani quoted in his book (Al Awsat): "Lies are sins except when they are told for the welfare of a Muslim or for saving him from a disaster" (p. 247).

Shaikh Abdullah Ghoshah, Chief Judge of the Hashemite Kingdom of
Jordan

Opening Speech

Experience has proved that what is taken by force can only be restored by force, that necks twisted with arrogance can only be straightened by blows dealt by us, Arabs and Muslims. With Allah's leave and help we can achieve victory, thanks to our potentialities in terms of wealth and men, of lands vast and rich, of a history shining with glories and drives for struggle, of a religion tolerant but stern and noble, including all principles of perfection. . . .

Your honourable conference has been an Arab, Islamic and patriotic necessity in view of the present circumstances in which the Arabs and Muslims face the most serious difficulties. All Muslims expect you to expound Allah's decree concerning the Palestine cause, to proclaim that decree, in all clarity, throughout the Arab and Muslim world. We do not think this decree absolves any Muslim or Arab from Jihad (Holy War) which has now become a duty incumbent upon the Arabs and Muslims to liberate the land, preserve honour, retaliate for [lost] dignity, restore the Aqsa Mosque, the Church of Resurrection, and to purge the birthplace of prophecy, the seat of revelation, the meeting-place of Prophets, the starting-point of Isra,[1] and the scenes of the holy spirit, from the hands of Zionism—the enemy of man, of truth, of justice, and the enemy of Allah.

[1] The Prophet's nocturnal ascension (Koran 17:1), during which he visited the farther Mosque (allegedly Jerusalem) in a dream.

The well-balanced judgement frankly expressed with firm conviction is the first step on the road of victory. The hoped-for judgment is that of Muslim Scholars who draw their conclusions from the Book of Allah, and the Sunna of His prophet. May Allah guard your meeting, and guide your steps! May your decisive word rise to the occasion and enlighten the Arab and Muslim world, so that it may be a battle-cry, urging millions of Muslims and Arabs on to the field of Jihad, which will lead us to the place that once was ours (p. 20).

If good wishes are hoped for this society [umma] and its righteous members intend to drag it from its fall, that will be accomplished only and at first through guidance, education and information.

However this way is not adequate for a nation that has become an easy prey to the dogs of humanity and has been an easy victim to deserted people in addition to the corruption of its society. Besides this activity of information, guidance, education and the spirit of manliness should be raised and the powers of practical Jihad and of patient struggle should dash onward. . . .

Islam is the religion which has been sent satisfactorily by Allah for all the peoples to be the foundation of their lives upon the Earth and to be the general programme of their transactions throughout ages and events. Allah has made the Islamic nation the best one for the people by enjoining what is right, forbidding what is wrong and believing in God. Therefore Allah entrusted the leadership and guidance of mankind to it so as to lead all peoples through the ways of goodness and the obedience (of Allah) in accordance to that rule and that programme which includes a perfect comprehensive depiction of the target of the whole existence and the aim of the human existence in particular (p. 132).

Therefore, All the peoples in the farthest and the nearest places upon the earth have the right to be informed of this heavenly call without being distracted from it or deprived of its care.

When this Call touches and illuminates their hearts, all the peoples have the right to be free to decide what they please and to select what they wish in an absolute liberty which is not limited by authority or power or paralysed by any privilege.

He who embraces it should not be molested by anyone or compelled to abjure it by all means of power and authority. He who adopts this Call should not impede it from prevailing. That aim can be achieved only when the Muslims perform their duties. . . . They are to enable the correct Faith to continue and prevail. This keen watch can impossibly be ascertained without Jihad and thus Allah, the Almighty, has enjoined it upon the Muslims [sic] (p. 133).

So Jihad consolidated the religion and increased the number of the worshippers of Allah and thus Jihad is considered one of the main supports of Islam, and the Believers pay much attention to adopt it and to adhere to it to a great extent. When the enemies occupy an Islamic area suddenly expose the affairs of the Muslims to danger, try to usurp their property, and try to rape the modesties of the Muslim women, Jihad then becomes an enjoinment in person. Every able person of the Muslims should fight by all means to rescue his country. He should defend his religion, his honour, and his homeland.

To those who are far away, Jihad is an enjoinment by proxy, namely, it can be executed or adopted by some persons on behalf of others, who are not obliged to take part in fighting.

The ways of supporting and consolidating the fighters of Jihad, such as providing them with money, employing their tongues and pens, resorting to political tactics, and urging the people to share in that fighting, are indeed part and parcel of the Jihad as an enjoinment in person. This is my viewpoint in this concern. . . .

Jihad has another meaning and it is then an enjoinment in person (Every person should adopt it by himself) upon all Muslims. This kind of Jihad is the struggle for saving money, which should be kept for the present battle between the Muslims and their enemies.

With money we can provide the Muslim fighters with arms, ammunitions, provisions, food, and medicine.

This kind of Jihad may mean also struggling with the pen and by all possible means of information. We can struggle as well by employing all intellectual powers which are possessed by the Muslims (individuals and groups) even if they are distant from the battle-field.

Some scholars view that the Muslims who are distant from the battle-field of Palestine, such as the Algerians, the Moroccans, all the Africans, Saudi Arabia people, Yemeni people, the Indians, Iraqi people, the Russians, and the Europeans are indeed sinful if they do not hasten to offer all possible means to achieve success and gain victory in the Islamic battle against their enemies and the enemies of their religion. Particularly, this battle is not a mere combat between two parties but it is a battle between two religions (namely, it is a religious battle). Zionism in fact represents a very perilous cancer, aiming at domineering the Arab countries and the whole Islamic world (pp. 136–37).

Sheikh Hassan Khalid, Mufti of the Republic of Lebanon

Our Muslim Community is closely attached to a creed and a system that had never been contrived by man, and thereby they are beyond any mistaking or misapprehension. She is attracted to her glorious past and linked up with her great Apostle. Her present-day enemy is (the self-same enemy of old) identical with the one who had confronted her Prophet in the early days of Islam. Thus she is bound to oppose him, until the Almighty inherits the earth and all who are thereon (p. 508).

Throughout the long ages of Muslim history, the Jews had been quite powerless under the rule of Islam. But in modern times the Colonialist Powers could put into effect their designs. Once Muslim Jurisprudence had been discarded as a rule of life, the Jews could establish a State of their own in the heart of the Muslim World, to defy Muslims, and to gain victory over the Arabs in three consecutive battles (pp. 523–24).

Hence present-day Muslims should never treat with them for peace, since it has been proved beyond doubt that they [the Jews] are a mere gang of robbers and criminals, to whom trust, faith, and conscience mean nothing.

Our return to (the true teachings of) Islam would restore to the Muslim Community its vital principles, the force of which would realize endurance and steadfastness, confidence and will, courage and faith. Thus could be established the equitable power that would be a factor in promoting peace and prosperity for the world at large.

There would be built up inside the World of Islam armament plants, so that Muslims might be in no need of importing them from enemy countries, which would certainly make a ban on such exports for fear of their possible use against them (p. 526).

Sheikh Abdul-Hamid Attiyah Al-Dibani, Rector of the Islamic University of Libya

Various Grades of Jihad

Jihad, as already maintained, had been decreed to repel aggression and to remove obstructions impeding the propagation of Islam in non-Muslim countries (p. 61).

Bringing the War to an End

Jihad would never end, because it will last to the Day of Resurrection. But war comes to a close so far as a particular group of people is concerned. It is terminated when the war aims are realized, either by the repulse of aggression and the enemy's surrender by the signing of a covenant, or a permanent peace treaty or truce, etc.; a topic we have already dealt with fully in a separate paper [which] God the Almighty helped me to write (p. 88).

Jihad is not confined to the summoning of troops and the establishment of huge forces. It takes various forms other than regular armies. From all the territories of Islam there should arise a group of people reinforced with faith, well equipped with means and methods; and then, let them set out to the usurpers, harassing them with incessant attacks until the land they had seized turns to be for them an abode for everlasting torment instead of being the country they had intended to be flowing with milk and honey.

If our enemies have wrought havoc throughout a portion of our Muslim territories, let us (in retaliation) raze their colonies to the ground. We should not despair of God's help. The strong will would restore what they had destroyed. There would be no other way to recover our lost territory save by offering our lives in the struggle. So let us make the sacrifice. This is the scope of activities for those who toil and strive, and in the field of honour and jihad, let Muslims vie with one another. "O ye who believe! If ye help God, He will help you and make your foothold firm" (Koran 47:7) (p. 103).

Sheikh Muhammad Abu Zahra Egyptian member of the Academy of
Islamic Research

113. Khomeini on Government, Jihad, and Impurity

An Islamic government is government by Divine Right and its laws cannot be changed, modified, or challenged (p. 19).

The legislative power is held exclusively by the Holy Prophet of Islam and none other than he can impose a law; any law that does not stem from him must be rejected (p. 20).

Holy War (*Jihad*) means the conquest of non-Muslim territories. It is possible that it may be declared after the formation of an Islamic government worthy of the name, under the direction of an imam or at his command. It will then be incumbent upon every adult able-bodied man to volunteer for this war of conquest, whose final goal is the domination of Koranic law from one end of the earth to the other. However, the world must understand that the universal supremacy of Islam differs considerably from the hegemony of other conquerors. Consequently, the Islamic government must first be established on the authority of the Imam in order for him to be able to undertake this conquest, which will be different from other wars of conquest of an unjust and tyrannical nature, which ignored the moral and civilized principles of Islam (pp. 22–23).

Impurity of the Infidel

Eleven things are unclean: urine, excrement, sperm, blood, a dog, a pig, bones, a non-Muslim man and woman, wine, beer, perspiration of the camel that eats filth (p. 59).

The whole body of a non-Muslim is unclean, even his hair, his nails, and all the secretions of his body (p. 62).

A child below the age of puberty is unclean if his parents and grandparents are not Muslims; but if he has a Muslim for a forebear, then he is clean (p. 63).

The body, saliva, nasal secretions, and perspiration of a non-Muslim man or woman who converts to Islam automatically become pure. As for their garments, if they were in contact with the sweat of the body before conversion, they will remain unclean.

It is not strictly prohibited for a Muslim to work in an establishment run by a Muslim who employs Jews, if the products do not aid Israel in one way or another. However, it is shameful [for a Muslim] to be under the orders of a Jewish departmental head (p. 160).

Ayatollah Seyyid Ruhollah Khomeini

114. Arafat on Religious Brotherhood and Jihad

The question of Palestine is crucial among those just causes fought for unstintingly by masses labouring under imperialism and oppression. I am aware that, if I am given the opportunity to address the General Assembly, so too must the opportunity be given to all liberation movements fighting against racism and imperialism (p. 183).

The Jewish invasion of Palestine began in 1881. Before the first large wave of settlers started arriving, Palestine had a population of half a million, most of these Muslims or Christians, and about 20,000 Jews. Every sector of the population enjoyed the religious tolerance characteristic of our civilization.

Palestine was then a verdant land, inhabited by an Arab people in the course of building its life and enriching its indigenous culture (p. 185).

It pains our people greatly to witness the propagation of the myth that its homeland was a desert until it was made to bloom by the toil of foreign settlers, that it was a land without a people, and that the settler entity caused no harm to any human being. No, such lies must be exposed from this rostrum, for the world must know that Palestine was the cradle of the most ancient cultures and civilizations. Its Arab people were engaged in farming and building, spreading culture throughout the land for thousands of years, setting an example in the practice of religious tolerance and freedom of worship, acting as faithful guardians of the holy places of all religions. As a son of Jerusalem, I treasure for myself and my people beautiful memories and vivid images of the religious brotherhood that was the hall-mark of our Holy City before it succumbed to catastrophe. Our people continued to pursue this enlightened policy until the establishment of the state of Israel and their dispersion. This did not deter our people from pursuing their humanitarian role on Palestinian soil. Nor will they permit their land to become a launching pad for aggression or a racist camp for the destruction of civilization, culture, progress and peace. Our people cannot but maintain the heritage of their ancestors in resisting the invaders, in assuming the privileged task of defending their native land, their Arab nationhood, their culture and civilization, and in safeguarding the cradle of the monotheistic religions (p. 186).

While we were vociferously condemning the massacres of Jews under Nazi rule, Zionist leadership appeared more interested at that time in exploiting them as best it could in order to realize its goal of immigration into Palestine (p. 187).

We distinguish between Judaism and Zionism. While we maintain our opposition to the colonialist Zionist movement, we respect the Jewish faith [because this religion is a part of our heritage][1] (p. 187).

Extracts from Yasser Arafat's speech at the General Assembly of the United Nations (New York), 13 Nov. 1974. In *JPS* 4 (1975): 181–94. See also *International Documents on Palestine (1974)*, (Institute of Palestine Studies, Beirut, 1977), pp. 134–44.

Arafat Cables Khomeini

I pray Allah to guide your step along the path of faith and Holy War *(Jihad)* in Iran, continuing the combat until we arrive at the walls of Jerusalem, where we shall raise the flags of our two revolutions.

France-Soir (Paris), 13 February, 1979

[1] This phrase appears in the French translation of Arafat's UN speech, as published in Switzerland (Lausanne, 1975) by the *Comités de Soutien au Peuple Palestinien.*

115. Egyptian Copts Appeal to President Sadat (1972)[1]

The National Assembly of the heads of the Copt-Orthodox, Copt-Catholic, and Copt-Evangelical churches met at the Orthodox-Coptic Patriarchate in Alexandria. The delegates were shocked by recent provocations and the planned persecutions publicly announced by the Ministry of Waqfs (Muslim Ministry of Religion) and its various sections. These projects are intended to inflame the populace to hatred and to discrimination which can only lead to our annihilation. In spite of all this, no responsible department of the administration has done anything to stop these perfidious intrigues against national unity. . . .

We, members of this Assembly, subjected to considerable pressure engendered by all these injustices which are occurring throughout the country, conscious also that the Constitution guaranties liberty to all citizens, we request, Sir, that:

1) Sectarian and mischievous projects of the Ministry of Waqfs and other departments of this Ministry cease.

2) Restrictions imposed by the officials of the Administration concerning the construction of new churches be abolished. The argument used according to which this prohibition is based on an old Ottoman decree is invalid as this law was abrogated by the new Constitution.

3) Entrance to the Universities must be based solely on the final examination results at secondary school and not on a private interview. Furthermore, it should be forbidden for University courses to be held in mosques and Islamic Institutions.

4) Studies of our religion from a negative viewpoint, such as "Israel and Universal Zionism" and "Conference on Christianity," should not be published.

5) All discrimination regarding employment in certain departments of the Universities and the Institutes of Advanced Studies should be abolished, as well as the QUOTA system applicable to Christian students in specialized schools and similar institutions.

---

[1] After the anti-Copt riots (1980–1981) in which hundred were killed and wounded, several churches burned and looted, President Sadat arrested (6 Sept. 1981) 1500 Muslim fundamentalists as well as 150 Copts, including priests and bishops. Pope Shenouda III was exiled to a desert monastery and has not yet been released. The increasing power of fundamentalism in Egypt has increased anti-Christian hatred, and has aggravated the situation of the Copts, designated by traditional pejorative terms as "Associationists" and Nazarenes (the Europeans are referred to as Crusaders). Muslim religious and political leaders insist that Koranic law should be the only source of government, which for the Christians would mean the revival of the traditional rules applied to the *dhimmis*.

CROWNING OF COPTIC PATRIARCH SHENOUDA III (1971)
(Keystone)

6) It should be forbidden to publish books or articles attacking our faith and our Holy Scriptures, in particular the Old Testament.

7) It is essential to apply the (National) COVENANT and protect the Christian family against the dangers which menace it through the pretext of granting legal protection. Divorce must be made more difficult in that part of the law relating to the personal status of non-Muslims.

8) The projects which are aimed at preventing Christians from acceding to high (government) posts should be abolished.

Sir, we await your reply, as soon as possible, to our just requests. We do not accept to be humiliated in this country which is ours. The delegates have called a further assembly in Cairo for TUESDAY 29 AUGUST 1972. There is thus sufficient time for our just requests to be accepted. If this will not be the case, martyrdom is preferable to a life of servitude.

We are sure of your wisdom, as we are sure that you will overcome this dangerous situation. May God protect you and through your efforts grant victory to our nation.

(signed)

For the Copt-Orthodox Patriarchate: The Reverend MENA, Patriarchal Vicar

For the Copt-Catholic Church: The Reverend GIBRAEL GHATTAAS, Patriarchal Vicar

For the Copt-Evangelical Church: Pasteur LABIB QALDAS (pp. 91–92).

Telegram (July, 1972) sent to President Sadat by the Assembly of Christian Churches in Egypt. English text in Masriya, *A Christian*, pp. 91–92

116. Lebanon: Statements by Archbishop Ignace Mubarak (1947) and Bashir Gemayel (1982)

. . . Here in the Middle East, which is for the most part Moslem, if the present Lebanese Government is recognized as having an official right to speak on behalf of the Lebanese nation, we should feel disposed to answer and prove that the present rulers represent only themselves and that their so-called official statements are dictated only by the needs of the moment and by the imposed solidarity binding this preeminently Christian country to the other Islamic countries which surround it on all sides and enclose it, *volens nolens,* in their politico-economic orbit.

By reason of its geographical position, history, culture and traditions, the nature of its inhabitants and their attachment to their faith and ideals, the Lebanon has always, even under the Ottoman yoke, kept itself out of the clutches of the other nations surrounding it and has succeeded in maintaining its tradition intact.

Palestine, on the other hand, the ideological center of all Old and New Testament propaganda, has always been the victim of all the troubles and persecutions. From time immemorial, anything with any historical significance has always been ransacked, plundered, and mutilated. Temples and churches have been turned into mosques and the role of that eastern part of the Mediterranean has, not without reason, been reduced to nothing.

It is an incontestable historical fact that Palestine was the home of the Jews and of the first Christians. None of them was of Arab origin. By the brutal force of conquest they were forced to become converts to the Moslem religion. That is the origin of the Arabs in that country. Can one deduce from that that Palestine is Arab or that it ever was Arab?

Historical vestiges, monuments, and sacred mementos of the two religions remain alive there as evidence of the fact that this country was not involved in the internal wars between the princes and monarchs of Iraq and Arabia. The Holy Places, the temples, the Wailing Wall, the churches and the tombs of the prophets and saints—in short, all the relics of the two religions—are living symbols, which alone invalidate the statements now made by those who have some interest in making Palestine an Arab country. To include Palestine and the Lebanon within the group of Arab countries is to deny history and to destroy the social balance in the Near East.

These two countries, these two homelands, have proved up till now that it is both useful and necessary for them to exist as separate and independent entities.

The Lebanon, first of all, has always been and will remain a sanctuary for all the persecuted Christians of the Middle East. It was there that the Armenians who escaped extermination in Turkey found refuge. It was there that the Chaldeans of Iraq found a place of safety when driven from their country. It was there that the Poles, in flight from a blazing Europe, took refuge. It was there that the French, forced out of Syria, found protection. It was there that the British families of Palestine, fleeing from terrorism, found refuge and protection.

The Lebanon and Palestine must continue to be the permanent home of minorities.

. . . Major reasons of a social, humanitarian, and religious nature require the creation, in these two countries, of two homelands for minorities: *a Christian home in the Lebanon,* as there has always been; *a Jewish home in Palestine.* These two centers, connected with each other geographically, and supporting and assisting each other economically, will form the necessary bridge between West and East, from the viewpoint of culture and civilization. The neighbourly relations between these two nations will contribute to the maintenance of peace in the Near East, which is so divided by rivalries, and will lesson the persecution of minorities, which will always find refuge in these two countries.

That is the opinion of the Lebanese whom I represent; it is the opinion of this people whom your Committee of Enquiry was unable to hear.

Behind the closed doors of the Sofar Hotel you were able to listen only to the words dictated to our so-called legal representatives by the lords and masters of the neighbouring Arab countries. The real voice of the Lebanese was smothered by the group who falsified the elections of 25 May.

THE LEBANON DEMANDS FREEDOM FOR THE JEW IN PALESTINE—AS IT DESIRES ITS OWN FREEDOM AND INDEPENDENCE.

Archbishop Ignace Mubarak

Extracts from a letter dated 5 August 1947, from Ignace Mubarak, Maronite Archbishop of Beirut, to Mr. Justice Sandstrom, Chairman of the Committee of Enquiry, UNSCOP, Geneva, Switzerland. See *Official Records of the Second Session of the United Nations General Assembly Ad Hoc Committee on the Palestinian Question;* Summary Records of Meetings 25 September–25 November 1947 (New York) pp. 57–59.

. . . In the name of all the Christians of the Middle East, and as Lebanese Christians, let us proclaim that if Lebanon is not to be a Christian national homeland, it will nonetheless remain a homeland for Christians. Above all a homeland for Christians, though one for others as well if they so choose a homeland to be protected and preserved, in which our churches may be rebuilt at the time and in the manner we desire.

Yasser Arafat has transformed the church of Damur into a garage. We forgive him, and though they defiled, sullied, and pillaged the church of Damur, we will rebuild it. Had we been in Egypt or Syria, perhaps we would not even have had the right to rebuild a destroyed church.

Our desire is to remain in the Middle East so that our church bells may ring out our joys and sorrow whenever we wish!

We want to continue to christen, to celebrate our rites and traditions, our faith and our creed whenever we wish!

We want to be able to assume and testify to our Christianity in the Middle East!

And whatever may be the difficulty in offering this testimony, we will never renounce it. We will testify to our Christianity in Lebanon! We will testify to our Christianity in the Middle East! . . .

So that Lebanon may truly be the Lebanon we desire, it must perforce remain the land of freedom, the homeland of civilization. Otherwise it will resemble Yemen or those countries wherein there remains not the slightest trace of our existence, nor the least reason for it. As a Christian part of the Middle East, we want to be different from others and possess a land which, without being—let it be repeated—a Christian national homeland, shall be a country for Christians, where we may live in dignity, without being forced by anyone to deny our faith, as we were in the time of the Turks when we were ordered to walk on the[ir] left because we were Christians. We do not want to be forced to wear any sort of discriminatory badge on our body or on our clothes—so that one might know that we were Christians—and we do not want to be transformed into citizens existing in the "dhimmitude" of others!

Henceforth, we refuse to live in any "dhimmitude"!

We no longer wish to be under any protection!

Our martyrs have defended us!

Our martyrs have defended our cause!

For eight years, our martyrs have defended our freedom and our presence in the Middle East, during which the whole world repudiated us, during which the whole world disinherited us, during which the whole world ignored us; and when we emerged victorious, all became our friends, all sought to befriend us.

In the future, it is our duty to deal with the whole world devoid of any sort of complex.

No one can outwit us!

No one can outrank us in bravery!

And no one has defended his country more than we have defended ours!

No civilization is superior to ours to be imposed upon us, pretending to be closer to the truth than we.

We are not backward.

We are not Bedouins; we have no camels.

Have we not a history of 6,000 years of which to be proud, and do we not know what is to be done to preserve this heritage?

. . . and my wish is that from this day forth, as Lebanese, we may no longer have any complex toward anyone, without fearing to speak the truth to anyone.

Only the truth will redeem us now.

Only the truth will allow us to abide in dignity.

Because we have mocked the world for forty years, the world has mocked us.

Because we have deceived the world for forty years, the world in turn has deceived us.

Because we deemed ourselves totally insignificant, the world has disregarded us.

. . . And just as we vanquished through our resistance, so we must today conquer all Lebanon, all its 10,452 square kilometers! We must conquer the whole country and this land must be free unto all its sons, without distinction of religions, beliefs, and opinions. Above all, this country must remain a haven of security and tranquillity for the Christian society of the Middle East, for we are no longer prepared to suffer exile in the United States or in Europe; we are no longer prepared to step to the[ir] left, nor get down on our knees, nor to suffer defeat!

We want to live here in dignity!

We no longer wish people to preach morality or philosophy to us, to give money or inform us of the proper manner in which to act.

We alone knew what was expected of us, for had we not done what we did, we would not be here today and there would not have remained a single nun, priest, or cross! . . .

B. Gemayel, " . . . Notre droit."

Extracts from the recorded speech (14 September 1982) of Bashir Gemayel, pronounced at Dayr-Salib. He was assassinated the same afternoon in East-Beirut, three weeks after his election as President of Lebanon.

Bibliography

Books and Articles Mentioned in Text, Notes, or Documents

Abd al-Qadir as-Sufi. *Jihad: A Groundplan.* London, 1978.

Abel, A. "Dar al-Harb." *EI²* 2.

Abitbol, M. "Zionist activity in the Maghreb." *JQ* 21 (1981).

Abraham, S. "The Jew and the Israeli in Modern Arabic Literature." *JQ* 2 (1977).

Abu Yusuf, Ya'qub. *Kitab ul-Kharadj* (Le Livre de l'impôt). Translated by E. Fagnan. Paris, 1921.

al-Adawi, Ahmad ad-Dardir (al-Malikı). *Fatwa.* Translated by Belin. *JA* 19 (1852).

Aldeeb Abu Sahlieh, S. A. *Non-Musulmans en pays d'Islam: cas de l'Egypte.* Fribourg, 1979.

Ali Bey (Badia y Leblich, D.). *Travels of Ali Bey in Morocco, Tripoli, Cyprus, Egypt, Syria and Turkey, between the years 1803 and 1807, written by himself.* 2 vols. London, 1816.

Anon. *The Exodus from Yemen.* Tel Aviv, n.d.

Anon. "Voyage en Palestine. II: Excursion en Terre Sainte" (1859). In *Le Tour du Monde* (Paris, 1st sem. 1860).

Anon. *Het Ellendigh Leven der Turcken,* 1663.

Arberry, A. J. *The Koran Interpreted.* Oxford, 1964.

Ashtor, E. "Levantine Jewries in the Fifteenth Century." *BIJS* 3 (1975).

———. *A Social and Economic History of the Near East in the Middle Ages.* London, 1976.

———. (Strauss, E.) "The Social Isolation of Ahl adh-Dhimma." In *P. Hirschler Memorial Book.* Budapest, 1949.

al-Asnawi. *Al-kalimât al-Muhimma fi mubâsharat ahl adh-dhimma (An earnest appeal on the employment of the Dhimmis.)* See Perlmann. *BSOAS* 10 (1939–1942) and "Asnawi's tract . . ."

Attal, R. "Le Juif dans le proverbe arabe du Maghreb", *REJ* 122 (1963).

———. *Les Juifs d'Afrique du Nord: Bibliographie.* Jerusalem, 1973.

———. "Croyances et préjugés; image du Juif dans l'expression populaire arabe du Maghreb." In *Les Relations entre Juifs et Musulmans en Afrique du Nord* (Actes du Colloque International de l'Institut d'Histoire des pays d'Outre Mer). Paris, 1980.

———, and Tobi, Y. *Oriental and North African Jewry: An Annotated Bibliography (1974–1976).* Jerusalem, 1980.

al-Azhar (Academy of Islamic Research), ed. *Kitab al-Mu'tamar al-Rabi'li-Majma' al-Buhuth al-Islamiyya.* 2 vols. Cairo, 1968.

———. (Ibid., English ed.) *The Fourth Conference of the Academy of Islamic Research.* 1 vol. Cairo, 1970.

Baer, G. "The Development of Private Ownership of Land." In *Studies in the Social History of Modern Egypt.* Chicago, 1969.

al-Baladhuri. *Kitab Futuh al-Buldan (The Origins of the Islamic State).* Translated by P. K. Hitti. New York, 1916.

Baron, S. W. *A Social and Religious History of the Jews.* 2d ed. 15 vols. New York, 1952–1973.

Barton Lord, P. *Algiers, with Notices of the Neighbouring State of Barbary.* 2 vols. London, 1835.

Bashan, E. *Shivyah u-fedut ba-Hevra ha-Yehudit be-Arzot ha-Yam ha-Tikhon (1391–1830) (Captivity and Ransom in the Mediterranean Jewish Society)* (Hebrew). Jerusalem, 1980.

Bat Ye'or. "Aspect of the Arab-Israeli Conflict." *WLB* 32, n.s. 49/50 (1979).

———. *Yehudei Mizrayim (Jews in Egypt)* (Hebrew). Tel Aviv, 1974. See Masriya

———. "Zionism in Islamic Lands: The Case of Egypt." *WLB* 30, n.s. 43/44 (1977).

———. "Terres Arabes: Terres de 'Dhimmitude' ". In *La Cultura Sefardita* (vol. 1). RMI 49, nos. 1–4 (1983).

Bazin, R. *Charles de Foucauld: Explorateur du Maroc, Ermite au Sahara.* Paris, 1921.

al-Bazzaz, A. R. *This is Our Nationality* (Arabic). Cairo, 1974.

Becker, J. *The PLO: The Rise and Fall of the Palestine Liberation Organisation.* London, 1984.

Bekhor-Husayn, S. (Letter on Jews of Baghdad). *ha-Zefirah* (Hebrew) (Warsaw, 1877). 3d year, no. 9, 22d Adar.

Ben Bella, A. "Tous contre Israël." *PI* 16 (Paris, 1982).

Benjamin, I. J. *Eight Years in Asia and Africa (1846–1855).* Hanover, 1859.

Bensimon-Donath, D. *Immigrants d'Afrique du Nord en Israël.* Paris, 1970.

Ben Shimon, R. A. *Ahabat ha-Qadmonim (Love of our Ancestors)* (Hebrew). Jerusalem, 1889.

Ben Zvi, I. *The Exiled and the Redeemed.* London, 1958.

Bible. *King James Authorized Version* (1611).

Binswanger, K. *Untersuchungen zum Status der Nichtmuslime im Osmanischen Reich des 16. Jahrhunderts: mit einer Neudefinition des Begriffes "Dimma".* Munich, 1977.

Bonar, A. A., and M'Cheyne, R. M. *Narrative of a Mission of Inquiry to the Jews from the Church of Scotland in 1839.* Edinburgh, 1842.

Bonsal, S. *Morocco as It Is.* London, 1891.

Boody. *To Kairwan the Holy.* London, 1885.

Bowring, J. *Report on the Commercial Statistics of Syria.* London, 1840, reprint, New-York, 1973.

Brawer, A. J. "Damascus Affair." *EJ* 5.

Brooke, A. de C. *Sketches in Spain and Morocco.* 2 vols. London, 1831.

Broughton, E. *Six Years Residence in Algiers.* London, 1839.

Bruun, D. *The Cave Dwellers.* London, 1898.

Bryant, W. C. *Letters from the East.* New York, 1869.

Bryce, J., ed. *The Treatment of the Armenians in the Ottoman Empire (1915–1916).* London, 1916.

Buckingham, J. S. *Travels in Palestine.* London, 1821.

al-Bukhari. *Al-Sahih (Les Traditions islamiques).* Translated by O. Houdas and W. Marçais. 4 vols. Paris, 1903–1914.

Cahen, C. "Histoire économico-sociale et islamologie: le problème préjudiciel de l'adaptation entre les autochtones et l'Islam." In *Les Peuples musulmans dans l'histoire médiévale.* Damascus, 1977.

——. "Dhimma." *EI²* 2.

——. "Djizya." *EI²* 2.

——. "Kharadj." *EI²* 4.

Campbell, P. *Report.* (1839). See Bowring

Campbell, T. *Letters from the South.* 2 vols. London, 1821.

Canard, M. "Arminiya." *EI²* 1.

Carré, O. "Juifs et Chrétiens dans la Société islamique idéale d'après Sayyid Qutb" (d. 1966), *RSPT* 68 (1984).

Carrouges, M. *Foucauld: Devant l'Afrique du Nord.* Paris, 1961.

du Caurroy. "Législation musulmane sunnite, rite Hanéfi", *JA* 17, 18 (1851) and 19 (1852).

Cazès, D. *Essai sur l'Histoire des Israélites de Tunisie.* Paris, 1888.

Charles Roux, F. *Les Échelles de Syrie et de Palestine au XVIIIe siècle.* Paris, 1928.

Chouraqui, A. N. *La Condition juridique de l'Israélite Marocain.* Paris, 1950.

——. *Between East and West: A History of the Jews of North Africa.* Philadelphia, 1968.

Cohen, A. *Palestine in the Eighteenth Century: Patterns of Government and Administration.* Jerusalem, 1973.

de Contenson, L. *Chrétiens et Musulmans.* Paris, 1901.

Corpus Scriptorum Historiae Byzantinaea. (Bonn, 1892).

Crawford, J. V. *Marocco at a glance.* London, 1889.

al-Damanhuri. *Iqamat al Hujja al-bahira ala hadm kana' is Misr wa-l-Qahira (Presentation of the clear proof for the obligatory destruction of the churches of Old and New Cairo).* See Perlmann

Dandini, J. *Voyage du Mont Liban.* Paris, 1685.

De Amicis, E. *Le Maroc.* Paris, 1882.

Dennet, D. C. *Conversion and the Poll-Tax in Early Islam.* Cambridge (Mass.), 1950.

al-Dibani, A-H. A. "The Jewish Attitude towards Islam and Muslim in Early Islam" (1968). See al-Azhar

Djaït, H. *La Personnalité et le Devenir Arabo-Islamiques.* Paris, 1974.

Doutté, E. *Missions au Maroc: En Tribu.* Paris, 1914.

Dulles, J. W. *The Ride through Palestine.* Philadelphia, 1881.

Fagnan, E. "Arabo-Judaïca." In *Mélanges Hartwig Derenbourg (1844–1908).* Paris, 1909.

———. "Le Signe distinctif des juifs au Maghreb." *REJ* 28 (1894).

Fattal, A. *Le Statut légal des non-Musulmans en pays d'Islam.* Beirut, 1958.

Fellah. "The Situation of the Jews of Tunis, September 1888." *Ha-Asif (The Harvest)* (Hebrew) 6 (Warsaw, 1889).

Fenton, P. B. "Jewish Attitudes to Islam: Israel Heeds Ishmael." *JQ* 29 (1983).

Feriol, A. *Explication des Cent Estampes qui représentent Différentes Nations du Levant avec de Nouvelles Estampes de Cérémonies Turques qui ont aussi leurs explications.* Paris, n.d. [ca. 1714–15].

Février, L. "A French Family in Yemen." *AS* 3 (1976).

Finn, J. *Stirring Times, or Records from the Jerusalem Consular Chronicles (1853–1856).* 2 vols. London, 1878.

Fischel, W. J. *Jews in the Economic and Political Life of Mediaeval Islam.* London, 1937; reprint, 1968.

———. "The Jews in Medieval Iran from the 16th to the 18th Centuries: Political, Economic and Communal Aspects." Paper, International Conference on Jewish Communities in Muslim lands (Institute of Asian and African Studies. Ben Zi Institute, Hebrew University). Jerusalem, 1974.

———, ed. *Unknown Jews in Unknown Lands: The Travels of Rabbi David d'Beth Hillel.* New York, 1973.

Fontanier, V. X. *Voyage dans l'Inde, dans le Golfe Persique par l'Egypte et la Mer Rouge.* 2 vols. Paris, 1844/1846.

de Foucauld, C. *Reconnaissance au Maroc (1883–1884).* Paris, 1888.

Franco, M. *Essai sur l'Histoire des Israélites de l'Empire Ottoman depuis les origines jusqu'à nos jours.* Paris, 1897.

Frank, L. "Tunis, Description de cette Régence". In *L'Univers. Histoire et description de tous les peuples. (Algérie, Etats Tripolitains, Tunis).* Edited by J. J. Marcel. Paris, 1862.

Fuller, J. *Narrative of a Tour through Some Parts of the Turkish Empire.* London, 1829.

Fumey, E. *Choix de correspondances marocaines (50 lettres officielles de la Cour chérifienne).* Paris, 1903.

Galanté, A. *Le Juif dans le proverbe, le conte et la chanson orientaux.* Istanbul, 1935.

Ganiage, J. *Les Origines du Protectorat Français en Tunisie (1861–1881).* Paris, 1959.

Gaudefroy-Demombynes, M. *Mahomet.* Paris, 1969.

Gedaliah of Siemiatyce. *Sha'alu Shelom Yerushalayim (Pray for the peace of Jerusalem)* (Hebrew). Berlin, 1716.

Gemayel, B. "Libérer le Liban." *PI* 16 (Paris, 1982).

———. "Liban: il y a un peuple de trop. . . ." *Le Nouvel Observateur,* Paris, 19 June 1982.

————. "Notre Droit à la différence" (Le discours-testament de Bachir Gemayel). *Bulletin d'information* (Union libanaise—Suisse) no. 1 (Dec. 1982).

Ghazi b. al-Wasiti. "An answer to the Dhimmis and to those who follow them". See Gottheil

Ghoshah, A. "The Jihad is the Way to Gain Victory" (1968). See al-Azhar

Gidney, W. T. *History of the London Society for Promoting Christianity amongst the Jews from 1809 to 1908.* London, 1908.

Gil, M. "The Constitution of Medina: A Reconsideration." *IOS* 4 (1974).

Givet, J. *The Anti-Zionist Complex* (with an introduction by D. P. Moynihan). New Jersey, 1982.

Godard, L. *Le Maroc, notes d'un voyageur, 1858–1859.* Algiers, 1859.

Goitein, S. D. "Evidence on the Muslim Poll Tax from non-Muslim Sources: A Geniza Study." *JESHO* 6 (1963).

————. *Jews and Arabs: Their Contact through the Ages.* 3d ed. New York, 1974.

————. *A Mediterranean Society: The Jewish Communities of the Arab World as Portrayed in the Documents of the Cairo Geniza.* 4 vols. Berkeley and Los Angeles, 1967/1971/1978/1984.

Goldberg, H. E. *The Book of Mordechai: A Study of the Jews of Libya.* Philadelphia, 1980.

———— . "The Tripolitain Pogrom of 1945." *PS* 8 (The Hague, 1977).

Goldziher, I. *Le Dogme et la Loi de l'Islam: Histoire du développement dogmatique et juridique de la religion musulmane.* Translated by F. Arin. Paris, 1921; reprint, 1973.

Gorgi, M. *Qorot ha-Zemanim (Chronicle of Afghan Jewry)* (Hebrew). Jerusalem, 1970.

Gottheil, R. J. H. "Dhimmis and Moslems in Egypt." In *Old Testament and Semitic Studies in Memory of W. R. Harper.* 2 vols. Chicago, 1908.

————. "An Answer to the Dhimmis." *JAOS* 41 (1921).

Goulven, J. *Les Mellah de Rabat-Salé.* Paris, 1927.

Green, D. F. ed. *Arab Theologians on Jews and Israel: Extracts from the Proceedings of the Fourth Conference of the Academy of Islamic Research 1968.* 3d ed. Geneva, 1976.

Guérin, M. V. *Description de la Palestine.* 7 vols. Paris 1868.

Guillaume, A. *The Life of Muhammad (Ibn Ishaq's Sirat Rasul Allah)* Translated, with introduction and notes. Oxford, 1955.

Haim, S. G. ed. *Arab Nationalism: An Anthology.* Berkeley: University of California, 1976.

Hakohen, M. *Highid Mordekhai (Mordechai Narrated)* (Hebrew). Jerusalem, 1968.

Halévy, J. "Mission au Maroc" (1876). Archives *AIU* (France IX A73). Also in *BAIU* (1st sem. 1877).

ha-Levi, Se'adyah. (A Hebrew Chronicle). See Tobi

Halpern, M. *The Politics of Social Change in the Middle East and North Africa.* Princeton, N.J., 1963.

Harkabi, Y. *Arab Attitudes towards Israel.* New York, 1972.

———. *Palestinians and Israel.* Jerusalem, 1974.

———. *The Palestinian Covenant and Its Meanings.* London, 1979.

von Hesse-Wartegg, E. *Tunis, the Land and the People.* London, 1882.

Hill, D. R. *The Termination of Hostilities in the Early Arab Conquest* (A.D. *634–656).* London, 1971.

Hillel, David d'Beth. *The Travels of Rabbi David d'Beth Hillel from Jerusalem through Arabia, Koordistan, Part of Persia and India to Madras.* Madras, 1832.

Hirschberg, H. Z. *A History of the Jews in North Africa.* 2 vols. Leiden, 1974/1981.

Hizkiya, *Arnes mi-Hizkiya (Hizkiya's elegy).* Ms. 341, Collection Elkan Adler. Translated by W. Bacher. *REJ* 48 (1904).

Hyamson, A. M. *The British Consulate in Jerusalem in Relation to the Jews of Palestine (1838–1914).* 2 vols. London, 1939.

———. "The Damascus Affair—1840" Transactions, *JHSE* 16 (1945–51).

Ibn Abdun. *(Traité sur la vie urbaine et les corps de métiers).* See Lévi-Provençal

Ibn Abi Zayd al-Qayrawani. *La Risala (Epître sur les éléments du dogme et de la loi de l'Islam selon le rite mâlikite).* Edited and translated by L. Bercher. 5th ed. Algiers, 1960.

Ibn Aqnin. *Tibb an-nufus (Therapy of the Soul)* (Judeo-Arabic). Bodl Ms. Neubauer 1273 (Oxford).

Ibn Askar. *Dawhat al-nasir (The Dawn of Victory).* See Vajda, "Un Traité . . ."

Ibn Attar, H. *Zikkaron li-benei Yisrael (In Memory of the Sons of Israel).* See Hirschberg

Ibn Battuta. *Rihla (Voyages).* Edited and translated into French by C. Defremery and B. R. Sanguinetti. 4 vols. Paris, 1854; reprint, Paris, 1979.

Ibn Ezra, Abraham. *Ahah yarad al sefarad* (Poem: "O, there descended . . ."). See Hirschberg

Ibn al-Fuwati. *Al-hawadit al-jami'a (Comprehensive History of Baghdad)* (Arabic). Baghdad, 1932.

Ibn Khaldun. *Al Muqaddima (An Introduction to History).* Translated by F. Rosenthal. 3 vols. New York, 1958.

Ibn an-Naqqash. "Fetoua relatif à la condition des zimmis et particulièrement des Chrétiens en pays musulmans, depuis l'établissement de l'Islam, jusqu'au milieu du 8e siècle de l'Hégire". Translated by Belin. *JA* 18 (1851), 19 (1852).

Ibn Qayyim al-Jawziyya. *Sharh ash-shurut al-Umriyya (Commentary on the Covenant of 'Umar)* (Arabic). Edited by S. Salih. Damascus, 1961.

Ibn Abd ar-Rabbih. *Al-Iqd al-Farid* (Arabic). Cairo, 1884.

Ibn ar-Rijal, *An-Nusus az-zahira fi ijla al-yahud al-fajira (The Plain Explanation of the Expulsion of the Wretched Jews)* (Arabic). Edited by A. al-Hadi al-Tazi. *JYCSR* 4 (1980).

Ibn Taghribirdi. *An-Nujum az-Zahira fi-Muluk Misr wa'l-Qahira (The Brilliant Stars in the Kings of Misr and Cairo).* See Fagnan, *Arabo-Judaïca*

Ibn Taymiyya. See Laoust, Shreiner

Ibn al-Wazir. *Tabaq al-Halwa (The Pleasant Plate)* (Arabic). Ms. Br. Museum, entry for 1115 H. (1703).

Idris, H. R. "Contributions à l'histoire de l'Ifriqiya" *(Riyad an-Nufus d'Al-Maliki). REI* (1935).

Isaac b. Samuel of Acre. *Osar Hayyim (Treasure-Store of Life)* (Hebrew). Ms. Gunzburg 775 fol.27b. Lenin State Library, Moscow.

al-Jili. *Al-insan al-kamil (The Perfect Man)* (Arabic). Cairo, 1970.

Karpat, K. H. "The Status of the Muslim under European rule: The eviction and settlement of the Cerkes." *JIMMA* 1, no. 2, 2, no. 1 (1979–1980).

Kattan, N. *Adieu Babylone.* Montreal, 1975.

Kedourie, E. *Arab Political Memoirs and Other Studies.* London, 1974.

Kepel, G. *Le Prophet et Pharaon: Les mouvements islamistes dans l'Egypte contemporaine.* Paris, 1984.

Kerr, R. *Pioneering in Morocco.* London, 1894.

Khadduri, M. *War and Peace in the Law of Islam.* Baltimore, 1955.

Khalid, H. "Jihad in the Cause of Allah" (1968). See al-Azhar

Khomeini, S. R. *Principes politiques, philosophiques, sociaux et religieux.* Translated and edited by J.-M. Xavière. Paris, 1979.

Koran. See Arberry

Laffin, J. *The PLO Connections.* London, 1982.

Landau, J. M. *Jews in Nineteenth-Century Egypt.* London, 1969.

———. "Ritual Murder Accusations and Persecutions of Jews in Nineteenth-Century Egypt." *Sefunot* 5 (1961).

———. "Ritual Murder Accusations in Nineteenth-Century Egypt." In *Middle Eastern Themes: Papers in History and Politics.* London, 1973.

Landshut, S. *Jewish Communities in the Muslim Countries of the Middle East.* London, 1950.

Lane, E. *The Manners and Customs of the Modern Egyptians.* 2 vols. London, 1836 (1 vol. London, 1963).

Laoust, H. *Le Traité de droit public d'Ibn Taymiyya,* Beirut, 1948.

Leared, A. *Morocco and the Moors.* 2d ed. London, 1891.

Lebel, R. *Les Voyageurs Français du Maroc.* Paris, 1936.

Lemprière, W. *Tours from Gibraltar to Tangier, Salle, Mogodore, etc.* London, 1793.

Leven, N. *Cinquante Ans d'histoire: l'Alliance Israélite Universelle (1860–1910).* 2 vols. Paris, 1911/1920.

Levi-Provençal, E. "Séville musulmane au début du 12e siècle" (Traité sur la vie urbaine et les corps de métiers d'Ibn Abdun). In *Islam d'hier et d'aujourd'hui.* Vol. 2. Paris, 1947.

Levtzion, N., ed. *Conversions to Islam.* New York, 1979.

Lewis, B. *The Emergence of Modern Turkey.* London, 1968.

———. "The Ottoman Archives as a Source for the History of the Arab Lands" (1951). In *Studies in Classical and Ottoman Islam (7th–16th centuries).* Reprints. London, 1976.

Littman, D. G. "Jews under Muslim rule in the Late Nineteenth Century." *WLB* 28, n.s. 35/36 (1975).

————. "Jews under Muslim Rule, II: Morocco 1903–1912." *WLB* 29, n.s. 37/38 (1976).

————. "Jews under Muslim Rule: The Case of Persia." *WLB* 32, n.s. 49/50 (1979).

————. "Quelques Aspects de la condition de dhimmi: Juifs d'Afrique du Nord avant la colonisation." (d'après des documents de l'*AIU*) *YOD* 2, no. 1 (1976). Enlarged reprint, Avenir, Geneva, 1977.

————. "Mission to Morocco (1863–64)." In *The Century of Moses Montefiore.* Edited by S. and V. D. Lipman. Oxford University Press, 1985.

Loeb, L. D. *Outcaste: Jewish Life in Southern Iran.* New York, 1977.

Lokkegaard, F. "Fay." *EI²* 2.

Lortet, L. *La Syrie d'aujourd'hui.* Paris, 1884.

Mac Donald, D. B. "Djihad." *EI¹* 1.

al-Maghili, *Ahkam ahl al-Dhimma (Regulations of the Dhimmis).* See Vajda, "Un Traité . . ."

al-Maliki, Abu Bakr. *Riyad an-Nufus.* See Idris

Ma'oz, M. *Ottoman Reform in Syria and Palestine, 1840–1861: The Impact of the Tanzimat on Politics and Society.* Oxford, 1968.

————, ed. *Studies on Palestine during the Ottoman Period.* Jerusalem, 1975.

Marcel, J., and Ryme, A. *Egypte.* Paris, 1848.

al-Marrakushi. *Al-mu'jib fi talkhis akhbar al-maghrib (Histoire des Almohades).* Translated by E. Fagnan. Algiers, 1893.

Masriya, Y. *Juifs en Egypte.* Geneva, 1971.

————. "A Christian Minority: The Copts in Egypt." In, *Case Studies on Human Rights and Fundamental Freedoms: A World Survey.* Edited for *SPS* by W. A. Veenhoven. Vol. 4. The Hague, 1976. (French, Geneva, 1973).

al-Mawardi. *Al-ahkam as-sultaniyya (Les Statuts gouvernementaux).* Translated by E. Fagnan. Algiers, 1915.

Memmi, A. *The Colonizer and the Colonized.* New York, 1963.

————. *Dominated Man.* New York, 1966.

van der Meulen, D. *Aden to the Hadhramaut: A Journey in South Arabia.* London, 1947.

Miège, J. L. *Le Maroc et l'Europe (1830–1894).* 4 vols. Paris, 1961–63.

———— *Documents d'histoire économique et sociale marocaine au 19e siècle,* Paris, 1969 (Index to 4 vols.)

Ministry for Foreign Affairs (Research Division). *The Arab View.* Jerusalem, Sept. 1971.

Misrahi, R. *La Philosophie politique et l'Etat d'Israël.* Paris, 1975.

Mitchell, R. P. *The Society of the Muslim Brothers.* Oxford, 1969.

Momen, M., ed. *The Babi and Baha'i Religions (1844–1944): Some Contemporary Western Accounts.* Oxford, 1981.

Moreen, V. "The Status of Religious Minorities in Safavid Iran (1617–1661)." *JNES* 40 (1981).

Morison, A. *Relation historique d'un voyage nouvellement fait au Mont Sinaï et à Jérusalem.* Paris, 1705.

Moses b. Maimon (Maimonides). *Iggeret Taiman (Epistle to Yemen)*. Edited by A. S. Halkin. Translated by B. Cohen. New York, 1952.

Muslim. *Al-Sahih (Traditions)*. Translated by A. H. Siddiqi. 4 vols. Lahore, 1976.

Muyldermans, J. "La Domination arabe en Arménie", extrait de l'*Histoire Universelle de Vardan*. Louvain and Paris, 1927.

Naipaul, V. S. *Among the Believers: An Islamic Journey*. London, 1981.

an-Nasiri, A. *Kitab el-Istiqsa li Akhbar doual el-Maghrib el-Aqsa (Recherches approfondies sur l'histoire des dynasties du Maroc)*. Translated by E. Fumey. 2 vols. In *Archives Marocaines* 9 and 10. Paris, 1906.

Niebuhr, K. *Travels through Arabia and Other Countries in the East (1761–1767)*. 2 vols. Edinburgh, 1792.

Obadyah, D. *Fas we-Hakhameha (The Sages of Fez)* (Hebrew). 2 vols. Jerusalem, 1979.

Obadyah, the Norman. *Chronicle*. See Scheiber

Oliphant, L. *Haifa or Life in Modern Palestine (1882–1885)* (London, 1887). Reprint, Jerusalem, 1976.

———. *The Land of Gilead*. London, 1880.

Parliamentary Papers (P.P.)

———. "Despatches from Her Majesty's Consuls in the Levant, respecting Past or Apprehended Disturbances in Syria: 1858–1860." 1860 [2734] LXIX.

———. "Correspondence relating to the Affairs of Syria: 1860–1861." 1861 [2800] LXVIII

———. "Reports by Her Majesty's Diplomatic and Consular agents in Turkey respecting the condition of the Christian subjects of the Porte. 1868–1875." 1877 [C. 1739] XCII.

———. "Further Despatch respecting the State of Affairs in Bosnia 1877". [C. 1768] XCII.

———. "Further Correspondence respecting the Affairs of Turkey. 1877". [C. 1806] XCII.

Paton, A. A. *History of the Egyptian Revolution*. 2 vols. 2d ed. London, 1870.

Pearlman, M. *Mufti of Jerusalem*. London, 1947.

Perlmann, M. "Asnawi's Tract against Christian Officials." In *Ignace Goldziher Memorial Volume*. Edited by D. Löwinger et al. vol. 2. Jerusalem, 1958.

———. "Eleventh-Century Andalusian Authors on the Jews of Granada." *PAAJR* 18 (1948–49).

———. "Ghiyar." *EI²* 2.

———. "Notes on Anti-Christian Propaganda in the Mamlûk Empire." *BSOAS* 10 (1939–42).

———. "Notes on the Position of Jewish Physicians in Medieval Muslim Countries." *IOS* 2 (1972).

———. *Shaykh Damanhuri on the Churches of Cairo (1739)*. Berkeley: University of California, 1975.

Péroncel-Hugoz, J. P. *Le Radeau de Mahomet*. Paris, 1983.

Perrot, G. "Souvenirs d'un voyage chez les Slaves du Sud (1868); IV: Une promenade en Bosnie". In *Le Tour du Monde* 21. Paris, 1st sem. 1870.

Peters, R. *Islam and Colonialism: The Doctrine of Jihad in Modern History*. The Hague, 1979.

———. "Jihad in Mediaeval and Modern Islam". In *Nisaba* 5. Leiden, 1977.

de Planhol, X. *Les Fondements géographiques de l'histoire de l'Islam*. Paris, 1968.

Poliakov, L. *Le Racisme*. Paris, 1976.

Proust, A. "Moeurs Turques. II: Le Cydaris" (1862). In *Le Tour du Monde*. Paris, 2nd sem. 1863.

Quaresmius, F. *Elucidatio Terrae Sanctae historica, theologica et moralis*. 2 vols. Rome, 1639.

Reischer, M. M. *Sha'are Yerushalayim (The Gates of Jerusalem)* (Hebrew). Warsaw, 1879.

Rey, F. *La Protection diplomatique et consulaire dans les Echelles du Levant et de Barbarie*. Paris, 1899.

Riley, J. *Loss of the American Brig Commerce: Wrecked on the Western coast of Africa, in the month of August, 1815. With an account of Timbuctoo and of the hitherto undiscovered great city of Wassanah*. London, 1817.

Romanelli, S. *Massa ba-'Arav (The Oracle of Arabia)* (Hebrew). Berlin, 1792. See Hirschberg

Rosenmüller, E. *Ansichten von Palästina oder dem Heiligen Lande, nach Ludwig Mayers*. Leipzig, 1810.

Roumani, M. M. *The Case of the Jews from Arab Countries: A Neglected Issue*. Tel Aviv, 1975.

Rubens, A. *A Jewish Iconography*. Revised Edition. London, 1981.

———. *A History of Jewish Costume*. London, 1973.

Russell, M. *History and Present Condition of the Barbary States*. Edinburgh, 1835.

Rustum, A. *Al-Mahfuzat al-Malikiyya al-Misriyya (The Royal Archives of Egypt)* (Arabic). 4 vols. Beirut, 1940–1943.

Samuel b. Ishaq Uceda. *Lehem dim'ah (The Bread of Tears)* (Hebrew). Venice, 1606.

Schechtman, J. B. *On Wings of Eagles*. New York, 1961.

Scheiber, A. "Fragment from the Chronicle of Obadyah the Norman proselyte." *AOH* 4 (1954).

———. "The Origins of Obadyah the Norman Proselyte." *JJS* 5, no. 1 (1954).

Schiller, E. *The First Photographs of the Holy Land*. Jerusalem, 1979.

———. *The First Photographs of Jerusalem and the Holy Land*. Jerusalem, 1980.

———. *The Holy Land in Old Engravings and Illustrations*. Jerusalem, 1977.

Schreiner, M. "Contributions à l'histoire des Juifs en Egypte" (Ibn Taymiyya). *REJ* 31 (1895).

Sémach, Y. D. "Charles de Foucauld et les Juifs marocains" (Conference, Institut des Hautes Etudes Marocaines). In *Bulletin de l'Enseignement Public du Maroc* 23 (June 1936).

———. *Une Mission de l'Alliance au Yémen*. Paris, 1910. Also, *BAIU* 35 (1910).

————. *A travers les communautés israélites d'Orient: Visites des écoles de l'Alliance Israélite.* Paris, 1931.

Serero, Saul ben David. *Dibray ha-Yamim (Chronicle of Fez).* See Hirschberg

ash-Sha'rani. *al-Bahr al-mawrud fi l-mawathiq wal-uhud (The Sea of Promises)* (Arabic). Cairo, n.d.

————. *al-Bahr* . . . (Cambridge Univ. Lib.), Arabic Ms. 1000.

Sharon, M. "The Political Role of the Bedouins in Palestine in the Sixteenth and Seventeenth centuries." In *Studies on Palestine during the Ottoman Period.* Edited by M. Ma'oz. Jerusalem, 1975.

Shaybani, *Siyar (The Islamic Law of Nations).* Translated by M. Khadduri. Baltimore, 1966.

Shaler, W. *Sketches of Algiers, Political, Historical, and Civil.* Boston, 1826.

Shamir, S. "Muslim Arab Attitudes Towards Jews: The Ottoman and Modern Periods". In *Violence and Defence in the Jewish Experience.* Edited by S. W. Baron and G. S. Wise. Philadelphia, 1977.

Silvain, G., ed. *Images et Traditions Juives.* Paris, 1980.

Slouschz, N. "Israélites de Tripolitaine." *BAIU* (1906).

————. *Travels in North Africa.* Philadelphia, 1927.

Smith, W. C. *Islam in Modern History.* Princeton, N.J., 1957.

Spicehandler, E. "The Persecution of the Jews of Isfahan under Shah Abbas II (1642–1666)." Paper, International Conference on Jewish Communities in Muslim Lands (Institute of Asian and African Studies, Ben Zvi Institute), Hebrew University Jerusalem (1974).

Spoll, E. A. "Souvenir d'un Voyage au Liban" (1859). In *Le Tour du Monde.* Paris, 1st sem., 1861.

Stephens, J. L. *Incidents of Travel in Egypt, Arabia, Petrea and the Holy Land.* New York, 1897; reprint, University of Oklahoma, 1970.

Stillman, N. A. *The Jews of Arab Lands: a History and Source Book.* Philadelphia, 1979.

Strauss, E. See Ashtor

Streck. "Armenia." *EI¹.*

Stutfield, H. E. M. *El Maghreb, 1200 Miles'Ride through Morocco.* London, 1886.

al-Tabari. *Ta'rikh al-Rusul wa'l-Muluk (History of the Prophets and Rulers)* (Arabic). Edited by M. J. de Goeje et al. Leiden, 1879. See Stillman

————. *Kitab al-Jihad (Book of Holy War).* edited by J. Schacht (Arabic) Leiden, 1933.

al-Tall, A. *Khatar al-Yahudiyya al-Alamiyya Ala al-Islam wa-al-Masihiyya (The Danger of World Jewry to Islam and Christianity).* Cairo, 1964. See Harkabi, *Arab*

Thevet, A., *Cosmographie Universelle.* 2 vols. Paris, 1575.

Theophanes. See *Corpus Scriptorum Historiae Byzantinaea.* Bonn, 1892.

Tibawi, A. L. "Russian Cultural Penetration of Syria-Palestine in the Nineteenth Century." *RCAJ* 56 (1966).

Tobi, Y., ed. *Toledot Yehudei Teman:mi-Kitvehem (History of the Jews in Yemen from their Chronicles)* (Hebrew). Jerusalem, 1979.

Le Tour du Monde. See Anon. *Voyage,* Perrot, Proust, Spoll.

Tritton, A. S. *The Caliphs and their Non-Muslim Subjects: A Critical Study of the Covenant of Umar.* London, 1930; reprint 1970.

———. "Islam and the Protected Religions." *JRAS* (1931).

Trotter, P. D. *Our Mission to the Court of Morocco (1880).* Edinburgh, 1881.

Tyan, E. "Djihad." *EI²* 2.

Vajda, G. "Ahl al-Kitab." *EI²* 1.

———. "L'Image du Juif dans la tradition islamique." *NC* 13–14 (1968).

———. "Juifs et Musulmans selon le hadit." *JA* 219 (1937).

———. *Un Recueil de textes historiques Judéo-Marocains.* In *Hespéris* 12 (1951).

———. "Un Traité maghrébin 'Adversus Judaeos': Ahkam ahl al-Dimma du Sayh Muhammad b. Abd al-Karim al-Maghili." In *Extraits des Etudes d'Orientalisme dédiés à la mémoire de Lévi-Provençal.* Vol. 2. Paris, 1962.

Volney, C. F. *Travels in Egypt and Syria (1783–1785).* 2 vols. London, 1787.

al-Waqidi. *Kitab al-Maghazi (The Book of Expeditions)* (Arabic). Edited by M. Jones. 2 vols. London, 1966.

Watt, W. M. "Muhammed." In *The Cambridge History of Islam,* edited by P. M. Holt, A. K. S. Lambton, B. Lewis. 2 vols. Cambridge, 1970.

Weill, G. "Le Juif des sables," *NC* 13–14 (1968).

Wellsted, F. R. *Travels in Arabia.* London, 1838.

Weyl, J. *Les Juifs protégés français aux Échelles du Levant et en Barbarie sous les règnes de Louis XIV et Louis XV. (D'après des documents inédits tirés des archives de la Chambre de Commerce de Marseille). REJ* 12 and 13 (1886).

Wilkie Young, H. E. "Notes on the City of Mosul." ed. E. Kedourie *MES* 7, no. 2 (1971).

Wilson, C., ed. *Picturesque Palestine, Sinai and Egypt,* 5 vols. London, [1882].

Wolff, J. *Narrative of a Mission to Bokhara in the Years 1843–1845.* Edinburgh, 1852.

———. *Researches and Missionary Labours (1831–1834).* London, 1835.

Wyman Bury. C. *Arabia Infelix, or the Turks in Yamen.* London, 1915.

Yodfat, A. H., and Arnon-Ohanna, Y. *PLO: Strategy and Politics.* London, 1981.

Zahra, M. A. "The Jihad" (1968). See al-Azhar

Zwemer, S. M. *Law of Apostacy in Islam.* Cairo, 1925; reprint, New Delhi, 1975.

Addendum:

Gibb, H. A. R. and Bowden, H. *Islamic Society and the West: A Study of the Impact of Western Civilization on Muslim Culture in the Near East.* Vol. 1: 2 Parts: *Islamic Society in the Eighteenth Century* (Oxford, 1950–57).

Muslim Historians and Theologians mentioned in this study: a selected list

Abu Yusuf, Ya'qub (d. 798). One of the founders of the Hanafi school of law Author of a basic treatise on public finance.

al-Adawi (18th century). Ahmad ad-Dardir. Maliki theologian, author of a *fatwa* against the *dhimmis*.

al-Asnawi (d. 1370). Theologian and teacher, head of Egyptian Shafi'is.

al-Baladhuri (d. 892). Renowned historian.

al-Bukhari (d. 869), Author of the most important compilation of traditions, being the acts and sayings attributed to the Prophet Muhammad.

al-Damanhuri (d. 1778). Egyptian theologian and head of al-Azhar.

Ghazi b. al-Wasiti (alive in 1292). Iraqi author of a treatise on the *dhimmis*.

Abu Hanifa (d. 767). Founder of the Hanafi school of law.

Ibn Abdun (d. 1134). Spanish jurist, author of an authoritative legal treatise.

Ibn Abi Zayd al-Qayrawani (d. 996). North African Maliki jurist, author of a celebrated legal compendium.

Ibn Askar (d. 1578). Moroccan hagiographer.

Ibn al-Athir (d. 1233). Famous historian, author of the *Kamil*.

Ibn Battuta (d. 1369). Renowned Moroccan traveler.

Ibn al-Fuwati (d. 1323). Historian, active in Baghdad.

Ibn Hanbal (d. 855). Jurist and theologian. Editor of a corpus of traditions and founder of the Hanbali school of law.

Ibn Hisham (d. 883). Famous biographer of Muhammad. See Ibn Ishaq.

Ibn Ishaq (d. 768). Author of the most influential biography of Muhammad, reproduced and edited by Ibn Hisham.

Ibn Khaldun (d. 1406). Renowed philosopher and historian. Born in Tunis, died in Cairo.

Ibn Miskawayh (d. 1030). Famous philosopher and historian.

Ibn an-Naqqash (d. 1362). Egyptian preacher, author of an important *fatwa* on the *dhimmis*.

Ibn Qayyim al-Jawziyya (d. 1351) Theologian, follower of Ibn Taymiyya.

Ibn Taghribirdi, Abu'l-Mahasin (d. 1469). Historian of the Mamluks.

Ibn Taymiyya (d. 1328). Reputed Egyptian theologian and Hanbali jurist, active in Damascus.

Ibn ar-Rijal (d. 1681). Yemenite theologian.

al-Jili (15th century). Yemenite mystic.

al-Maghili (d. 1504). North African theologian.

Malik b. Anas (d. 795). Jurist. Founder of the Maliki school of law.

al-Maliki, Abu Bakr Abd Allah (11th c.). Tunisian historian, author of famous chronicle, *Riyad an-Nufus.*

al-Marrakushi (d. 1224). North African historian of the Almohads.

al-Mawardi (d. 1058). Shafi'i jurist of Baghdad, author of important treatise on constitutional law.

Muslim (d. 874). Disciple of al-Bukhari and compiler of a basic corpus of traditions, being the acts and sayings attributed to the Prophet Muhammad.

an-Nasiri (d. 1897). Important Moroccan historian.

ash-Sha'rani (d. 1565). A well-known Egyptian mystic and religious writer.

al-Shafi'i (d. 820). Jurist and founder of the Shafi'i school of law.

al-Shaybani (d. 805). Jurist, author of an important work, *The Islamic Law of Nations.*

al-Tabari (d. 923). Famous historian of *Annals.*

al-Waqidi (d. 823). Historian, one of the main sources for Muhammad's raids and military expeditions.

British Secretaries of State
Ambassadors, Consuls, Vice-Consuls,
and Agents: a selected list

ABERDEEN, 4th Earl of, George Hamilton Gordon (1784–1860). Ambassador Extraordinary at Vienna (1813), Foreign Secretary (1828–30, 1841–46), Secretary for War and the Colonies, Prime Minister (1853–54).

BRANT, James, Vice-Consul, Trebizond (1831–36)–traveled through Persia 1832, and Asia Minor, 1834), Consul, Erzerum (1836–55)–traveled Kurdestan, 1836, Damascus (1855–60).

BULWER, Sir Henry William Henry Lytton Earle Bulwer, 1st Baron Dalling and Bulwer (1801–72). Attaché Berlin, Vienna, and the Hague, Chargé d'Affaires Brussels, Secretary of Embassy Constantinople (1837–39), Paris, Ambassador Madrid, Ambassador Washington, Minister Florence, Ambassador Constantinople (1858–65).

CAMPBELL, Colonel Patrick (1779–1857), Columbia (1826), Agent and Consul-General in Egypt (1833–41).

CANNING, Sir Stratford, 1st Viscount Stratford de Redcliffe (1786–1880). Entered Foreign Office (1807), Denmark, Constantinople (1808–12), Switzerland, Washington, St. Petersburg, Ambassador at Constantinople (1825–29, 1831–32, 1842–58).

CLARENDON, 4th Earl of, George William Frederick Villiers (1800–1870), Attaché at St. Petersburg (1820–23), Minister at Madrid (1833–39), Lord Privy Seal, President of the Board of Trade, Lord Lieutenant of Ireland, Foreign Secretary (1853–56, 1865–66, 1868–70).

DICKSON, John (1854–1906). Vice-Consul Mosul (1872), Acting Vice-Consul Damascus (1875–76), Vice-Consul Beirut (1876–82), Consul Damascus (1882–84), Consul Jerusalem (1890–1906).

DUFFERIN, Earl of; 1st Marquess of Dufferin and Ava, Frederick Temple Hamilton-Temple Blackwood (1826–1902). Vienna Conference (1855), Commissioner to Inquire into Massacres in the Levant (1860), Governor-General of Canada, Ambassador St. Petersburg, Constantinople (1881–84), Viceroy of India, Ambassador Rome, Ambassador Paris.

ELDRIDGE, George Jackson, C.M.G. (–1890). Consul Kertch (1856), Consul-General Beirut (1863–90).

ELLIOT, Sir Henry George, P.C., G.C.B. (1817–1907). Entered Diplomatic Service (1841), Copenhagen, Naples, Greece, Turin, Ambassador Constantinople (1867–77), Ambassador Vienna.

FINN, James (1806–72). Consul Jerusalem (1845–62). Author of *Stirring Times, Sephardim, Byeways in Palestine, Orphan Colony of Jews in China*, etc.

FINZI, Moses d'Abraham. Consular Agent, Acre (1837–79).

FREEMAN, Edward Bothamley, Chancellor at Diarbekir Consulate (1858–60), at Bosna-Seraï Consulate (1863–76), Acting Consul Bosna-Seraï at intervals (1863–76), Acting Consul, Bosna-Seraï (1876–78), Consul for Bosnia and Herzegovina, stationed at Bosna-Seraï (1878–91), Consul-General, Bosnia and Herzegovina (1891–1905).

GRANVILLE, 2nd Earl, Granville George Leveson-Gower (1815–91). Attaché Paris (1835), Under-Secretary of State for Foreign Affairs (1840–41), Secretary of State for Foreign Affairs (1851–52, 1870–74, 1880–85), President of the Council, Secretary of State for the Colonies.

HAY, Sir John H. Drummond (1816–93). Entered Diplomatic Service (1832) serving under his father, who was Political Agent and Consul-General, Tangiers. Under Lord Ponsonby and Sir Stratford Canning at Constantinople (1840–44). Successively, Consul-General, Chargé d'Affaires, and Minister at Tangiers (1844–86).

HOLMES, Sir William Richard. Consul, Diarbekir (1852–60), Consul in Bosnia (1860–77), attended Constantinople Conference (Dec. 1876–Jan. 1877).

MALMESBURY, 3rd Earl of, James Howard Harris (1807–89). Foreign Secretary (1852, 1858–59), Lord Privy Seal.

MOORE, Niven C. B. (1795–1889). Constantinople (1822), Consul Beirut (1835–41), Aleppo, Beirut (1841–53), Consul-General Beirut (1853–62).

MOORE, Noel Temple, C. M. G. (1833–1903). Beirut (1851–62), Consul for Palestine (1862–90), Consul-General Tripoli (1890–94).

ROSE, Colonel Hugh Henry, 1st Baron Strathnairn (1801–85). Field Marshal. Special military service in Syria (1840–41), Consul-General Beirut (1841–51), Secretary of Embassy Constantinople (1851–54).

RUSSELL, Lord John, 1st Earl (1792–1878). Home Secretary, Colonial Secretary, Prime Minister (1846–52, 1865–66), Foreign Secretary (1852–53, 1859–62), President of Council.

SKENE, James Henry, Vice-Consul, Constantinople (1852), Consul, Aleppo (1855), attached to Alison Mission to inquire into state of Syria, visiting Aleppo, Damascus, Jerusalem, and Beirut; returned to Aleppo Consulate and retired 1878.

TAYLOR, John George; Agent and later Vice-Consul, Bussorah (1851–55), Acting Consul, Teheran (1859), Consul, Diarbekir (1860–65), Consul in Kurdestan at Erzerum (1865–74).

WERRY, Frank Howard Stephen, Acting Consul Aleppo (1837–41), Vice-Consul, Mytilene (1842–52), Vice-Consul, Benghazi (1852–56), Vice-Consul, Tunis (1856–69–Acting Consul-General at intervals 1859–69).

YOUNG, William Tanner. Vice-Consul Jerusalem (1838–41), Consul Jerusalem (1841–45).

Index A
(Persons, Peoples, Tribes, Institutions)

Words of frequent occurrence, such as dhimmis, *Jews, Christians, etc., have not been indexed. Both the Arabic definite article "al-", and "b." (for* ibn*), have been disregarded. Inconsistencies in the translation in the text or documents are not necessarily reproduced in the indexes.*

Index B
(Places)

432

Index C

(Selected Arab and Turkish Technical Terms)

Index D
(General)

Divided into MUSLIM attitudes towards *Dhimmis;* and DHIMMI(S)' situation.

(i) MUSLIM

A

Abduction
—of women, orphans, 44, 61, 75–6, 151, 209, 241, 264, 268, 271, 278, 285, 293, 347
Abrogation (of *dhimma*), 52, 101, 120, 179, 183, 193, 199, 204, 269, 364
Activities (forbidden in the service of *dhimmis*)
—as masseur, cleaner, stableman, donkey-driver, 187
—patient, 62
—servant, 62, 109, 184, 197
Апостазу
—punishable by death, 177, 183
Arabization, 67, 86, 122
Assault(s), 44, 101, 247, 282, 292, 307, 318, 319, 343, 352, 362, 366, 371, 373

C

Charity (to *dhimmi*, prohibited), 197
Colonization, 67–8, 105
Comfort (prohibited to comfort *dhimmi* mourners), 190, 204
Covenant of Umar, 48, 71, 154

D

dhimma
—legal texts, 163, 166, 169, 176, 304

E

Edict (confirming "Covenant of Umar"), 336, 340–1

Emancipation
—reactions to, 84, 86, 91, 100, 103, 105–7, 109, 121, 241, 251–2, 261, 269, 321, 336

G

Greetings (to *dhimmis*, prohibited), 87, 183, 187, 190, 197, 203–4, 215, 237

H

Honor (prohibited to honor *dhimmis*), 197, 204

I

Impunity (for crimes), 282, 294, 295, 310, 359. See also *dhimmi*(s) (murder of)
Inquisitions, 206, 210, 347
Islamization, 86

J

jihad. See Index C
jizya. See Index C
—Collection of, 169, 188, 192, 201, 297
Justice, 56, 224, 271, 277, 280, 294, 343, 352

L

Land, 166–8

P

Pacts. *See* Covenant and Edicts
Pan-Islamism, 93, 109, 121

439